Shamanism

ALSO BY GARY EDSON

Mysticism and Alchemy through the Ages: The Quest for Transformation (McFarland, 2012)

Masks and Masking: Faces of Tradition and Belief Worldwide (McFarland, 2005; paperback 2009)

Shamanism
A Cross-Cultural Study of Beliefs and Practices

Gary Edson

McFarland & Company, Inc., Publishers
Jefferson, North Carolina

The present work is a reprint of the illustrated case bound edition of Shamanism: A Cross-Cultural Study of Beliefs and Practices, *first published in 2009 by McFarland.*

LIBRARY OF CONGRESS CATALOGUING-IN-PUBLICATION DATA

Edson, Gary, 1937–
Shamanism : a cross-cultural study
of beliefs and practices / Gary Edson.
p.   cm.
Includes bibliographical references and index.

ISBN 978-0-7864-9547-4 (softcover : acid free paper) ∞
ISBN 978-1-4766-1694-0 (ebook)

1. Shamanism.   I. Title.
BF1611.E36   2014   201'.44 — dc22   2008030076

BRITISH LIBRARY CATALOGUING DATA ARE AVAILABLE

© 2009 Gary Edson. All rights reserved

No part of this book may be reproduced or transmitted in any form or by any means, electronic or mechanical, including photocopying or recording, or by any information storage and retrieval system, without permission in writing from the publisher.

On the cover: George Catlin, *Medicine Man, Performing His Mysteries Over a Dying Man*, oil on canvas 29" × 24", 1832 (Smithsonian American Art Museum, Washington, D.C.)

Front cover by TG Design

Manufactured in the United States of America

McFarland & Company, Inc., Publishers
Box 611, Jefferson, North Carolina 28640
www.mcfarlandpub.com

To M

Acknowledgments

This book is in large part the result of the interest, support, and kindness of friends and colleagues around the world who contributed assistance and special knowledge to the writing. My sincere thanks and appreciation go to the following persons for their time and effort in responding to my request for information, images, or contacts related to this project.

In particular, I wish to acknowledge and thank Andrew Wheatcroft, distinguished author, teacher, scholar, and dreamer (in the visionary sense of the word) who has been a friend and sounding board for almost 15 years. He and I first discussed this book project five years ago.

I wish also to thank Bill Mueller at the Museum of Texas Tech University who provided help with images from the Museum's collections. At the National Anthropological Archives, Catherine O'Sullivan and Daisy Njoku located material and assisted with photographs from that institution. Sirkku Dölle and Marja-Leena Hanninen at the National Museum of Finland were extremely helpful with photographs from that excellent museum, and Dr. Dorothee Schäfer at the Photographic Archives of the Staatliches Museum für Völkenkunde made photographs from that museum available. At the National Museum of Mongolian History, the Vice Director, Dashdendev Bumaa was extremely generous with her time and effort to allow me to photograph items in that museum and to provide supplemental images. Also in Mongolia, special thanks must go to Tsevegjav Enkhchimeg for her willingness to escort me from store to store looking for books and items relating to Mongolian shamanism. I wish also to acknowledge and thank Ebba Brännback in Finland, Lucia Astudillo in Ecuador, and Wanchen Liu in Taiwan. They are colleagues and friends who provided much needed assistance on request. I wish also to include a special remembrance of the late Dirk Huber, a friend, teacher, mentor.

I would be remiss not to recognize the Museum of Texas Tech University, my professional home for over two decades, and the talented staff that make everyday a learning experience.

Finally, I wish to thank my wife Miriam for her constant support. She kept the cats occupied and patiently allowed me time to work on this manuscript. Without her kind consideration no writing could have been accomplished. It is to her that this book is dedicated. Thank you!

TABLE OF CONTENTS

Acknowledgments	vi
Preface	1
1. Spiritual Exaltation	5
2. Shamanism and Belief	22
3. Shamanistic Power and Magic	46
4. Shamanistic Symbolism	68
5. Shamanism and Imaginative Representation	92
6. Shamanic Ritual and Transformation	118
7. Shamanic Divination and Curing	140
8. Spirits, Dreams, and Ecstasy	161
9. Transformation and Shape-Shifting	184
10. Life, Death, and Sacrifice	207
11. Transcendental Shamanism	230
Notes to the Captions	243
Notes to the Text	245
Bibliography	263
About the Photographs	277
About the Drawings	279
Index	283

PREFACE

Shamanism is a subject of which most people have heard and which is yet a mystery. The ideas associated with spirits of the natural world (some call it animism) are accepted in some cultures; whereas, in other locations belief in intervention by friendly or unfriendly spirits is viewed as alien, naïve, or "primitive." At the same time, contemporary society has a fascination with the spirit world and the assumed supernatural authority vested in persons such as the shaman, mystic, fortune-teller, soothsayer, and clairvoyant.

Belief as an attitude of acceptance without intellectual knowledge has been an intriguing element of humanity from earliest times. It was for generations a fundamental part of survival. Popular beliefs and magical practices accompanied ordinary people throughout life and into death as they followed the prescribed rituals to guarantee security in the present or a place in the afterlife. The measures a people employed to validate and defend their beliefs are well documented. Blood sacrifice and self-mortification were common practices.

The artifacts, sites, and markings discovered in numerous locations attest to the importance early people placed on recognition and veneration of their chosen spirit deities. Those relics were often validated by myths, stories, and legends that were fundamental to the sacred beliefs of a certain time and place. Shamanism was, in its various forms, the foundation of those early practices. The shaman provided the means for his or her people to live in balance with the world. It was believed that by living in the proper way and observing the appropriate rituals, practices, and taboos, an individual could keep the world in balance and attain maximum personal power.

The chapters of this book address these complex issues but do not presume to present a systematic study of the vast world of shamanism, nor do they attempt to describe all the varied aspects of the spirit world. Instead, they offer a level of insight into humanity's attempt to understand and control the forces of nature, and many of the shamanistic practices associated with those activities.

Shamanism and the power of the supernatural as a personal interest started with that exposure normally attributed to traditional medicine, "old wives tales," or myth. All rural communities like the one in northwest Missouri where I spent my early years had such beliefs, and those forces guided local practices. The people believed there was a greater power—an omnipotent presence with the wisdom and authority to guide and ameliorate life's issues. They looked to the heavens for escape from life and salvation from death. The primary issues that challenged the thinking of those ordinary people were renewing the crops, surviving illness, and having knowledge of the unknown, in particular knowing what tomorrow would bring. Those issues were assigned to the supernatural regardless of the professed belief or spirit/deity called upon.

Some years later as a graduate student at Tulane University, my exposure to beliefs about supernatural phenomena became more focused. New Orleans was at that time an exuberant place. It was a city of paradox and contrast — a unique blend of cultural elements with an undertone of spiritism. The *Vieux Carré* was a city within the city, and a place of artists and writers that brought forth a stimulating respect for the creative process reminiscent of early writers such as Walt Whitman, Sherwood Anderson, and William Faulkner. It was also a place where people spoke openly about their beliefs, both traditional and nontraditional, and the influences those forces had on life and creativity. An array of overlapping practices called upon the supernatural world to provide inspiration, guidance, and hope. The range of beliefs included voodoo, shamanism, and spiritualism as well as the more conventional institutionalized religious practices.

Work and study opportunities after graduate school allowed further exposure to different beliefs and the supportive practices. Several months were spent in Mexico followed by two years in Korea. The "Land of the Morning Calm" in the mid–1960s was still recovering from the war, and people were struggling to regain a sense of wholeness in their lives. There was a feeling of emergence that called upon the traditions of the past and the need for belief in the future. The influences of Buddhism, Shintoism (a residual of Japanese occupation), Shamanism, and spiritism as well as various forms of local belief were commingled with Christian practices. The shamanism drew from the land and the people and had a similar feeling to the beliefs and expectations found in the farm communities of the mid-western United States.

Residency in Korea was followed by fourteen months in Ecuador. Time in the Andean country granted exposure to different attitudes about the impact of natural and supernatural forces on human existence. Popular beliefs extended into the distant past to the time of the Inca. The Ecuador sojourn included time in the rain forest on the inland slopes of the Andes and interaction with the indigenous peoples of that region. Those practitioners of traditional beliefs verified the diversity of needs that shamanism (or spiritism) addressed as a necessary complement to an ever-evolving survival process.

Travel and research during the past thirty years has allowed me to return to Korea for nine months for research and to renew my association with Ecuador. In addition, I was fortunate to have time in Taiwan, Paraguay, Costa Rica, Russia, and Mongolia. Each of those experiences reinforced my interest in those social and cultural activities perpetuated by belief in ancient spirits and shamanistic practice.

Every encounter with believers in the spiritual world reinforced the notion that shamanism is as much an art form as a religion, belief, or supernatural phenomenon. Though shamanistic practice served the interests of many people, each occurrence required a different interpretation, performance, and outcome. Perhaps for that reason the books written on the subject often resort to either the suppositional theory of shamanistic practice or description of particular events within specific groups of people.

The unusual nature of shamanism is often viewed as curious and unsophisticated. Some individuals view it with humor and skepticism and others advocate it as a substitute for ecclesiastical dogma. Shamanism fits neatly into neither of these categories. It is likely that it is a part of all people and an element that resides in the subconscious waiting to emerge. It is constantly present in different forms and serves different functions as needed.

Shamanism is about belief and reality. Such issues inhabit a dominion of knowledge that is poorly defined and difficult to recognize. Consequently, people often choose the narrower path of societal acceptability, leaving the spirit world unattended. It is true, however, that humankind has for generations endeavored to reach into the regions of spirituality to understand the forces that influence the world in which they live. It is for that reason that no belief, however marginal and peculiar it may seem, is truly insignificant.

A Note About the Illustrations

A decision was made to include both drawings and photographs in this book for the purpose of better illustrating certain features of shamanistic practice. Where possible the people associated with each piece are identified by name; however, some images reference early sites and the cultural affiliation is more generic.

A section at the back of the book, "About the Drawings," describes the model(s) I used for each drawing. The pieces illustrated were chosen to symbolically represent fundamental emotional and spiritual perspectives, as well as document different styles and cultural affiliations. The drawings are representations of the images, not exact presentations of the original objects, allowing in some instances the spiritual integrity of the object to remain undisturbed.

Another section at the back, "About the Photographs," describes the source of each photograph. The photographs were selected to better illustrate shamanic attire and supporting accessories. The use of drawings to describe the shaman's coat, drum, and mirror did not adequately illustrate the detail of those special items.

(Note: Permission to include the photographs in this publication was granted by the providing institution where appropriate. Some images were determined to be clear of copyright restrictions due to age and common use. However, reasonable effort was made to ensure against copyright infringement.)

A Final Note About the Book

As indicated by the extensive bibliography and the lengthy endnotes, much of this book is literary; however, a significant portion is based on direct field observation. There are many publications on the subjects of shamanism, religion, spiritualism, dreams, divination, and magic, and all provide insight into the underlying phenomenon of belief. My research attempted to draw from all these resources and to show the commonality of their intellectual and psychological merits. However, no matter how carefully I attempted to factually represent the available information, the choice of the data and the images used in the text are mine. When dealing with any subject that draws from diverse times and cultures, it is easy to make assumptions based on unintended ethnocentrism, and such errors are difficult to discover and correct. In general, this book is about people and the means they developed to deal with socially, culturally, and environmentally challenging occurrences that influenced their lives.

1

SPIRITUAL EXALTATION

Since the early ethnographic reports, shamans and their practices have attracted westerners. Characterized by hysteria, ecstasy, magic, and transvestism, shamanism is alien to the rational positivistic worldview of science and anthropology, dominated by the positivistic sciences, has failed until recently to understand it as an important dynamic force in today's world or to develop adequate theoretical models for comprehending it.[1]

Shamanism is the oldest form of magico-religion in Asia and possibly the world. It was found in "societies around the world with the exception of the region around the Mediterranean..."[2] It was practiced as far back as the historical record exists, and there are central ideas and a series of symbols that express it. The entire Asian region was once a single cultural area extending over Russia, China, India, Mongolia, Tibet, Nepal, and Persia, and for shamanism this was a unified culture. "Shamanism is therefore to be defined by reference to the elements of which it is comprised, and to its general motivation."[3] Siberian shamanism, the Bön religion, and Chinese ancestor-worship grew out of the original shamanism. When Buddhism spread throughout central Asia after 600 BCE, Tibet converted from (primitive, early, or Dö-Bön[4]) Bön to Buddhism about 800 CE. The resulting religion called Tibetan Buddhism embraced most of the elements of Bön. It was essentially a shamanistic religion. Tibetan lamas fall into trances, predict the future, and in many ways serve exactly like shamans. After 1300 CE, the Mongols converted to Tibetan Buddhism, and that faith spread into Siberia.

Although there are many similarities, there are also elements of Asian shamanism that do not appear in North and South America spiritual activities. There are, however, four important element of Siberian shamanism: "the ideological premise, or the supernatural world and the contacts with it; the shaman as the actor on behalf of the human group; the inspiration granted him by his helping spirits; and the extraordinary ecstatic experiences of the shaman."[5]

Hysteria, Ecstasy, and Magic

Spirits were often credited with knowledge of magic. They were believed to have handed it down to humans and sometimes used it in their relations with the people.[6] The desire to manipulate the spirits and the actions they represented caused the founding of the activity described as "magic."[7] When special assistance was needed, the people turned inward to identify an energy source (magic) that they could call upon to deal with supernatural, as well as natural powers. That need for help evolved into an elaborate system of spirit helpers (familiars) as intermediaries for conveying the wishing of humans to the all-powerful deities.

The power (applied magic) and authority of specific spirits were determined by myth and tradition and as with all such symbolic references, there was no attempt to justify the narratives or to render them plausible. The myth presented itself as an authoritative, factual account, no matter how much the narrated events or spirit interventions were at variance with natural law or ordinary experience. The myth was also used to refer to an ideological belief when that belief was reinforced by a quasi-religious faith. The myth helped the people to escape their menial, sometimes frightening, and normally difficult lives by allowing them to imagine a better existence in the inner sanctum of the spirit world.

Investigation of early cultures centered on such issues as material culture and the development of religion. This research identified systems of belief and action involving the supernatural that existed in all known human societies.[8] Because there is no doubt about the existence of spirituality and spiritual life among peoples at an early date, it was easier to view shamanism as a "religion," so it could be analyzed according to a fixed set of rules. Shamanism, as a religion, could be assessed based on its compliance with certain standards and practices. However, shamanism does not include many of the elements of organized religions including the Godhead, but it reinforces social values by divine sanctions and provides hope and consolation.

Belief systems are cultural, but individual acceptance or rejection is social, and it is often myth that influences the individual and society in the decision making process. Any form of occult knowledge regardless of how it is derived is associated with spiritual exaltation. It is also true that almost all belief systems that foster adoration of unearthly being (spirits) were motivated by a mystical concept. Nevertheless, "[m]any religious traditions exist parallel to one another and are nurtured in the midst of modern activity. Cults that came from the Stone Age still exist at the "gateway to the roof of the world.""[9]

Myths are an indispensable part of all cultures, and it was myths that govern the call, initiation, and training of shamans.[10] Heritage — the human condition — in most communal situations, is something that is partly material, partly human, and partly spiritual on which humans often rely to cope with circumstances, specifically challenges that face them. It is more than customs, ideas, and traditions, and often includes belief that is not necessarily limited to sacred considerations. Therefore, heritage (myths, beliefs, and practices) is most often a set of conditions adopted by a cultural grouping to meet the basic requirements of that group, such as providing food, shelter, and safety, as well as sanctioning procreation. The practices employed to meet these survival requirements are transmitted by means of imitation, social conditioning, and instruction. The use of secondary practices (shamanism) is reinforced as they are transmitted from one generation to the next. Belief in a higher authority that can render aid as needed is a common wish regardless of the name or method used to gain that assistance.

There are two parts to the past: "the temporal one that passes and is gone, and the metaphorical 'past' that is held in the memories and traditions of a society and its surroundings."[11] Maurice Halbwachs included a related concept in his 1980 publication, *The Collective Memory*. He noted that a person has two aspects of the memory process — one individual (personal) and one collective (social).[12] Halbwachs proposes that individual memory is reinforced when others remember the same or similar objects, events, or activities (rituals and ceremonies). This "collective" recognition of past circumstances (including myths) allows the individual to reconstruct a body of memories that is recognizable. The person has one memory process that reinforces individuality, and a second that "maintains impersonal remembrances of interest to the group."[13] In all probability, the two memories converge at that time when the individual locates himself or herself within the collective present by evoking his or her past. The social memory (myth) can be relied upon to fill the gaps in individual recollection when needed.

> And why should it be that whenever men have looked for something solid on which to found their lives, they have chosen, not the facts in which the world abounds, but the myths of an immemorial imagination — preferring even to make life a hell for themselves and their neighbors, in the name of some violent god, rather than to accept gracefully the bounty the world affords?[14]

The concept of the world, among most peoples, was that it was divided into two distinct realms, the seen and the unseen, the physical and the metaphysical, or the sacred and the profane. The same divisions continue today, and in this bipartite environment many people subscribe to traditional values that are more relevant than scientific truths because they represent seemingly real solutions to personal problems. The acceptance that something is true or real is the basis for an emotional or spiritual sense of certainty. Sociologically, participation in communal rituals identified a person as a member of the community and integral to the group that accepts the system of beliefs. Working within the shamanic concept the "real" world that existed beyond the mundane was highly significant; therefore, "attempts were made, in the form of the trance, to penetrate into the spiritual world and exercise an influence on it."[15]

The shaman fulfilled different roles in different communities — political, mystical, and religious. He or she was a communicator who breeched the void between the social and the spiritual in some societies, and in other locations, he or she was a healer or the source of a malevolent appeal to a supernatural being for harm to come to someone or something. Black or white, good or bad, the role of the shaman fulfilled the need of the community in which he or she lived.

> Although the describing and explaining of the phenomenal complex going under the name shamanism has been one of the central themes of research into ethnology, comparative religion and anthropology, ethnomedicine and folklore, no consistent answer has been found to the question "what is shamanism?"[16]

Pursuing the Spirits

To understand the development of the shaman as an element in the early social structure it is necessary to consider the survival strategies of humans. The first peoples were primarily hunters that depended on opportunity to provide their primary food source and this attitude can still be found today. Over time, a more stable order was established and people developed a planter culture that involved planning. This calculated form of existence is the basis of modern civilization. The hunter sought the available product of nature and seizes them as a means of surviving. The hunter culture adjusted its activities to find compatibility with the forces of nature and adopted an attitude of sharing rather than domination. In contrast, the planter culture strived to develop methods for regulating the forces of nature and the environment. Productivity was a concern as was the accumulation of tangible property.

Shamanism is a widespread concept that is known literally all over the world and has left traces in all major religions. It is a recognized and endorsed belief system, and although shamanism is not considered by many purists to be a religion, it is often described as a "religious complex."[17] Shamanism is a term used to designate a form of belief or magico-religions activity, by which physical nature was brought into a cooperative relationship with humans. It existed among Turanian, a cultural group occupying regions of southwest Kazakhstan and northwest Uzbekistan and Mongolian peoples, Native Americans, and a number of other cultures around the world. T. M. Molhilov describes shamanism as "a natural religion, and the degree of its transformation into societal religion among various peoples is what defines its character."[18] Molhilov contends that "even among the most advanced peoples of Central and Northern Asia, it remained an idolization of the forces of nature and preserved ritual as its major, but not only component."[19]

Shamanism blended with traditional beliefs and customs, reinforced myths, and provided a sense of empowerment for individuals and communities. Most subscribing cultures believed that shamanism was created by the gods to assist humans in their struggle against the evil spirits. Other peoples believed that shamans entered their vocation for different purposes and in different ways. Some shamans received their calling from a family member, a hereditary transition known in many locations. Other persons were "marked" for shamanhood through unusual birth conditions, or the spirit-mediated recovery from life-threatening illness. Persons in some cultures, such as the Native American, pursued shamanic enlightenment through vision quests, and finally, there were those individuals called to the "practice" through initiatory dreams.

The forces encountered by the shaman were often beyond the understanding of ordinary people, and the authority they commanded exceeded that of a normal individual. The shaman had a special gift that was described as supernatural power. Perhaps the shaman filled the gaps in human sensibilities that were left vacant by lack of knowledge, or as likely he or she provided a means of expression for human wants, needs, and desires. The shaman granted protection from known and unknown enemies, predicted the successful hunt, foretold life and death, and prophesied feast or famine. The extremes of most circumstances were seen in a vision received during a state of ecstasy that was induced by sound, movement, meditation, or stimulants.

The spiritual worldview of many early cultures included belief that "shamans," (also described as medicine men, witch doctors, magicians, psychopomp, mystics, and spiritual leaders) could provide healing, guidance (i.e., divination), or wisdom through the supernatural (occult), spiritism, or altered states of consciousness. The shaman's soul was believed to leave the body during a trance, and at that time the shaman might speak with beings from the other worlds or assume animal forms to converse with ancestors.

The word "shamanism" may be derived from *shaman* or *saman,* a word that comes from Manchu and means "an excited or raving man." However, some scholars contend that "*saman*" is a Tungus word, and others believe that it is a later dialectic form of the Sanskrit *sraman* and meaning "a worker or toiler."[20] According to the writings of John T. Driscoll (1912) the Buddhist Mongols call shamanism *shara-shadshin* (the black faith), and the Chinese identified it as *tjao-ten* (dancing before spirits). The Tatars, a Turkic-speaking people living in west-central Russia, call shamans *kam,* among the Samoyeds living on the West Siberian Plains they are known as *taryib*, the Ostjaks, a people now known as Khanty living in the Ob River basin of central Russia, refer to shamans as *tadib*, the Buriates a people living south and east of Lake Baikal use the word *boe*, Yakut Turks in far northeast Russia say *oyun*, and shamans among the Native American peoples are generally called *medicine men*[21] (actually the term "medicine man" is thought to be of French origin and not of the indigenous cultures). In the *Bhagavata Purana*, the most celebrated text of Hindu sacred literature, the Jains called them shramans, and in Persian-Hindu the term "shaman" means an idolater.

Although there are thousands of words written about shamans and shamanism, "even the origin of the word 'shaman' is disputed, though often attributed to Siberian, especially Evenk (Tungus), culture."[22] According to the Encyclopedia Britannica, the term shaman (*saman*) comes from the Machu-Tungus language and literally means "he who knows." This origin is the most often quoted in scholarly publications. However, Birket-Smith[23] states that shaman is perhaps derived from the Manchu word *hamman* meaning a person in ecstasy or the Sanskrit word *çramana*, meaning an ascetic. The Encyclopedia Britannica follows its proposed word source with the explanation that "[t]here is no single definition of shamanism that applies to the elements of shamanistic activity found in North and South America, in southeastern India, in Australia and in small areas all over the world, as well as in the phenomena among the northern Asian, Ural-Altaic, and Paleo-Asian peoples."[24]

Andreas Lommel, writing in *The World of the Early Hunter* (1967),[25] contends that the shaman was a distinctly different person from the ordinary "medicine man." That conjecture was based on an assumption that the shaman was of a higher level of intellectual intensity and reflected an affiliation with the early hunting community. Regardless of the name by which a unique individual was known, the shaman was a person believed to be in communion with the spirits. The shaman's energies were outwardly oriented and "directed toward the community so that the trance [visionary journey] serve[d] as a medium of communication between the supernatural or non-ordinary reality and the community of men [people]."[26] The shaman and the audience were integral parts of the visionary journey, and the "ecstasy" ended if the connection was broken.

Stanley Krippner writing in the *Proceedings of the Ninth International Conference on the Study of Shamanism and Alternate Modes of Healing*, states, that, "Shamans can be defined as socially sanctioned practitioners who deliberately alter their consciousness to obtain power and knowledge from the 'spirit world.'"[27] Krippner continues by noting that shamans used the acquired information to "help and to heal members of their community and to fulfill other community needs."[28] He contends that, "In psychological terms, shamans regulate their attention to obtain information not ordinarily available. Shamans use this information to reduce stress and ameliorate the living conditions of members of the social group that give them shamanic status."[29]

> Shamanism — the powerful psychological and spiritual process for re-creating the cosmos and turning death into life in all the dimensions of Regality — was the driving force behind every aspect of ancient Maya life.[30]

Shaman as Spiritual Mediator

Regardless of the way a person made the determination to become a shaman, the training period usually lasted for several years. It was normal practice for the neophyte to apprentice with a master shaman to learn the names and functions of deities, spirits, and power animals. The apprentice must learn the history of the particular people, the rituals required for each intervention, and the names of plants used for medicinal purposes. A part of the training included the mythology of the people as well as drumming, chanting, dancing, and other aspects of shamanic practice.

The shaman was a mediator between the inspiriting world of myth and reality. As a spiritual leader, healer, and social regulator he or she was a necessary respondent to the supernatural world. The recognition of that position acknowledged the mystique of ever-present spirits and demons. It was in that environment that the vocation of the shaman developed. If humanity was to endure, the shaman, as a special person, had to enter a state of altered consciousness that allowed access beyond the limitations of the natural order and into the world of spirits and ancestors. Once he or she had transcended that gap, the shaman could gather the symbols of ritual recognition that influenced the physical conditions of the people. When the survival scheme components were assembled, the people could participate in rituals that reinforced the shaman's communicative activities.

The shaman as priest, psychopomp, messenger, and guide of religious-magical practices regulated relations between the spirits (supernatural) and the community to ensure the community's wellbeing. The shaman was a person the people allowed to influence their lives. He or she represented an unequaled power whether it was over objects; the way information was conveyed about objects, spirits, or activities; or the beliefs and perceptions of people. The shaman discovered or foretold what was otherwise hidden from the human eye, and influenced or manipulated objects or natural phenomena to satisfy actual or assumed human needs. Perhaps most importantly, the shaman also contested the various evils, real or imaginary that afflicted humankind.[31] Those activities were wide ranging depending on the needs of the society the shaman served. The more ideal and non-threatening the surroundings were the fewer demands there were for shamanistic intervention.

It is believed that the shaman exerted more control over his or her altered state and the spirits he or she meet than other magico-religious practitioners such as priests or mediums, although the division between these individuals is often elusive.[32]

The concept of "mastery of the spirits" is noted in several books and articles relating to shamans and shamanism. There are, however, an equal number of writings that speak about summoning, cajoling, conjuring spirit beings. Åke Hultkrantz writes "For all we know, the spirits may exist side by side with the shaman, as his called-on informants, his escorts during the shamanistic journals or (when they have animal-form) riding animals...."[33] Hultkrantz also speaks of "a controlling or main spirit who often took up residence inside the shaman, and this spirit was in may cases identical with the shaman's ancestor or his dead predecessor."[34]

In contrast with the ideas expressed by Hultkrantz, Lawrence Krader posits that there are two types of shamans having different relationships with the spirit world. In his opinion shamans were good and evil, white and black, and "that the black shamans were less the masters of and more in the service of the evil spirits."[35] The Buryat believed that white and black shamans fought with each other from distances of hundreds of miles. The white shaman served the fifty-five good gods of the West and had charge of the ceremonies held at birth, weddings, illnesses, and death. On the other hand, the black shaman served the forty-four wicked gods of the East. These (black) shamans were thought to have power to bring illness and death upon humanity. They were not liked, but much feared by the people who sometimes killed them.[36]

The shamans in the hunting-and-gathering societies were ritual practitioners who "enter altered states of consciousness to achieve a variety of ends that include healing the sick, foretelling the future, meeting spirit-animals, changing the weather, and controlling real animals by supernatural means."[37]

Mircea Eliade offers the perspective that "[s]hamanism in the strict sense is pre-eminently a religious phenomenon of Siberia and Central Asia."[38] Although other scholars disagree with this notion (as already noted above), whatever shamanism may be, the dependency on it is probably similar for all people and all groups of people. There may be differences in its expression. One group may appear more mystical or spiritual and another less. One culture may attempt to appease local ghosts, another may worship a remote god, and a third may seek spiritual assistance to open the rain clouds and lure the game. However, all peoples gave signs of satisfaction with their observances, and a society without some form of belief system has not been found.

It is likely that shamans could be "men and women, old and young, sympathetic and tyrannical, strong and weak, oriented toward good ('white') and bad ('black') spirits."[39] Marjorie Balzer explains in *Shamanic Worlds* (1997) that to "understand shamanism, one must explore the art and symbolism inherent in many shamanic ritual performances: an enactment of usually sincere belief in shamanic ability to be sacred intermediaries between human and supernatural worlds."[40]

The Shaman and Shamanism

> It seems that the evolution of the human mind has only been biologically possible for so long because we continue to believe that existence has meaning and some sort of a cosmic reference.[41]

Efforts to systematize the religious theories and practices were undertaken at a relatively early stage in the history of human society. These arrangements lead to the separation of those persons officiating at the ceremonies (priests, medicine men, shamans, and seerers) into a special social group consistent with that practice. It is likely that shamans appeared among the southern Siberian peoples, in the middle of the first millennium of our era.[42]

According to Stanley Krippner in the book compiled and edited by Gary Doore, "shamans were the world's first healers, first diagnosticians, first psychotherapists, first religious functionaries, first magicians, first performing artists, and first storytellers."[43] Krippner also states, "Shamans can be defined as native practitioners who deliberately alter their consciousness in order to obtain knowledge and power from the 'spirit world' which can then be used to help and to heal members of their tribe."[44]

Mircea Eliade writing in *Shamanism: Archaic Techniques of Ecstasy* (1974) is in general agreement with that assessment. Mariko Namba Walter and Eva Jane Neumann Fridman write in *Shamanism: An Encyclopedia of World Beliefs, Practices, and Culture*, volume I (2004), that "[t]he shaman knows the spirit world and human soul through 'ecstasy,' the power of an altered state of consciousness, or trance, which is used to make a connection to the world of the spirits in order to bring about benefits to the community."[45]

It is reasonably certain that the activities performed by the shaman were resident in many areas of the world before the notice of shamanism as a communal service gained cross-cultural acknowledgement. Piers Vitebsky notes in his book *The Shaman* (1995) that the word "shaman" was most likely "...first used only to designate a religious specialist from this [hunters and reindeer herders in Siberia] region. By the beginning of the twentieth century it was already being applied in North America to a wide range of medicine-men and medicine-women, while some New Age practitioners today use the word widely for persons who are thought to be in any sort of contact with spirits."[46]

In addition, Marjorie Balzer writes in *Shamanic Worlds* (1997), "[m]any writers would agree that shamans are medical and spiritual practitioners. Disagreement comes as people struggle to understand the political, mystical, and religious roles shamans played and sometimes still play in communities no longer easily defined as 'traditional.'"[47] Ruth Benedict observed that, "the shaman is the religious practitioner who, by whatever kind of personal experience is recognized as supernatural in his tribe, gets his power directly from the gods."[48] It is also a fact that "...man [humankind] has a drive to organize unexplained external stimuli into some coherent cognitive matrix."[49]

The idea of "the shaman" has become generic in the commonality of its use and implications. The concept of shamanism is further "decontextualised, universalized, and romanticized (and in some cases honored) by Westerns wanting to be shamans."[50] Publications, both popular and academic, use the words "witch doctor" "medicine man," "magician," or "sorcerer" as synonymous with the word "shaman." All these terms denote an individual possessing certain magico-religious powers. While there may be some similarities between the activities of all these persons, the shaman is described as being called into shamanism by "the spirits."

"Shaman," the word identifying the practitioner, has, in general, replaced words such as "medicine man" and "witch doctor." Witch doctor was apparently coined by eighteenth century Westerners and the term is now considered pejorative and anthropologically incorrect. The medicine man designation for curing practitioners was used by early French traders and settlers to describe the activities of the shaman. The French used the "medicine man" terminology when they observed the shaman using herbal remedies to cure. Because the French lived in or traveled through regions where doctors were rare they made use of the shaman's curing skill and the medicine man name continued to be used.[51]

Shamans differed considerably in quality and power. The difference in quality was due to the type of spirits the shaman commanded. The difference in power or authority, as least among the Yakut people of northeastern Siberia, depended on the placement of the souls of future shamans upon the high tree in the Upper World. It was believed that the souls nest at various heights and that the greatest shamans were placed near the top of the tree, while the intermediate ones were located in the middle and the lesser ones were on the lower branches.[52]

There is also some evidence of an overlap between shamanistic experiences and culture-bound mental illness.[53] Early researchers considered shaman to be afflicted by a nervous disorder and a form of intellectual dysfunction that allowed the individual to absorb the sickness or demons of the clan or community. The shamanic condition was described as hysterical. The erratic drumming, unintelligible chanting, and strenuous gyrations associated with the shaman's ecstatic performance, often reinforced that belief.

Persons given to metaphysical practice and belief were often considered mentally deranged, and shamans were no exception to this perspective. Opinions differ on this issue. Some researchers propose that shamans were persons with disordered minds and that it was the psychosis that manifested itself in the shamanic activity. V. G. Bogoraz wrote in 1910, and is quoted in *Shamanic Worlds* as saying, "that among the shamans known to him many were almost hysterical, and some were literally half-insane."[54] It was proposed that a sane person could not become a shaman. D. K. Zelenin stated in 1935 (also quoted in *Shamanic Worlds*), "the shaman ... is a neuropath, obliged by the community of the clan to assume a peculiar medical function — to personally absorb the demons of disease from the sick of the community."[55]

An equal number of researchers view shamans as cleaver manipulators that took advantage of trusting tribesmen with slight-of-hand tricks, visual manipulation, and careful investigation. It has been suggested by various researchers that the shaman feigned trance-like conditions, pretended to be induced into an ecstatic condition, and faked demonic possession as a part of the act performed for the audience. It would seem obvious, assuming these pronouncements are correct, that the shaman could not be insane, and might be very cleaver to perpetuate a hoax of such proportion.

Supposition aside, shamanism for the Jivero in South America was an all-embracing way of life and thought. Jivero youth, as young as six years of age, sought admission into the spirit world by standing under the cascade of the sacred waterfall awaited a vision. If the vision quest failed, they ingest a hallucinogen called *maikua*[56] (from the *Datura* genus of plants that includes jimsonweed). The Jivero youth searched for a power-giving spirit and the related supernatural power in the form of an invisible dart that could be shot a people. The spirit world and the supernatural realm were "considered so pervasive and all-inclusive that even hunting dogs were given their own special hallucinogens to provide them with the essential contact with the supernatural."[57]

In reality but no one knows for certain, shamans embodied all the aspect of human nature. There were quite possibly persons with unstable minds and charlatans as well as serious and honest medical and spiritual practitioners. It can be verifies by first-hand observation that whatever the shaman's mental condition he or she was a person who fulfilled the activities determined by the norms of the resident culture.

Although precisely analogous ideas of the supernatural were not found in every culture, a distinction between the sacred and profane was almost universal.[58] The status of "supernatural" was attached to unnatural or phenomenal happenings among practically all people. Extraordinary incidents were seldom regarded with emotional detachment, as they were thought to be the result of social or cultural transgressions. Accordingly, most cultures had activities or acts that were considered taboo and believed to be dangerous. Those activities evoked emphatic emotional responses that were different from those assigned to commonplace occurrences.

People in many cultures are guided by spiritual or religious beliefs and practices that have evolved from ancient times.[59] Indigenous tradition often imbues everything with spirit. The shaman believes that the university exists on, above, and below ground, and that they were in communication with the spirits on all three levels.[60] This belief pattern was consistent with most organized religions. Humanity existed on the surface plane while heaven and hell constituted the upper and lower worlds. The lifeways, of many early people, appear to have centered on beliefs and practices emanating from this divisional arrangement that involved supernatural forces. A balance had to be achieved and maintained between the ethereal and material worlds for the people to survive. That equilibrium was sought through ceremonies, rituals, and various forms of self-privation or mutilation.

The shaman aided in this existential process as an intermediary between the living and the spirit worlds and a medium for communication with spirits. "Shamanism seem[ed] to occur in almost every area where an early hunting economy ... continued virtually to our own days; that is to say, in Siberia, North America, South America, various regions of Africa, and also in certain zones of Australia."[61] Once the supernatural connections were established between the material and spiritual worlds, a "pact" or contract was consummated. To initiate that contract and to further its purpose, the shaman was the agent for calling the spirits and convincing them to perform his or her bidding for the good of the group.

Fear, Uncertainty, and Shamanism

One of the greatest changes in human existence was the extraordinary revelation of self-awareness.[62] As earlier peoples became aware of themselves and their relationship with nature, and they transformed the vastness they encountered to meet their purposes. Out of that consciousness came the understanding that human existence was predicated on numerous factors, many of which were beyond the control of mortals. This realization carried the seeds of hope and fear, and laid the foundation for systems of belief. The phenomenon of self-awareness promoted the need regulate those things that influenced daily life.

Probably the single most significant influencing factor for human activity was fear. People generally feared the unknown more than the known and consequently, they constructed barriers against the undefined forces of evil (darkness) that filled the spaces in which they lived. Concern about the unknown aspects of existence was a consuming condition because every activity, event, or circumstance was laden with potential danger. Fear comes from a threat that was more powerful than the individual or the group. Fear announced that this threat might harm the individual or the group either physically or emotionally.[63]

Fear was a force and all organized remedial belief systems (including all forms of organized religion) capitalized on the insecurity of ordinary people. "There was fear of uncertainty, fear of the taboos that other people broke, and fear, finally, of the dead and of the malevolent ghosts."[64] An extra-human force was necessary to mitigate that thinking and to explain the unknown elements that influenced human survival both physically and emotionally. With the transfer of emotion insecurity to the supernatural, people developed a new attitude toward existence and gave substance to basal emotion. By giving "fear" a tangible form, it could be confronted, manipulated, placated, hated, and sometimes bribed and abated.

For early people, the more uncertain the food supply, for example, the greater the feeling of insecurity and, consequently, the more intense the emotion of fear. In such instances, the dread of hunger was often the solidifying bond that united the members of the community. Insecurity caused community members to share the need for survival, and that need guided them to the priest, medicine man, or shaman.

The control of the spirits and the actions they represented caused the founding of the manipulative activity described as "magic."[65] The relationship between magic and religion has been debated for years, and the association was one that differs from culture to culture. Magic is the belief that individuals may directly affect or impact nature or other beings, for good or bad, by their own efforts, actions, or deeds. Religion seeks to do the same thing but through prayer or sacrifice to a greater (divine) power.[66]

Magic is a generally applied term to describe that supernatural energy that is beyond the ordinary powers of humans outside the common processes of nature. Peoples in all areas of the world recognized a similar energy of occult power for which they had specific applications and unique systems of belief. According to those beliefs, both positive and negative

DRAWING 1.1—A skeletonized figure that referenced the shaman's journeys to the Underworld. The figure has "rods" or "horns" extending from the top of its head that may signify power or a mystical connection available to certain people. The figure may be ascribed to the shaman's ancestor. (There are three traditional ways of representing the shaman ancestor: by the doll, the ämägyat, and the skeleton.) It is a rock painting from Monsell site, Salish, Nanaimo River, British Columbia.

forces were recognized, named, defined, and celebrated. Cultural groups knew and respected the forces of the supernatural, and each developed ritual and ceremonial practices for dealing with those powerful and often unpredictable forces (see drawing 1.1).

As an inclusive belief system, magic facilitated communication with immutable "greater beings" in contrast to the world of human beings that was in constant realignment. As a means of dealing with routine uncertainties, magic was considered an alternative to more structured belief systems. In its primary application, magic was direct and thereby facilitated action. The results of magic were believed to be the automatic outcome of properly performed rites and correctly recited spells. Other belief systems required a spiritual intermediary to receive the request for action, and the spirit messenger may or may not choose to accommodate the request. Magic, in most societies, was a part of a complex belief system that sought both direct and indirect interventions on behalf of the requesting individual or group. It provided explanations that met the human need for an understandable and responsive world.

Although early humans were undoubtedly afraid of the uncertainties of the struggle of life, and that one of their great fears was death, Émile Durkheim writing in *Elementary Forms of the Religious Life* (1947) contends that religious belief was not in its origination base on fear, but on forces "very near to him [the shaman/practitioner] and confers upon him very useful powers which he could never acquire by himself."[67] Durkheim continues, "However, it may be objected that even according to this hypothesis, religion remains the object of a certain delirium. What other name can we give to that state when, after a collective effervescence, men believe themselves transported into an entirely different world from the one they have before their eyes?"[68]

There seem to be no organized group of *Homo sapiens* that rejects the idea of the supernatural powers aiding the lives of those persons subscribing to the pre-established rituals of devotion. The perception of threat from unknown forces has been and continues to be a major factor in the lives of all people. There is a continuing concern about events that might happen, or situations that might impact an individual's or group's existence. Contemporary society has developed a number of protective measures to counter potential threats that lurk in the minds of citizenry. As an example, authority over some aspects of personal existence has been granted the governing body, and laws have been established to regulate the interaction between individuals. The transfer of responsibility is both a solution and a problem for the uncertainty that constantly influences human existence. Insurance is to protect against personal liability, collisions, property loss, and in a special way death. The range of protective mechanisms designed to guard against the unknown and unseen but imagined catastrophes increases daily.

Some societal factions promote fear to demonstrate power, and to validate the need for a force greater and more dominant than the impending threat. This disposition is demonstrated by the secret societies communities in Papua, New Guinea as represented by the *Tami-Huon* bark-cloth masks (see drawing 1.2) or in the Igbo culture of Nigeria (see drawing 1.3).

Left: DRAWING 1.2— Tami-Huon bark-cloth mask from New Guinea constructed of a palm wood armature over which was stretched bark cloth. The red and black painted masks, used as spirit symbols, were placed on the roof of the men's house. These masks were a tangible representation of spirit power as controlling elements of a secret society. They represented a generally accepted authority and verified the control of that society over the spiritual life of the group.

Right: DRAWING 1.3— An Ekoi, a people of southeastern Nigeria, mask made with antelope skins and worn by members of the "Ekpe" (Egbo) or Leopard society. Membership in this secret society was available to wealthy men who could meet the expense involved. Members of this society participated in ceremonies concerned with ancestral spirits and were believed to protect the community through magic and religious rituals.

1. Spiritual Exaltation 17

The influence of these societal factions (and secret societies) increases or decreases depending on the belief system of the community, a system encompassing the physical, social, and spiritual worlds of those individuals indoctrinated into that structure.

Shamanistic Non-Orthodoxy

"The spirit of man was different, it was like this shadow. A man or woman might have two or more spirits. One spirit of a man might be good and the other bad. One might be brave and the other cowardly. One might be true and the other false."[69]

There is no prototypical shaman or shamanic practice. Though there are books and articles that describe field studies emphatically reporting the role of shamanism in a particular society and the realities of shamanistic practices for a specific people. Each report describes a different situation and a different application of the powers assigned to the shaman. The study of shamanism depends on storytelling, that is, the relating of particular events describing the activities of a particular shaman in a specific situation.

The shaman may have had a special gift that could be described as supernatural. Probably the shaman did fill the gap in human sensibilities that is left vacant by lack of knowledge and ensure protection against enemies, predict the successful hunt, foretell life and death, and prophesy feast or famine. These services were often the results of visions received during a state of ecstasy that was induced by sound, movement, meditation, or stimulants.

There is no certifiable time or place that marks the beginning of shamanism. "Shamans are globally distributed and shamanism is an ancient spiritual practice"[70] (see drawing 1.4). The ambiguity of origination is understandable when shamanism is view not as an organized pan-regional phenomenon or a religion in the traditional use of the word, but an attitude or series of beliefs that find their way into many religions and numerous practices. "Although there are some broad constraints involving trance and the spirit world, there is no set pantheon, no dogma, and no set ritual."[71]

Although not considered a true religion, shamanism was maintained by beliefs and unregulated rituals. Like religion, it has myths and practices and thought they vary from place to place and culture to culture, there is a common notion of interaction with the spirits (or gods). Shamanism generally had its ceremonies, sacrifices, prayers, chants, and dances. The beings that the shaman invokes and the forces with whom he or she communicates

DRAWING 1.4—Anthropomorphic figure incised into a stone surface at Bol'shaya Kada, Angora during the Neolithic period. The figure has an animal mask or features and chevron chest marks may be a bird reference. The "V" or chevron was associated with both the female figure and the bird as early as the seventh millennium BCE and that relationship continued through the Neolithic.

DRAWINGS 1.5 AND 1.6— Petroglyph rubbings from the Ussuri area in Russia depicting masks with connecting "rods" or "rays." These images were incised (pecked) on a basalt cliff during the fourth or third century before the current era in Sheremetyevo, Viazemsky district, Khabarovsk territory.

were often similar to those inhabiting the traditional religion. However, it is significant to acknowledge that shamans traveled in spirit form to confront the spirits (gods) or to retrieve a wandering soul, whereas, the tradition religion simple requests assistance from a benevolent interlocutor (see drawings 1.5 and 1.6).

Shamanic beliefs were common to certain peoples and they were often dedicated to adhering to and practicing the rites associated with the particular group. The beliefs were not only received individually as members of a group, they belong to the group and were communally endorsed. This collective belief unified the group and gave them confidence to think in the same way about the "sacred" world and its relationship with the profane world (see drawing 1.7).

When that belief system was monotheistic and the shaman claimed to be a representative of the gods, shamanism might be viewed as a religion. However, there was no dogma — no common message to be held as truth — no godhead — no divine being in whom all things were manifest, and no edifice of sacred observance. As an emissary of his client or community, the shaman confronted, cajoled, begged,

DRAWING 1.7— Lower Pecos pictograph of the "white shaman" figure typical of the cave and shelter paintings found in the Pecos River area of Southwest Texas. This figure represents Period 3 of the Pecos River style. These images may have been made as depictions of deities encountered during spiritual activities while under the influence of hallucinogens.

threatened, and challenged the requisite spirits to retrieve a lost soul, determine a course of action, find a lost object, promote wellbeing, or heal the sick and injured. The shamanism was the servant of the people whereas the traditional religion is intended to serve the designated god.

Shamanism in the Beginning

The origin of the world and the three major spirits of shamanism were issues of great interest to early Mongols. According to legend the three spirits were: (1) the "queen" earth, (2) the "king" heaven, and (3) the "prince" water,[72] and they dwelled within the three worlds of the universe (see drawing 1.8). The Mongol shaman's invocation known as the "fire prayer" state:

> Once upon a time, both the Earth and Heaven was a single thing of disordered structure, from which fire and all the universe were formed. During this formation, the force, which created everything with its own form, was the feminine creator Earth and the one which animated, or gave them a spirit, was the male creator or Heaven.[73]

People having common ancestry shared a sympathetic association with past events, though the current generation had no direct connection with those resources. Nevertheless, the association was firmly embedded in the collective memory, and it was possible to remember in detail, activities, events, or objects that were described, identified, or defined by others. There were many examples of this phenomenon, and among the most common are those found in self-perpetuating activities such as group ceremonies (birth, puberty, and death), organizational structure (tribe, clan, and moiety), and procedural affirmations (rituals). These elements, though generally intangible and generic to most societies were aspects of the collective memory and routinely associated with cultural heritage.

Early societies had a number of ways for promoting group integration and regulation, but they often relied on specialists to assist with regulatory procedures. The peoples of the Americas, Africa, or some parts of Asia assigned a position of honor such as the priest, shaman, and mystics to those persons performing those specialized duties. The range and scope of cultural practices, conventions, and values varied greatly, and they were shaped by many real and imagined forces. The notion of transcendent power was aligned with social-cultural belief, and the assumption of power allowed humans to manipulated circumstantial influences.

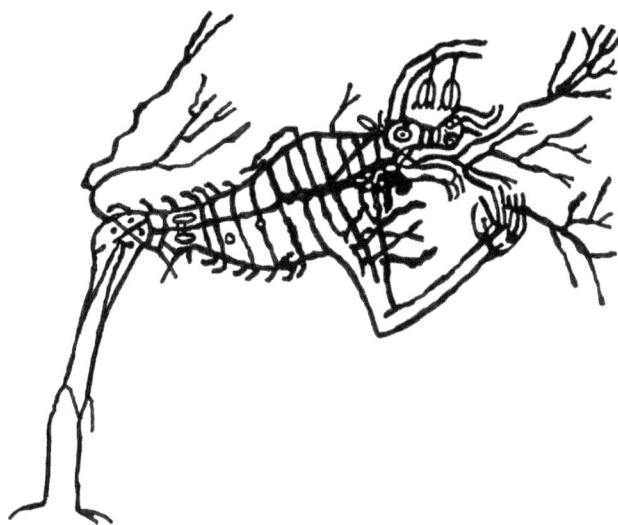

DRAWING 1.8—Petroglyph incised into a rock slab in the seventh century BCE, and found in a Byrganov, Khakasta (Siberia) burial mound. This fantastic creature combines animal and bird features. It has been attributed to the Bronze Age (c. 1000 before the current era) and interpreted as a beast-deity symbolizing the Lord of Three Worlds.

The power for survival was often vested in tradition, belief, and related ceremonies. The shaman, priest, or mystic was granted the responsibility for maintaining oversight and compliance with those established practices. Shamanism prevailed among the Turanian (a linguistic populations including Ural-Altaic peoples), Mongolians, and American Indians, and blended with their varied beliefs and traditions. Shamans were believed a class created by the deities to struggle for good against evil spirits. The belief that shamans practiced this magic art was universal among early people.

A shaman according to theory was born, not made. The suggestion that he or she was a shaman possessing supernatural powers often came in dreams. The neophyte saw grotesque faces or figures (see drawing 1.9) and heard songs that he or she was able to reproduce when awake. He (a male neophyte) often reported that when out hunting he lay down to sleep without ammunition and awoke to find a flask of powder by his side. This experience made him an object of attention, and afterward he was likely to find many things by his side without making serious exertion to obtain them. These experiences were proof that he possessed extraordinary faculties.[74]

DRAWING 1.9—Image of a helping spirit called Isitog or Giant-eye. The spirit was said to be a specialist in finding people who had broken a taboo.

An early publication (1923) written by John Lee Maddox described the shamanic "calling" and initiation process followed by the Chimariko, a native people of Northern California now believed to be extinct. Maddox explained that the first sign that a person was destined to become a shaman was a series of dreams. These dreams were for a male often the results of solitary visits to remote mountain lakes, in which the individual bathed at dusk. In the dreams various supernatural beings gave instruction the neophyte that had to be followed exactly.[75]

Mongol shamans once selected were thought to possess supernatural powers, and able to act as intermediaries between humans and the invisible forces of life. Shamanism is thought adopted in Mongolia during the eighth century before the current era. In his book *Mongolian Shamanism* (2007), Professor Otgony Purev concludes there are two ways for a person to become a shaman: hereditary and non-hereditary. The hereditary shaman was often identified from an early age and trained for shamanistic practices. The non-hereditary shaman was a person suffering a "Shaman disease" and overcame these natural forces with shamanistic power. Professor Purev also posits a second method of non-traditional shamanistic ascendancy. He states that it is possible for a person to become a shaman "by facing an unusual natural phenomenon...."[76]

Among the Quechua of South America, supernatural forces chose shaman candidates, and those forces became guiding spirits.[77] The selection process required the candidate to be struck by lightning three times. It was believed that the first charge killed the aspirant, the second reduced his or her body to small pieces, and the third strike reassembled the shattered body.[78] This ritualistic selection process involving death and resurrection also was common among the peoples of Central Asia and Siberia.

Korean shamanism is rooted in the folk traditions. Historical records confirm that during the Koryo Dynasty (935 to 1392) the court established ten state shrines for the performance of rites to evoke peace and prosperity for the nation. Shamans danced and played music at the shrines for national wellbeing.[79] The Korean shaman was a professional mediator between the forces of good and evil spirits. The female shaman in Korea is called a *"mudang"* and male shamans are known by the name *"paksu."* However, both male and female shamans dance to enter a trance — altered state of consciousness. Their soul is said to depart their bodies in this state and venture to the realm of the spirits. The shaman in a state of ecstasy could communicate directly with the spirits and often displayed supernatural strength and knowledge.[80] The duties of Korean shamans differ based on gender, availability, and power.

Korean shamans are divided into two categories: those who are chosen by the spirits, and those who inherit the practice from their ancestors. The chosen shamans have the power of divination and curing. They communicate directly with the spirits. These shamans wear different costumes according to the spirits they embody.[81] The possessed shamans fell into an ecstatic state by dancing to the accompaniment of a drum and gong. Whereas, those who became shamans by inheritance did not possess transcendental power, and the rites they officiate did not involve ecstasy for communication with the supernatural. Hereditary shamans did not worship specific spirits.[82]

The influence of the shaman was often based on the theory of disease and the local attitude toward the spirit world. Disease was believed to be the activity of hostile spirits that might be under the control of a shaman, sorcerer, or witch. The malevolence spirits operated upon the victim's body by affecting his or her spirit.

Life was a temporary union of different parts, which could easily be disordered or unbalanced. In all this there was no clear separation of the physical from the mental, or of the mental from the emotional.[83]

2

SHAMANISM AND BELIEF

Creator gods receive greater social consideration and ritual attention when they are also believed to be interested in assisting man [humanity] to attain his [or her] worldly goals. Gods active in human affairs have shrines or houses of worship, priests, or other religious specialists who will attend to them, and often are depicted in images.[1]

The definition of shamanism proposed by Kim Tae-kon in the book titled, *Korean Shamanism—Muism* (1998), is that "shamanism is a traditional, natural religious phenomenon that is being passed on by the central figure of the shaman."[2]

Belief in the Supernatural

Belief is a part of the biological process. People are what they believe, and those beliefs are always relative to a people's intellect and range of experience. The connection between ideas and outcomes is true only for the experience prevailing at a particular moment. Later the connection is replaced by new beliefs in conformity with the world of things and attitudes to which those beliefs belonged. Both the positive and negative aspects of human reality are included in extant beliefs.

Belief generally refers to the attitude that considers something to be true, and motives of creditability are the justifications for believing something has really happened or will happen. People believe because they wish to believe and because not believing would create a void and deny hope. Shamanism promoted belief. It acknowledged the threats and challenges that filled every part of the world and offered ritualized ways for confronting those circumstances. Early cultures required an interlocutor — a go-between — to carry the problems of humanity to the gods. It is logical, therefore, that shamanism was the forerunner of organized religions because the needs addressed by the shaman were on a local level and did not require the concept of universality or the omnipotent figurehead. The shaman entered the realm of the spirits and personally carried the massage to the deities — spirits (see drawing 2.1).

Belief in the supernatural acknowledged a force that addressed basic questions about existence that were unanswerable in other ways. If evil spirits were the source of human problems, then the removal of negative beings should assure a better life. The shaman in that process performed a crucial service in attracting or exorcising spirits. The performance of duties and

2. Shamanism and Belief

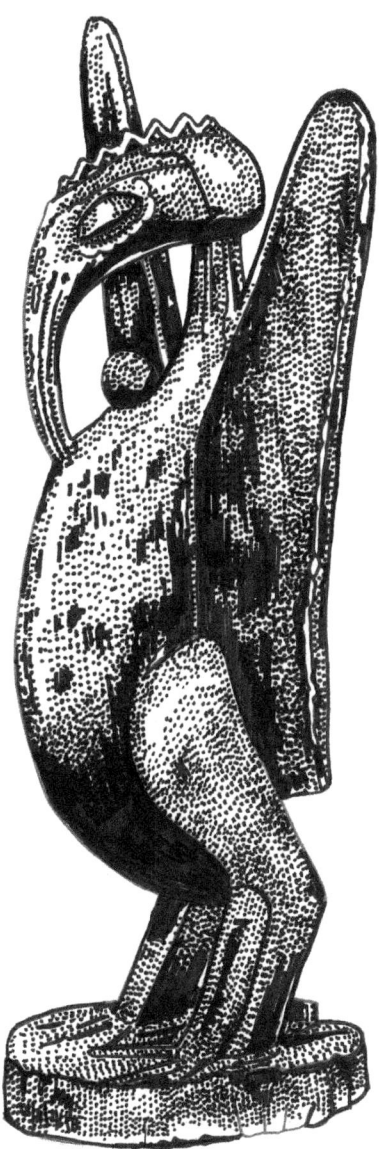

rituals based on traditional beliefs and myths concerned with supernatural powers were the shaman's tools.[3] Those powerful intangible elements along with other suitable (tangible) paraphernalia were used in response to circumstances that challenged the community's resolve (see drawing 2.2). That approach recognized existent belief systems, as well as continuing those traditions that influenced earlier generations.

Left: DRAWING 2.1— Carved wooden bird made by Senufo (also spelled Senoufo) people of Ivory Coast. Birds played an important role in their ritual and ceremonial life. The bird form was a well-defined symbol of fertility and an image of one of the five primordial creatures in Senufo creation mythology. Some Senufo myths also note that it was the first animal killed by man for food. Birds were a symbol for the men's secret society known as Poro during initiations and at funerals for senior members.

Right: DRAWING 2.2—*Nkisi* (fetish) figure made of wood with embedded iron blades, pieces of metal, and nails. This anthropomorphic figure had a stomach cavity that contained spiritually activated "medicines." A mirror covers the cavity to reflect unwanted intruders. These figures were found in the region of the Congo River and were made by the Kongo, Yombe and Songye peoples of West Africa. The *nkisi* were believed to have great power for divining and healing.

Shamanism appears to be based on the notion that events are related and that they will be related in the future in the same way they were in the past. The shaman manifested the idea that everyone believed in this repetitive process and that by performing the proper ritual he or she could interrupt or moderate the cycle. Although there is no demonstrative proof by either empirical observation or reason that beliefs are factually based, people are bound to believe in them and they are rational to do so. Concern for the dead that they might influence the actions of the living and belief that witches cause undeserved misfortunes are reasonable justification for granting the shaman the power to intercede with the malevolent forces. What mattered was the apparent success of shamanic intervention not its conceptual foundation.

The shaman was a healer or diviner but generally performed a greater service to the community — the reduction of anxiety. Shamanic power was believed to come from a supernatural force; however, division of the world into natural and supernatural realms may confuse our understanding of shamanism, which does not make this distinction.[4] Working within the natural world and not beyond it, a spirit, often associated with a particular animal, was said to take possession of the shaman and gave him or her extraordinary powers, often after transposition to a spirit world. It was the shaman's function through rituals or transcendental activities to regulate relations between the spirits and thereby to ensure the community's wellbeing (see drawing 2.3).

Belief in the supernatural has been a part of the human psyche for as long as people have observed the changing cycles of nature. It gave reason and understanding to those occurrences that were beyond human control. Endorsement of the supernatural had a primary influence on the lives of people. No other force was remotely equivalent to the raw impact upon the existence of individuals and communities as that generated by acknowledgement of the transcendental world. Those phenomena that occurred outside the rule of natural law were both wondrous and terrifying because they reinforced the belief that life as a transcendental concept had meaning.

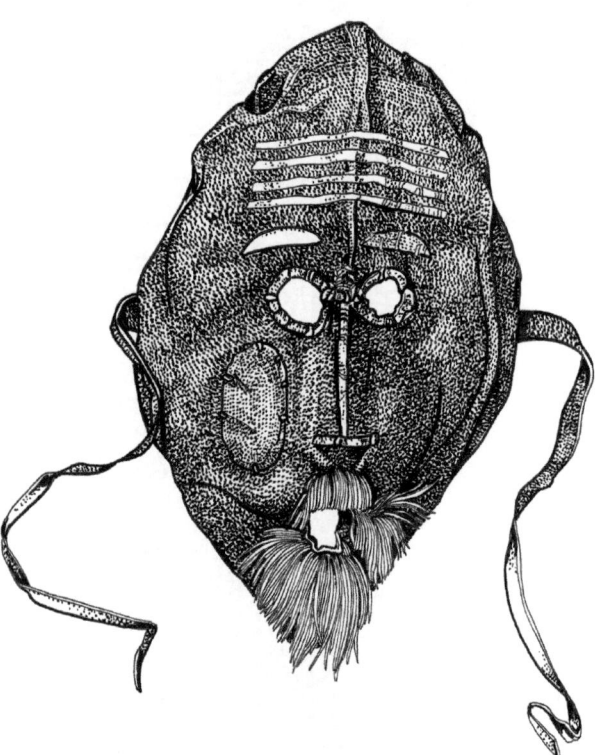

DRAWING 2.3 — Shaman's mask made in East Greenland in the early twentieth century. The mask made of sealskin, fur, twine, and sinew ties around the head covering the entire face to change the shaman's appearance. Such masks symbolized the spiritual force and its power. It also demonstrated the special relationship between the shaman and that spirit.

The notion of transcendental power is synonymous with institutionalized ecclesiastical authority in most contemporary societies. Generally called religion, this attitude is used to describe a range of beliefs and activities; however, acknowledging the supernatural and justifying phenomenological events are seldom associated with the institutionalized church, temple, or mosque. Nevertheless, supernaturalism or belief in the otherworldly realm is related to all religions. Consistent with this sociological affiliation, the shaman was an intermediary between the supernatural and natural worlds. That relationship was much akin to traditional religious practices. Alice Beck Kehoe elucidates this point in *Shamans and Religion* (2000) where she states, "Siberian shamanism is a well-formulated set of religious practices that, as recorded by literate travelers, has endured for at least five centuries."[5] It is likely that the practice of shamanism extends well beyond the historic horizon, but because of the verbal traditions of the people, no conformation of that assumption is known to exist.

> Whether shamanism is a religion ... well, of course it is, I have to say yes. But you have to define what religion is. How do you define religion? [quoting Urgunge Onon].[6]

Although a universally accepted definition of religion is difficult to find, attempts continue to be made to determine the essential elements of all religions. Beyond describing religion as a system of practices related to the divine, almost all definitions refer to belief in transcendental power, that is, they acknowledge mystical or supernatural experience that is outside the material world. The paranormal authority (power) is called upon to allay conditions or circumstances that cause anxiety, insecurity, dissatisfaction, and vulnerability.[7] These emotional conditions constitute an unpleasant feeling of apprehension or distress commonly described as fear.

The word "religion," like the concept, is used in most societies to validate deference to paranormal authority, rituals expressing that belief, group worldview or cosmology, and myths explaining the works of the transcendent power. Religion reinforces the human need to come together, and to ensure a level of comfort by indulging in "group thinking." It fulfills, in most circumstances, the sociological and physiological need of people to associate with a union of like thinkers. Thus, religion is the term societies affix to selected human behavior that is derived from a public source and communally accepted. It is probable that early humans, like contemporary society, embraced the supernatural, that is, religion-like activities as a way of understanding and validating daily existence. Life acquired meaning.

Every social group develops its own beliefs and values that the people continually recreate, and those beliefs are a mixture of pride, unity, ethnic loyalty, and nostalgia. As the world's cultural and natural heritage expands and contracts, societal values and historic indicators evolve to meet contemporary needs. Most societies have a short cultural memory, and that which remains was often modified by subjective and selective recollection. Objects, places, and other physical and ideological manifestations reinforced group identity, but might not in themselves constitute a true element of cultural or social validation.

> In Christianity the God created everything, isn't that so? But for us [Daurs] there is nothing greater than heaven and earth. So how can you ask who created them? In our own way, I think we [the Daurs] were advanced. We understood that no one created the sky and earth. They just are [quoting Urgunge Onon].

Belief is a product of social action although its producers are not always easily identified. When belief is more interesting or serviceable than reality, the belief is remembered and is often transmitted as myth. It is normal for people to embrace those beliefs that make their life more acceptable, livable, and secure regardless of the source of that authority. Different names are given to the belief process and all are intended to reinforce ideological acceptance that something or someone is true or real. The notion of reality reinforces the belief that positive intervention is eminent.

Defining a System of Beliefs

Shamanism is a complicated subject that involves "belief, rituals, myths, the psychic states of the shaman (with 'alternative consciousness' and aberrant behavior), social organization, political epiphenomena, and material objects (drums, idols, masks, headgear and ceremonial costumes, etc.). Shamanism could easily be described as a whole culture complex."[8] The shaman, as the primary element in shamanic practice, is the messenger between the invisible realm of the spirits and the manifest world of human life.

Two psychogenic aspects of humanity appear to be universal — they fear the unknown and they have a limitless capacity for belief. For thousands of years the primary motivating force for humans was very likely emotion, and the most dominant emotion is fear. The world was cruel. It inflicted many forms of suffering, both natural and human-made, on every person. It is, therefore, understandable that people invested much of their time and energy in avoiding situations that promoted fear and suffering. The avoidance process resulted in psychological and spiritual paralysis that aggravated the fear factor. The Maya believed that fear "keeps the soul off balance so that it cannot feel centered or express itself with dignified grace."[9] The Chinese gave importance to balance and the equalizing forces of the yin and yang. Humans in all regions of the world assigned their fears to the deities or demons and with that transfer, beliefs were formed to avoid imbalance in their life (see drawing 2.4).

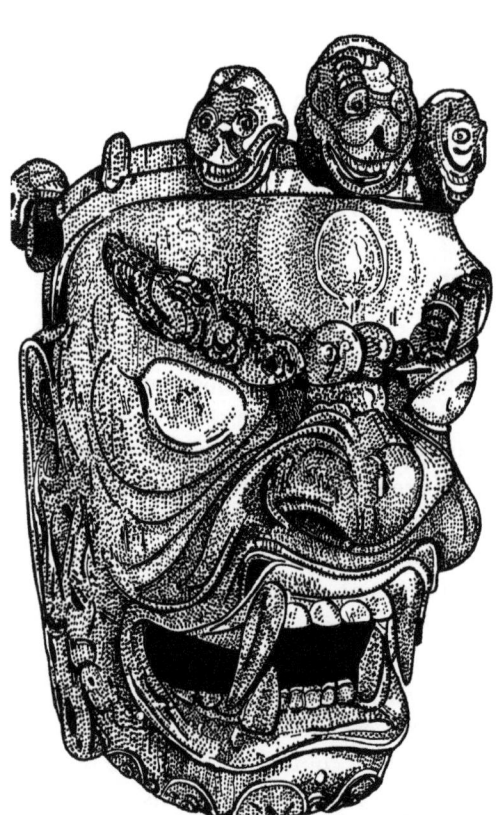

DRAWING 2.4—Carved and painted wood mask of Dharmapala (defender of the Buddhist faith). Masks of this type were used in ceremonies in which protector deities were utilized to scatter negative forces. These masks made between the fourteenth and seventeenth centuries were worn in ceremonies involving the transfer of evil or misfortune. Individuals were called upon to accept the evils of the community and were subsequently chased away in a ceremony that included masked Buddhist monks.

According to John Oman writing in *The Natural & the Supernatural* (1931), humans won three victories over the fluctuation of experience with the distinction of sacred and profane. He contends that the first victory was that "death is not an absolute end, but a part of man continues to exist; the second, that his conduct was not measured by the immediate situation, but had a relation to a wider society of the living and the dead."[10] Oman believes that the third victory was that there was an "invisible reality, which, though of uncertain and various manifestations, was more continuous and more reliable than mere material events, and was akin to man himself and responsive to his purposes, whereby purposes, otherwise impossible, may be realized."[11]

Commonly endorsed beliefs included communion with the divine, and the most generally used method for communication was prayer. The recitation of prayer or chants is one of the most ancient expressions of belief. These manifestations of divine are generally acknowledged repeatedly as incantations. Prayers commonly focused on personal achievement and well-being, and were practical requests directed to the celestial beings for food, protection, life, wealth, et cetera. Prayers, in some societies, gave hope to the living and accompanied the deceased so they may reach the preferred final resting place — a prayer for the dead. Prayers also may be directed to the spirits of ancestors to request wisdom, strength, or resolve.

The physiological and emotional needs of early people undoubtedly exceeded the limits of their understanding, and therefore, they required paranormal intervention to find acceptable solutions to challenging situations. This level of intellectual accommodation extended beyond commonplace experience and created situations where emotional interpretation was given full-range to augment an imperfect reality. The acceptability of that attitude on both the physical and mental levels was continually modified by group tradition, myth, and experience. A sympathetic understanding had to exist between all elements for the situational accommodation to be effective. The shaman provided that balance through rituals and ceremonies to reinforce expectation of acceptable outcomes.

A factor allied with the emotion of fear and a similarity shared by most people was the concept of good and evil. Inherent in that notion was the difficulty of validating the existence of evil. It was everywhere. Evil threatened the existence of every human, but if it existed then the acknowledged gods were not almighty, else it would be obliterated. Reason and belief determined that evil resulted from the activities of humans (witches, sorcerers, and black shamans). The attempt to reconcile the goodness of a god with the observable facts of evil and suffering in the world challenged the thinking of early peoples. The conflict arose when society assigns worldly measures to celestial activities. Group defined rituals and belief influenced by observation of natural processes guided the thinking of many early cultures.

The gods, according to early belief, were to serve the interests of the people, and the process for gaining assistance normally took the form of rituals. The nature of ritual activities included prayer and coercion to self-mutilation and sacrifice. Although the rituals were often extreme in their differences, they were grounded in and related to the social environment in which they were observed.

The levels and manifestations of belief took many forms. It was possibly because of the inconsistencies of the gods (masters) and the need to identify with particular deities that early people gave the otherworld beings human or animal shapes and attributes. Once the characteristics were established, selected members of the group acted as intermediaries. This humanization supported the notion of formulizing the supernatural, a natural human trait, that is, naming the unknown to gain control.

Belief in the supernatural was a universal condition, as was the tripartite structure of the universe — heaven or paradise (the place of the gods), earth (the place of humans), and the underworld (the place of the dead and demons). Humans endorsed some form of spiritual reverence as a means of addressing the social, physical, and emotional issues they encountered (see drawing 2.5). "[T]here is no satisfactory historical evidence that since man was man there have been peoples who did not attempt to enter into social relations with the extra-human powers of the universe."[12] The belief systems of many traditional people found reality in practices involving the placation of spirits to divert their energy for benevolent purposes.

Making Visible the Invisible

The need to make visible the invisible lead to the creation of symbols, and the symbols became elements of the ritual process. The symbols of religion arose as "collective representations" of the social sphere and rituals function to unite the individual with society. "Each kind of ritual is a patterned process in time. The units of which are symbolic objects and serialized items of symbolic behavior."[13] Although there are differences in its expression, the significance of religion-like activities is probably similar to all people and to all groups of people. One group may appear more spiritual, another less. One people may strive to placate local ghosts, another may worship a distant god, and a third may rely on magic to open the rain clouds and lure the game. However all cultures give signs of satisfaction with their own observances.

Regardless of whether the intention was to gain practical benefits or to sense communion, a person might seek to communicate with divine beings through a specialist or independently. Individual or independent communication was not considered appropriate or possible in some societies. In those cultures with a structured communication process, it was common to place the responsibility of communicating communal concerns in the hands of persons with special skills. That role in orthodox religion was consigned to the priests, pastors, rabbis, and mullahs. These were clearly distinguishable positions that were identified with specialized training and particular clerical duties. Shamans, diviners, medicine men, healers, sorcerers, and an assortment of other names were given to persons with similar roles in different cultural configurations. In this aspect most researchers agree that shamanism is certainly a tradition based belief system, but with no Godhead as is common in organized monotheistic belief systems.

Nevertheless, certain similarities exist among all religions and religious-like practices. One very specific similarity is that the real purpose of religion is not to make believers think, nor is religious dogma intended to enhance the believer's knowledge. Rather it is to make the individual act (or react) according to pre-established rules, and to consequently aid them in determining life activities. Shamanism did the same. The shaman gave the people a sense of hope and security that was, for the believer proof of his or her beliefs. That conformation satisfied one of the essential requirements for religious endorsement — the verification of belief.

DRAWING 2.5 — "Helping spirit" mask from the Kuskokwim River region of Alaska made in the mid-nineteenth century. It is made of wood and originally painted, but has faded. The "helping spirit" mask represented a transformation of the shaman's psychic structure. The spirits were to influence the people of the shaman's group and were associated with techniques of trance and ecstasy.

There is an attitude among many people that belief in shamanism is less creditable than belief in "religions of the book." This opinion reflects the practices of cultures that recount their heritage by means of the written word. However, shamanism, although often viewed as being "primitive" is recognized as having contributed in substantive ways to the development of so-called "higher" religious forms such as Christianity, Buddhism, and Islam. Shamanism is the foundation of many social and cultural practices including ancestor worship, animism, and other transcendental postulations found in most established ecclesiastical practices. Belief in a higher authority that can render aid as needed is a common wish regardless of the name pronounced or method used to gain that assistance. It is within this concept that the shaman, like the priest, pastor, rabbi, or mullah, attempts to "penetrate into the spiritual world and exercise an influence on it."[14]

The difference between priestly and shamanic activities is that, "The shaman communicates with mystical beings directly, as by visions experienced in trance [altered state of consciousness]; the priest communicates through carrying out established rituals and does not necessarily have any vision or other direct communication."[15] The priest represents power through office, whereas, the shaman maintains authority through inspiration. I. M. Lewis writes in *Ecstatic Religion* (1989), "The shaman is an inspired priest who, in ecstatic trance, ascends to the heavens on 'trips.'"[16]

The Earliest Form of Supernatural Veneration

Researchers have speculated that shamanism was the world's earliest form of supernatural veneration beginning at least 50,000 years ago.[17] Most scholars have agreed the term "shaman," as well as the practice, probably originated in Siberia. Scholars also associate shamanism with the notion of "a master of spirits," because the shaman (man or woman) acted as an intermediary between humans and the supernatural. As the true origin of shamanism is obscure and because it may have been practiced during the Upper Paleolithic period and perhaps goes back to the Neanderthals, the location of the first ascetic is difficult to ascertain.[18] However, ideas about shamanism have influenced the philosophical foundations of reverential systems across Asia, North Africa, and areas of North and South America. "In the shamanistic world everything [is] alive, and all life [is] part of one mysterious unity by virtue of its derivation from the spiritual source of life — the life force."[19]

It is assumed that the early hunter cultures were the source of the first shaman despite the vagaries of its origination. The logic for this assumption is drawn from several sources including the need of hunters to relate to the animals they hunted and killed. The shamans transcended the limits of normal existence, or perhaps more accurately, the normalcy of existence, to control the animals of the hunt and to become intermediaries between the hunters and the hunted.

Shamanic ritual practice involved related symbolic references, and it was during an early state of sacred symbolism "that we find the first substantially concrete evidence of shamanism still manifest on exquisitely decorated cave walls, displaying an aesthetic sensibility rivaling anything we produce today."[20] The representations of the shaman as "summoner" of beasts are found in the caves of Les Trois Frères. The so-called "Dancing Sorcerer" dates from the Magdalenian Period (18,000 to 11,000 BCE). This human figure with antlers of a deer (*Cervidae*), the ears of a wolf (*Canis*), beard of a goat (*Capra*), tail of a horse (*Equidae*), and paws of a bare appears to represent the quintessential beast. It is the amalgamation of the hunter's query (see drawing 2.6).

Discussion about shamanism is often confined to Siberia and regions of North America. However, shamanic practices were widespread, and were found where early hunter cultures have survived.[21] Andreas Lommel speculates that the "figure of the shaman grows out of the world-picture of the hunter."[22] The basic belief was that every living creature has two component parts — the physical and the spiritual. This concept was manifest in the practical world that was divided into two distinct realms, the seen and the unseen, the physical and the metaphysical, or the sacred and the profane. This division continues today in most so-called sophisticated societies. The belief system incorporated into many organized populations can be described as the deification of society and its structures.

The earliest recorded reference to shamanism in Japan is the Chinese document, the *Wei Chih*, written in the third century of this era. The writing describes the land of the *Wa* (the Japanese people), and provides information about the customs and manners of the people. This chronicle describes the female rulers as a shamanistic diviner.[23]

The early Japanese believed in a three-dimensional universe. The upper realm was called "The Plain of the High Sky (*Takama-no-hara*)."[24] That was the land where the spirits (*kami*) dwelled. The lower realm was the "Nether World (*Yomotsu-kuni*), the habitat of the unclean and malevolent spirits."[25] The land where humans and other animate and inanimate being lived was called the "Manifested World (*Utsushi-yo*)."[26] Religious observations to honor the kami often took place around a holy tree (*himorogi*).[27] The cosmic tree is a symbol found in many locations.

The Japanese believed charismatic (as opposed to hereditary) power was divinely bestowed by the *kami*. The shamanic diviner (*miko*), as a recipient of that power, was the contact between the Manifested World and the places of the spirits. The important role of the shaman during the

DRAWING 2.6—"Sorcerer," a figure found in the subterranean chamber of Les Trois Frères, France. This Middle Magdalenian figure dates from ca. 14,000 BCE and is an early depiction of a masked figure in a ritual (dance) posture. The cave painting combined human and animal shapes that probably had shamanistic significance. The nude male figure was drawn wearing a mask with antlers, a long beard, and wolf ears. The animal disguised might have been a way of identifying with helping spirits that were imagined in animal shapes.

early period of Japan was described by a Chinese writer who said that the "people of Japan have profound faith in shamans, both male and female."[28] The record shows that the mother of the first emperor of Japan was called "*Tama-yori-hime*, a common name given to female shamans meaning 'a woman (*hime*) in whom dwelled (*yori*) the spirit (*tama*) of the *kami*.'"[29] Eventually, shamanic diviners came from hereditary families and others (charismatic persons) were individuals without training. However, whether of noble birth or common origin, they were usually women exhibiting certain psychological characteristics.

Alice Beck Kehoe concludes in *Shamans and Religion* (2000) that it was presumed that all cultures that did not raise crops through plow agriculture were unsophisticated and not evolved much from animal ancestors. Consequently, the spiritual practitioners of Siberia, Lapland, the Himalayas, Australia, and most of the America were lumped together as "shamans" or "medicine men."[30] This assumption attracted an amount of endorsement from various scholars; however, it is an over simplification of a complex survival process. There were undoubtedly similarities between the shaman and medicine men, but there are differences based on social and cultural requirements. The medicine man in some societies was also a mystic — a shaman — who called upon paranormal forces to aid in the healing process. Whereas in other cultures he or she might be superseded by a "wise man or woman" and have no interaction with the supernatural.

Andreas Lommel, writing in *The World of the Early Hunters* (1967),[31] insists that the shaman was a distinctly different person from the common "medicine man." That opinion is based on an supposition that the shaman was of a higher level of intellectual intensity and reflected an affiliation with the early hunting community. Regardless of the name by which the person was known, the shaman was an individual believed to be in communion with the spirits. That individual's energies were outwardly oriented and "directed toward the community so that the trance [visionary journey] serve[d] as a medium of communication between the supernatural or non-ordinary reality and the community of men."[32] The shaman and the audience were integral parts of the visionary journey, and the "ecstasy" ended if the connection was severed.

"Shamanhood implies something more than prescribed sacred action. It is an intimate, mystical encounter with the fields of life and death and the forces that fuse these realms."[33] The psychological and physiological elements are unified in shamanic activities (see photograph 1). "Their bodies are left behind while they fly to unearthly realms."[34] The shaman traveled the spirit world seeking guidance, whereas, the medicine man awaited inspiration to be visited upon him or her in a vision or dream.

> The shaman was not merely a medicine man, a doctor, or a man [or woman] with priestly functions, he [or she] was above all an artistically productive man [or woman], in the truest sense of the word creative — in fact, he [or she] was probably the first artistically active man [or woman] known to us.[35]

Natural and Supernatural Cognition

"One hears much of the voice 'low and out of the dust' which is so characteristic of the ecstasy of true shamanism."[36] The shaman in a trance-like state was possessed by a spirit and given the powers of healing and divining. The shaman concentrated his or her imaginative powers into an intense mental image of an anticipated outcome to control and direct that

Left: PHOTOGRAPH 1—A female shaman in native costume and with face paint. She is a Toraja, a group of people living in the central Celebes (Sulawesi), regions of Indonesia.
Right: PLATE 22—Painted Canadian Indian shaman's rattle. The rattle has a number of geometric designs painted on the surface, but of particular interest are the two birds (eagles). Among the indigenous peoples of North America the eagle has particular significance as the conveyer of mysteries and magic.

energy. Masks, rattles, and drums were used to facilitate the connecting process. The ceremonial regalia allowed the shaman to assume a certain characteristics thought to be agreeable to spiritual powers.

Joan Halifax observes that, "Shamanic knowledge is remarkable consistent across the planet. In spite of cultural diversity and the migration and diffusion of peoples across the earth, the basic themes related to the art and practice of shamanism form a coherent complex."[37] I. M. Lewis explains that, "...mystical experience, like any other experience, is grounded in and must relate to the social environment in which it is achieved."[38] Consequently, the unique aspects of shamanic belief narrate how different societies and cultures treat the ecstasy and rituals associated with spirit possession.

Humans are a reflection of the environment in which they live. For that reason, they are constantly investigating and assessing that universe, as they know it. They are at once the same but different with their world, because the energy that activates their physiological and intellectual essence—the soul or spirit—and identifies them as who they are, is derived from their surroundings. Neither person nor soul can be called whole and complete without the other. Setting aside race, gender, age, and ethnicity, and ignoring social stereotypes, it is relatively easy to ascertain the nature of an individual by their attitudes toward the world in which they live. Interestingly, individuals differing from this pattern are generally viewed as anomalies—someone strange and difficult to understand—the other worldliness that often marks the shaman.

The human species lives in a profane state that is made understandable by a paradigmatic, mythically sacred setting. It is an environment where reality is contextually defined. A distinction is made between the sacred and the profane based on belief, and it is only the acceptance of this separation that allows the supernatural and the natural to be acknowledged. It is said that the shaman performs his or her activities in a trance or ecstatic state, and that the plane of communication is achieved by various means including monotonous sound such as chanting and drumming accompanied by dancing. Some shaman use both sound and motion to achieve an ecstatic state, and others use neither. However, a primary aspect of shamanistic performance is audience participation. The transcendent state must be transmitted to the audience. Therefore, shamanism is an intellectual and emotional attitude that requires a psychological investment. It is in fact a cultural, historical, and ethnological phenomenon, but its psychological side cannot be overlooked.

It may be assumed that confrontations between humans and supernatural beings whether physical or psychological could be dangerous, as well as fortuitous. Stories passed from generation to generation telling of the unpredictable nature of supernatural power, and how humans were tested by the spirits beings occupying the cosmic realm. The stories or myths surrounding these exchanges served to bind the levels of the mystic universe and reinforce belief.

Although shamans are viewed as being connected with the "other" world, as we presume the supernatural to be beyond normal understanding, they often live ordinary lives. They are allied with the physical as well as the metaphysical environment. The two worlds are the "true" nature of things. According to Piers Vitebsky, "many people may be shamans to a greater or lesser degree, according to their insight into this reality."[39] In cultures such as the San of South Africa there were no official shamans. Apparently "all adult males seek shamanic power."[40] They pursue this special status by dancing for hours until they succumb to exhaustion or achieve a state of ecstasy.

The author, Alice Beck Kehoe, observes that early anthropologists attempted to identify laws of such human behavior that were as qualified as the laws of physics and chemistry. Belief as a ubiquitous element of human behavior defies empirical classification; nevertheless, shamanism can be described as being among the most primitive religious elements in that hypothetical structure. It is embodied in the so-called Law of Progress. Kehoe goes on to say that because shaman lacked "formal schooling and written texts, [they] were supposed to act spontaneously and their beliefs were assumed to be irrational and deluded."[41] However, it is likely that early humans were quite rational and spiritual people, and that they were not "primitive" in the way people of different times and places often imagine (see photograph 2).

Shamanism is about belief in spiritual forces that existed beyond the control but not outside the influence of humans. "It represents the innate wisdom which warned humanity against straying too far from the fact of the preconscious and the harmonious relationship with the larger world it holds."[42] Those worldly forces were more powerful than humans and controlled the elements in life that were important to survival. Such beliefs were fundamental to supernatural acceptance. In most communities that acceptability was part of social tradition, and was passively endorsed by both the individuals and the group. Therefore, belief in the supernatural was an important way of maintaining the basic qualities of life, because it preserved the values accepted by the people. As with all religions and religious-like beliefs shamanism was a conservative factor in culture. It sustained tradition.

In Pursuit of Reality

It can be presumed that early shamans believed fully in their abilities and the magical arts they practiced, for they were of the same people and time as their audience. The forms of magic they employed were considered "sympathetic" in nature. This idea has been explained as a process where "...things act[ed] on each other at a distance through a secret sympathy, the impulse being transmitted from one to the other by means of what we may conceive as a kind of invisible ether...."[43]

Belief in similar or imitative actions had a very real application in most early cultures, and those attitudes were used extensively in shamanistic activities. If it was believed that destroying a figure in effigy caused harm to the individual, then it was equally conceivable that dancing in a way that mimicked an animal's movements aided in the hunt or contributed to the abundance of the herd (see drawing 2.7).

The concepts of similarity and contact were considered to have universal application. Therefore, magic was viewed as a system of natural laws that ruled the events of the world, and when viewed from the pre-scientific viewpoint the idea appeared plausible. According to J. G. Frazer,[44] the Laws

Left: PHOTOGRAPH 2— Snake Priest of the Antelope Fraternity, Hopi. The Hopi Snake Dance ritual is held in August, and during that event dancers performed with live snakes in their mouths. The dance was a religious ceremony (not social), and most of the rite was conducted secretly in kivas. Edward Curtis took this photograph circa 1900.

Right: DRAWING 2.7— Cherokee animal effigy masks representing the buffalo were worn in ritual activities to symbolize the group members as hunters. The ceremonial events endorsed the prowess of the hunter as well as calling upon the spirit of the buffalo to ensure an adequate supply of food for the people.

of Similarity and Contact had far reaching influence on magic and by extension to shamanistic practices. The Law of Similarity assumed that an act or action could be recreated by imitation, and the Law of Contact inferred that whatever was done to an object affected equally the person with whom it came into contact.[45]

Shamanism was also a process of cause and effect. It was the necessary basis of early human reasoning and experience. It was magical and illusionary, and the first requirement for belief in illusion was desire. The transfer of human suffering or pain to an inanimate object or distant spirit was a psychological incentive to relieve the physiological condition (see drawing 2.4). Native American shamans (medicine men, magicians, or jugglers) handled hot coals during healing rituals, and in so doing gave the patient confidence in their "special" powers. While there were spiritual usurpers in many lands and among many peoples, to assume that all ritual performances were no more than "slight-of-hand acts" is to ignore the power and purpose of the shaman, and to disregard the cultural foundation that motivated them.

Shamanism as a social phenomenon worked with symbols, both real and inferred. It appeared to be a celebration of symbolic energy, a half-exuberant, half-terrified flexing of magical powers, and a discovery and exploration of its remarkable potentiality. Masks, chants, songs, and power words were a part of the act of magical instigation performed by shaman to achieve specific results. Shamanism was a social event that involved practices recognized by society for achieving established goals, and although those activities could be negative for some persons, they were understandable by the group as being motivated by traditional belief.

> Every man [as the hunter/provider] would at some time or another feel impelled to consult the shaman and ask for revelation or blessing. This was usually at some point in life when he was not sure of his own power over the spirits of the animals he wished to hunt, and felt the need for reassurance.[46]

It is likely that in the beginning stages of human development an abundance of spirits was believed to inhabit the world, and their presence was reflected in every aspect of life. They inhabited the trees, sky, and rain as well as the animals and most animate and inanimate objects with which the people interacted directly or indirectly. The supernatural was the source of all positive and negative occurrences. It gave life and brought death for humans, animals, and nature. Every object, action, or person was subject to the power of supernatural forces. Everything possessed a form of associated power that emanated from the supernatural, and it was the shaman's role to serve as the intermediary between the distinct yet closely joined natural and supernatural influences.

Consequently, reality might be gauged against the anthropocentric attitudes that perceive it. The activities of the shaman were associated with the culture in which he or she lived. Beliefs were determined to be "real" when they satisfy and nourish the interests and needs of the people. Some cultures required only an external form of shamanic assistance to facilitate dominance over worldly circumstances. Elements of this assistance might be a successful hunt (domination of animals), a safe voyage (domination of the elements), or a victorious clash with an enemy (domination of others). Those services might require the shaman's spirit to search the cosmos for assistance, but where the culture did not have a belief in a celestial deity, there was no requirement for the shaman's extraterrestrial treks.[47] In other cultures ascending into the "outer world" to confront a malevolent ancestor or angry deity was a routine requirement. Similarly, the host community might require the shaman to descend into the bowels of the earth to retrieve a lost soul from the land of the dead — the "inner world."

The shamans of the Gurung, a people of Nepal living on the south side of Annapurna, visited Khrō-nasa, the underworld by "going down the nine ladders."[48] The shamans also ascended to the upper world by nine ladders where they arrived at the "mansion of *Mu*," the Gurung word for sky.[49] It was believed that the middle world, the land of humans, was "connected to the upper world by a tree in the sacred grove at Tapje village...."[50] The journey from one world to the other was similar to the ecstatic travels of the Siberian shaman.

People apparently understood the balance between the elements that occupied the space in, on, and above the earth. All elements of that crowded environment performed their roles in a harmonious relationship according to socially established norms. Humans had a central role, and animals were kin in that setting. The animals had souls that lingered when the physical remain were taken to feed the properly prepared hunter, and the souls or spirits of dead relatives or clanspersons were also present. Great harm could come to the living if the souls (spirits) of the dead were improperly treated. It was in that environment that the shaman found a societal responsibility. The shaman's role, although defined in different terms, existed and perhaps still exists, in all cultures.

People may experience a feeling of elation, generally associated with happiness and wellbeing, at times, or they may have a sense of anxiety and dread at other times. It is the latter that is the most pervasive, the most difficult to control, and the least logical. Most, if not all, people are capable of placing an identifiable attitude or action within the emotional responses to elation. It is a pleasant experience with friends and family, the new child, a successful journey, or the avoidance of some unanticipated disaster. It is the euphoria associated with a real situation that activates a person's sense of wellbeing. In contrast, anxiety or fear is most often identified with the unknown. It is an unpleasant emotion characterized by a feeling of vague, unspecified harm. It can be the fear of what might be hidden in the shadows, or the unanticipated crises that might wait around the next corner. It is death and destruction — the fearsome arrival of the calamitous four horsemen of the Apocalypse — that is determined, without reason beyond feeling or belief, to be inevitable. Anxiety lowers a person's ability to perform most tasks and as anxiety increases, behavior becomes more chaotic and ineffective.

The people in archaic times undoubtedly had apprehensions about many things both natural and supernatural. One of their primary anxieties, from a pragmatic perspective, must have related to physical debilitation. Illness was feared because of its mysterious nature and because it deprived people of the ability to participate in activities necessary to sustain life. The causes of infirmity in all probability were thought to be either the result of magical inducement or spiritual intervention. Even injuries occurring during warfare or hunting were believed to be due to spiritual influence. The shaman's role was identified with anxiety and the amelioration of that condition.

The shaman aligned physical maladies with cultural beliefs to give meaning and reason to the patient's bewilderment and distress, as well as a prescription for relief.[51] A part of the healing process often related to the mythological record of the people. That referential reliance allowed the patient to identify with mythical beings and to discover both the cause and solution for the distress causing conditions.

Consistent with this anxiety about life and death, people have a need to embrace the idea of salvation and resurrection. Stories, beliefs, and practices endorsing the concept of reemergence, rebirth, or life after death can be found in all cultures regardless of intellectual, economic, or sociological status. Although the conviction may not apply to all individuals, the group as a communal body holds fast to the belief of some form of life beyond the grave.

Different cultures promote different solutions for the question of immortality, but it is central to all belief systems.

Early hunters "invented" the immortal soul according to Andreas Lommel.[52] He surmises that the concern for eternal life was to free the hunter from the guilt associated with the animals "murdered" in fulfilling the necessities of life. The logic appears to be that the animals were not really killed, only the flesh was taken and that when the bones were treated properly, the animals would be resurrected. This reasoning required a "world beyond" where the soul of the animals could wait until they reemerged. The shaman's role in this process was to visit the land of souls and to encourage the animals to return so hunger might be avoided. Eventually, the "life after death" concept was granted to humans as well as animals. It is also believed that the shaman must experience death and dismemberment before being reborn or resurrected.

Many daily activities in the tri-parted universe included a certain amount of inherent risk. Simple occurrences might cause apprehension and anxiety. Undoubtedly leaving the security of home or community for a trip to a distant land, no matter how distant, could be the source of concern and consequently, the basis for solicitation of supernatural intervention. Shamanism was a unifying element in times of social distress or communal insecurity in addition to relieving the anxiety of the individual. Shamanic influence provided the means for affecting the course of events. The shaman acknowledged the uncertainty of life and emphasized societal belief as the basis for an emotional sense of certitude. Sociologically, participation in communal rituals identified a person as being inside and integral to the community that accepts the system of beliefs.

Because the people residing in an anxious state sought reassurance, they wanted answers to unanswerable questions, and they preferred to be guided by belief and spiritual intervention. The methods used in responding to these situations were varied; however, dependency on the supernatural was universal. The shaman was often the central figure in this process, whereas, in some cultures he or she lived and worked in the shadowy fringe of society.[53] Some cultures that employed the services of a shaman also made use of psychotropic drugs to deal with anxiety and to alter the behavioral responses of individuals to or within the transcendental environment. The consumption of psychotropic drugs was an early mind or attitude altering practice. Marijuana, opium, rauwolfia, tobacco, and various other hallucinogenic compounds were used in practically every known culture. Hallucinogens, such as mescaline, were taken in conjunction with religious ceremonies and are reported to enhance insight and heighten the ecstatic experience.

People at different cultural plateaus separated their social conditions into subsections and arranged those elements into an order of preference. Emotion and passion in that differentiated state were tempered by basic experience and reason, and individual reaction was moderated by group requirements. Despite the values assigned to certain aspects of survival, all people separated those things that had a direct impact upon their lives from those conditions that influenced everyone else. Human existence was a response to the interaction between the two halves of that equation, and ritual observance guided those fundamental but complex interactions.

The shaman, as an intermediary, summoned mythical beings and spirit deities to reach the transcendental state that joined the profane and sacred worlds. He or she became an imitator or narrator of myths and an expression of group tradition during the ecstatic episodes. Shamans achieved an extraordinary state of semi-consciousness in which they experienced phenomena beyond their mortal identity and outside their time and place. That mystical information provided a paradigmatic imprint that members of the group were expected to observe and perpetuate in order to assure the continuity of life, society, and the world. These models of social acceptability were often presented in mystical form with the cultural hero as the mediator.

Shamanism and Communal Necessities

Shamanism, like most human institutions, did not commence anywhere as a fully developed belief system. Certain "beginnings" may be assigned to simplify the process of defining history, but like other socially significant activities, shamanic belief and rituals undoubtedly evolved from traditional practices, superstitions, and the necessities for survival. Shamanism as an attitude and practice was highly social. It involved both the potential to heal and to cause sickness and death. It aided in foretelling the future, influencing the weather, and determining the movement of game animals. Typically, the functioning of the shaman was by passing to a state of trance or ecstasy, thus enabling direct communication with spirits. The extraordinary similarity of shamanic practices in different regions of the world suggests they were conceived as pragmatic responses to the necessities of psychological, sociological, and physiological survival.

The foundation of Mongolian shamanism was closely related to the interaction between people and nature. The human capacity for direct physical and mental communication with nature was believed to be much greater in early society. During the initial stages of social development, people had to interact with nature with direct means so natural obstacles and difficulties were overcome by physical and mental capacities. In that environment, humans were subject to natural selection in much the same way as other species.

Many early cultures embraced some form of shamanistic practice. Those observances were generally associated with hunting and gathering cultures that were migratory and generally without specialized social organization. The shaman, or perhaps more precisely, shamanism as a socially endorsed doctrine was ideally suited for a number of cultural groups living in different regions of the world. Though shamanistic activities was believed to originate among the inhabitants of Siberia, related practices are found in distant lands. Ruth Benedict observed in *Patterns of Culture* (1934) that, "Shamanism is one of the most general human institutions."[54] It was a practice that offered maximum benefit for a minimum amount of organized societal investment.

Benedict also notes that, "The shaman is the religious practitioner who, by whatever kind of personal experience was recognized as supernatural in his tribe, gets his power directly from the gods."[55] While this statement reflects the language of the time (1934), it identifies the shaman's link to "power and the gods." The spirits were believed to choose the shaman, and a spirit force, sometimes associated with an animal was believed to take possession of the shaman during a trance (altered state of consciousness). The spirit was the source of the shaman's powers; consequently, the spirit determined the type of services performed and the clothing the shaman wore, as well as the symbols, instruments, and equipment used including the drum.

The societal endorsement of the shaman is nearly as old as human consciousness itself, predating the earliest recorded civilizations by thousands of years.[56] As noted previously, the

PLATE 8—A shaman from Lake Sadra in the Russia Altai, a mountain range that extends across much of Central Asia. (A Turkic-Mongolian word, *altan* means "golden.") The shaman appears to be in ordinary attire with a cloth tied around his head. The drum has considerable adornment with a head-like shape at the top suggesting a figure formed by the handle and the crossbar draped with ribbons. Both ends of the crossbar have "jinglers." K. Hildén took this photograph in 1914.

word "shaman" is derived from the Tungus word *saman*[57] meaning "he who knows" or "one who is excited, or raving."[58] The Tungus, also know as Evenki, are a people originally from the Amur River valley in eastern Russia. The Tungus live mainly in Siberia and speak dialects of Tungus-Manchu subdivision of the Ural-Altic language family. In *The Shaman: Patterns of Siberian and Ojibway Healing* (1983), John A. Grim maintains that the root word for shaman has been traced to the Turko-Tartar word *kam*.[59] According to Vitebsky,[60] the name was first used to designate a religious specialist from Siberia. Michael Harner explains that, "This word [shaman] was specifically chosen by anthropologists and given a precise technical definition in order to accurately describe certain individuals in native societies who perform specific part-time functions in the community."[61] Dictionaries generally describe a shaman as somebody who acts as a go-between for the physical and spiritual worlds.

The magico-religious life of the people centered on the shaman throughout the immense northeastern Asiatic region. However, as mentioned, shamanic practices are also found in regions of Africa, Oceania, Australia, the Americas, and parts of Northern and Eastern Europe. It was an integral part of every hunting-gathering culture and remained an important force for all those who maintained the traditional attitudes. Although shamanism is a magico-religious concept, and not, as already stated, a true religion, it is in practice a psychological technique that existed within the framework of many religions and many ideologies. It emerged primarily within early religions and predominately within the beliefs of hunting peoples.[62]

William Howell states that, "Shamans seem to flourish, as might be expected, mainly among people whose religion was not highly organized and whose social structure was also simple and loosely knit."[63] This statement is followed by an explanation that when shamanistic activities occurred in other cultures, it was apt to be subservient to a form of higher authority. The indigenous religious conceptions of the Mongols including shamanism were exposed to a range of influences and describing this process in chronological order is difficult because of the absence of old sources. Even so, what was important for the shaman (and the people) was the ability to join with the spirits, journey to the inner and outer worlds, and know what ordinary people could not know. For the Daur Mongols, the shaman was someone, male or female, who was differently constituted as a person from ordinary people by the ability to fulfill these requirements. This meant not simply undergoing a public consecration ritual but experiencing an inner metamorphosis.[64]

The early people of Siberia and Northern Europe seemingly had complex sociological, as well as physiological needs that demanded satisfaction. There was little distinction between the physical and spiritual worlds for many cultures; so, there was a profusion of spirit beings present in every aspect of life. The phantasms manifested themselves in many ways, and were responsible for fulfilling or frustrating different functions. The Buryats living south and east of Lake Baikal had a more elaborate form of shamanic practices than in most Siberian communities. The Buryats revered spirits of natural phenomena and also had "a complex pantheon consisting of ninety-nine divinities as well as their numerous ancestors and offspring."[65]

Whether the shaman receives his or her status directly from celestial spirits as some traditions propose, or inherit the "authority" from a family member or mentor, the person invested with the position had a primary role in the host community. "The shaman was not a haphazard figure in the history of humanity. He [or she] was a person who took on the functions dictated by the norms of his [or her] culture."[66] There were benevolent and malevolent shamans that were aided by auxiliary spirits in specialized activities. There were an equal number of functions that caused people to seek the services of the shaman. "Many writers would agree that shamans were medical and spiritual practitioners. Disagreement comes as people struggle to understand the political, mystical, and religious role shamans played and sometimes still play in communities no longer easily defined as 'traditional.'"[67]

Consistent with the thinking of other regions, the world had three levels for the people of Siberia, and a river linked the three parts.[68] The middle world was inhabited by a plethora of "masters" (deities) that occupied the whole of nature. There were masters of the trees, mountains, animals, fish, and rivers, and it was the shaman's role to establish contact with the various masters and to regulate their actions by force of his or her will. The contact with the masters or their spiritual manifestations was generally achieved through trance induced by song and dance. During these activities the shaman wore a special costume, which in form often represents his or her "familiar" or animal helper[69] (see drawing 2:8).

2. *Shamanism and Belief* 41

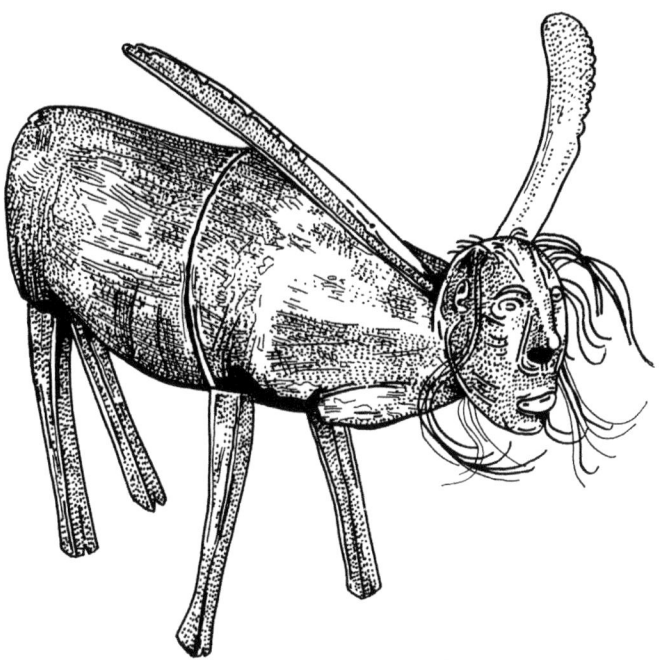

DRAWING 2.8—Caribou person (fetish) from Bristol Bay. The carved wooden piece has strands of hair and traces of paint. The figure calls attention to the human/animal relationship that was prevalent in shamanic ritual.

Particular spirits were involved with those privileges assigned to all members of the societal group. Other spirits were concerned with the activities of daily life, and some interacted with the extraordinary powers granted to shaman, sorcerers, and magicians.[70] Many of the latter spirits, described as "familiars," were believed to inhabit masks, drums, rattles, and other paraphernalia used for ritual events described as séance.

The beliefs of the Selkups and Kets (indigenous people of Siberia) like those of the Buryats centered on shamanism, and among these Siberian people, the special costume of the shaman was highly developed. It consisted of a long coat with ribbons and metallic objects representing the bones of skeleton, sun-discs (mirrors), and birds. The attire included an iron-framed open crown shaped like wings or antlers. The shaman's drum had design depicting the layers (levels) of the real and spiritual worlds.[71]

Mongol shamans performed many normal activities wearing ordinary dress, but for ritual acts, a special costume was worn. Henry Hansen wrote in *Mongol Costumes* (1993) that, "The costume consisted of trousers, a caftan, supplemented either with breast-cover or a round collar, hat, gloves, and footwear."[72] The garments were made of cloth or the skins of sacred animals or birds. They often had elements made of both fabric and skin. Hansen continues by stating that "All parts of the costume [were] provided with decorations of different kinds: metal objects, cowry shells, wadded cloth birds and snakes, and fluttering decorations in the form of loosely hanging streamers and fringes."[73] The streamers were cloth or strips of leather.

The decorations on the costume were intended to give the shaman the likeness of an animal, and by different types of decoration, different animals were acknowledged, including deer, bears, and birds.[74] Reportedly, many shamans' costumes represented birds. Those costumes were easily recognized because the hats were affixed with eagle, owl, raven, or other bird feathers (see drawing 2.9).

The deer style costumes include a metal band round the head with two horn-like protrusions. In some examples, a metal bird may be a part of the deer costume. A square piece of cloth with long streamers was placed on the back of caftans as the tail of the shaman, "by means of which he regulates his flight through the realm of the spirits."[75] Some costumes reinforced the impression of flight with small bundles of feathers (wing-like) attached to the back

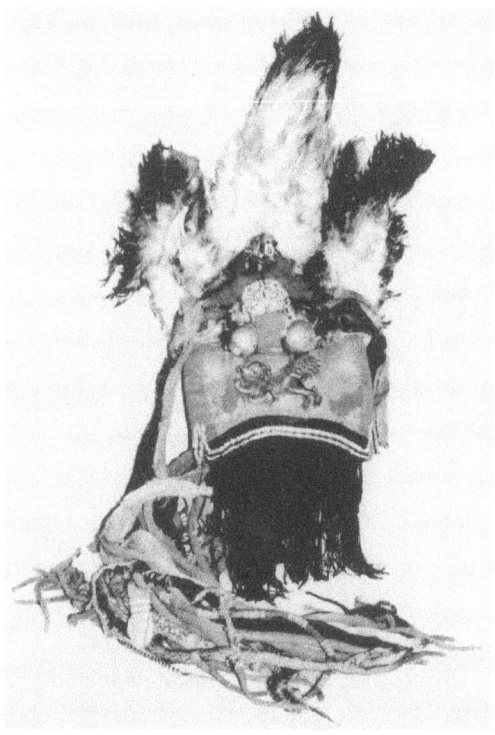 

Left: PLATE 24—Male shaman's head cover with owl feathers attached to a black wool cap. The band across the front is red fabric on which a winged lion is mounted. The lion is of chased copper and above it are two round brass bells. The black silk fringe covers the face and long fabric "snakes" are attached along with several rattles.[a] The fringe is not to prevent the shaman from seeing, but to protect his eyes from the sight of others and to allow him or her to concentrate on seeing another world.

Right: DRAWING 2.9—Mongolian (Tuva) shaman's head cover with long-eared owl feathers. Two of the feathers—called "horns"—were positioned to project from the headband. The fringe around the bottom of the headband is to cover the shaman's eyes.

of the coat or dress. These symbolic "wings" gave the appearance of being extensions of the shaman's scapula (see photograph 3 and plate 4).

Mongolian shaman's caftans (robes) were "decorated" with metal objects, such as, bells, flat copper discs (mirrors called "*toli*"), iron chains, cowries, and wadded cloth birds. There were also "octagonal plates with a hold in the middle representing the earth, flat figures representing human beings and animals ... flat iron bars representing the bones of the body...."[76]

The shaman in costume journeyed to the "Owner of the Earth" to ask for the soul of a reindeer in the Siberian hunting ritual. When his or her request was granted, he or she returned to the land of the living and presented the soul to the hunter. Although the hunter could not see the soul of the reindeer, the shaman placed it on the head of the hunter, and tied it with an invisible bandage.[77] The correlation between this ritual and that of the Yaqui Indians of Northern Mexico is interesting. The Yaqui dancer tied the head of deer atop his head (a male hunter), and performed a ritual of gratitude. He thanked the spirit of the deer for feeding the people and asked forgiveness for taking the lives of the animals (see drawing 3.2).

As an element of societal service, the Siberian shaman was reportedly to leave his or her body and to travel to other parts of the cosmos in search of spirits. It was believed that the

Left: PLATE 4 — Seated female shaman in costume. The symbolic "wings" are clearly visible on her shoulders.
Right: PHOTOGRAPH 3 — Apsaroke eagle medicine man (shaman) wearing an eagle headdress. The Apsaroke are a band of Crow Indians living in Montana. A basic element in Crow belief was the supernatural vision, induced by fasting. A person attaining a vision was thought "adopted" by a supernatural guardian (friendly spirit) that instructed him in gathering objects to be placed in his medicine bundle. Edward Curtis took this photograph circa 1908.

shaman's soul could fly to the upper world or could descend to the underworld without becoming an instrument of the spirits encountered in an altered state of consciousness.[78] The ability to move about freely was often reflected in bird or bird-like images associated with shamanism. The bird or feathers as a symbolic element is found in almost every culture. Shamanism has sometime been described as a gift from a great god in the form of an eagle.[79]

Mongolian shamans revered the eagle and falcon as powerful heavenly creatures. Professors Otgony Purev and Gurbudaryn Purvee wrote in *Mongolian Shamanism* (2007), that Mongolian shamans "generally tied feathers to their headwear."[80] The authors state that owl, eagle, and wood grouse feathers were commonly used. The Black Darhad shamans "fixed nine feathers separately onto their headdresses."[81] It is reported that the Sharnuud shamans also wore nine feathers but in three groups, and the Huular shamans "fixed twenty-one feathers in three groups onto their headwear."[82]

Different species of birds have been venerated by tribal cultures as "envoys that carry prayers and supplications to the sky spirits."[83] Birds were believed to be symbols of the soul as well as intermediaries to the gods. Avian objects and images were worn as talismans for protection and power from early times. Although feathers were believed to be the most potent part of the bird, the skull, talons, and in some instances, the entire body was used to attract and retain the bird spirit.[84] Symbols representing "the bird" are found on shaman coats, headwear, and drums (see drawing 2.10). Araucan shamans of South America believe they can transform their auxiliary spirits into the form of a bird.[85]

The significance of the bird is not overlooked in Christian religions. The dove represents the Holy Spirit, and in Acts of the Apostles, the fifth book of the New Testament written in the seventh to ninth decade of this era, attention is also given to flight and the numerous outpourings of the Holy Spirit, called *Paraclete*. The Acts define the activities of the Spirit as healing, prophesying, expelling demons (exorcism), and speaking in tongues. These activities may be linked to the Old Testament reference to the Spirit of Yahweh; however, there is no explicit belief in the "spirit" as a separate anthropomorphized manifestation. One suggestion is that the Spirit is the intercessor (*paraclete*) or helper described in the Gospel According to John. In 381 of the current era, the Council of Constantinople attempted to define the position of the Holy Spirit, and to give it equal substance to the Father and the Son.[86]

Contacting the Spirit World

During the period of the patriarchal clan structure among the people living in the vicinity of Lake Baikal in central Russia (middle third — late first century before the current era), when livestock raising developed and metal began to be used, shamanism took shape as an illusory form of representation of the existing socioeconomic system.[87] That circumstance promoted a hierarchy in "spirit-owners," and embraced shamanic practices as cult recognized activities. The shaman in this setting may have been the only spiritual specialist in a particular group and it fell to him or her to contact the spirit world and to make use of supernatural power. Though the Siberian path to becoming a shaman differed according to group tradition, in certain circumstances the selection was hereditary. A blood relative of the shaman was selected to inherit the "practice" once the older person died or retired (retirement might be the result of age, health, or the loss of power). The novice accompanied the shaman; assisted with the different activities; and learned the required chants, drum beats, and incantations. As the trainee's skills improved he or she was given more complex choirs until full shaman status was attained.

Among the inhabitants of the Andaman Islands, the spirits selected the shaman; nevertheless, the

DRAWING 2.10 — Stylized bird figure (eagle) on a Canadian shaman's painted rattle. The North American eagle is an important image as the bird that brought mysteries and magic to humanity.

transformation required a transitional process. The person might "die" and come back to life retaining some of the qualities of the spirit he (in this case a male) temporarily became.[88] This encounter with death and subsequent rebirth were commonly recognized initiations for shamans. Whether the event was real (figuratively) or took the form of an inner experience, the resurrection closely corresponds with actual biological birth.[89]

Shaman in other locations found their direction (or calling) in a dream or vision, and entered the realm of the dead to return with a greater sense of purpose. The dream of death was often experienced during the time of a critical accident or severe illness, and was believed that the shaman made a spiritual connection during this time of personal crisis. It was from that contact that a bond with the supernatural was initiated. "The crisis of a powerful illness could also be the central experience of the shaman's initiation."

The vision quest is recognized as a practice for gaining spiritual guidance employed by indigenous people living in the Central Plains of North America. Fasting, sun gazing, solitude, and other forms of physical deprivation were thought to grant the believer access to the spirit world. The guiding energy often came in the form of an animal to serve the shaman as a connecting force—a link between the natural and the supernatural. Whereas among the people living in a verdant environment, it was the jungle spirits that capture a person and reward him or her with special powers. There were certain "tests" that the person had to accomplish before being identified as a shaman regardless of the location and selection process. The tests might be physiological or psychological. They might result in a compromised physical condition or a state of mental disorder. Whether the maladies were the result of the selection process or the selection was the result of the spoiled mental and physical condition is unclear. Nonetheless, it was normal for the neophyte to experience a sense of rebirth or renewal whether physical or mental, and that encounter facilitated a spiritual linkage that was to be the basis for future shamanic practices.

Reportedly, the training of shamans required many years of preparation, including a period in which the candidate experiences intensive physical suffering.[90] The debilitating process was to prepare the candidate spiritually for the responsibilities associated with shamanistic duties. The training in some locations included long periods of solitude for communion with the supernatural and introspection. These solitary interludes were accompanied by rigid physical requirements such as fasting, the avoidance of sexual relations, and the observance of other taboos depending on tribal or clan practices. Some neophyte were said to prefer death to enduring shamanic training.

3

SHAMANISTIC POWER AND MAGIC

Anciently, men and spirits did not intermingle. At that time there were certain persons who were so perspicacious, single-minded, and reverential that their understanding enabled them to make meaningful collection of what lies above and below, and their insight to illumine what is distant and profound. Therefore the spirits would descend into them. The possessors of such powers were if men, called *hsi* (shamans), and if women, *wu* (shamanesses).[1]

Invisible Beings with Power

Shamans, as social functionaries, were capable of attaining an altered state of consciousness to establish a relationship with the supernatural world, and by that means obtained power and knowledge to help members of their communities. The shamanic help—aid or assistance—given to the resident community often involved dealing with issues of magic and witchcraft. The cause of illness was often attributed to witches using a form of magic to inflict pain and suffering on individuals. Witch-magic was believed responsible for infertility in humans and animals, crop failure, disease, and death. The world was made a difficult place in which to survive with mysterious forces and invisible beings of awesome power that could be commanded by those with the proper skill.

Witchcraft was viewed as anti-social and not usually a part of the shaman's undertaking. However, because he or she had a protective role for the social group to which he or she belonged, the Lapp shaman, for example, was often called upon to counteract or reverse the negative influence of the sorcerer (witch). At the same time, the Lapp shaman was believed to be dangerous because he (in this instance a male) had dangerous and morally indifferent helper spirits. The shaman, when angry, might transform his spirits into wolves or bears, and if he wished, he threw the transformed spirits at others. He might have them run as wolves or bears through the woods and fields hunting domestic animals.[2] This manifestation of imagined evil was a variation on the traditional werewolf theme that was prevalent in most of Europe at that time.

It was believed from earliest times that people shared the world with a profusion of spirits that influenced every aspect of life. Those spirits manifested themselves in various ways

3. Shamanistic Power and Magic

and were seen as fulfilling different functions. Some spirits granted special privileges; some concerned themselves with everyday life, and others conferred powers on the shamans and sorcerers. The shaman was the intermediary to deal with the complex interaction between distinct yet closely joined aspect of the natural and supernatural worlds.

Ruth Benedict wrote in *Patterns of Culture* (1934) that shamans of Siberia are individuals who by submission to the will of these spirits have been cured of a grievous illness — the onset of the seizures — and have acquired by this means great supernatural power.[3] Whereas, John Lee Maddox explains that the priests and exorcists (shamans) in China possessed a special power, "the so called 'Yang power' of good, through which they were expected to avert droughts and other troubles by rendering harmless the evil-force of darkness or 'Yin.'"[4]

Power for the Apache of the Southwestern North America was a very elusive substance, and defied most attempts to harness its energy. Power could render good and valuable services including weakening the enemy, protecting the group from attack, and when it chose, warding-off arrows and bullets. It is said that power enables Apache shamans to find missing objects, discover hidden adversaries, and controlling natural phenomena[5] (see drawing 3.1).

Power in parts of Africa, was equated with magic, and for the Asante, people of south-central Ghana, power could be found in minerals, rocks, plants, animals, and human beings — everywhere in nature. This power was neither good nor bad and could be activated by any person that found the right asking place, and asked in the correct way. It was possible by these properly worded requests to initiate magical actions and discover remedies of different types and of differing intensities.[6] "If these powers are locked into certain objects — such as pots, figurines, horns, or bottles — and brought to life with blood sacrifices, they gain in effectiveness and can be used magically"[7] (see drawings 2.1 and 2.2).

> Everything possessed power, or spiritual force, be it a pebble on the beach, a rock, tree, animal, or man himself; abstract qualities, such as beauty, had a similar force, as did the sun, moon and stars, and the lakes and rivers. Although this power originated in the spirit-world, it manifested in the realm man occupied.[8]

The insurmountable power of nature has been acknowledged from early times, and people recognized their inability to change or alter that primal energy with the means available to them. Consequently, they demonstrated their deference to nature by the belief systems they maintained and the objects they venerated to sustain their existence. That recognition reinforced the

DRAWING 3.1— An Apache dance mask made in southwestern North America. These masks were made of fabric (or animal skin), wood, paint, and feathers. Most of the early Apache people believed in the Mountain Spirits that represented good power. The spirits could protect people (believers) from illness. Four masked dancers selected by the group shaman were a part of the healing ceremony. The dancers circled the patient four times as a drum sounded, then waited as the shaman examined the ailing suppliant. The shaman directed the dancers to perform a series of dance steps and to "blow away" the illness.

separation of humans and the deities that controlled their daily existence. The people turned inward to identify an energy source that they could call upon for assistance to deal with those powerful forces. This survival process evolved into an elaborate system of spirit helpers (familiars) to serve as intermediaries for conveying the wishes of humans to the all-powerful deities. Those helpers were aligned with the shaman.

Magic, as it related to power, is a part of human history and an undeniable ingredient in the development of social order. It, like power, is an aspect of survival. "Spiritual beings are often credited with a knowledge of magic. They handed it down to men and sometimes use it in their relations with men."[9] Magic is considered to be an art so ancient that there is no known originating source other than revelation by a power associated with magic itself—a spirit being or deity. Shamanism and magic may have evolved together because they were practical activities used to achieve desired results or to avoid unwanted outcomes. Often shamanism and magic were the same activities, performed by the same person, and based on the same beliefs. They played a special role in human existence by filling the uncertainty caused by the lack of knowledge.

The Andaman Islands shaman gets his (usually a male) power from contact with the spirits. The traditional pattern of shamanic initiation of this land located in the southeastern part of the Bay of Bengal was for the aspirant to "die" and return to life. The shamans subsequently gained their reputation through acts of healing and the ability to regulate the weather. The shamanistic initiation might occur on a transcendent level or on a practical level. While the candidate was in a death-like trance, "the body was cut into pieces by the spirits of the Yonder World or submitted to a similar trial. The reason for cutting up his body was to see whether he had more bones than the average person."[10]

Shamans in many locations received power from involuntary dreams, and from voluntary quests. It was commonly believed that certain places such as caves, mountains, or other secluded locations were where power could be acquired. However, depending on local tradition, only power for certain undertakings could be sought in some of those places, whereas in other locations several types of power (spiritual assistance) could be found. Tradition might also dictate the tests that were imposed on the seeker according to the place where the power was sought.[11]

The shaman as the possessor of power was the heart of a community, but shamans fulfill different roles in different locations. He or she often had important political, mystical, and religious roles that were far from traditional in the sense of being underdeveloped. The shaman, for some people, was a communicator who breeched the void between the social and the spiritual, and in other societies, he or she was a healer or the source of a malevolent appeal to a supernatural being for harm to come to someone or something. Black or white, good or bad, the role of the shaman fulfilled the need of the community in which he or she lived.

For the Daur Mongol shaman "the vision of the world as divided into ordinary and hidden realms was not an idle cosmology, but a powerfully generative theodicy."[12] Mongolians believed there were different types of heavens to accommodate the spirit/soul when it left the dead body, and there were different spirits/souls according to social rank. It was thought that the spirit of a family master or tribe chieftain remained as leader of all the spirits of that family or tribe. The shaman might perform a ceremony called *ukhan-budla* to protect a child during his or her infancy or preside at the ancient spring festival called *urus-sara* that celebrated the renewing of all things. The shaman also had the responsibility to heal and to make contact with the pervasive forces of the macrocosm.[13]

Shamanistic attributes often included interpreting dreams, divining, guiding the souls of the dead, telling the future, and directing ceremonies or rituals to appease a violated spirit. Those and other paranormal abilities came as a calling from beyond the realm of the visual world. "In that other world the shaman [was] taught certain symbolic gestures that [were] used later in ritual activities to impart a sustaining or healing energy to individuals or the community."[14]

It was believed that the influence of the shaman did not cease with his or her death. The shaman was buried but retained consciousness in the grave, and knew everything that happened in the village. In acknowledgment of this belief, a person about to take a drink of water first poured a part of it upon the ground, and when in eating, a small portion of the food was first laid by in the same way.[15] This practice was to nourish the dead, and it was often for deceased shamans to solicit their favor.

One of the incongruities of shamanic activity was time as it related to the physical or metaphysical events. The physical activity such as a ritual had a time and place that could be identified. It was possible to say the event took place at a certain location and certain individuals observed it. In contrast, the outcome of the ritual, as a metaphysically generated event might occur in a location distant from the physical arena. Consequently, it was frequently possible to qualify the metaphysical phenomenon as a coincidental occurrence and not the result of shamanic intervention.

"The things of the world had the function of stabilizing human life."[16] They addressed the metaphysical as well as the physical questions about the relationship of the people and the spirits that held an essential position related to individual and group identity. When the parallel tracks of mind, body, need, and the supernatural converge, a physical and spiritual catharsis occurs and a path emerged. However, that union might satisfy the need of only one person. Selected elements were endorsed and "explained" to those persons seeking the security of sociocultural reference and thereby promoted the sense of group identity. Objects and practices "give concrete evidence to one's place in a social network as symbols of valued relationships."[17]

Secret Knowledge Was Power

> For the shaman, all that exists in the revealed world has a living force within it.... The knowledge that life is power is the work of the shaman. Mastery of that power; this is the attainment of the shaman.[18]

Although early people might have believed they were powerless to deal with the perilous and often unpredictable forces that surround them, certain individuals had or acquired a unique ability — a power — that allowed them to overstep the boundary between the known and unknown. That ability did not denote physical strength or mental dexterity, it was of a different nature that often was acquired at the expense of physical well being. That power transcended ordinary limitations and was beyond normal understanding. "A limited number of people were inspired by stronger spirit powers than others.... They formed an elite [group] since the numbers of men and women with shamanistic abilities were very small, and they were sometimes considered as outsiders to the community."[19]

The shaman, for preliterate people, was a mediator between the inspiriting world of myth and "ordinary" reality. As the archetype spiritual leader, healer, and social regulator, the shaman was a creative response to the supernatural. The recognition of that unique position acknowledged the incomprehensibility of the activities of spirits, deities, and demons. It was in that environment that the vocation of the shaman developed. However, "...secrets like power must be hidden from public view."[20] The shaman provided direct access to the supernatural. His or her special ability within the group was to make personal contact with the supernatural by use of a sacred language that was different from everyday speech. It was, in part, that privileged form of communication that separated the shaman from other members of the community.[21]

Ari Kiev notes in his book, *Magic, Faith, and Healing* (1964) that the provenance of power was not good or bad; rather, its asset was its potency.[22] As an example, if an Apache could control an amount of spiritual power, he (it was the male member of the group that was involved according to this report) could perform important spiritual or secular services. The Apache understood that the human was weak therefore he sought spiritual help. After the "contact" was made, the spirit appeared to the Apache in a "personified guise and offered a ceremony or supernatural aid to the person.... The power offered him a ceremony, and, if he accepted it, the songs and prayers which establish the rapport between the power and the practitioner were revealed."[23] It was in this exchange that the details of the ceremony and its uses were explained. Thereafter, the individual became the conduit through which the spiritual power served the needs of the people.

"The idea that a shaman received his powers directly from the supernatural also involved the concept that prospective shamans were regularly singled out for their tasks by the spirits."[24] It was also believed that certain attributes were indications of shamanistic prowess. Early attitudes, abilities, and maladies related to group beliefs, and therefore, marked an individual for possible service as a shaman. A people that gave special significance to drumming might detect that ability in an individual, and place that person in the care of an elder shaman for training. It was also possible that the group might identify a person suffering from epileptic seizers or having a debilitating disease from which they miraculously recover as a future shaman. Often the selection was neither anticipated nor sought by the individual chosen because the training as well as the life style was demanding and often physically and emotionally consuming (see photograph 4).

The Paviotso (Northern Paiutes) shaman derived supernatural power from the spirits of animals, birds, snakes, and fish. In a few instances power was also received from natural phenomena such as clouds and thunder.[25] Power acquired from ghosts and spirits of dead relatives was another concept that appeared among the Paviotso. Further to the east in the land of the Shoshone (Seed Eaters), it was ghosts that were the source of the strongest shamanic power.[26] Whereas, the Klamath people of south central Oregon believed that healing was only possible with the power derived from certain culturally identified spirits.

The ghosts and spirits of the dead were extraordinary sources of power. They granted that energy to shamans or protected the power that exists within the shaman. Dreaming about a dead person, relative, friend, or one who has been a shaman, was a means of connecting with the ghost or spirit. Power for the Wintu, a Penutian-speaking California people, came to the shaman from the spirits of his dead children. Many of the western North American tribal groups appear to have considered ghosts as a primary source of shamanistic power. However, in northern California, the Hupa believed in the existence of "pains."[27] These human- or animal-like forms inhabited rocks, streams, lake, and mountains. "They were the cause of all disease, death, and trouble, [and] became the guardians of the shamans, who were often inherited by them."[28]

Power also came from other transcendental sources. Polished pyrite crystals held the secret world of the Mayan shamans. They used reflective mirrors to help them see more deeply into the three levels of the universe. "They gazed into their mirrors and saw the deeper layers of reality hidden within their own souls and behind the illusory surface of the created world."[29] Similarly, charms, fetishes, and masks as tangible objects were ingredients in the shamanic process because power was often associated with prescriptive objects. Once the connection between the seen and the unseen was made, it was possible to transfer qualities from one sphere to the other or to influence one by actions performed on the other. The power of the image (the visual material or "seen" element) was greatly increased when it was used as an element of a ritual activity to influence the spiritual ("unseen") entities. Symbolic numbers, colors, sounds, gestures, names, times, and places also had an affiliation with magic. Although there was nothing particularly magical in most "magic activities," the psychological influence of magico-religious manifestations had a tremendous impact upon receptive participants.

Emotional receptivity influenced what people's saw, and what they saw reinforced their beliefs. The circular concept of this process was contrary to the linear

PHOTOGRAPH 4—Navajo medicine man from the southwestern region of North America. The belief system of the Navajo was complex. Some of the simple rituals were performed by individuals for luck or for the protection of crops and herds. The more complex rituals for curing bodily and psychiatric illnesses required the services of a specialist and production of a dry painting made with pollen and flower petals. This photograph was taken circa 1915.

progression that regulated most mundane activities. The non-linear approach directly influenced the two principles upon which magic was based — misdirection and supposition. The imagined can be made real, but the real was an illusion. By giving fear a name (and sometimes a face), it became real and in that established reality it could be avoided or destroyed. The Komi people in the Ust-Sysolsk area of Russia believed in a forest monster called "Vörsa." They alleged it had a "living soul" called an "*ort*" that followed people through their lives and appeared before them at the moment of their death.[30] Although the Komi people had a Christian priest who conducted public rituals, in their private lives, they looked to the old shamanistic practices for relief from such menacing traditional fears.[31] The forest monster had a name and shamanistic assistance could keep it appeased.

Real life attitudes and practices acknowledged daily existence and perpetuated the true history of the people. Daily challenges and achievements were formed by tradition and custom, and that process imitated the past. Similarly, it was tradition that explained the unknown — the monsters that confounded all societies — and released the people from their tenuous lives by allowing them to imagine a different existence within the secure confines of the spirit world.

The Status of the Supernatural

The shaman was a person the people allowed to influence their lives. He or she represented an unequaled power whether it was over objects, the way information was conveyed about objects, spirits, or activities, or the beliefs and perceptions of people. The shaman foretold what was otherwise hidden from the human eye, and manipulated objects or natural phenomena to satisfy human needs. Perhaps most importantly the shaman also contested the various evils, real or imaginary that afflicted humankind.[32] Those activities were wide ranging depending on the needs of the society the shaman served. The more ideal and non-threatening the surroundings were the fewer demands there were for shamanistic intervention.

Belief in the supernatural acknowledged a force that explained fundamental questions regarding existence that were unanswerable in other ways. If evil spirits were the source of human problems, then the removal of negative beings could assure a better life. The shaman in that facilitating process had a primary role in attracting or exorcising spirits. The performance of duties and rituals based on traditional beliefs and myths concerned with supernatural powers were the shamanic tools.[33] Those powerful elements along with the appropriate paraphernalia were used in response to phenomenological occurrences. The shaman's activities embraced existent beliefs, as well as continuing those traditions that influenced the earlier generations — the ancestors.

Ritual activities also had very practical purposes. For instance, the primary function of shamaness in Bronze Age China (most of the shamans at that time were female) was to bring rain. It was believed that the shamaness could convince the deity to descend from his home in the clouds and visit the terrestrial world. The shamaness while in a trance spoke with the voice of the spirit and danced to bring the rain to the arid regions of northern China.[34] Different spells and magical practices were used, but the shamanic activities were not without consequences. When other form of placation failed, "[s]hamans were burned publicly to bring rain to drought-stricken fields...."[35]

By the third century before the current era, the Han Dynasty in China organized an official state religion based on old traditions including the worship of nature gods and ancestral spirits. The "official" cult was established to insure the authority of the Emperor and his appointees. Although that belief system was to set aside earlier practices, many shamanic elements continued. The dynastically endorsed religion included the god of the Five Direction — North, South, East, West, and Center.[36] At that time, "[p]rivate communication with the gods through a shaman was discouraged and sometimes prohibited; [nevertheless] even in official circles the use of shamans was reserved for occasions of extreme peril."[37]

Eventually, the Chinese government established Confucianism as the acceptable way of life of the Han gentleman. Other forms of religious belief, such as shamanism, were treated as superstition, and it was the duty of governmental officials to destroy all manifestations of unsanctioned cult activity. However, that policy was never completely effective because popular religion practices grew out of the primitive roots of the ancient beliefs. The common people continued to seek assistance from the thunder gods, fish deities, and forest trolls.[38]

Identity with the four directions is found in the design of the cross. Although associated with the Christian religion, the cross was a traditional form for marking the four directions of the universe and a clear reference to the cosmic center and the tree of life. (In fact, the cross was not considered a Christian symbol until the seventh century and was not fully accepted until the ninth century.[39]) Belief in the cosmic directions is also a part of the religious practices of the people of southwestern Chihuahua state in northern Mexico. The Tarahumara (also called Ramámuri) observe the four directions — North, South, East, and West as part of their Eastertide feasting a ritual that often included the services of an *owirúame* or shaman.

The Yaqui festival mentioned in Chapter Two joined the influence of Christian belief with animism and shamanism. The dancer with a deer's head attached to his head seeks the forgiveness of the animals killed during the past year (see drawing 3.2). The deer's antlers were wrapped with red ribbons to signify blood, and the dancer wore deer hooves attached to his waist and cocoon rattles tied to each leg to create a rhythmic sound as he moved though the village calling both the natural and supernatural to acknowledge the request for forgiveness.

This Yaqui performance was a form of sympathetic magic. The people believed that pantomiming an event with an adequate amount of passion and devotion would cause that event to take place or repair damage done. The hunter stalked an animal in a pre-hunt ceremony and symbolically killed the beast with arrow or spear to ensure success in the hunt. Whereas, the Plains people of North America sought the return of animals killed for food — a revitalization of the animal population. The successful completion of the ceremony assured the desired results. Beliefs and magic were necessary and purposeful parts of survival.

Dance, performance, and special paraphernalia were elements that pro-

DRAWING 3.2 — Deer Dance mask worn by Yaqui and Mayo people living in northern Mexico. This extraordinary mask, made of a stuffed deer head with the horns attached, was used in *la danza del venado*, a popular *pascolas* dance. It was worn on top of the dancer's head and secured with leather thongs tied under the chin. Streamers of red ribbon were tied to each horn to accentuate the dance movements and represented the blood of Christ. Performers simulated the hunt that ends in the killing of the deer. It was a dance that celebrated the deer and asked forgiveness for taking its life. The Deer Dance combined elements of Christian religion with the magico-religious practices. The deer was slain — sacrificed — to nourish humankind.

moted the believability of the shamanic activities. Performances were enhanced by subtle but important visual elements there made the viewer a willing participant in the ritual process. These visual manipulations might be considered magical in the sense that they deceived the eye to reinforce belief.

The notion of sympathetic magic as a performance was pervasive. Magicians called "cunning men," "charmers," "sorcerers," or "witches" performing services including healing of the sick, fortune telling, and divination were active in sixteenth and seventeenth century England. Those activities were not unlike those attributed to shamans in other times and locals. These magicians (some said charlatans) relied on common sense, medicinal plants, charms, and regional knowledge to fulfill their designated roles.[40] It is believed that the clever diviners sent an assistant into the village before his or her arrival to discern the appropriate factual information and thus to prepare for the divining (séance).

Shamans use sympathetic magic, on the principle that association in thought must involve connections to reality similar to the hunting rituals of the Native American, or making an image of a person to bring about his or her death. Similarly, Mongol shamans sought an altered state of consciousness by fasting and ritual chanting often in an ancient or unknown language. The shaman called on the spirits by imitating the various sounds of objects in nature wherein the spirits are believed to reside, such as, the whispering wind, the growling bear, or the screeching owl.

Shamans, unlike the local magicians, were thought to have direct exchange with the gods. As Mircea Eliade writes in *Shamanism: Archaic Techniques of Ecstasy* (1974), "A shaman was a man [or woman] who had immediate, concrete experiences with gods and spirits, he [or she] saw them face to face, he [or she] talked with them, prayed with them, implored them — but he [or she] did not 'control' more than a limited number of them."[41]

Certain modes of communication with the spirit world were possible on an individual basis. The hunter, whether Yaqui or Siberian, observed the proper ritual before embarking on the hunt or an expectant mother performed the appropriate ceremony to ensure a successful, and painless child delivery. Assurance of a positive response by the deities often required sacrifice, prayers, ritual, dance, or dramatization using the proper costumes. The services of a shaman were used, and group ceremonies were performed for more demanding interactions with the spirits.

Because magic was believed to cause illness and death, the healing often required the services of a shaman to prescribe a curative. The Arunta of Australia believed the shaman accomplished the curing process by extracting the foreign object that was the cause of the affliction. The removal process required the shaman to suck the object from the ailing individual's body. Should the shaman fail to accomplish a cure, it was assumed that the person (shaman or witch) causing the illness had greater power or stronger magic. Another service provided by the shaman was the use of sorcery (dark or black shamanism) to harm another person and to determine who was responsible for a death or illness.[42]

Although magic, in its earliest form, was a part of the daily life of every person as intervention expectations grew and the practices became more complex; the magic-related practices generally were assigned to one member of the group. This decision corresponded to the natural evolution of social order — specialization through the division of labor or duty. The shaman or medicine man, in that societal structure was recognized as the practitioner of magic, that is, contact with the supernatural, and in fulfilling that role, it is possible that the shaman was also the maker of the first mask[43] (see drawing 3.3).

It is only in recent history that people have proclaimed existence apart from the supernatural world. Magic for most people pertained to all supernatural powers that influenced natural events. The concept of magic was often employed broadly in the sense that it was used to describe acts that transcend rational explanation. The shaman, as the central figure of the societal belief system, was the mediator between the two worlds — the natural and supernatural. His or her role was to serve the interests of a particular community. Magical practice included attitudes associated with the concepts of "white" or "good" magic. However, black magic was a practice of enchantment that corresponded to the sorcerous activities and was intended to do harm. Voodoo (vodun, vodu, or vodau) was a form of sorcery that originated in West Africa and was generally associated with fetishes (see drawing 2.2). Magical practices described as witchcraft were associated with powers derived from evil spirits.

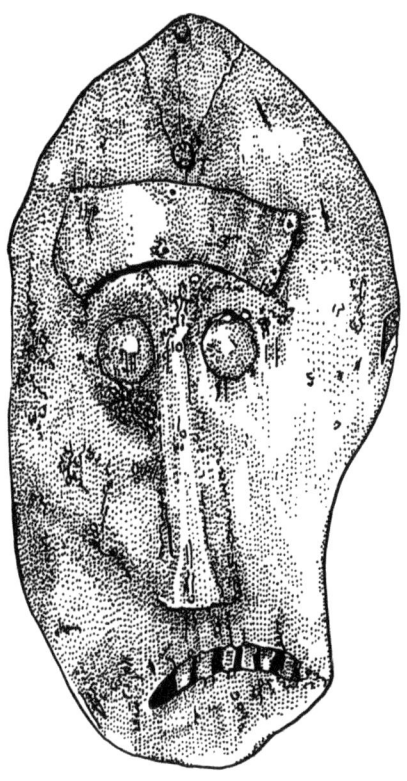

Magic as an Element of Shamanism

Spiritual beings were credited with knowledge of magic. They were believed to have used it in their relationships with people and thereby to have passed that skill to humans.[44]

Magic is a form of power. It is a generally applied term to describe that supernatural energy that is "beyond the ordinary powers of man, [and] outside the common processes of nature."[45] Sorcery, witchcraft, magic, or alchemy was believed to be responsible for all unexplainable phenomena. Illness, drought, famine, as well as life and death were viewed as magical manifestations unexplainable in human terms. Peoples in all parts of the

DRAWING 3.3—Carved wooden Nganasan female shaman's mask called *hua hora* ("wooden face") that belonged to a collection of shamanistic accessories called *N'aley kandachera* ("Sledge N'aley"). Wooden masks from this region are quite rare. This mask was found on an abandoned sledge (hence the name), and probably demonstrates the influence of Tungus tradition on the Nganasan and Enets people.

world recognize a concept of occult power for which they have specific applications and unique systems of belief. According to those culturally specific belief systems, both positive and negative forces were recognized. Each cultural group knew and respected the forces of the supernatural, and each developed ritual and ceremonial means of dealing with those influential resources. The results of magical intervention were easily observed when the magician or shaman could compel the spirits to comply with his or her wishes. If the patient died, the magic failed; or, if the rains came and the crops flourished then the magic was a success. The vengeance against an unknown wrongdoer could be claimed as successful with the illness or death of anyone. A call for a good crop or successful hunt could be termed a success with minimal outcome or the failure was easily explained by the disregard of a taboo. The process was self-fulfilling and every magical activity was situation or circumstance oriented. People motivated by the need to vitalize personal success (the birth of a male child, an increase in livestock, or the taking of an animal for food) or ameliorate social insecurity relied on magic as a way of fulfillment of their wishes.

George Vetter wrote in his book *Magic and Religion* (1973), that "the ancient Iranian medicine men, shamans, magicians, or priests were called *magi* in the plural form; singular: *magus*."[46] Vetter continues by saying that "[t]hese fellows were equipped with a considerable 'bag of tricks,' a combination of medical and practical knowledge, with an impressive ritualism bolstered by an imposing array of devices for deceiving the eye."[47]

The wish to control the spirits and the actions they represent stimulated the further development of magic. To suggest that shamanism and magic were the same is inaccurate, but to declare that they were two separate and unrelated aspects of human existence is equally incorrect. There was an element of magic as a special or mysterious skill in many shamanic activities, and the illusionary element was used to give creditability to ritual performances. A difference that can be found between shamanism and practices such as magic and witchcraft is that this latter group attempt to influence surrounding activities through covert means, whereas, shamanism tended to be open and often involved members of the community.

Nonetheless, the various applications of magic were recognition of the metaphysical influence capable of being controlled, directed, and used by humans. Magic as a practice was the utilization of that authority for private or public purposes, and its significance varied according to the values assigned by a particular society at a particular time.[48] Magic, or magic inspired beliefs, often came from the distant past, and those beliefs were bequeathed as a precious legacy from mythical ancestors to the people. No culture was exempt from such legacy.

Magic, though a part of daily life, is described as pseudo-action in that it is a substitute for true action. Magical activity provided a means of "proposing" an alternate action in situations where humankind could not alter the effects of natural or physical phenomenon. Magic changed emotional attitudes to reflect the anticipated outcome of the magical procedure. Belief was justified in this way, and an assumption of human power was maintained. Faith and trust were elements of every belief system and when the welfare of the group depended on magical achievement, the magician or shaman was elevated to a position of importance and influence. Magic in the form of spells, chants, potions, and rituals was an accepted intervention for otherwise uncontrollable circumstances.

Using magic was a way to change something—a situation, an attitude, or destiny. It altered the subject (object, practice, or activity) through magical intervention, and the alteration might be positive or negative. One way of activating the magical process was the use of verbal notification. Normally no "real" action took place when oaths of allegiance or curses were spoken, but because of the psychological and sociological association of the process to the anticipated outcome, the requested action may follow the "magical" invocation. That acceptance reflected the process of sub-conscious programming. "But far from saying that these rituals were therefore all non-action, the psychoanalysts found they [had] remarkable effects that could be arranged on a continuum from almost-action through various degrees of defective action to almost effective social action."[49]

Magic belongs to a domain where the things that happened appeared to be the result of chance or accident and where human activities were never certain of fulfillment. Early people looked inward to identify an energy source on which they could call upon to deal with those uncontrollable forces. The societal requirements helped to identify a system of spirit (shamanistic) helpers to convey their wishing to the spirits. Magic offered people a way of "dealing with forces and phenomena that otherwise appear incapable of control or were believed to contain an element of mystic danger that must be removed and nullified."[50] The desired outcome was offered by magic reinforced by belief.

The imagined becomes real when magic was viewed as a mode of thinking that utilized invisible forces to influence events, effect change in material conditions, or present the illusion of change. When a phenomenal event occurred, shamanism might be said to include an element of magic. Certain shamanic activities such as divination, spirit intervention, and some forms of curing appeared to have magical elements, and the same might be said of Hinduism, Buddhism, and Taoism. All material life is an illusion and therefore subject to manipulation by cosmic forces. The real world is in the imagination, whereas, the mundane is a world governed by unnatural circumstances. "To communicate truth of this kind, shamans must make the audience see what they see. Just as importantly, miraculous performances help the viewers see reality reflexively, the way the shaman sees it."[51]

The magical implications associated with shamanism is illustrated in the Paleolithic caves of southern France and northern Spain that are dated circa 30,000 to 10,000 before the current era. The depictions refer to hunting magic as well as ritual activities involving shamans with bird-like masks (see drawing 3.4). The magical connection is also shown in the rock engraving from Bessov-Noss, Lake Onega, Russia. This ritual illustration depicts a shaman with a drum and wearing a wolf's mask behind a reindeer[52] (see drawing 3.5).

Shamans used magic (a pseudo-action as a substitute for true action) to demonstrate the illusory quality of material reality and direct awareness to the spirit world. This purposeful deception was a way to demonstrate the spuriousness of human trepidation about the future or future events. The mystical elements or attitudes of magic also appeared in Tantra and other more esoteric sects of Hinduism and Buddhism that used mystical signs and symbols in ritual activities. The notion of "magic" as an activity, especially relating to its communal dimension, required an understanding of the cultural context in which it was used.

Magic might be a primary element of survival. Traditional people attempted to alter the world in which they existed by using magic. It was, for them, a blend of coercion, manipulation, placation, and wishful thinking, and the "first explanation of the interaction of the ego and the object."[53] The application of magic in the form of mystical influence had primary importance in satisfying the demands for food, shelter, and physical wellbeing. This

Left: DRAWING 3.4—A figure with what appears to be a "bird" head (mask) and an erect phallus. Beside the supine figure is a stick with a bird ornament as a finial. The figure found in a cave at Lascaux (in France) is dated to the late Aurignacian (Perigordian) period (c. 15,000–13,000 BCE) and is believed to be a representation of shamanistic practice.

Right: DRAWING 3.5—Rock face image of shaman with a drum and wolf's mask pursuing a reindeer. The image located near Lake Onega, Russia is believed to portray a magical or shamanistic ritual.

use of external power (spirits) to affect or serve the interests of others was inherent in the various activities that were part of the shamanistic presence in a community.

Engaging the Spirit World

Shamanism did not attempt to manipulate the spirit world through human techniques instead it generally drew upon the strengths and weaknesses of the social situation from which it evolved. It is safe to say that emotional (instead of intellectual) endorsement was required in all aspects of belief for it to be effective, and shamanistic practice was no exception. The practitioner (shaman) must believe in the effectiveness of his or her technique, the patient or victim must believe in the power of the practitioner, and the resident group must believe in the reality of the process for it to succeed.

The causes of misfortune, illness, and death were often too complex or too unimaginable to understand. The incalculability of these calamities validated the influence of magic on daily life. The successful intervention by the shaman in mundane activities such as helping the ill to recovered, correcting a wrong, or resolving an overwhelming situation was proof of the positive influence of magic. The details of how the results were accomplished were irrelevant. There were no inquiries into the laws of chance or probabilities, the powers of suggestion, or the natural course of events. When shamanic intervention was sought, the desired results were either achieved or they were not. For those times when the ideal outcome was not gained, any number of outside forces could be blamed for interfering with the magical process.

Shamanism and magic were inherent elements of many social activities. Hutton Webster[54] reported that part of the training given Maori neophytes joining the "priestly" society (shaman) included various forms of magic and ventriloquism. Among the indigenous peoples of North America, the handling of potentially dangerous objects (black stones, human skulls, and glowing embers) or animals (poisonous snakes, lizards, and spiders) was a part of the initiation process. Sleight-of-hand manipulation was used to give credibility to healing and divining activities, and various forms of prestidigitation enhanced the believability of certain rituals.

Connecting the supernatural to magic, as a part of shamanic ritual was an activity carried out on behalf of an individual or a community at times of difficulty. Creating the illusion of self-inflicted wounds to demonstrate the commitment as well as the power of the shaman was part of the magical repertoire of the shaman. It was believed in many cultures that the "mysteries of the future were revealed at the borderline between life and death, therefore the shaman also resorted to self-torture."[55] However, self-mutilation or physical abuse to gain a vision of the future was not as common as dancing or the "monotonous sound of the rattle and drum."[56] The shamanic "magic" of predicting the future was a part of human history and an undeniable element in the development of social order (see photograph 5).

Whether an act is called magic or shamanism the related activities were intended to help people with their daily problems. However, a difference between the two (magic and shamanism) might be explained by acknowledging that spirits or other supernatural powers do not control magic. The shaman might use magic as a means of controlling the supernatural and willing the spirits to do things that humans could not. Shamanism was an active effort to be in touch with supernatural forces, to influence them, and to do their bidding (or vice versa) as required to achieve and to maintain an environment in which survival was possible. Although some cultures chose to distinguish shamanic activity (magic in the broadest sense of the word) from ordinary activities, it was not entirely separated from many aspects of daily life. It was a necessary element of the most survival schemes.

The Energy of the Supernatural

People in all areas of the world acknowledged the energy of supernatural power for which they had specific applications and unique systems of belief. It was according to those beliefs that both positive and negative forces were recognized, named, defined, and celebrated. Cultural groups knew and respected those mystical forces, and each developed ritual and ceremonial practices for dealing with those influential and often unpredictable powers. It is, therefore, reasonable to assume that early people believed that if they performed proper rituals, observed prescribed

PHOTOGRAPH 5—A Navaho shaman taken by John K. Hiller between 1872 and 1885 (the exact date is unknown).

taboos, and venerated the appropriate spirits, they might compel certain things to happen. This connection between request and outcome was possible only as long as the proper observances were made and only for the current experience. The prescriptive practices had to be ritualized, and the relationship with the spirit world was usually defined by tradition but could be replaced by new beliefs to conform to the changing needs of the individual or community.

Magic made it possible for people to develop and implement a system that allowed them to believe that what they desired was within reach. It is certain that belief influenced what people saw and what they saw or thought they saw reinforced what they believed. The power of belief galvanized a societal force that was both emotional and physiological. It should not be denied that the intensified self-confidence produced by genuine magical observance could influence daily existence. Numerous acts and activities, natural or human caused were attributed to magical intervention. Unexplainable phenomena were assigned to the will of a particular deity or to sorcery, witchcraft, magic, or alchemy. Illness, drought, famine, as well as life and death were viewed as magical manifestations unexplainable in human terms.

People motivated by the need to boost an economic activity, cure an illness, or ameliorate social friction relied on magic or shamanic intervention as a way of deliverance from their dilemma. When the primary purpose of magic was to compel the spirits or deities to comply with the wishes of the shaman, then the results could be observed.

The successful shamans coordinated his or her actions with nature, the physical environment, and people to give reassurance and confirm accepted practices. In some locations almost every action or activity required the proper accompanying blessing or curse as an appeal for assistance. The sinew used to sew a garment required a request for strength and durability. A cooking pot, tool, or weapon was formed while the appropriate words were chanted to ensure strength and durability. The enemy will die; crops will grow; and animals will be captured or slain when the right narration accompanied the act.

The use of certain words or phrases as part of the magical scheme was practiced in many locations. The most common type of verbal declaration was an appeal for assistance. The words might be spoken, chanted, or sung by a shaman, but without being voiced the activity being performed could not succeed. An object belonging to a particular individual may be burned, pounded, or fed to animals, and the person's name must be spoken in a forceful and frightening manner to cause personal harm. Only with the pronouncement of the name would harm befall that person. As another example, when asking for assistance in gaining the affection of a particular individual, a bundle of carefully selected herbs are placed in a location frequented by that person, and the person's name was stated along with an explanation of the desired outcome of the spiritual intervention.

The power of words, whether spoken by a shaman or layperson, was so much a part of the cultural tradition among some people that care was taken not to revel a person's real name. This precaution stems from the belief that an evil spell could not be imposed on a person if their name is not included in the oath. Names were also changed to avoid potential disaster, and women were often known by the family name or the husband's surname (a custom that continues today in some locations). This practice was also associated with the naming of children who might remain un-named for some time after birth, so they could avoid injury or death by magical intervention. This attitude was also associated with the using of nicknames.

Shamans also utilized verbal assistance in completing their tasks. Gaining the attention of the power source was accomplished in many ways (drum, rattle, chant, or dance), but once the contact was made, words (often spoken in different tongues) were needed to focus the energy and complete the appropriate action. Words were a part of oath making in the Hawaiian Islands where priests (shamans) sought the aid of spirits to locate persons guilty of committing crimes and to inflict pain and suffering on those persons. The malefactors were literally "prayed to death." However, words or chants were only "one component of a magical rite. The actions that accompanied the words, and the objects used in rituals were equally important."[57] Similarly, the shaman used different symbols and actions to embody the essence of his or her power (authority). A special feature of shamanistic activities among the Chukchee was ventriloquism.[58] The shaman projected the voices of animals and spirits, and often had an extended "conversation" with the spirit world.

Because magical acts required a visual expression to be effective, the shaman often caused something to happen as a demonstration of his or her power. Shamanic activity included a visually oriented activity (event) in which certain steps were taken to achieve the anticipated result. The means/ends approach reinforced the assumption that certain acts or actions could be recreated by imitation or play-acting. Masks and costumes were visually inspired elements used to imitate the actions of spirit or invoke their assistance. Proper paraphernalia aided to the symbolic transformation of the shaman and his or her request from the natural to the supernatural realms (see drawing 3.6).

The level of shamanistic credibility increased when people acknowledged life activities from two fundamental perspectives — one relating to matters of the natural world and the other dealing with matters of the supernatural. When the alignment of supernatural elements was part of existence, the shaman could change forms, adopt another persona, and control the various manifestations of human or animal anatomy. Belief granted the shaman the ability to achieve physiological and psychological transformation. That attitude altered the deterministic process and facilitated emotional liberation for both the shaman and the lay constituency from the restrictions of daily existence.

Shamanism was about power and influence, and it was successful often enough that the people believed in the practice. It demonstrated the concept that there was more to the universe than was readily perceived, and that power or authority over things natural and supernatural was achievable. The possibility of power was perhaps the reason that shamanism was such a vital force in the life of early people.

Magic to Accept the Unacceptable

If by *magic* we mean the efforts of a human being (the magician) to control the course of events by non-rational means, mostly in the form of enforced ritual actions designed to affect spirits, gods, and the secrets of nature, then the shaman was certainly a magician in this sense.[59]

DRAWING 3.6—*Meninaku* mask made of painted wood, fiber, and feathers. This mask was probably used in the curing ceremony. The Meninaku, a central-Brazilian Arawakan tribe (Upper Xinga River), believed sickness was the result of having the person's soul taken by spirits of the forests and lakes. The patient sponsored a ceremony to counteract the illness and to prevent the offending spirit from returning. This spirit mask, possibly a cayman, was used in the ceremony to dissuade the maleficent spirit from making anyone else ill.

Magic is so ancient that there is no known initiating source—no beginning. It was nonetheless an influencing element of early life. Magic was probably not the single most important aspect of shamanism and in some communities it played a very minor role it was, however, an ingredient in many shamanistic activities. Magic that configured illusions to made seemingly impossible or unlikely things to occur was an element of shamanic ritual. Examples of visual manipulation are abundant and include transformation from human to animal, cuts and stabs to arms or abdomen, and extraction of deadly projectile by sucking.

Whether magic and shamanism evolved as a unified element cannot be verified; however, as with shamanism, it was inevitable that early people believed in some form of magic and the secret arts. Magic reinforced many basic beliefs and validated the acceptance of necromancy—communication with the spirits of the dead. Magic was an accepted way of explaining, empowering, and manipulating the material and spiritual elements of human existence. It accomplished that goal by using spiritual intermediaries—emissaries of the supernatural. Those supportive intermediaries (familiar spirits) had different appearances, and when not directly involved in magical intervention, they provided the appropriate charms, incantations, or spells to empower the magician or shaman.

Even during prehistoric times magic had primarily utilitarian objectives. People probably developed ideas about their environment and the conditions in which they existed from the beginning of human consciousness. They undoubtedly had thoughts about the world in which they lived and what they could do to alter their existence and thereby to achieve greater security. They may have considered what outcomes were desirable and imagined how to achieve those results. The effort to control life circumstances and the multitude of beings that influenced daily life brought about the founding of magic as a ubiquitous practice. Magic in most locations was the accepted method for resolving problems regulated by forces that seem to have no mortally recognized or socially accepted solutions.

The application of magic during shamanic performances or séances was often illusionary, and the first requirement for belief in illusion is desire. The shaman crumbled stone in his or her hand to make pebbles, symbolically mutilated his or her body, or transformed his or her physical appearance to that of a wolf, bear, or fox. Masks and other paraphernalia helped to gave substance to the illusion that fulfilled the wishes (expectations) of the people (see drawing 3.7). Magic promoted the belief that there was a greater meaning and purpose to the universe than was readily perceived. Magic gave the illusion of facilitating access to power over things natural and supernatural. The promise of power was one of the primary reasons that magic and shamanism were such essential forces in the life of early humanity. Magic as a part of shamanic belief was about power over the intangible, and it was successful often enough that until there was a more effective way of gaining the desired results, people continued to believe in magic-inspired practices.

The shaman as an instrument for ameliorating the unforeseen events of daily life came to be associated with magic because of the spiritual element, the unknown, and the dependence on collective belief. Scholars argue that shaman were not magicians in the historical sense; however, few can argue that they used illusion, misdirection, and audience manipulation in their divination and soul recovery routines. Shamanic activities caused things to happen as a demonstration of power just as magic required a visual manifestation for a magical activity (occurrence) to be effective. Magic, like shamanism, was a means/ends process in which certain predetermined steps were taken in a systematic progression (means) to achieve a calculated or anticipated result (ends). The means/ends process often was applied without total understanding of either the means or the projected outcome (end) despite the degree of social development. This approach reinforced the assumption that certain acts or actions could be recreated by imitation or playacting, and the ritual performance was an integral element of shamanism. Magic in all its manifestations promoted the idea that there was more to the universe than was readily perceived, and that power over all things natural and supernatural was the ultimate goal. The similarity to shamanism is obvious.

DRAWING 3.7—Eighteenth or nineteenth century animal spirit mask from Tibet or Bhutan that may be an animal incarnation of Padmasambhava. Masks of this type were used in ritual activities.

Reality was a challenge for people, and by necessity, life involved traditions and customs that imitated the past. Conversely, imaginary life found reasons for the unknown, unexplained, and unorthodox. It took the people from their menial, sometimes frightening, and normally difficult lives by allowing them to imagine a better existence in the spirit world. Magic was a process of cause and effect. It was the psychological basis of early human belief and experience.

Although magical activities were situation or circumstance oriented, magic, as contact with the supernatural, offered a view of life that was less complex. It revealed ways of managing everyday activities, and provided the means for people to meet and accommodate the uncertainties they regularly confronted. All things, tangible and intangible, were potential sources of magical interaction. The mingling of the physical and metaphysical, human and animal, external and internal, or life and death provided an abundant range of opportunities for magical influence.

Unusual occurrences in Greenland were believed controlled by spirits, and those spirits were controlled by formulas or charms that were in the possession of the medicine man [shaman], although certain simple charms might be owned and used by anyone.[60] The old men among the Nanai people (also called the Golds) living in the Amur region of northeastern Asia were believed to speak directly with animals. According to Urgunge Onon and as described in *Shamans and Elders* (1996), "[t]here were particular things to be said to each kind of animal and fish."[61]

Magical intervention was believed to aid in identifying the causes of human misery and offering hope for deliverance in the most desperate circumstances. It was a way for humans to deflect or redirect the forces of fate. Magic, as previously noted, was a pseudo-action in that it was a substitute for real action. It simulated a personalized protection system and allowed people to believe that what they desired was within reach. It also accepted self-delusion when circumstances were too distorted to achieve a desired outcome. The power of belief energized a force stronger than reality that permitted any number of acts and activities, natural or human to be attributed to magical intervention. Unexplainable phenomena were assigned to the will of a particular deity or to sorcery, witchcraft, and magic (see photograph 6).

Rituals associated with shamanic activities and those for magical observances were often detached from the activities of daily life. Although they took place in a common location, the atmosphere during these performances had a paranormal character that added to their special nature. The rituals were performed in a time-honored method and often to the accompaniment of chants, songs, and dances. The overriding purpose of magical activities was to explain, direct, or control the real and unreal worlds by ordering and validating societal experience in terms of its own rationalization. Social systems and magical practices were mutually reinforcing, and it was that sense of magical release that freed the people from the responsibilities and reality of daily life. That attitude and the processes for reinforcing and acknowledging that belief were closely intertwined. It is likely that dependence on the supernatural caused magic and shamanism to merge into a single attitude of recognition and placation when needed to appease the malevolent spirits.

People have always investigated the limits of the world in which they live. They searched for confirmation of their environment because the energy that activated their physiological and intellectual essence, and identified them as whom they were, was derived from their surroundings. It was in this setting that the phenomenal power of nature generated magic, but it was the people who enhanced, refined, and used it. Neither humanity nor the environment was capable of finalizing this creative process without the corresponding contribution. The Mayan people offered regular devotion to their core concepts about the essential order of the cosmos, its patterns, purposes, and the place of human beings in it.[62] Maya shamanism survived for two and a half millennia as a social institution, because the shamans helped their followers to re-create a vital view of reality over and over. They healed sick children, blessed new homes, and renewed the nurturing bonds between the inhabitants of this world and those of the Otherworld.[63]

Magic to the Kwaio, living on the volcanic island of Malaita (Mala) in the Solomon Islands, was viewed "as one kind of technology, a form of pragmatic action distinct from more directly physical work (fencing or weeding a garden, cutting sago pith as food for pigs, plotting and executing a pig theft) which was added to such physical work to achieve success."[64] Daily activities included a certain amount of risk and magic allowed people to adjust to the societal circumstances in which they existed. Simple occurrences caused anxiety that could be alleviated by magical observances that intensified self-confidence and actually influenced situational outcomes. An unanticipated change in familiar or communal conditions was a source of concern, and was, therefore, the basis for solicitation of supernatural intervention. In times of social distress or communal anxiety, the shamanic intervention and magical influence were unifying elements. Shamanism was also an element of social control that enforced group behavior.

Shamanism had a distinct role in matters of life and death. Here again, the Kwaio took a pragmatic attitude. "[L]iving as they did in an uncertain world. A curer [shaman] might have considerable faith in his magic [that may include applying a poultice or spitting chewed leaves, therefore having a pharmaceutical element], but he still must face the fact that it sometimes works and sometimes does not."[65]

PHOTOGRAPH 6—Hami—Koskimo costume. A Koskimo individual wears a full-body fur garment, oversized gloves, and the mask of a Hami ("dangerous thing") during the numhlim ceremony. Edward Curtis took this photograph circa 1914.

When the cure failed, the shaman, as a psychopomp, was responsible for escorting the soul of the departed into the underworld and to its proper location. The spirit helpers were necessary accompanying voyagers on this journey that was often long and dangerous for the shaman, the soul of the departed, and those left behind. If the soul of the deceased was not taken to its predestined location, it might wander the world of the living causing harm to family and friends. In a similar way, the mortuary magic of the Egyptians was to win for the dead a pleasant life in the hereafter.[66] The World of the Dead was in the west according to Egyptian tradition. It was the land where the Sun god disappeared in the evening. As a result of this belief, the dead were spoken of as the "Westerners."[67] It was also understood by the Egyptians that death soared into the sky disguised as a bird, and it was there that the heavenly barge of Ra, the Sun god, awaited them "and transformed them into stars to travel with him through the vault of the heavens."[68]

The Chukchee living in the northeastern part of Siberia, like most other Siberian peoples, practiced a form of animism as well as mystical shamanism. They believed that invisible spirits inhabited the universe and that the spirits were extremely mobile and capable of changing their size and appearance.[69] The stealing of a person's soul by malevolent spirits was believed to cause Illness and death. The Chukchee used amulets, incantations, and rituals to protect against spiritual intrusion. Amulets were considered invested with special powers, protecting their owners against evil spirits. They were fastened to clothing, hung in the dwelling, attached to hunting and fishing implements, and painted on the dwelling walls and covers.[70] A special place was given to these magic objects as protection against the intervention of spirits.

Chukchee also made sacrifices to the spirits as a further guard against the unknown. The reindeer-breeders sacrificed reindeer and the coastal Chukchee sacrificed dogs. Those rituals were held in the autumn. People and sleds were anointed with blood following the slaughter, and the meat was distributed among guests. The ritual required the cooking and eating of the meat. Following consumption of the meat from which the spiritual elements had been withdrawn, members of the family struck the tambourine (single-faced drum) to announce to the deities the ritual fulfillment. The shaman, as a part of the host community, took part in these events, but wore no special costume. Even so, he or she was easily recognizable by the array of amulets and tassels sewn to their clothing.

Witchcraft and Evil Magic

No culture is without myths and tales relating to witchcraft, and the following themes seem to appear always and everywhere:

1. Were-animals who move about a night with miraculous speed, gathering in witches' Sabbaths to work evil magic.
2. The notion that illness, emaciation, and eventual death can result from introducing by magical means some sort of noxious substance into the body of the victim.
3. A connection between incest and witchcraft.[71]

According to Joseph Ennemoser in his book *The History of Magic* (1970), the word *Hexe* (witch) comes from "*Haegse*, a wise woman; and *Haegse* from Hygia ... which means wisdom."[72] Ennemoser explains that the word was changed into "*Hesee*, witch, and then signified a wicked woman who had a spirit of sorcery and divination...."[73] The meaning of the word and the person changed significantly after the introduction of the Christian religion. At the beginning of this era these women were considered unpleasant and ridiculous. It was later when magical potions were believed to produce impotence or abortion, and witches were credited with nocturnal riding through the air, the changing of a person's disposition from love to hate, the control of thunder, rain, and sunshine, the transformation of a man into an animal, and the intercourse of incubi and succubi with human beings, that the church condemned their activities and eventually sentenced hundreds to death by burning.

Witchcraft as the notion of malevolent individuals intent on doing harm co-existed with and gave creditability to the positive influences of shamanism and magic. The malevolence identified with witchcraft was taken in by organized religions as representative of the universal evil against which the righteous was to resist. The concept of good could not exist without a comparable negative ideology.

"Witchcraft and sorcery are ... close to magic as are processes of oracular consultation, divination and many forms of curing."[74] They were concerned with producing effects that were beyond the natural powers of humans. Witchcraft was however involved with the idea of a deceitful activity that appeal to the intervention of malevolent spirits. Supernatural aid might be invoked to cause the death of a person, to awaken the passion of love in an individual who is the object of desire, to call up the dead, or to bring calamity upon enemies or rivals. This is not an exhaustive enumeration, but these activities represent some of the principal purposes that witchcraft was made to serve. Witchcraft was associated with the interests of the malicious and vengeful forces during all periods of the world's history.

The power to do "good" might be transformed to the purposes of evil — the savior of souls may become the thief. When a shaman used his or her special powers to harm others or to manipulate them, they were called warlocks (*bokshas*) or witches (*bokshis*).[75] The Navajo witches were thought to be living Earth Surface people who acted in an evil manner for personal gain. Their most heinous activities were eating human flesh and incest. The Navajo witch might be anyone, because during the daylight hours they looked and acted like a normal person, but at night they roamed the countryside dressed in the skin of wolves, bears, coyotes, or foxes. The witch that was also a shaman made people ill (as a witch), so they could be cured (by the shaman).[76] It was a lucrative practice. To avoid that deception, shaman (*jhankris*) in Nepal must swear an oath to their teacher (*guruji*) that they will use their ability for good.

Tlingit witches also appeared to be normal men and women, and they were believed to have the power to cause illness and death. They were a constant threat to the people because they could strike without warning. "When the witches wanted to harm a person, they would obtain something closely associated with him [or her] — a hair, a fingernail, spittle — and bury it near a grave house."[77] It was believed that when the witch completed this activity the person became ill and sometimes died. The Tlingit also believed that illness could be cured only by supernatural means. It was the shaman that had the power to combat the maliciousness of witches.

The belief in witchcraft existed as an important force among many peoples. It played a conspicuous part in ancient Egypt and Babylonia. Witches, according to tradition, had preternatural powers such as the ability to assume different shapes at will, and to torment their chosen victims, while a "familiar spirit" performed any service that might be needed to further their nefarious purposes. It was in the role of the tormentor and troublemaker that witches and witchcraft ran afoul of shamanism.

Lucy Mair wrote in the book titled, *Witchcraft* (1971), "that the belief in witchcraft reinforced confidence in magic for curing sickness, since failures could be ascribed to the interference of witchcraft rather than its inherent inadequacy...."[78] The witch was thought to be capable of every heinous act conceivable, therefore people could contemplate such acts without undue emotional or intellectual constraint. The activities of witches served the community by defining what was bad and socially unacceptable. However, because of its unique nature witchcraft was often a convenient element of social control.

> Witchcraft [was] strong all over North America, and the Native Americans traced many diseases to the activities of witches. Among the Tlingit practically all severe disease were believed to have their origin in witchcraft. The most important task of the shamans was to reveal the witches.[79]

People believed that dangerous diseases — the most common form of disaster — were caused by witchcraft, and most individuals were acquainted with the practices of witchcraft and magic. It was the witch that used magic to shot a pathogenic object into a person or cause the soul to go astray. It was generally imagined that diseases caused by intrusions were the work of a witch exerting power over an individual. If the person was to recover, the object had to be removed by sucking through a hollow bone or by the mouth being placed directly on the patient's body.[80]

Among the Kwaio people magic as a form of human manipulation "was used to achieve a wide range of ends; it fell into a series of types or complexes; and it employed a wide range of substances and procedures."[81] An exact verbal formulation was required to enact a magical procedure — a spell. A sequence of comments was required to validate the spell, and to make it "work." The validation process required naming the ancestors beginning with the first to originate the magical procedure to the present. "The typical spell consisted of a list of objects or acts and goals constructed in a verbal formula. Sometimes they were purely arbitrary [for instance]: 'two coconuts, two *cordylines*, two areca nuts, two *pandanus*,' naming eight or ten or twenty pairs in a specified order."[82]

The Zande (also spelled Azande) of central Africa were of the opinion that some people were witches (*baloi pl. muloi sl.*), and they had the power to cause harm by virtue of an inherent quality. The Zande witch employed no ritual or spell. The act of witchcraft was a psychic act[83] that could kill cattle, cause illness and death, cause pregnant women to abort, bring unseasonable rain, and rob men of sexual prowess.[84]

Like shamans, the Zande *baloi* employed the assistance of familiar spirits. These helper spirits, called "shades," were stolen from the recently deceased. The *muloi* raised the corpse from the grave by magic and restored it to life. The witch then ceremonially killed the person again, thereby gaining possession of the shade, and subsequently allowing the corpse to return to the grave.[85] The *muloi* carved a figure to represent the shade, and although the spirits were called by different names, they had much the same features and perform the same functions. The familiars were believed to wander the countryside at night in search of victims, and a meeting was presumed fatal.

Witches in rural areas of the Philippines were called *aswang*, and when not transformed into one of his or her special guises appeared to be an ordinary human. With the power of the *aswang* came the ability to perform miraculous feats, and the capacity to be a menace to others.[86] They were believed to be able to transform themselves into an animal at will, and to assist with their nefarious activities, they were said to keep a special "helper pet."[87] These pets called *sigbin* were said to cause illness and could kill. The appearance of the *sigbin* varied according to belief and opinion. Some people believed they took any animal form and others contended that they looked like rabbits or kangaroos.[88] People also believed that *aswang* could fly without changing into a bird "with only his [or her] head and intestines aloft, and the rest of his [or her] body left behind."[89]

4

SHAMANISTIC SYMBOLISM

The symbol has a long-established relationship with myth (sacred stories that define the human condition and man's relation to the sacred and holy). Often containing a collection of symbolic forms, actions, expressions, and objects, myths describe gods, demons, men, animals, plants, and material objects that are themselves bearers of symbolical meaning and intentions.[1]

Social life takes place through time. It is the inevitability of change that causes society to endorse self-defining symbols to represent its heritage. Although these symbols may be arbitrarily, or randomly selected, they often are qualified by time. The temporal concept of "then" and "now" allows past practices to validate the present and impart knowledge to influence the future. Situational necessity promotes the invention or rediscovery of heritage as traditional practices. In times of social distress or civil strife in which group identity or territory is threatened, heritage, including myths, rituals, and beliefs gain new or renewed meaning. Often, the meaning and purpose are sought as empowerment — situational authority. Heritage in both complex and basic societies is the essence ingredient for group identity, cohesion, and the development of a belief-based society.

Because tradition is socially conveyed behavior, the related human practices and thought are a part of heritage. Consequently, the heritage of each human is the product of language, habit, gesture, and shared mythology, and the total of which identifies each person as a member of a particular culture or society, and the environment in which they live and work. That totality called "heritage" may be either tangible or intangible. Objects, places, and other physical and ideological attitudes and practices reinforce that heritage, but may not constitute true elements of cultural or social validation.

Symbols of the Human Condition

Symbols as the embodied presence of the sacred have societal influence regardless of what the essence of the symbol may be. Symbolic thinking is consubstantial with human existence. "It came before language and discursive reason. The symbol reveals certain aspects of reality — the deepest aspects — which defy any other means of knowledge."[2] Symbols, like myths, are not irresponsible creations of the human condition, but a response to an identified need.

4. Shamanistic Symbolism

They fulfill a function by illuminating the hidden meanings of cultural attitudes and beliefs. Symbols are an inherent part of all mythology. "The symbol translates a human situation into cosmological terms and reciprocally, more precisely, it discloses the interdependence between the structure of human existence and cosmic structures."[3]

The Cosmic Tree (world pole, god-pillar, Tree of the World, or Tree of Life) was the symbolic link between earth and the upper sphere ("heaven") for the Central and Northern Eurasian shamans (see drawing 4.1). The tree was believed to grow through all layers of the natural and spiritual worlds. Climbing the tree (actually or symbolically) signified the shaman's ascent to heaven and his or her connection with the deities. A ladder might be used to symbolize the tree, or an actual tree was prepared with seven to nine "notches" to aid in the climb. As the shaman climbed, he or she declared that he or she was going up to heaven and described all that could be seen at each step. "At the sixth heaven he worshiped the moon, at the seventh, the sun. Finally, at the ninth, he prostrated himself before Bai Ulgän, the Supreme Being, and offered him the soul of the horse that had been sacrificed."[4] The shaman might also use the roots of the tree to descend into the lower world in search of the dead.

DRAWING 4.1— Siberian shaman's hut (tent) with birch tree (cosmic tree) and helper spirits.

The tree and the ascent were symbolic, but the ideology was real and the "message," transmitted had real meaning within the endorsing community. The tree spoke of the time when the spirit world above and the human world were closely placed. It was believed that humans might climb the tree or scale a mountain to enter the realm of deities. It was later that the worlds separated leaving humans in isolation. Numerous myths and cultural practices were based on ascending or descending to interact with deities or spirits.

The Mongol shaman believed the birch to be a "tree from Heaven" because it was never struck by lightning.[5] "The use of the birch [wood] meant that Heaven's blessing covered *ger* [traditional Mongol dwelling], property, tools, instruments, weapons, fire-hearth, and holy text."[6] It was also from a branch of the Cosmic Tree (the birch) that according to legend the shaman received the wood to make his or her drum. The symbolic association between the tree and the drum promoted the magical functions of both. "By the fact that the shell of his [or her] drum was derived from the actual wood of the Cosmic Tree, the shaman, through his [or her] drumming, was magically projected into the vicinity of the Tree."[7]

An extension of the cosmic tree concept is found among the Mongols and some Siberian peoples. The "silver pole" (*mungen bahana*) was a pole erected outside the "golden womb" a type of shrine made in a cave.[8] The tree with its branches that interconnect mundane life with the supernatural is a "natural symbols," not unlike the phallus, silver pole or Hinduism's "lingam." The meaning assigned to such symbols constituted the enhancement of mythological understanding.

An example of a natural sign is an animal track.[9] That symbol, as reproduced in ritual activities, had a direct reference for the hunter/gatherer peoples. It was not difficult to assume that archaic hunters visualized the animals as they viewed the tracks. That approach was "conceptual" in that the animal was an imagined beast shaped according to the intellectual (referential) comprehension of the individual. The tracks made the animal present in the mind (imagination) of the hunter although it was outside the field of normal vision.

The "symbol" for the Ndembu of Zambia (central South Africa) is the "smallest unit of ritual which still retains the specific properties of ritual behavior."[10] With this specification in mind and regardless of the limitation imposed by a particular society or culture, symbols are often representative of the "meaning" derived from an emotional connection with an elevated traditional beliefs and practices. Societies are often imbued with traditional activities or events that constitute meaningful symbols to serve as mnemonic stimulants.

Because it had a primary role in social life of most people, symbolism was found, in some form, in all human societies.[11] Symbols defined certain values common to people and aided in sustaining an emotional commitment to that which was determined to be of special importance to the group. Symbols added a new or different value to objects and acts without violating related immediate or historical validity. The object or action as symbol became an "open" event that had immediate reality for the resident community.[12] That relationship correlated with the notion of a symbol representing or causing something to be recalled due to analogous qualities or associations in fact or thought. Symbols, in that context, were an integral part of society and the socializing processes. They were aligned with human interests when explicitly formulated as in a ritual activity or casually inferred by circumstances and practices. As an example, *ongons* (birds, animals, and anthropomorphic images believed to contain the spirits of dead ancestors) derived their symbolic meaning from their association with certain practices of social and cultural life and from the transference of specific ideas and qualities. There was a magical or symbolic relationship in the process of shifting emotions and desires between the *ongons* and the emotion it represented.

The use of symbols was a general human attribute that entered into "all mental activity and the physical activity it empowered and guided."[13] Consequently, symbolic reference was a tool for analyzing cultural attitudes when examined in relation to fundamental beliefs (including shamanism) and the way they were conceptualized and formulated. A part of conceptual thinking, and therefore an integral part of the cultural process, was the ability to use symbols and to recognize the idea of one thing or image as representing another.[14] Although most people communicate in words with symbolized meanings, non-literal symbology was also used. However, symbols were elements of communication only as long as they had the same value to both parties — the presenter and the receiver. Commonly accepted symbols, such as those associated with rites and rituals communicated group-recognized messages and thereby stimulated group acknowledgement and response. Because most speech was learned by imitation, it was reasonable to believe that the symbols associated with culturally specific rituals were also learned.

Mircea Eliade[15] describes a symbol as an "autonomous mode of cognition" since it aids the viewer in seeing both what is represented and what is perceived. Human sensibilities in most circumstances are inclined to "see" or recognize the anticipated objects disallowing the overriding authority of reason.[16] (This limited visual acuity is a necessary factor in most conventional illusionary magic.) As an example, a ritual object used by the shaman might be a facsimile (a symbolic representation), but it was the similarity between use of symbols and the associated mental image that promoted identity and subscription. It (the symbol) acquired validity and purpose by that association. An example of a similar and more direct association is the (cosmic or world) tree. A tree has long life therefore the shamanic ritual projects the concept of immortality.

Symbolism plays an important role in societies because people use symbols to express beliefs, desires, expectations, affiliations, and loyalties. Symbolic representations have many forms from the simplest reference to the most complex expression. Some symbols are broadly recognizable and only a few people knew others. Culturally acknowledged figures, shapes, and colors are enhancing elements of differing importance to people, as are sound symbols. However, nonverbal language was the universal referent for signifying the spiritual and emotional content of most cultures. For instance, body alterations are ubiquitous elements of nonverbal communication. Scars, tattoos, amputations, or extractions have recognized meaning among specific cultural groups.

The use of symbols allowed the shaman to evoke two worlds — the sacred and the profane — at the same time. A symbol might represent in a metaphysical sense an entity of a higher order, that is, a thing or attitude of extraordinary emotional or sentimental value. However, on the practical level, the symbol represented nothing more than itself except when placed or used in the proper circumstance it could become an integral part of an invaluable emotional experience that asserted itself as a special form of the sacred.[17] The symbol had extraordinary power in those circumstances.

The shaman might not deliberately "manufacture" symbols instead he or she made a "representation" of a group-identified object of belief. It was because of their special nature that symbols cannot be deliberately made. It was through the ritual and ceremony that the symbol became the means of "integrating with a higher reality and consciousness."[18] The symbol influenced cultural, social, and conditional understanding that did not generally transcend societal boundaries. Nevertheless, symbolic awareness opened the observer to new perspectives that went beyond the mundane to an inclusive "reality" linked to the spiritual realm. The shaman used symbols to link the three worlds and to establish a spiritual continuance.

Words, sounds, objects, and gestures had a definite symbolism, and cultures used a range of symbols to convey both positive and negative meaning. The Tuvan people of Western Siberia believed that, "If the cry of a raven is heard at night, this meant the soul of a person was going away. By imitating the voice of the raven, the shaman predicted the imminent passing of a person with his soul."[19] The Tuvan shaman relied on word sounds associated with a particular thing or action to convey a particular meaning. The shaman might, as a related use of sound, chant or speak onomatopoeic words in a quite voice to communicate with the spirits.

It was common practice for shamans to deliver distinctive word symbols (sounds) in different voices. The raven, crow, magpie, wolf, or bear intoned the message while the shaman flapped his or her arms to simulate flight, ran with the loping gait of the wolf, or waved his or her arms in the menacing gesture of the standing bear. The sound of the voice as well as the associated gestures reinforced and clarified the meaning of the spoken symbols. The delivery of these symbolic messages was often accompanied by other visual and sensual symbols.

A drum or rattle provided an auditory accompaniment, and light, smoke, tobacco, snuff, alcohol, or narcotic stimulants often influenced the senses.

Sacred or "magical plants" that induce visions and trances were used as stimulants in locations where they were available. "In Colombia, the Siona-Tukano, a South American indigenous people, spent a month in isolation so their memory of the ordinary world was free. During that time, they drink *ayahuasca* ... a drink made from the bark of the *banistoriopsis* vine."[20] Shamans living in verdant areas often used sacred plants along with dancing and drumming to reach an altered state of consciousness and to establish communication with their deities. In the far north where vegetation was sparse, shamans generally relied on the rhythmic beating of a drum or monotone chants to induce the trance. Plains Indians sought supernatural guidance through fasting, exposure to the elements, and other forms of self-imposed discipline, hardship, and pain. The use of various forms of mortification to gain shamanic insight was widespread.

"Whether the symbol [was] a spoken word, a drawing in the sand, or a mimetic dance, the principle [was] the same, the act of symbolizing, particularly when ritualized, actually 're-present' its object, that means 'bringing it before us by calling it back from whatever place it may have reached.'"[21] Cultural symbolism revealed events and attitudes that occurred in another world and therefore, could not be compared or explained by experiences in the material world.[22]

Symbolism is a language, from the perspective of basic communication, because it discloses dimensions that are not provided by the tangible object or the fully enacted activity. Consequently, the shamanic headgear, drum, mask, coat, and rattle could be seen as symbols of social importance or elements of local custom. Gestures, dance, and actions conveyed the ideas of flight, climbing, swimming, struggling, and protecting when included in rituals and ceremonies. Those shamanic "signs" had situational importance because they gave new value to objects and activities without removing or altering their practical purpose or meaning. The shaman's drum had a practical purpose as a membranophone instrument with a frame (shell) and a membrane cover. The shal-

PHOTOGRAPH 7—Edward Curtis took this photograph of the Peyote drummer in 1927. Peyote came to the people of the Plains of North America as a power to "open the walls of space and release to the mind visionary realities such as in primeval times had been known to the shamans."[b] The use of hallucinogens was not as common among Plains peoples as in other regions. Most vision quests involved fasting, sun gazing, isolation, and other forms of self-deprivation.

low "tambourine" style drums used by shamans were often crudely formed but acquired special meaning and purpose associated with ritual activities (see photograph 7).

Symbolic and physical aids aside, the greatest factor influencing the role of the shaman among people in all societies was the ecstasy of belief. That aspect of humanity has not changed since belief in a societal influence was introduced thousands of years ago. However, when the symbol was a word conveyed in a symbolic language, it was often difficult to discern the reference because meanings changed according to inferred or real combinations, situations, and circumstances. The shaman or clan elder in many cultural groups directed the creation of symbols, and thereafter had to interpret them.[23]

Although symbols were used to express ideas that were beyond the range of human understanding, they were also used to bolster commonly held beliefs. The human psyche required constant reinforcement and recollection reactivation. "There are ... unconscious aspects of our [human] perception of reality. The first is the fact that even when our senses react to real phenomena, sights, and sounds, they are somehow translated from the realm of reality into that of the mind."[24] Shamanic activities depended on psychological fulfillment. The patient or client required symbolic justification for belief and the shaman provided that assurance by his or her actions and the objects (symbols) used as a part of the ritual performance (see drawing 4.2).

Symbols to Reinforce Shamanic Identity

The symbol has a long-established relationship with myth (sacred stories that define the human condition and man's relation to the sacred or holy).[25] Myths are stories filled with culturally significant gods, demons, men, animals, plants, and material objects that are bearers of symbolical meanings. Consequently, it is often difficult to distinguish between a myth and the assemblage of symbols arranged in story form. Myths or stories about sacred stones, animals, plants, and drums represent traditional beliefs and guarantee the continuity of those social functions. The origin of many such symbols clearly indicates the unity that was presumed to have existed between the symbol and the sacred in an earlier time.

It may be assumed that objects, places, and other physical and ideological manifestations (symbols) reinforce identity, but are not always true elements of cultural or social validation. Every group develops its own heritage, beliefs, customs, values and usage, which the incumbent population continually remembrances or recreates. Sha-

DRAWING 4.2 — Carved wood *shurama* figure from the Chucunaque River region of Panama. Shamans used these male figurines in curing ceremonies. The design may have had a relationship to the patient but the features were traditional and stylized.

manism was perpetuated because it met the needs of the people, and as needs changed shamanic practices were revised to be current with evolving societal requirements. The practices of the group (clan, tribe, or community) are a mix of pride, unity, ethnic loyalty, and nostalgia that were symbolically associated with social life. It was because societies had short cultural memories that myths and rituals were needed to reinforce recollection. "[S]ymbolic culture [was] a product of past social action although its producers [were] not always easily identified."[26] When myth was more interesting (or entertaining) than reality, the myth was remembered and transmitted.

Every group requires an element of identity, and in every society, people act or react according to the examples given to them by their history, including the myths, beliefs, and practices of the past. An essential part of the shamans' role was the presentation of the mythological images of the group, and to use those images to strengthen the community. The shaman relied on acting, singing, and dancing to fulfill that responsibility and to affix the mythical ideology in the conscious of the group. Mongol shaman often used the *ongon*, drum, rattle and other aids to go beyond the limits of daily life. They relinquished their ego with the assistance of these objects and allowed the spirits to enter their psyche. Through this emotional metamorphosis, they positioned themselves to be conduits of information and energy derived from the spirits. The act of preserving heritage resources whether real or imagined is an expression of resilience for a people or a country.

According to James Forsyth writing in *A History of the People of Siberia*,[27] the Buryat shamans (a people living south and east of Lake Baikal in south central Russia) were mainly a hereditary caste, and were of two kinds. There were "white" shamans who served the heavenly divinities, and "black" shamans who served the interests of the underworld. The Buryat shamans differ in practice from those of the Tungus (also called Evenk, Evenki, or Evenky, people living in Mongolia, Russia, and China) or Kets (indigenous people of central Siberia) by not relying on the drum to accompany their ecstatic dance. Instead, they used a small bell and a horse-stick.

The symbols of cultural heritage reflect the interests, traditions, and beliefs of the people. It was often those symbolic indicators that exemplify the distinguishing character of groups and that distinction was essentially psychological. The defining time in the history of the people, according to shamanic tradition, was when attitudes and characteristics change to establish the distinction between humans and non-humans. It might have been at that time that the moieties for organizing the Tlingit social universe and identifying the taboos and practices to appease the spirits were established. Tradition reinforced beliefs and explained the steps required for shamans to ascend to the top of the spirit world or descend to the regions of the dead.

Historical practices were subverted for many Siberian peoples when the influences of Buddhism from Tibet replaced shamanism during the late sixteenth century. However, according to Middleton in his book, *Gods and Rituals* (1981), the Buryats remained fundamentally shamanist. Nonetheless, it is difficult to separate traditional forms of belief and ritual from evolving practices among any people, but the range of social activities that retain ideologies established in the distant past were often impossible to determine. It was the retention of tradition that allowed humankind as a species, to transcend individual destiny and to achieve cultural continuity.

It is certain that the heritage of a people involves knowledge and attitude as a holistic approach to existence that includes the inherent system of ideas and values that define visions of the world, personal and group perceptions, and ways of life. Shamanistic activities were events of social narration where traditions were preserved and communicated. By sharing that communal legacy of traditional shamanic practices, people envisioned the possibilities of their lives, and changed the way they viewed the world. A range of tangible or intangible symbols psychologically reinforced shamanistic traditions.

Bird Symbols and Shamanic Flight

The shaman often presented himself or herself in many different symbolic manifestations. The wolf, jaguar, as well as the bird were favored symbols and helpers that served as guides for the practitioner's spirit journeys. The bird was a meaningful symbol because of the significance of flight and feathers were a part of the shaman's regalia in many cultures. Stylized feathers in the form of ribbons or rods were used as connecting elements to link the practitioner with the air or space — the great beyond.

The sacred bird that brought blessings and removed evil is a myth found in many cultures. Ritually recognized references to that sacred symbol appeared in the form of stylized bird fetishes, feathers, or other avian references. "The tawny owl (or owl) played an important role in shamanism, appearing as the assistant of the shaman in the struggle with evil spirits."[28] According to Buryat legends, "the first shaman was an eagle who sent good spirits to protect people from bad spirits."[29] However, the people could not understand his speech, so the eagle asked for human speech or to give his mission to a Buryat. Reportedly, "the good spirits granted him his second request, and upon their command, the first shaman sprang from the union of the eagle and a Buryat woman."[30]

John A. Grim notes in *The Shaman: Patterns of Siberian and Ojibway Healing* (1983), that the "Yakut shaman's costume display[ed] a complete bird skeleton of iron amplifying this flight symbolism."[31] Flight allowed the shaman to maintain the relationships between the cosmic worlds.[32]

Bird images were identified with the shaman's ability to cross supernatural frontiers; similarly, certain ritual paraphernalia had expanded wings to suggest the capacity to soar. The avian characteristics symbolically reinforced the shaman's capacity to maintain an extended connection with the transcendental world. Various birds (real and metaphorical) were considered "spirit helpers" and messengers that moved freely between the natural and supernatural worlds. Bird images, like culturally defined images and fetishes, such as ongon, were symbols of transformation that had a presence in many societies and can be traced to pictographs originating in the Late Paleolithic Period.

There was widespread belief among many traditional peoples that after death the soul left the body in the form of a bird. It was also believed that "Siberian, Eskimo, and North American shamans [could] fly."[33] Birds are included in Brähmanic literature, however these symbols of flight do not belong only to the Indian tradition, since they are at the very heart of shamanic symbolism — the symbolic transports to the "center of the world" and magical flight.[34] Two strong traditional symbols in Tibetan Buddhism — the bird and serpent — are combined and given a human head with horns known as the Garuda (eagle and vehicle of Vishnu) and destroyer of Naga, the snake god and evildoer.[35] This configuration of elements is classic good and evil symbology. It is possible that this hybrid creature found further manifestation as a dragon in Japanese and Chinese mythology (see drawing 4.3) and may refer-

PLATE 1— Crow male, Medicine Crow, in native dress with ornaments and holding an eagle feather fan. The elaborate costume has ermine "tassels" similar to those worn by Mongolian and Siberian shamans. The hair arrangement (topknot) identifies Medicine Crow as a shaman. Charles Bell took this photograph in 1880.

ence the snake as a symbol in the Garden of Eden.

Shamans wore an array of items as symbols of their positions within the community as spokespersons for the spirits. For instance, shamans often wore metal ornaments represent such diverse elements as the internal organs, bones, female breasts, the Sun, and the Moon; but the objects common to Eurasian shamans were metal mirrors. The surface of the mirror reflected the souls of the dead and provided a vision of the future. These symbols of shamanic authority (and power) were of many different sizes, and some shamans wore several for communication and protection. The mirror (*toli* in Mongolian) was a symbol of authority such as the masks of the Eskimo or the feathered headdress of the Plains people and often had a more specific symbolic meaning to the people within a particular culture. As a particular example, the symbol of shamanic acceptance for the Puyuma people of Taiwan was the *tamararamaw's* (shaman's) bag. The bag held the shaman's tools as well as the guardian spirit.[36]

It was a person in the transcendental state that became "the sha-

DRAWING 4.3 — Dragon. Some people believe this bronze figure represents the oldest portrayal of the *bixie* the mythical winged feline believed to overcome evil. Other persons consider this spiraling serpentine pathway a dragon that represents the essence of *chi* (energy). The Chinese dragon, *lung*, represented *yang*, the principle of heaven, activity, and maleness. It was the emblem of the Imperial family. The dragon is popular in Korea because it is associated with rain and the success of the annual rice crop. The dragon in Japanese symbolism is able to change its size at will and is identified with the spirits of the air. In other areas of the world the dragon is viewed as a serpent and a symbol of evil. The Egyptian god *Apepi* was the great serpent of darkness. In the Christian world the dragon came to be symbolic of sin and paganism. The dragon is a common feature in Hungarian folk tales and mythology, and in Uralic shamanism it is believed to be both good and evil. Dragons are among the deified forces of nature in Taoism.[c]

man — the medicine man — whose magical practices and flights of intuition identified him as a primitive master of initiation. His power resided in his supposed ability to leave his body and fly about the universe as a bird."[37] The prospect of flight suggested physical levitation and implied a range of fantastic activities including spiritual flight that allowed the shaman to navigate without the restrictions imposed by gravity. The shamanic spirit was believed to take wing and join the atmosphere with or without human endorsement or consent. The use of bird images, masks, and connecting antlers or rods (snakes) reinforced the idea of the ethereal transcendence instead of the physical assumptions of flight (see photograph 8).

The *Ghyabre* (shamans and death cult specialists) and *Paju* (shamans and specialist in exorcism) of west-central Nepal had "bird" tutelary deities to assist them in their efforts to promote a world harmony that benefited the community in which they lived.[38] These traditional experiences were symbolized by projecting the human spirit into an ethereal setting. Such symbolic projections were often associated with dogma and theological sentiment. Examples of that connection were found in literally every cultural environment and at all levels of socio-cultural development. It was most apparent in Buddhist doctrine and the Christian teaching of the Last Judgment as exemplified by punishment of sin, hell and purgatory, and eternal reward (Paradise).[39]

There are also marks that reinforce culturally recognized ritual elements. The "V" is an example of this symbology. It was used as a single sign or repeated as a chevron. It was connected with the bird or with anthropomorphic bird sculptures in Siberia, from the time of the Upper Paleolithic. Other examples of this symbology appear on the "waterbird figurines from Mal'ta in Siberia marked with rows of incised V's, [and] faceless anthropomorphic waterbirds carved on mammoth ivory from Mezin near Chernigov in the Ukrane, are marked with dashes or V's."[40] The simplified bird symbols appear on shamanic objects in graphic form (see drawing 2.10), or as symbolic "shorthand."

There are references to shamanic flight and bird in the mythological records found in many locations. This tendency was exemplified in ancient Egypt where the myth of Osiris (also called Usiri) includes the shamanic transformations of Osiris.[41] It was said that upon his death, the ruler of Egypt became Osiris, King of Duat. Thereafter, the pharaoh in the mystic embodiment of Horus (the hawk) assumed a new manifestation as monarch of the Underworld.[42] It was noted in a related reference that Osiris' brother Seth killed him, cut his body into fourteen pieces, and scattered it throughout Egypt. Isis (also spelled Aset or Eset) the wife of Osiris transformed herself into a bird and in mystical flight collected the pieces of his body, and returned him to life by a magical spell.[43] This symbolic ritual of death and resurrection is consistent with shamanic practice. "Shamans [among Siberian people] were believed to have been killed by the spirits of their ancestors, who, after 'cooking' their bodies, counted their bones and replaced them fastening them together with iron and covering them with new flesh."[44]

The shamanic association with afterlife is included in both the religious and profane literature of Egypt. There are twelve chapter of the *Book of the Dead* devoted to providing the deceased with words of power, the recital of which will enabled him or her to transform himself or herself into a divine hawk, a phoenix, a heron, a swallow, the serpent *Sata*, or a crocodile.[45] Once granted this mystic

PHOTOGRAPH 8— Two Whistles, an Apsaroke man, (a band of Crow Indians living in Montana) is described as a medicine man. He is wearing face paint and a medicine hawk headdress. The hawk may represent his supernatural guardian spirit. Edward Curtis took this photograph circa 1908.

power, the deceased could swim or fly any distance in any direction. The Egyptians gave special attention to particular birds and animals because they were believed to embody the characteristics of certain gods. It was the gods or the mystic power associated with those gods that was a defense against the negative forces that inflict pain and suffering on the people. The transformational element as well as the reconfiguration as a bird or animal has distinct shamanic reference.

Mongol shamans often attached eagle feathers to their headwear. It was the eagle that was the most often represented in avian symbology. The Buryat people living east of Lake Baikal in Siberia called the bird they held in high esteem "*yekhe-Shubun*"— the eagle. It was the sacred bird that occupied an important place in the shamanistic mythology and cult of the Buryats.[46] To the southeast, the inhabitants of Hatra in the Al-Jazirah region of northern Iraq carved eagles to symbolize a Syrian deity. Hatra was called *Beit "Elaja"* ("House of God") in the first century of this era, because of the numerous temples.

An eagle or some other bird often carried the hero from the depths of the underworld to the surface of the earth in Siberian folklore. The Goldi (Golds) shaman did not undertake an ecstatic journey to the underworld without the help of a bird-spirit (*koori*) to ensure his return to the surface. The shaman was reported to make the most difficult part of the return journey on the back of his *koori*.[47]

> In Siberian societies animals and plants with some anomaly were attributed with supernatural qualities, giving life. Such animals gave success, and the plants or objects were used as amulets. At the basis of all these ideas is the attempt to express, through the singular, i.e. the departure from the norm, the *maximally universal*— principle of life itself.[48]

The ability to turn into a bird was frequently associated with shamanism in the Arctic, North America, India, and Oceania. Flight allowed the shaman to surpass the limits of the mundane world and to reach the place of the gods. Related concepts are found in Chinese and Japanese stories that tell that the souls of the dead were transported to Paradise by birds, and in India the vehicle of Vishnu, the man-eagle Garuda was the healer and destroyer (see drawing 4.4). In Persian mythology the *simurgh* had a similar role, as did the Japanese *Gario*, the woman-bird with crane's legs, and "the Babylonian eagle that was given the responsibility of carrying the hero Etana to heaven."[49]

As a further reference to avian symbols, small bird figure were sewn on the costumes of Yakut, Vogul, and other Asiatic shamans, and posts surmounted by wooden models of birds are found in many locations. The Yakut shaman's costume was often adorned with iron or copper bird "bones" to symbolically represent flight.

DRAWING 4.4— The Garuda or "sun bird" of the upper world is one of two traditional vehicles of Vishnu, and a form of symbolic transfer of evil deeds. The transport of the lower world is the serpent Ananta. The Garuda as a manifestation of Hindu mythology is found in many cultures. As a representative of Vishnu, especially in one of his favored incarnations — Krishna — the Garuda is described as the "filth eater." In that persona, the Garuda rids the world of foul words and deeds.

The Akawaio Caribs of Guyana in the Western Hemisphere believed the shaman's spirit attached itself to the swallow-tailed kite, known locally as the "clairvoyant woman," to help it soar aloft to commune with the other spirits.

Divers (also known as loons) are placed at the four corners of the coffin of a Tungus shaman. Those birds also had an important role in folklore and mythology. The bird's diving ability played a part in many myths about the beginning of the earth. It was believed by the Faroese (inhabitants of a group of islands in the North Atlantic Ocean between Iceland and the Shetland Islands) that the diver was a companion of the soul. The birds held an equally important place in the tradition of Siberian peoples. Graves found at Ipiutak culture sites in northwestern Alaska included "skulls not only of human beings but also of divers, suggesting that the birds were regarded as companions or guides for the soul and that the destinies of divers and men were regarded as linked."[50]

Terrestrial beings have always been fascinated by the extraterrestrial. The ability to move about without restrictions whether in air or water has appealed to the fantasies of most humans.

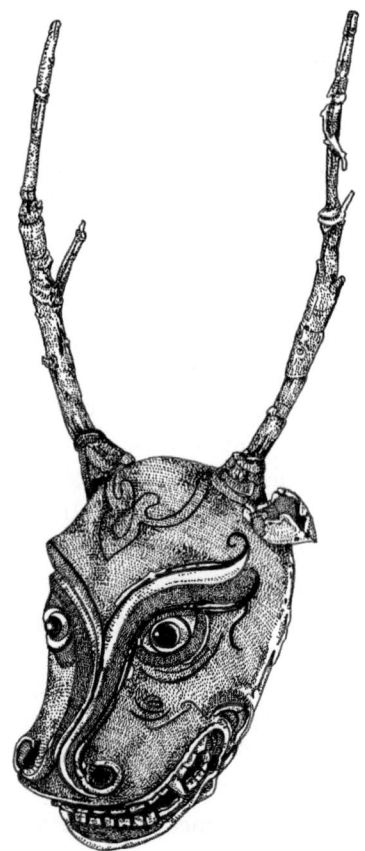

Left: PLATE 23—Female shaman's head cover with three owl feathers, face-covering fringe, and silk "snakes." The two outside feathers stick outward and may represent horns, although this related costume is identified as a "bird-style."

Right: DRAWING 4.5—Stag mask made of papier maché. This mask from Tibet was painted green and blue and had bamboo horns that were wrapped with paper. Masks of this type were worn in "devil" dances. They have standardized features that represent a particular evil spirit from Tibetan mythology.[d]

It is reported that some Siberian shamans wore caps or headpieces with feathers and ribbons, and other shamans in the area have iron horns on their heads to represent reindeer antlers. The Teleut shaman in Siberia wore a head cover made from the body of a brown owl, and Japanese shaman wore caps with eagle and owl feathers.[51] Tibetan monks and shamans wore masks with horns made of wood and wrapped with bright colored paper (see drawing 4.5). Native people living on the Northwest coast of North America wore masks (a type of head cover for transformation) made in the image of birds to recognize the intermediary role performed of the human spirit.

Feathers were sacred in Egypt where it was believed that each soul would be weighted at death against the Plume of Maat, "the mother whose name meant Truth."[52] An Egyptian's soul was seen as a bird (*ba*) that could fly in and out of the tomb because the feather was also the symbol for air. Buddhist text also speaks of magical powers and the ability to fly, and the feathered or flying figure was found in the Southern Cult art of the Mississippian culture (starting about year 800 of the current era). The mystic role of flight is widespread in the Western Hemisphere and may have evolved from Mexico or the Adena-Hopewell religious cults (200 years before to current era to 550 of the current era). Often the "flying" figure has a bird-like headdress and a tail extends below the feet.[53]

The bird image and the cosmic tree (god pillar *shiwangdae* on Cheju Island ROK) were common element associated with Siberian shamanism however it is possible that the notion of flight had a too literal context. The meanings assigned to symbols were often various and inconsistent, and the concept of flight might have been no exception to the generality. Ambiguities reflect both the historic association of the symbol and the social context in which it was used. The idea of flight as physical levitation or transmigration suggests a whole range of fantastic performances. Whereas spiritual flight allowed the shaman to navigate the ethereal world without the restrictions imposed by terrestrial gravity. The spirit could take wing and the breath (as quintessence of the soul) could join the atmosphere with or without human endorsement or consent. Symbols such as bird images and connecting antlers (bone or metal) or rods (cloth) reinforced the concept of spiritual transcendence and granted the shaman the ritual assumption of flight.

This presumption of flight as associated with shamanic activities may be viewed as an illusion, but the concept of rising above the natural world (the earth plane) to engage the spirits in the "Overworld" was an important part of the shaman's repertoire and his or her ability to perform the requisite mystical duties. The shaman of the Tapirapé, a South American forest people, reportedly traveled to the villages of the dead in the form of a bird, and other forest peoples traveled the sky in their canoes as "Jaguars of the Skies."[54] The symbolic connection of flight and animal embodiment had many manifestations in shamanic practice.

It is likely that the idea that birds and flight are connected with spirit transcendence. It is also logical to assume that people observed the behavior of birds and were fascinated by their ability to move from place to place seemingly without effort. Spirits were able to move effortlessly in a manner similar to birds; therefore, nearly every winged being was symbolic of spiritualization. As an example, in areas of West Africa the bird figure was symbolically associated with witches and witchcraft. Masks made by the Yoruba include the Ibis image, and Senufo masks intended to ward off witchcraft had birds on the top (see drawing 2.1). Conversely, the Temne (people) believed that the "witchbird" was responsible for making children ill and causing bad luck, and to protect against witchcraft they wore feathers in their hats.[55] The symbolic associations gave a physical presence to a mystic entity thereby joining the material and spiritual worlds.

Feathers, horns, rods, antlers, and streamers are ubiquitous energy symbols. They are found in Judao-Christian symbolism and represented in other cultures as the crescent. They are generally viewed as connections to the Overworld—the ethereal or the supernatural (see drawing 4.6). According to the notation in *Shamanism: Selected Writings of Vilmos Diószegi* (1998), edited by Mihály Hoppál, "ethnographic, linguistic, and archaeological evidence show that the shaman headgear with antlers goes back to very early times; and from this it follows that the conceptions shaping our object were rooted in one of the ancient layers of Man's view of the world."[56]

Shamanic Connections to the Universe

At some time in ancient history, people endorsed the belief that possession of human bone, particularly the skull, brought the protection and help of the dead.[57] Apparently from that time forward, the skull was viewed as a primary symbol of mortality in many localities. The head bone was a part of two very prevalent beliefs; (1) bones were centers of psychic energy, and (2) the head was the dwelling place of the spirit. Consequently, the skull and the protrusions from the skull (horns, antlers, and hair) were assigned great importance in the spiritual life in numerous cultures.

A dead person's bones were thought to retain elements of the soul. The bones were considered to be the seeds of renewed life, and although there are more than 200 different bones in the human body, the skull was of primary importance. The fascination with the head as the center of life was found in most cultures and it manifested itself in various ways. Skulls, as symbols of recognition or power, were arranged on poles, tree branches, and specially prepared racks to emphasize the unity of the material and spiritual worlds.

The spiritual or supernatural association with the head extended to the keratinized filaments that grew from the epidermis of humans. Peoples in New Guinea believed their ancestral spirits lived in their hair, and their

DRAWING 4.6—*Mgbedike* mask made by the Igbo culture of Nigeria. This mask of wood, fibers, vegetal paste, and pigment was used to dramatize the interaction between the worlds of the living and the living dead. These masks called attention to the elders of the group as being living ancestors and illustrated the interchangeability of man and spirits. The underlying message addressed the duality of all things—life and death, youth and old age.

presence made it grow. The males of those societies darkened their faces with charcoal to emphasize the beard area and to give themselves an unearthly disguise. Their ancestors "came to their faces" in this altered condition. The people transformed themselves through the shaded elements of their self-decoration. The darkened features were not to represent another person, spirit, or animal, rather they were to imbue the individual with exemplary qualities.[58] The light and dark sides of human nature accommodated the inconsistencies of the spirits. The darker concept of spirits as "shades" or shadows was also found among certain African peoples.

Early people also gave special attention to animal skulls believing they related to a form of hunting magic, whereas, human skull veneration was closely connected with ancestor worship. The shaman often employed the skull as a connection to a particular region above or below the plane occupied by humans. Skulls, horns, and antlers were important connecting elements in shamanism. Those object symbols were present in implicit form as well as actual. Chinese guardian figures from the Zhou dynasty, Warring States period in the fifth century BCE China were shaped to represent birds, deer, and mythical figures with antlers. Native Americans of the high plains presented the buffalo skull in a shamanic observance to appeal for replenishment and success.

The animal horn was an energy symbol, and had great symbolic importance. It was an accepted sign of strength that had a phallic outside and hollow inside giving the complex symbolism of giver and receiver — the *lingam* and the *yoni*— the sexual manifestations of the male and female elements. Bones of different shapes and sizes had an important role of shamanic ritual. A trumpet made from a human or animal bone was used to contact the dead,[59] and hand and finger bones were employed for protection and divination.

Horns of various shapes, sizes, and materials have been assigned power or energy in many cultures. The shaman in the Northwest Coastal region of North America frequently had iron antlers attached to their head covers (hats) as representations of the wild reindeer. The antlers and rods also served to connect shamans with the cosmic energy source. Similarly, statuettes of Osiris, the Egyptian deity, were made with crowns that included ram horns as a manifestation of authority (power). The Celtic deity, the Daghda, is shown on the Gundestrup Cauldron (found in a peat bog in Denmark) as the Lord of the Wildwood with the horns of Cernunnos on his head.[60] Kali ("She who is Black"), the Hindu goddess, has a necklace of fifty human skulls and a girdle of human hands.

The significance of horns and antlers has many explanations. One theory suggests that various hoofed and antlered mammals had mythical affiliation among early people and that the affinity continued as the cultures evolved. That notion may be reflected in the Indo-European word "deer" that is the basis of a range of derivatives meaning "to rise in a cloud," as dust, vapor, or smoke, and related to semantic notions of breath.[61] These associations suggest a connection with the spirit world.

Different religions have deified or demonized horned and cloven-hoofed animals. Buddhism associates the deer with the Buddha and spiritual enlightenment, and the bull, Apis, was sacred to Ptah creator god of the Memphis pantheon and cohort of Sakhmet, the goddess associated with disease and healing. The ram has been portrayed as both good and evil. The satyr was the foremost manifestation of debauchery but as the Egyptian god, Khnum (also spelled Khnemu), the ram, god of fertility and the cataract region. Khnum, worshiped from the first dynasty 2925–2775 before the current era, was believed to have created humans from clay using a potter's wheel.[62] However, the quintessential nefarious demon is the cloven-hoofed and horned fallen angle (Satan), a concept that found its way into Christian doctrine as described in the Old Testament (Book of Job, Chapters 1 and 2).

> The shaman's life-soul assumed the shape of a *xargi*, that is, a deer, but the soul, or spirit of the shaman's ancestor was also *xargi*, or deer-shaped.... Consequently, the shaman and the animal symbolized by his headgear were very closely related....[63]

It is certain that skulls, both human and animal, played an important role in various manifestations of belief. The mystical significance of the skull was not restricted to one region or culture. Human heads were associated with the cult of the dead, ancestor worship, warfare, magic, and the rites of survival. Reportedly, early Germanic peoples preserved heads by fastening them in trees, and the Celts hung the heads of slain enemies from house rafters to gain protection from the dead person's spirits. Greeks, Jews, Semites, and Norsemen kept human heads as oracles.[64] In addition, headhunting to gain the supernatural power contained in the skulls of the enemy was a prominent part of the historical record of the Celts.[65]

The Mochica culture of Peru observed a ritual practice of decapitation, and elsewhere in the world cannibalism, headhunting, and various forms of head taking and human sacrifices were embraced to appease the deities or transfer evil. In Mexico, Aztecs adorned temples with skulls of sacrificial victims, and people of the Southern Pacific covered skulls with a mixture of clay and oil and modeled the surface to a likeness of the deceased. The Hindu Goddess Kali wore a garland of skulls, and Tibetan Buddhists shaped containers from skulls. In West Africa, the skull of the deceased was set on a pole to mark the grave. Jivero headhunters in the Amazon region collected heads to obtain the power held by the rival warriors.

Bones were a life substance and there was a discernible affinity among shaman, magicians, and mystics and such symbols. Eskimo shamans had rods and ribbons as part of their headdress, and shaman in Ecuador wear "puma" (jaguar) masks made of cloth with rod-like extensions (see drawing 4.7). The shamans of the Huichol people of Central Mexico were often portrayed with antler-like head covers or masks.

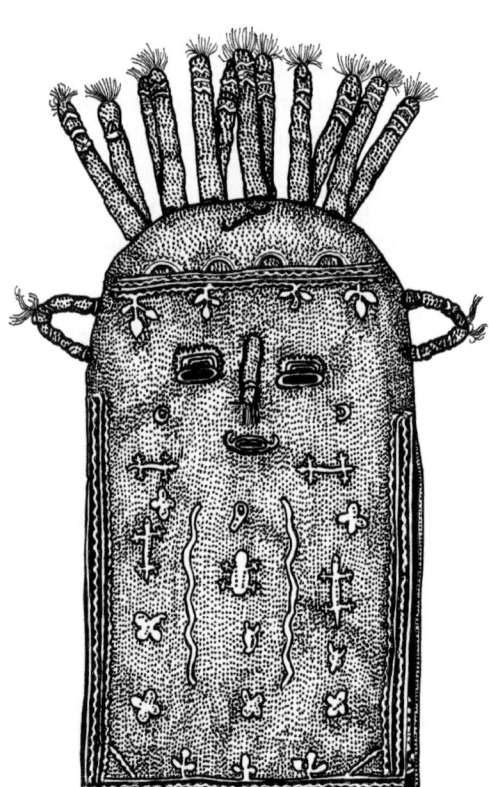

DRAWING 4.7—Contemporary representation of an Ecuadorian "puma" mask with connecting rods. This mask was made in the style of a traditional shaman/priest head cover.

Shamanic Amulets, Charms, Familiars, and Fetishes

Although described in different terms than those used in other areas of the world, the Yoruba and Igbo people of Western Africa believed there was "no area of the earth, no object or creature that had not a spirit of its own or which could not be inhabited by a spirit."⁶⁶ E. Bolaji Idowu wrote in *African Traditional Religion* (1975) that according to traditional belief there were spirit trees where spirits congregate and chatter like birds (another connection between birds and spirits). It was also possible for spirits to inhabit rocks, mountains, hills, and rivers.⁶⁷ Those spirits might be called upon to perform specific acts. Consequently, offerings were placed at the base of the tree, and passersby offered prayers requesting personal protection from unfriendly spirits, especially the spirits of witches.

Ordinary people as well as shamans carried charms and amulets for protection against spirits, disease, and misfortune. The protective and supportive talismans were either found or fabricated. Natural amulets included stones, bones, teeth, or plants. Fabricated talismans included small figures carved from wood, ivory, and stone (see drawing 4.8). In many areas, the small figures had a doll-like appearance but were believed to have significant supernatural power including the ability to cure disease or cause death. The number of charm and amulets carried by one individual was unlimited. Shamans carved and gifted amulets to aid in personal and communal activities. Individuals found, made, or received objects believed to promote good fortune and as long as success prevailed the objects were retained. Although the fetishistic power depended on the symbols or devices drawn on the object, there was a mystic connection between nature, humankind, and the spirits assigned to all fetishes. Among people in some areas of the world there was often an added relationship between fetishism and totemism — the kinship between man and animals.

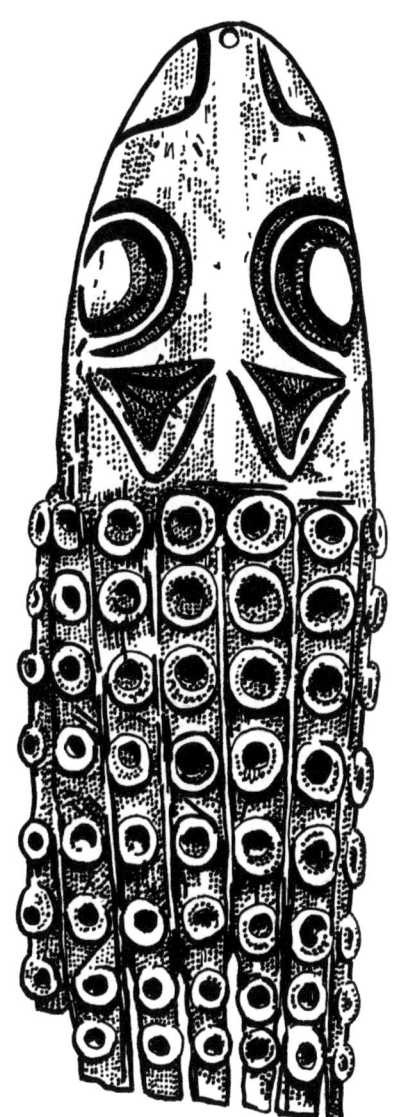

Protection from spirits as well as requests for assistance were a necessary part of life, consequently, shamans depended on amulets, charms, familiars, and fetishes to aid in the execution of their spiritual activities. Dorothy Jean Ray wrote in *Aleut and Eskimo Art* (1981), "Amulets and charms of wood or ivory were made in abundance by the shamans for supernatural protection or aid."⁶⁸ The charm, for the Eskimo, was intended to influence the helping spirit. According to Ray, "charms were used by shamans in curing and magical performances and were often hung in ceremonial houses and individual dwellings or attached to boats."⁶⁹ The dwelling place of the Mongolian shaman's helper spirit was the *ongon* (see drawing 4.9).

A charm and amulet in their various manifestations were thought to enhance the shaman's spiritual power. Those talismans were to aid the shaman in the execution of his or her activities.⁷⁰ The Eskimo shaman wore a belt from which suspended special items such as animal bones and teeth, strips of cloth, ribbons, and small-carved figures rep-

DRAWING 4.8—Ivory shaman's charm (amulet) in the shape of an octopus. This small, carefully carved piece is from the Northwest Coast of North America.

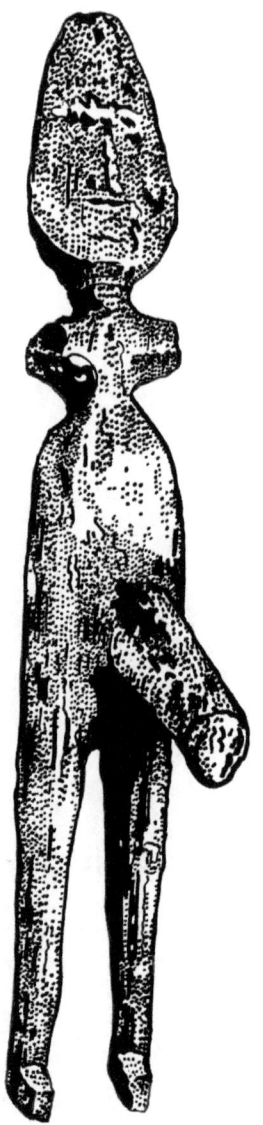

DRAWING 4.9—Drawing of a late nineteenth century man's *ongon* figure. The use of these special figures was widespread among different peoples in Siberia. *Ongon* means "sacred" or "pure." They are believed to keep spirits of dead ancestors. "There were ancestral, medical, hunting, territorial, cattle-breeding, and many other ongons, devoted to various protecting spirits."ᶜ This image has an association with fertility rituals. Such "spirit aids" were used by shamans

resenting spirit helpers. Shaman from the Jemez Pueblo in the Southwestern North America wore neck rings with tokens of animals and birds that were believed to be shamanic helpers.[71] Similarly, Zuni and Hopi medicine man (shaman) carried prayer sticks to aid in performing ceremonies to restore equilibrium to the cosmos, cure diseases, exorcise ghosts and witches, and ensure success in the hunt.

Hutton Webster in his book titled *Magic: A Sociological Study* (1948) said there was a clear distinction between fetishes and charms. The fetish, according to Webster, had an indwelling spiritual being—"a place of imprisonment of a subservient spirit"[72]—while the charm had no will of its own but acted automatically.[73] He acknowledged that it was difficult to tell the difference between charms and fetishes and contended that the distinction depended on the degree to which they were personified.[74]

Whether charm or fetish, both male and female Apache employ objects called *tzi-daltai*.[75] These highly valued "spirit pieces" were of wood from trees that had been struck by lightning. They were often decorated with incised lines to represent lightning. Among other peoples such as the Huron, a people originally living along the St. Lawrence River in eastern Canada, a fetish with its indwelling spirit might be any unusual object to which was assigned supernatural meaning. The Huron were believed to fear the possible theft of a treasured fetish by evil spirits. Lewis Spence wrote in *Myths of the North American Indian* (2005 [1914]), "The highest type of fetish obtainable by a Huron was a piece of the *onniont*, or great armoured serpent, a mythological animal revered by many North American tribes."[76]

Beadwork, shells, skins, and metal ornaments had supernatural significance to shaman and to ordinary members of North American societies. The great fetish of the Cheyenne was their "medicine" arrow. The head of the arrow was covered with waved and spiral lines to denote its sacred character.[77] An important object (charm or fetish) for some nomadic people consisted of "a mantle made from the skin of a deer and covered with feathers mixed with beadings. It was made and used by the medicine-men [shamans] as a mantle of invisibility, or charmed covering to enable spies to traverse an enemy's country in security."[78]

A preferred fetish of the northern Sioux, a high plains people living west of the Mississippi, was the buffalo head and neckbones that were preserved and protected to promote the belief that the buffalo herds would be prevented from leaving the area. Even horses were provided with fetishes, "in the shape of a deer's horn, to ensure their swiftness, [and] the rodent teeth of the beaver [were] regarded as potent charms, and [were] worn by little girls around their necks to make them industrious."[79]

Contacting the Spirits

The guardian and helping spirits were a necessary part of the shamanic activities and can be regarded as the authenticating sign of the shaman's ecstatic journeys in the spirit world. A shaman might have several helper spirits (familiars) or only one or two. The potency of the shaman determined the nature of the helpers and how they were employed. The shaman of the southwestern North America embarked on a vision quest to identify a helper spirit, and in South America the helper spirit entered the shaman at the time of his or her initiation. The helper might be as imposing as an eagle or as simple and unassuming as a pebble. The helper might come in a dream or require a process of fasting, self-mortification, or stimulants.

The gifts to shamans were an important part of their paraphernalia, and considered meaningful articles for contacting the spirit world. Such gifts included band-ties, shawls, tobacco-pouches, furs, feathers, or animal claws. "The most important of all were, at least for the people around Lake Hövsgöl [in northern Mongolia], colored cloth (ideally silk) band-ties called *Tsuudir*."[80] These white, red, blue, or green strips of fabric were "knotted three times in a clockwise direction"[81] and attached to the shaman's gown or robe.

Other articles of shamanistic regalia included animal headed human figures, and a variety of creatively joined animal and human elements. Many of those objects were derived from supernatural experiences as helper or totem beings and had meanings known only to their owner. These figures called *tupilak* by the Inuit of Canada were often imaginative creations with symbolic human and animal characteristics (see drawings 4.10).

Huge human figures of wood were made as charms and oracles to determine what success might be anticipated for the season's hunting and fishing in communities from the Aleutian Islands to Siberia.[82] These sculptures although made by ordinary people (as differentiated from those persons with shamanistic authority) reflected shamanic thinking. The spirit world influenced the survival of the living and granted peace to the dead. Another practice involving the carving of figures was found among the Russian peasants from the Petrovsk region of the Middle Volga. That ritual involved the making of a wooden figurine to symbolize the infant at the time of his or her birth. The figurine and the placenta were placed in a coffin and buried beneath the family home. This ritual was believed to guarantee long life for the child.[83]

The shaman might invoke gods

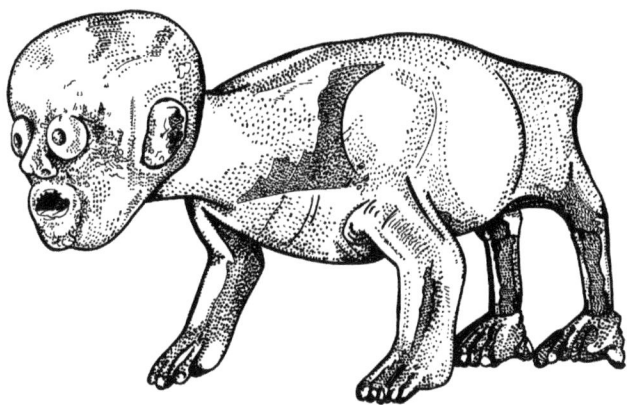

DRAWING 4.10—Shaman's spirit figure or "*tupilaq*" carved in the shape of a half-raven and half-dead-child. These Inuit figures were carved in various shapes and were used for both good and evil purposes. One of their tasks was to identify and eliminate the causes of illness.

and spirits to aid in a particular situation but they were not simply at his or her disposition. In contrast, familiars, guardian spirits, or helping spirits were "on call" to help with various shamanic activities. The majority of these helping spirits had animal forms, but some had a grotesque appearance that combines human and animal characteristics (as already described, see drawings 4.11). In some traditions the helping spirit (familiar) manifested itself in a vision or dream. It was the individual in other cultures that sought to discover his or her guide by undertaking a vision quest. It was possible, in some locations such as among the plains Indians of North America for anyone to acquire the assistance of a helping spirit, whereas, in areas of South America only the shaman could gain the services of a familiar.

Yakut shamans in the extreme northeastern part of Siberia were thought to have had, in addition to the helping spirits, the aid of tutelary spirits called *ämägät* in animal form that might be summoned (by voice or drum) as needed.[84] These tutelary spirits were usually "the soul of a dead shaman or a minor celestial spirit."[85] It was their role to instruct the shaman in his or her various duties. The activities of the *ämägät* was different from those of the helper spirit in that the "familiar" (helper spirit) took part in the shamanic activity while the tutelary spirit (*ämägät*) guided or directed the séance or performance.

The Otomí shamans, living on the central plateau region of Mexico, had animal companion spirits called *rogi* (also known as *tonal*). According to James Dow writing in *The Shaman's Touch* (1989), every person had one of more of these superhuman animal companions.[86] Only the Otomí shaman could tell how many *rogi* a person had and what animals they represented. In contrast with the powerful and good *rogi* (*tonal*), Otomí sorcerers employ the aid of evil-doing *puxijwaí* (*naguales*).[87] It was believed in some areas that powerful sorcerers could transform themselves into *nagral* (a deer, jaguar, or bird) for evil purposes. Although the words, *rogi* and *puxijwai*, were used inconsistently by the Otomi to describe good (shaman) and bad (sorcerers) animal helpers the concept is comparable to the "familiars" of Siberian people.

Probably influenced by Eurasian shamanic practices that traveled south through Mongolia, shamanism has been a part of the cultural fabric of Korea since at least the second century before the current era. It is thought that during the Silla Dynasty (57 BCE to 935 CE) that the kings might have had shamanic roles.[88] The female shaman in the northern part of Korea were called *mansin* and the male shaman were known as a *mugyök* or *paksu,* whereas, in other part of that country they were called by different names. Shamans in northern Korea commenced their practice when the spirits

DRAWING 4.11—A "*tupilak*" created by a shaman in Greenland to do harm to enemies. A spirit figure is believed to reside inside the *tupilak* and can be called upon by the shaman to perform services as needed. Most figures are in the form of small mammals but some are humanoid and grotesque.

entered them while in the southern part of the peninsula the transfer of shamanic practice was often hereditary.[89] Korean shamans gave much of their attention to healing, but unlike their Siberian counterparts, they did not ascend to the heavens to encounter spirits, instead the spirits descend and spoke through them. Korean shamans performed the ritual *kut* accompanied by music instead of the traditional trance.

> When shamans talk to other worlds, they [did] not mean that these [were] disconnected from this world. Rather, these worlds represent the true nature of things and the true cause of events in this world. The understanding [was] widely shared in the community, and many people [might] be shamans to a greater or lesser degree, according to their insight into this reality.[90]

Manitou represented to the Ojibwa (also spelled Ojibwe or Ojibway and sometimes called Chippewa) a people of North American and Canada, a pervasive power (spirit) that individuals could call upon for their own help and protection. Contact with the power of *Manitou* "usually occurred through the vision fast, which was undertaken before puberty and was the most important act in an Ojibway childhood."[91] This experience allowed the Ojibway to initiate contact with the surrounding spirit world. Although direct contact with spirit beings was possible, the shaman served these subarctic people as a part-time curer and diviner. The ability to perform the required duties came from dreaming of animals that taught the shaman to work with their assistance.

The Yanomami (also spelled Yanomamö or Yanoamö) are a South American people living in the Orinoco River basin in southern Venezuela and the Amazon River basin of northern Brazil. These tropical forest people relied on the shaman to enjoin their helper spirits (*hekura*) to either attack the souls of enemies or help them recover the lost souls of people from their village. "This was a constant battle, and the men [shamans] take hallucinogenic snuff—*ebene* [semen of the sun]—daily to do contest with their enemies through the agency of their personal *hekura*."[92] The spirits entered the chest of the *ebene* (or *epene*) user causing him to dance in ways specific to the possessing spirit.[93]

The Personified Face of the Spirits

Helper spirits were represented by both the costume of the shaman and the mask used for a particular ceremony. It is likely that early masks were designed to reinforce that symbolic purpose, and that the designs gave visual information (symbolic meaning) about the role of the masked figure in a ceremony and evoked the associated belief and the related spirit. Regardless of the exact "message" being conveyed, the image presented by the mask generally included implicit symbols (see mask 4.12) that were familiar to at least some of the participants.[94]

A necessary part of shamanic activity was the ability to change forms, to adopt another persona, and to control the various embodiments of human or animal anatomy. This ability implied mystical validation. The mask was a part of that metamorphic process as was voice (language, range, and ventriloquism) and gesture. It was a way of representing and regulating the spirits—the "real" face in which the spirits could reside. The symbolic realignment or reordering of these magical elements was a necessary part of shamanic practice.

Masks covered the face and functioned as idols. Among the Evenki (also written Evenk and Evenky) living on the Central Siberian Plateau, the mask was a "serving spirit of the shamans, a copper idol" or a "shamanistic fetish."[95] Many of the Evenki masks were oversize and were far too large to be worn. Existing photographs of Evenki shaman show the mask placed beside him or her. This arrangement confirms that the function of the mask was not that of an actual face covering, but represented the physical existence of the particular spirit.[96] It was a place for the spirit to reside.

The shaman often used masks to represent or suggest his or her helper spirits or to alter his or her persona. In addition to speaking in a voice representative of the familiar, the shaman dressed in the fur or hide of the helper, wore its claws, and inserted teeth into his or her mouth to aid in the transformation.[97] The altered appearance allowed the shaman to maintain a distance between himself or herself and the audience, and verified his or her special relationship with the supernatural.

A shaman's masks was often identified with a particular bird, animal, or being (real or imagined) associated with a spirit helper. The image evoked by the mask was a principal source of inspiration since the shaman in different cultures interacted with the supernatural in an animal guise. Masks were a part of the transposition from human to animal, as well as a sign to the viewers about the shaman's spiritual advisor and helper. Along the Northwest Coast of the North America this tradition was particularly strong. Shamans used animal and bird masks to symbolize the transformation of humans to animal forms. Transforming masks were powerful references to the duality of the human existence.

Masks made by the Kwakiutl, Nootka, Tlingit, and Haida people of the Northwest Coast of the United States are extraordinary examples of animal and human or bird and human masks. These masks were carved in wood and used in shamanic activities as well as social events. According to written records, it was thought that during the winter months supernatural beings came to live with humans, and it was during that time that social events using masks were held.[98] (See drawing 4.13). On the other hand, Mircea Eliade states that, "the mask plays no part in shamanism" among the Chukchee, Koryak, Kamchadal, Yukagir and Yakut people of Siberia."[99] However, it is believed that the Yukagir wore masks at funerals to avoid being recognized by the souls of the dead.

Sharpa shamans performed a masked "dance" in which they transformed themselves into *Mahakala* (Sanskrit meaning the "Great Black One") the great shamanic god. The *Mahakala* is one of eight *dharmapala* (defenders of the religious law) in Tibetan Bud-

DRAWING 4.12 — A *Udegei* Khambabo (shaman's) mask from the Amur River region of Siberia. The simple but very powerfully carved wood mask conveys a feeling of other worldliness that epitomized the shaman's role within the community. The painted lines on the forehead have the appearance of antlers representing either a link with animals or power rods of connection to the spirit world. This symbolic link between the material and ethereal worlds is found many locations as both a statement of power and a quest for supernatural energy.

dhism. Their grotesque appearance was to instill terror in evil spirits, and to promote this attitude; the worshipers of these defenders included the performance of masked dances. "Whatever was represented by the mask was made present in reality, and had a visible body."[100] The dance was a shamanic performance to join the two worlds — the spiritual and the mundane.

The influence of transformation masks in the shamans' rites was significant in Oceania (as the collective name for the islands scattered throughout most of the Pacific Ocean), as well as, along the Northwest Coast of North America. Masks in those areas expressed the dual nature of humans. The assumption of duality was also found in areas of West Africa,[101] where masks made visible the inner presence of the twin beings (human and animal). It was believed that these masks recalled the past and referred to the time when humans could change their appearance.

DRAWING 4.13 — Cannibal bird mask used during the *Kwakwaka'wakw Tsetseka* or winter ceremonial. This rite was to initiate young men into a ceremonial society and included individual masked enactments of totemic spirits.

Masks worn as a part of shamanistic activity represented spirit beings in the "power transformation strategy." Due to the personal and extraordinary nature of those special masks, they were placed in the shaman's grave or funeral house at the time of his or her death. These helping masks might combine anthropomorphic and zoomorphic images. The basic shape and look were human (anthropomorphic) with superimposed animal or bird (zoomorphic) forms. These dual-component masks were common along the Northwestern Coastal region of North America[102] and as transformation masks included an inner and outer image (see drawing 6.7). The symbolic meaning of one figure contained within another refers to the life and death process that influences the survival of all living creatures. People in all cultures are the consumer or the consumed — the predator and the pray. Shamanistic transformation called on the power of the inner being to be enhanced by the outer or more powerful spirit image.[103]

Unlike the Northwestern Coast of North America, shamanic masks were rare in much of Siberia (see drawing 3.3). The Altaians and Goldi shamans paint their faces with soot or cover their features with a cloth or the beaded fringe of a headband. According to Vilmos Diószegi,[104] Tofa (a linguistic group in north central Siberia) shamans wore three different head ornaments: the headband, hat, and crown. "The painting and the mask have a purely defensive character. The shaman would die if he could not conceal his [or her] face in the underworld, which he [or she] visits in his [or her] dream journeys."[105] Consistent with this idea of concealment, shaman masks often had no eye openings. This arrangement implies both inner vision and exclusion of the outside world.

> The symbol translates a human situation into cosmological terms; and reciprocally, more precisely, it discloses the interdependence between the structures of human existence and cosmic structures. This means that [so called] primitive man does not feel "isolated" in the Cosmos, that he [was] "open" to the World which symbolically [was] "familiar" to him.[106]

5

SHAMANISM AND IMAGINATIVE REPRESENTATION

One type of picture springing from shamanism is that in which parts of animals are combined more or less arbitrarily; for instance a stag is given several legs or heads, a panther is decked out with a stag's antlers, parts of these antlers are in turn the heads and hoofs of other animal. Such motifs occur frequently in the metal art of the nomads of Siberia and southern Russia in the first millennium B.C. and are undoubtedly connected with shamanistic ideas.[1]

That images of differently combined elements were made during the early horizons of human activity is a reality, because the objects exist and have been dated. The purposes they served, the cultural values they represent, and the natural or supernatural significance they may have served the "first users" is speculation. Scholars of different academic disciplines have theories about the meaning of this material that ranges from "art for spiritual devotion" to "art for art sake." Reality may be somewhere between the extremes. However, it is certain that some objects have been linked to shamanistic activity by qualified researchers, and other images suggest by their appearance a devotional quality consistent with the beliefs of the producing culture.

Imagination and Belief

Imaginative representation (art in the most general sense) for most early people was an essential feature of visual expression, but the resulting images were seldom viewed as aesthetic achievements. Objects had a purpose and a need to fulfill. Every object related to existence, and was assigned a place in life as a referent to the natural or supernatural worlds. Consequently, the importance and value of imaginative imagery were generally found in terms of the metaphysical reference to the group's survival. "If the perceptions of the originals ceased to be mystic, their images [two-and three-dimensional objects] would also lose their mystic properties. They would no longer appear to be alive...."[2]

Things visible and those imagined were often confused (or interchangeable), because of the symbolic meaning of shamanic objects. The imagined or believed became visible even to the inexperienced eye and the normal, that is, the usually recognized shapes of familiar objects were transformed. The knowing and understanding processes became more complicated when "believing by seeing" was a matter of personal convection. Rituals were intended to modify the viewer or participant's sense of space and time, reality and fantasy. "Siberian shamans performed rituals for success in hunting as well as to heal the sick, divined the future, and conducted offerings to local, family, and higher sprits."[3] Each of those "services" was a necessary part of community life and to promote societal continuity the skilled shaman created signs of spiritual contact with mimetic gestures, music, dance, and symbols.

Depicting the imagined was a special human activity that evolved into a separate and distinct type of work. It has been described as one of the most interesting and unique characteristics of the human being.[4] Although the making of images developed into a form of creative expression, it was seldom viewed as a separate and unique aesthetic activity. One of the extraordinary aspects of imagery was its symbolic quality because in normal circumstances, it was a human activity unlike any other. Image making as an effort to imitate nature was a part of nearly all early cultures. However, as a separate category of social activity, it likely had minimal meaning to most cultures. As the conscious arrangement of shapes and other elements in ways that influenced communal attitudes, it was an essential part of the recognition of beliefs and practices that was central to the lives of most peoples and most cultures.

The performance of ritual ceremonies that benefited the community acted as a catharsis. The feeling of spiritual release brought about by these intense emotional experiences generated a wide-range of objects to implement such activities. However, there was often little apparent relationship between the design and detail of the "art object" and its motivations and functions. The shapes were simple or complex, the surface rough or smooth, and the design expressive or symbolic. The objects, many of which were used by shamans, were symbols of power and considered to be representative of the spiritual energy granted for ritual purposes. The objects were manifestations of magic or "religion," but it was seldom simply art.

The Duwamish, a people living on the west coast of the North America, believed that the shaman could travel to distant places to recover lost or stolen souls. It was also thought that each shaman who had the power to go on such a quest had in his possession a carved figure obtained "as a consequence of his experience with a supernatural being in his younger days."[5] The figure was believed to embody the appearance of the beneficial being from whom the shaman had received his power. It was from that helper being (spirit) that the shaman learned the songs needed to release his power, and the other images that were to be painted on boards to assist in the ceremonial process.[6]

The connection between belief and art has received considerable attention. These two aspects of social consciousness are closely intertwined in many cultures, and in the environment guided by shamanic intervention the influence of art as a form of imaginative representation was a particularly intimate one. Early humans made images for protection from the negative powers that were to them quite real. The images reinforced belief and validated the societal link with the magical and surreal worlds. Psychologically, both belief and art invoked an emotional response that had no clearly explainable logic though there was an identifiable intellectual element.

The Duwamish shaman prepared for each ritual journey by repainting ceremonial boards and arranged them with carved helper figures in the outline of a canoe. The shaman used the ritual canoe to "embark upon an imaginary and highly mimetic voyage to the underworld in order to rescue the lost souls."[7] Each part of this dangerous journey was acted out in a performance that involved the audience/participants as well as the shaman. The audience generally knew what was happening and often they knew the shaman and the patient, so they were very emotionally concerned about the journey.[8] The soul recovery was eventually declared a success and the balance between the spiritual and mundane worlds was reestablished.

The carved figures, ceremonial boards, masks, and an array of other objects were essential elements in the shamans performance. They helped to perpetuate the *status quo*, and aided in validating the belief associated with cultural continuity. Although the objects were believed to be the source of shamanic power, there was apparently little artistic prerequisite for the carvings or boards, since they were simple in shape and style and gave no indication of aesthetic investment.

Societal practices dictated the shapes and refinement of objects (art) used for ritual activities. Some objects had crudely formed features, were devoid of details, and lacked aesthetic refinement. They were shaped and finished for "the economic, social, and/or political needs of the community, from materials thought to contain a vital force of their own."[9] It is that sense of social and cultural vitality that linked the complex web of relationships between the various parts of tradition into a unified whole.

> The process whereby the beings of this world are ordered according to their properties, so that the words of action and of spiritual and moral facts may be explored by analogy, is one which can also be seen, with the dawning of history, in the transition of the pictograph into the ideograph, as well as in the origins of art.[10]

People produced different symbolic systems as a means of social connection, but these connections were very intricate. Society embraced different languages, gestures, etiquette, and beliefs for better orientation and greater continuity. Societal messages could, therefore differ one from another according to their content, form, and affiliation. They were, however, the same in two aspects: people wanted to establish contacts with other beings even when that communication was one-sided, and the message was conveyed not just in one type of "language," but in more than one code at the same time.[11] An example of that communication was the ceremony in which the shaman used the drum and chant as a language to make contact with a supernatural being or deity. The shaman's coat, stick, and head cover added to the circumstances of communication in the magical-religion symbols, because a certain authority was attributed to that paraphernalia.

It is clear that "shamanic art had a wide variety of meanings to different people, so wide perhaps that the value of the term could be questioned."[12] Nevertheless, just as mythic being might be used to explain the traditions and practices of a people, art gave substance to those same elements. The images created and preserved by humanity reinforced the association between form and idea, belief and reality. The creation and re-creation of natural and supernatural connections between those elements that regulate life forces required constant vigilance. "Shamanism — the power psychological and spiritual process for re-creating the cosmos and turning death into life in all the dimensions of Reality — was the driving force behind every aspect of ancient Maya life."[13]

Maya shamans "were known as '*itzers*'— those who could bring forth the divine substance and direct it to create abundance and life."[14] It was the insights and ecstatic visions of those shamans/artists that lead the way on the road to immortality, and it was their guidance that shaped Maya art and spirituality.[15] Objects including paintings, sculptures, writings, and masks were designed to teach those willing to see "the secret instructions for surviving death and achieving resurrection."[16] In the Maya imagination, both the creation process and the sacrifice brought forth new life.

The shamanistic tendency to produce art with symbolic references or to think in terms of images that evolved from the emotional and intellectual past reveals an attitude that extended beyond the horizon of ordinary comprehension. That tendency has survived for eons and is apparent in contemporary art. Marija Gimbutas writes in *Language of the Goddess* (1989) that, "Symbols are seldom abstract in any genuine sense; their ties with nature persist, to be discovered through the study of context and association."[17] It is likely that early shamans and hunters saw in the images of animals and other symbols the cosmic soul or life force. The picture allowed the creator to believe that through the picture he (probably a male hunter) could capture or influence the soul and therefore the animal.[18] A similar relationship likely occurred with the masked or costumed priest or shaman. The appearance transformed the person, thereby allowing belief and imagination to superceded reality.

PLATE 19—Coat of the shaman Tulayev of the Karagass, Siberia. The coat demonstrates the care and attention give to the shaman's attire. There are downy feathers attached to the shoulders and fringe on the hem to aid in flight. On the upper chest are elongated metal rattles to gain the attention of spirits, and the long ribbons, strips, and snakes of fabric are representative of the number of spirit helpers to be employed by the shaman.

The animal figures associated with shamanic art forms reflected the use of natural symbols and iconography associated with the hunter-gatherer environment. Images that combined man with nature promoted the sense of unity with the known world. The images advanced a feeling of completeness that was enhanced and ritualized during activities performed in an altered state of consciousness. Man became the art whether the image was a painting in a rock shelter, a mask, or a costume (see drawing 5.1).

Creative Expression as Applied Magic

The early communities of which we have knowledge appear to have endorsed the idea of other worlds that had a direct influence on the activities of life, as they knew it to be. The mysterious events of this, the middle world, were easier to understand when assigned to the intervention of spirits, deities, and demons. It was apparently determined that humankind needed a means for influencing the supernatural beings and to gain their support. Therefore, they developed a societal arrangement for mediation services between the world of myth — spirits and the supernatural — and the earthly reality of human existence. The shaman helped to fill that role as the prototype of the artist, priest, and physician, and drew upon a wide range of creative practices to address the challenges of this multi-dimensional responsibility.

The shaman had a close relationship with his or her spirit helpers, and the results of that connection was an increase of power. When the shaman was an artist, musician, or storyteller, his or her talents were enhanced, and the healing power used as a medicine man or woman was increased.[19] Therefore, it was reasonable to view art, at least in its earliest forms, as synonymous with the human situation in historical terms, and as depicting the relationship between the patterns of human existence and cosmic belief. Although it was likely that the images produced by early people were drawn from things reveled in visionary experiences, the marks symbolically describe the world that was familiar. The art provided a means for social interaction and thereby ameliorated the sense of isolation imposed by the limitations of human existence.

A number of tools and implements were developed by early people that verified a certain dexterity and inventiveness, and perhaps more important, they demonstrate, the skill and imagination needed to make images. Along with this "talent" for "artistic" expression, they had an appreciation for music as shown by excavated bone whistles and flutes.[20] The challenges of survival stimulated the need for ceremonies and rituals by the Upper Paleolithic (perhaps 25,000 years ago), and music making, as an accompaniment to early forms of ritual activity, might have been practiced as early as the Aurignacian Period (begin-

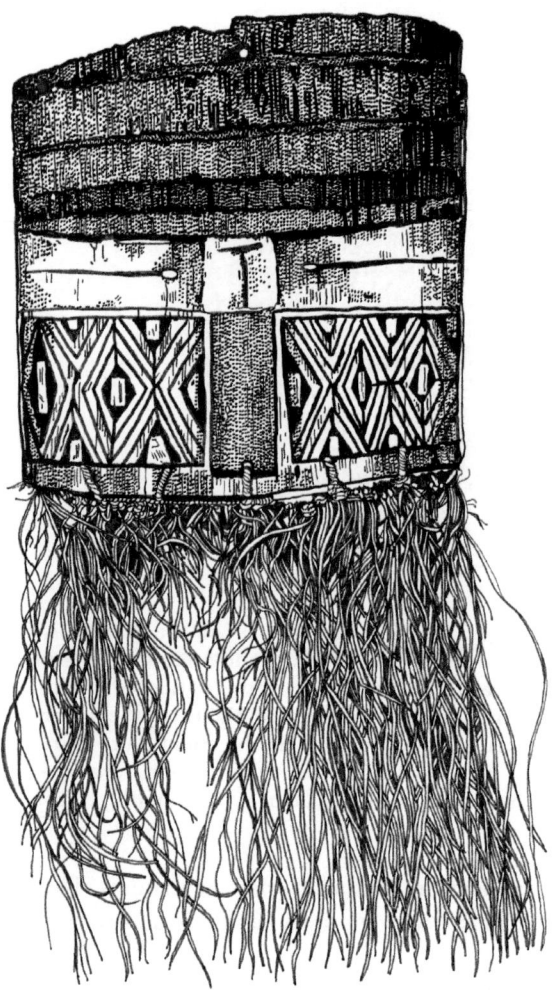

DRAWING 5.1— Fish Dance mask of the Kamayura from central Brazil made of wood and fiber and probably representing the fish spirit. The "T" marking on the nose "symbolises a shape visible on a fish" and the lower part of the mask has a "net-like drawing."[f] There is no clearly documented record of how these masks were used, but they were apparently associated with curing ceremonies.[g] They might have been used to cure illness brought on by the loss of the patient's soul. The masking ceremony was to attract the offending spirit to the village and to convince it to return the stolen soul.[h]

ning about 34,000 years before the current era). The Upper Paleolithic people, as well as the San (of the Kalahari in southern Africa) and Australian Aborigines[21] left evidence of image-making and musical apparatus.

Imaginative imagery created during the Upper Paleolithic included geometric patterns that have been attributed to shamanistic purposes. These "signs" are interpreted as having a variety of meanings, but none are totally acceptable or verifiable. However, contemporary with the signs and symbols were anthropomorphic figures, paintings and etchings that are of a male figure clothed in the skin of an animal, and wearing a mask identified with an animal (see drawing 5.2). The part-human/part-animal figures, although subject to interpretation, appear to document the use of masks for some form of early ritualistic practice. Regardless of the purpose these figures served, the renderings demonstrated a special skill and an appreciation for natural form. The images produced were undoubtedly symbolic of past experiences and probably delineated scenes of enjoyment or veneration. A significant aspect of those symbolic representations was the achievement and advancement of technical skill.

There are many Paleolithic representations of human figures with animal masks, features, or appendages. Probably the most interesting is the so-called "sorcerer" figures of *Les Trois Frères*—"The Three Brothers" named in honor of the boys who found the cave in France.[22] One figure was drawn with antlers, canine ears, a long beard, a horse's tail, and bear's paws instead of hands (see drawing 2.6). In the same cave is another figure with a bison headpiece and holding bison (bovine) hooves (see drawing 5.3). The figures are males with their genitals exposed, both appear to be robed in animal skins, and both have a dance-like posture. Joseph Campbell describes another element of the *Lascaux* pictograph as "a shaman depicted lying in a trance, wearing a bird mask and with a figure of a bird perched on a staff located beside him"[23] (see drawing 3.4).

Early cultures produced numerous depictions of animals and humans, and while the exact meaning of these images is often unclear, they seemingly represent the activities and beliefs of the people. It is generally believed that in the shamanistic world everything is alive, and all life was part of "one mysterious unity by virtue of its derivation from the spiritual source of life."[24] The shamanism bequest to the late Mesoamerican magico-religion practice was the fundamental assumption that all phenomena of the world were animated by a spiritual essence, "the common possession of which rendered insignificant our usual distinctions between human and animal and ever the organic and inorganic."[25]

DRAWING 5.2—Incised image of a man dressed in an animal skin performing what appears to be a "magical" dance that mimics the animal. The image is from the Mege shelter near Teyjat (Dordogne, France).

Evidence of early supernatural belief also has been found in the *Transbaykal* caves located in Eastern Russia. The sloping walls and ceilings of the caves are decorated with red-ochre drawings in a style dating from the Bronze Age. According to Levin and Potapov and as written in, *The People of Siberia*, the drawings illustrate "the cult of the sacred bird—an eagle or falcon—a magic group ritual aimed at ensuring the fertility of livestock, the growth of the clan and the welfare of its members."[26] It is not surprising that the drawing of the bird continued to appear in regional design into the twenty-first century.

Incised or painted images of sorcerer or shaman have been found in various locations from Altamira in Europe to sites in Africa and Australia. Attributed to different time, cultures, and circumstances, many figures have human qualities and appear to wear masks and other articles of specialized attire. The "shaman" figure paintings found in the rock shelters in the Lower Pecos region of West Texas are excellent examples of this application of illustrative expression. These black and red figures at Panther Cave and Rattlesnake Canyon have been described as "spirit beings" and "shamans" painted by persons emerging from a chemically induced trance or enraptured emotional state (see drawing 1.7).[27]

Symbolic expression can be viewed as a form of magic. It involves the transfer of thought as an abstract concept through applied physical energy and intellectual transformation to real (tangible) imagery that communicates visually and emotionally to not only the creator but to viewers. This magical practice manifested itself as a figure drawn upon or engraved into stone, ivory, wood, or other material to be used as a talisman, an amulet, or for casting spells. It was a mark of celebration or a marker to acknowledge the dead. The creation was an image, a word rooted in the Latin verb *imitari*, which means to imitate or imagine. "At some point in human prehistory, the ability to draw images and configurations came into being, and art was born."[28]

The important role assigned to art is not limited to one people or one location. "The ancient shamans and artists lead the way on the road to immortality, and it was their insights and ecstatic visions that shaped Maya art and spirituality."[29] Andres Lommel writes in *The World of the Early Hunter* (1967) about the representation of shaman and the exceptional nature of the images emanating from the early artistic

DRAWING 5.3—Masked figure from Les Trois Frères, France. This bison masked figure appears to dance or to make some kind of exaggerated movement across the rock surface. The image may represent an early form of totemism or celebration of the kinship between humans and animals. The figure was perhaps imitating a respected part of human existence or acknowledging the animal life that was taken so human life might continue.

expression. He calls attention to the "materially conceived assistant" of the Lord of the Animals. Elsewhere, the Tungus people carved an idol from wood to represent "either a small human figure without arms or a zoomorphic figure, most likely an elk."[30] It was a representation of energy. These special figures might be dressed in a deerskin cap and a "skirt of bear's ear skin"[31] according to the directions given the shaman.

The Siberian hunter appealed to the figure (idol) to elicit the help of hunter magic, before embarking on a hunt. The request for a successful hunt was not directly to the Lord of the Animals; instead, the idol was petitioned to carry the message and bring the response. Following a prescribed pattern of observances that included feeding and entertaining, the idol "messenger" was thrown into the air and allowed to fall to the ground. When it landed face upward, it foretold good hunting or fishing. A face downward landing was a sign that the hunt would not bring the desired results.

Shamanistic art that included human and animal shapes was found in many locations. The Inca made pottery vessels that incorporated human and animal elements (see drawing 5.4), and the indigenous peoples of Alaska made extraordinary masks and sculptures that endorsed the unity of humans and animals. The Mayan shaman like the early Egyptians relied on imaginative imagery that combined human and animal elements to depict deities and demons. Mayans also used ceremonial offering plates as roadmaps to otherworld destinations. These plates had intricate designs that illustrated specific places the shaman wanted to reach.[32] The plates were a blend of reality and imagination. They were emotionally activated maps to visionary locations inhabited by deities and demons.

Shamanic rituals also relied on the natural world for spiritual guidance. The Ogallala people, the largest of the seven independent bands of the Teton Dakotas, believed that there were spirits belonging to places, things, animals, birds, insects, and reptiles. In other lands, the Karagas shaman (a Turkic-speaking people of southern Siberia) considered his drum as a symbolic horse that he rode during rituals,[33] and in ancient China, Siberia, Japan, and Africa animals were sacrifices in ritual activities. A central ritual of Mongol shamanism was blood-sacrifice to the sky god *Tengri*. A horse (usually white) was killed in that ritual, and its skin was hung on a high pole to allow the spirit to escape that it might carry messages to the gods. The spirit released by the sacrifice was the vital force representing a chain or continuum of all individual spirits of that animal (horses) that had lived, were living, or were to live.

DRAWING 5.4—Ceramic stirrup spouted vessel symbolizing a curer performing her medicinal magic. The figure on this South American pot is thought to be holding hallucinogenic cactus used in shamanistic rituals. The image of the tethered llama is another symbol of magical curing. The shape incised above the llama may represent a diving bowl.

The relationship between humans and animals reflected the myths and legends found all over the world. It was the animal that carried the shaman, priest, or king into the jungle, tundra, or sky where the person died and was returned to life by the largess of benevolent spirits. The relationship between humans and animals was a dominant characteristic of Paleohunter belief. It was a shared believed that certain shamans could be transformed into animals, understand animal language, or share their occult powers. Each time this transformation occurred the shaman entered the mythical time when the separation between animals and humans had not yet occurred.[34]

Images of Belief and Sympathetic Magic

Art can be described as a human activity by which a person consciously and by means of certain external signs, passes to others feelings about life so they are influenced by those feelings and also experience them. To paraphrase Philip H. Lewis speaking at the Symposium held at the Royal Anthropological Institute in 1961, the early artist might be thought of as not one person, but many. The artist creates something that exists in the minds, thoughts, and beliefs of members of the resident society.[35] Interestingly, Mayan lore asserted that, "the shaman-scribes and shaman-artists were the inventors of writing, the mythmakers, the astronomers and astrologers, the curers, the seers, the spiritual explorers, the innovators, the architects, the keepers of the ancient wisdom and the creators of beauty."[36] It declared that, "all authentic human beings were shaman-creators in one way or another."[37]

The concept of the immortal soul quite possible contributed to the creative process of depicting animals. However, the individuals making images, although important at the time, were often forgotten. Among the art "makers" in all societies there were the skilled and the unskilled. Some artists were likely convinced that their carvings and drawings were completely realistic and lifelike. The artists (image makers) might have believed that their creations mirrored every detail of the animal portrayed. However, in spite of the wish to create a "realistic" representation, it was the impression and distinctive character of the animal that was idealized. What mattered most was the significance of the object and its meaning to the people of the community. The perception of an object was more than sensation; it was the impression of things, and the completeness of the visual experience was not determined by the concept, but the impression. It was when the work of art (carving or drawing) was viewed against its socio-cultural background and in relation to other objects that it was seen in its entirety.

That the early markings and symbols had a magico-religious purpose seems certain, and that they were viewed as having a "special" value or uniqueness within the producing culture, although seldom considered works of art. Many objects, though aesthetically pleasing and with recognizable forms, were not intended to represent an ideal of beauty or an expression of an emotional need. They were more likely to connect two very different worlds — one world relating to the natural needs of society, and the other rooted in myths, legends, and influences of the deities that regulated daily existence.

The relationship of imagery with shamanic practice was in early times very direct. The images and objects were believed to contain the animal's spiritual substance or soul. Treated properly, the species of animal portrayed would regenerate and continue to be available to the hunter. The image was a connector, a material link between the mundane and spiritual worlds.

According the Mircea Eliade, "one becomes what one displays. The wearers of masks are really the mythical ancestors portrayed by their masks."[38] The symbolized animal being attacked and killed by the hunter was a depiction of the reality to come.

In a similar way, the *ongon* was for the Mongolian shaman the dwelling place for helper spirits that offered a unique perception of the world of Siberian peoples. The *ongons* represented the idea of cosmic space and humanity. They foretell the future, provide information about forthcoming events, and predict the weather. Shamanistic connect with the spirit world through *ongons* was a necessary part of most activities. "The shaman *ongon* is a powerful and clever thing, which gives all kinds of information from all over the world...."[39]

Erwin Christensen speculates in his book *Primitive Art* (1955), that the "prehistoric hunter employed magical principles in his art in three ways: (a) to create new animals, or fertility magic; (b) to assist the hunter's aim, or death magic; (c) to appease dead animals, or propitiation magic."[40] Fertility magic was of concern since it referred directly to the multiplication of the animals and humans. Death magic assisted the hunter to trap and kill pray, and it also protected the hunter against becoming the victim of animal aggression. Life, death, and procreation were of primary concern along with the disposition of spirits. An improperly treated animal spirit might seek revenge on the hunter, thus causing hardship or death. Magic had to be employed to avoid such reprisal. The image was a means for initiating magic.

Art forms were dictated by the needs and interests of the community, and guided by the shaman, or the myths that defined the origins of the particular people. Interestingly, certain art forms appeared in diverse cultures that have strikingly similar imagery. These similarities defy attempts to explain their universality based on contact. The images appear to have mystical meaning, but whether they were dream or fantasy stimulated is uncertain. It is generally agreed that the exact purpose for which they were drawn, etched, scratched, or painted is unclear. It is equally unclear why some artists worked in hidden or secluded locations away for the activities of the surrounding population while others created images in open locations.

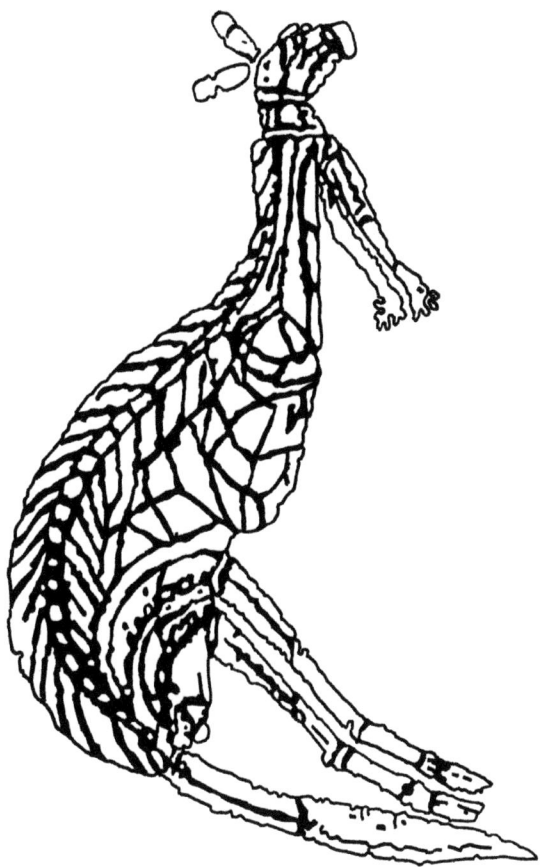

DRAWING 5.5 — X-ray style painting of a kangaroo from Goulbourn Island, North Australia. This bark painting shows the inner structure of the kangaroo according to aboriginal tradition. The backbone and ribs are clearly depicted, as are the bones in the legs. The x-ray style was found in many locations and is believed to relate to the notion that bones are the "seeds" of new life.

The so-called x-ray or skeletal style

Left: DRAWING 5.6—X-ray style drawing showing the internal organs of an elk. The ribs are clearly described and concentric circles depict the stomach and intestines. The image was incised into a basalt cliff on Klya River, Khabarovsk district, Khabarovsk territory during the fourth-third millennium before the current era.
Right: DRAWING 5.7—Zuni Pueblo deer design with "lifeline" extending from the mouth to the stomach or inner soul. The line is believed to show the path of life. Air enters through the mouth as a necessary element for life and the soul exits through the mouth as the life ends. These drawings made by Zuni Pueblo peoples of southwestern North America are a simplified form of x-ray imagery.

used to represent humans and animals is considered to be an expression of shamanistic belief current among early hunters. These drawings and painting show the skeletal frames and internal organs, including heart and lungs, and are thought to represent the shamanic belief in resurrection from anatomical components (see drawings 5.5 and 5.6). Representations of the animals or humans were not merely pictures but were believed to contain the animal's or human's vital substance.[41] "These were not mere beasts but spirit animals only vaguely resembling live creatures. They are amorphous, all but invisible, uncatchable, with the legs of other animals."[42]

The X-ray style can be traced to the Mesolithic art of northern Europe and originating in either Norway or Russia. Early examples were found on bone fragments in southern France dating from the late Magdalenian Period (13000–6000 before the current era). Paintings in this distinctive style have been found in the art of hunting cultures in Spain, eastern Siberia, the Arctic Circle, North America, western New Guinea, New Ireland, India, Australia, and Malaysia.[43] The X-ray style appeared in greater or lesser abstract forms in these locations. The "lifeline" animal motif seen on Pueblo pottery of the southwestern North America is a simplified extension of the style (see drawing 5.7). In these examples, a line was drawn from the animal's mouth to a place representing the heart or stomach. It is the path of breath that nourishes the spirit and prolongs life.

The Washo and Wishram people of Oregon made x-ray style carved wooden figures. The small pieces displayed the underlying skeletal structure with the facial and rib bones especially pronounced giving the "impression of seeing through the flesh."[44] The carvings included both human and animal figures. Although the exact purpose for these figures is not known, the marks that form the skeletal image are well recognized as fundamental elements of design that extended into the distant past. The chevrons and "V" of the rib cage are bird goddess symbols[45] and the zigzags of the skirt are identified with the symbol for water.[46]

The Buryat women's *ongon* figure pictured in the *Ancestors' Spirits in the Sounds of the Tambourine* catalog has a line drawing of a skeleton-like figure inside the wood surrounding shape. Though the wood and cloth image is not a true x-ray style figure, it has similar characteristics (see drawing 5.8).

Facing the Spirits

Earliest agriculturists might not have invented the mask, but it is as old and as universal as art and religion. Neolithic people followed a tradition established by their Palæolithic forebears, adopting the mask to their mode of ritual observance and imaginative expression.

Spiritual or demoniacal possessions were circumstances in which the shaman's help was necessary. Supernatural intervention was required to dislodge the possessing force of malevolent spirits. Shamanistic regalia including a mask, head cover, and robe, as well as a rattle, drum, fan, and other types of spirit attracting paraphernalia were used to capture or exorcise the disruptive visitant. Each piece of the supporting apparatus was said to transmit a special energy that was outside the understanding of normal people. As an example of the special character of the paraphernalia, the mask separated the shaman from his or her natural associations and established a supernatural relationship with the possessive spirits. Those masks were often frightening in appearance and had unearthly qualities.

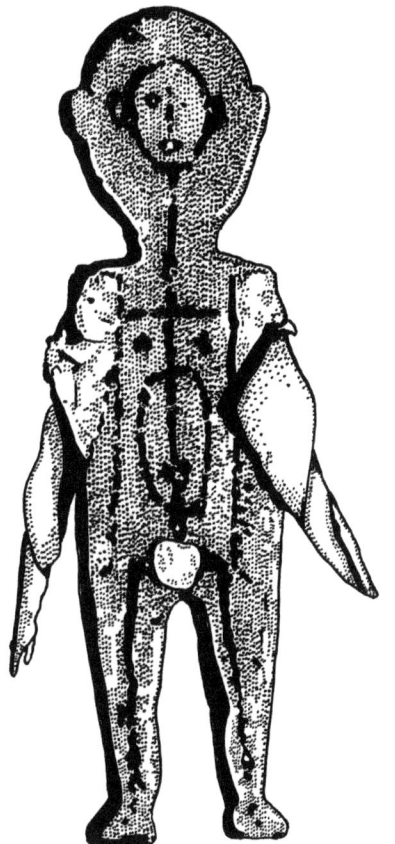

DRAWING 5.8—Drawing of an early twentieth century woman's *ongon*. The word *ongon* is used to describe the image of a spirit or the spirit itself that was supposed to dwell in the image, and also the souls of ancestors. The *ongon* were usually in human form and painted or drawn on wood, cloth, or rock. The skins of some animals also served as *ongon*. The shaman kept *ongons* in special boxes and offerings of food and wine were made to them.

> A unique shamanic society known as the *Windigokanak* is ... found among members of the Turtle Mountain Band [Ojibwa people]. This "clown mask" society wore strange masks in honor of the cannibalistic deity *Windigo*, and performed outlandish acts....[47]

It is not possible to describe with absolute certainty the purpose and meaning of masks among early people. That they existed in many cultures is verified by numerous sources. However, the use assigned to individual masks or groups of masks is subject to recent interpretation, and no matter how commanding the logic or reasonable the concept, it remains speculative. The same can be said of much of pre-literate history, but beliefs, myths, and practices appear to validate many suppositions about the lives and lifestyles of early people.

It is believed that archaic societies lived as much as possible in the sacred, that is, affixed in an attitude both physiological and psychological, of dedication to a deity or in close proximity to consecrated objects.[48] "The tendency is perfectly understandable, because, for primitives as for the man of all pre-modern society, the sacred is equivalent to a power, and, in the last analysis, to reality."[49]

Historic record confirms that shamans were believed to be visionaries who mastered death. They often communicated with the supernatural in animal guise using elaborate masks to fulfill their unique role in an increasingly complex cultural setting and to address the many demands of the natural worlds. The animal and bird masks made on the Northwest Coast of the North America to symbolize the transformation of humans to animal forms are well documented. These masks, as symbolic references to the duality of the human subconscious, opened to reveal the human face inside — the joining of two life forms. Other articles of shamanistic ceremonial dress included animal headed human figures, and a variety of creatively joined animal and human forms (see drawings 2.8, 4.10, and 4.11). Most of these objects were derived from supernatural experiences, and represented helper or totem beings that had meanings known only to their owner.

The images made by shamans were inspired representations of humanity and nature, as well as a statement of time and belief. They were a commitment to the future in that the images gave identity to the past in terms of the present. The masks, figures, and symbols were signs of continuation, and extensions of time linked to cultural survival. Human understanding undoubtedly had its beginning in the senses. Objects that were seen remained in the memory, and those memories could be called upon to stimulate related activities and events. Art, as image making, was instrumental in maintaining the memory of society. The transfer of cultural information often started with an image that stimulated group memory and subsequently generated endorsement and action.

The image making practice was likely drawn from the traditions of the people rather than an imitation of nature. Masks, for example, expressed the spiritual embodiment associated with beliefs or magic. They were often tied to "its function of mediation between the supernatural world and the natural world."[50] The image makers, among certain cultural groups, were "professionals" that inherited the their role from family members that had attained an elevated rank within the community or clan. The artisans (carvers and fabricators) in other areas were selected because of special talent and trained through an apprenticeship in the methods and techniques of image making.

The Mask: As an integral part of the "concept of human need," ritual paraphernalia often including masks was viewed as functionally interrelated elements of a society that contributed to the survival and well being of the people. The "need," in this instance, was considered as "something required" for the satisfactory functioning of the group, and because humans are inherently social beings, those needs were organized and addressed through cultural activities.

Because masks, as cultural phenomena, were a blending of two separate attitudes, the real and the imaginary, they were activated by the conditions in which they were produced. They were a manifestation of the imagination and yet they were drawn from traditional designs rather than a representation of the "real." The concept of a "different kind of perception" allowed the making of images that were free from the limitations imposed by mundane life. The anthropomorphic appearance of certain objects give them positive value, whereas, the same consideration might not be extended to other objects lacking those characteristics. The unknown and the unidentifiable were causes for concern and apprehension for many people, and the most commonly applied defense against those feelings was avoidance. Most shamanistic images were culturally guided impressions that responded to a time, place, and need.[51]

Masks like many sanctified objects were practical in that they provided a service to the community as mnemonic objects that referenced social and cultural heritage. The Pueblo people of the southwestern North America and their belief in kachinas exemplify the duality of masks as links between the sacred and profane worlds. These ancestral spirits — kachinas — were believed to act as intermediaries between humans and the appropriate deity. They were thought to live with the people for half of each year at which time, they were made visible by men performing traditional rituals while wearing masks. It was believed that the performers were transformed and became the spirits identified by the masks. Men carved small wood figures of the kachinas for the children so they can learn the practices and beliefs of the people. The identity of the spirit was demonstrated not by the form of the figure but by the color and ornamentation of the associated mask.

In some locations, only members of secret societies were allowed to make and to use certain objects. For instance, adult kachina society members had masks made for them by the other society members. Some masks were communal property and individual dancers owned others.[52] Kachina masks were often quite elaborate. The center of the mask is a leather hood that fits over the performers head. The identity of individual representatives of the 500 kachinas was made apparent by the addition of paint, feathers, sticks, and other accessories. The masks exhibited a great variety because some had fur or pine wreath collars, attached beards, protruding mouths, snouts, and horns. The leather hoods were retained from year to year but the attachments were normally replaced each season[53] (see photograph 9). Kachinas are not shamans, but conduits to the supernatural based on myth and tradition.

PHOTOGRAPH 9 — *Haschogan*, a masked Navajo spirit figure. Like other Pueblo people, the Navajo venerate a variety of gods, departed ancestors, and spirits. Masked impersonators represent the different deities (spirits) in communal ceremonies. Edward Curtis took this photograph in 1904.

The Tlingit, the northernmost people of the North Pacific Coast of North America, inhabiting the islands and coastal lands of southern Alaska from Yakutat Bay to Cape Fox have masked events over which the shaman preside. These events — potlatch — are held to celebrate important events such as marriages, births, deaths, and initiations into secret societies. Individuals who had suffered public embarrassment also used the potlatch as a face-saving activity. Potlatch activities often included masked dances "in imitation of the clan crests."[54] The shaman's role in the in these activities was to control forces of both natural and human origin for the benefit of individual community member or the whole lineage.

The shaman — usually a man but not always — had a special role in the Tlingit community. It was believed that his power came from spirits that inhabited living and non-living things. The shaman's "paraphernalia" includes masks, amulets, and rattles, but the most powerful component was the mask. "Each [Tlingit] shaman would possess four masks, one for each spirit, although the most powerful individuals might possess eight masks."[55] The masks were basically human in form, but each design included an attribute that related to a personal spirit such as a shark, octopus, or hawk.[56] Travelers and missionaries verified the use of these masks from the second half of the eighteenth century (see drawing 5.9).

Mongolian shamans did not generally use masks except for the *Avgaldai* mask of the bear ancestor. This special mask was used during the shamanic initiation ceremony.[57]

"Shamanism — the power psychological and spiritual process for re-creating the cosmos and turning death into life in all the dimensions of Reality — was the driving force behind every aspect of ancient Maya life."[58] Masks were an objectification of that life. They concealed the face of the wearer, either actually or symbolically, and presented a "new" face to the viewer. Masks identified the power or energy of significant persons in dramatic ways. Many "non–Olmec kings, including those of the early Maya, wore masks; and the first Maya royal headdresses with their magnificent flowing feathers were meant to depict the monarchs mystical oneness with the gods."[59] The mask was identified with the energy of position, and Maya kings were acknowledged as shamans and priests.

Masks had two identities. One related to the physical shape or the outer view. That aspect of a mask identified it with a particular entity, animal, human, or spirit and gave information about the reason the mask was being worn for a particular event. The second identity was its inner contents or "spirit." That element of the mask related to its force — its purpose for being. When the mask was worn, the masked person might assume the outward identity but only rarely the "spirit" of the mask. The "face" was more easily transformed than the inner being.

The significance of that duality, the inner and outer aspects of the mask, cannot be overstated. The two faces, the seen and the unseen, are a key part of many mythological traditions, and therefore, a primary image source for masks. The outer reality — the world of humans and nature — was a manifestation of the inner realm of the spirits.[60] When applied to humans, the duality referred to "the person with a double image." That pronouncement identified a person who gained an advantage by use of magic. This double perspective was a reflection of the spirit world and a notion closely associated with shamanism.

Masks were necessary elements of the social and ritual functions of peoples guided by tradition, and the validity of those traditions was of primary concern. However, just as the role of masks was a connecting element for social, as well as shamanic activities in some

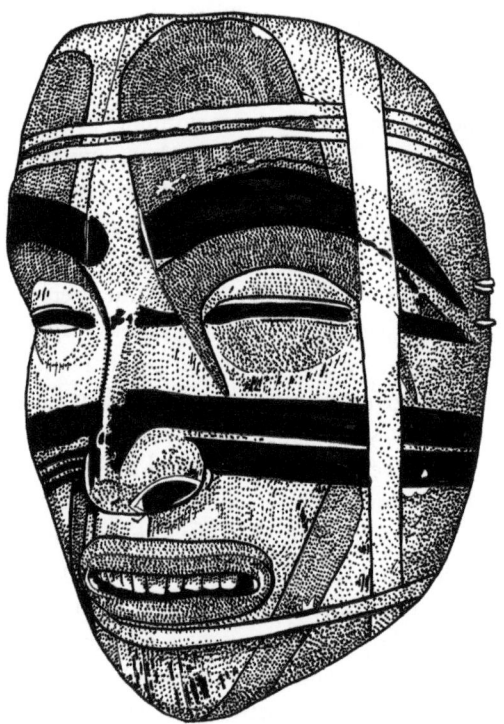

DRAWING 5.9 — This Haida portrait mask with designs similar to those used in facial painting was worn alternately with an animal mask to demonstrate the shaman's transformation from the natural to the supernatural state.

societies, other peoples avoided them. "[T]he mask plays no part in shamanism" among the Chukchee, Koryak, Kamchadal, Yukagir and Yakut people of Siberia,[61] according to Mircea Eliade in his book *Shamanism: Archaic Techniques of Ecstasy* (1974). The Yukagir were said to wear masks at funerals to avoid recognition by the souls of the dead.

Masking as a cultural related activity has been used throughout much of the world since the Stone Age. Nevertheless research has often approached masking as an interesting phenomenon of group activity instead of an integral part of a cultural whole. The needs of an individual changed according to the requirement of the society in which a particular individual existed, and those needs moved between the real and surreal worlds. They were inclined to be associated with the inner nature of things rather than their surface appearance. There was at times an overlapping of the requirements and desires of individuals, and both aspects of social survival related to ritual activities.

Masked dances were a part of the historic record of almost every culture, and essential aspect of these performances was one of communication with a spirit or deity. Sacred (ritual) dance was an ecstatic means of contact that involved cyclical rather than linear time, a reverie state, and transformation.[62] The physical and psychological were not separated in the dance, as a result, the distinction between physical interaction and psychological exchange like verbal and non-verbal communication between individuals and deities was not a limitation for shamanism.[63]

Ritualized activities that involve dance are believed to have served as an intermediary between people and the gods from prehistoric times. Japanese *Kagura* dances dedicated to native deities were performed before local Shinto shrines. Those dances were "in essence a symbolic reenactment of the propitiatory dance that lured the sun goddess *Amaterasu* from the cave in ancient myth."[64] The *Kagura* performances, as with other shamanic dances, were accompanied by drums, brass gongs, and flutes. Across the Sea of Japan, or East Sea, masked shamanistic dances were performed during the Unified Silla period (668–935) in Korea. Those dances called "The Five Displays" were described in a poetic composition of the ninth century.[65]

Sounds and Reflections of Shamanistic Activities

> The *pawo* [Bön medium] begins chanting, accompanying himself with a little drum or bell. He dances, first slowly, then faster and faster, and, finally, trembles convulsively. A being of another world, god, demon or spirit of a dead person, has taken possession of him. In a kind of frenzy he utters broken sentences, which are supposed to convey that which the invisible being wishes to communicate....[66]

The Paleo-Siberians shaman usually made his or her ritual accessories, but only after the spirits gave their permission. Not all shamans could wear the *manyak* (coat) and the owl-skin cap.[67] The spirits generally announced to the chosen man or woman when he or she might wear them. Because they were sacred, only the shaman was to use those accessories, otherwise, they were impotent to produce any results. Similarly, it was only a "real" shaman who was to possess the full shaman's attire.

The distinction between Paleo-Siberians and Neo Siberians influenced shamanic rituals as well as the paraphernalia associate with those activities. The designation Paleo-Siberian refers to peoples of northeastern Siberia believed to be remnants of earlier populations displaced by the later arriving Neo-Siberians. The Paleo-Siberians include the Chukchee, Koryak,

Itelmen (Kamchadal) Nivkh (Gilyak), Yakaghit, Ket, and Koryak peoples.[68] The Neo-Siberian population included Finnic, Samoyedic, Turkic, Mongolic, and Turgusic peoples of Central Asian origin.[69]

Drum: The most important object of shamanistic paraphernalia in Siberia was the drum. It was also a part of the ritual activities of both Asiatic and American Eskimo.[70] "The drum had the power of transporting the shaman to the superworld and evoking spirits by its sounds."[71] The drum used by the Chukchee was different from that adopted in northwestern Asia by the Yakut, Tungus, Koryak, Kamchadal, and Yukaghir. Drums used by those peoples were of a "southern type," large and rather oval in shape, and held by four loose bands fastened to the hoop of the drum on the inside.[72] The bands meet in the middle, and were tied to a small wheel or a cross that was without other support. The drum hung loosely when grasped by the handle. The drum was shaken as well as being struck, and its position was easily changed. The wooden drumstick used to strike the drum was covered with skin or cured leather.

Among the Chukchee (a Paleo-Siberian people) the senior female shared the role of shaman with the senior male in the family ceremonial. The female had charge of the drum and amulets, and she might perform the family sacrifices although that responsibility usually resided with the male—the father. Shamanism, at least among the Chukchee was not restricted to either sex. The gift of shamanic inspiration was be-

PLATE 5—A shaman of the Samoyed ethnolinguistic group that inhabited northwestern Russia. The Samoyed people were also called Nenets. They occupied a region that extended from the White Sea on the west to the Taymyr Peninsula on the east and the Sayan Mountains to the south. The northern limit of their homeland is the Arctic Ocean. The Samoyed had several classes of shamans with different abilities. Kai Donner took this photograph circa 1911–13.

lieved granted more frequently to women, though it was considered to be of an inferior nature. The higher levels of power and spiritual enlightenment were thought bestowed upon men.

The Chukchee drum had a wooden handle that was attached with sinews to the wooden hoop. The hoop was nearly circular in shape, and the drumhead was of very thin skin, usually from a walrus's stomach.[73] The drumstick varies according to its purpose. It was either a narrow, light strip of whalebone, or a piece of wood that was sometimes adorned with fur tassels. The whalebone stick was used during the magical performances held at night, and the wooden stick was employed during ceremonials performed in a tent during the day.[74]

The Darhad shaman's drum (*henggereg*) was a mount for their *ongons*. The drum was the means by which the Tsaatan (reindeer herders) and Toj shamans traveled to "heaven" to meet with their *ongons*.[75] Mongolian shamans of Halha Banners had circular, triangular, and octagonal drums. Professor Purev reports that shamans from the Dayan Deerh area had octagonal as well as circular and triangular drums.[76] "Thus, the shaman *henggereg* was transport for both the ongon and shaman and according to the animal skin it was covered with was for either kind or evil actions."[77] The round drum is thought to represent calmness and good action whereas the triangular drum symbolized anger and opposition to Buddhism (see photographs 10 and 11).

The shaman accessories of the Koryak, another Paleo-Siberian people, were said to be minimal. They had no special dress or symbols that distinguished their position, and they

Left: PHOTOGRAPH 10 — Drum used by a male shaman. The drum is made of two layers of birch wood with a leather handle wrapped with silk and cotton. Above the handle is a wire with seven coins of Chinese-Manchurian origin, as well as rattles and bells. The image on the drum face shows flames on a foggy mountain. To the left of the fire is a tiger and to the right is a lion. On the mountain amid the clouds burns a ritual fire with a doe on the left and bird (*Garuda*) and stag on the right. The symbols indicate how strongly Buddhism influenced the so-called "yellow shaman."[i]

Right: PHOTOGRAPH 11 — The back of a drum used by a male shaman showing the silk and cotton wrapped leather handle. Above the handle is a wire with coins, rattles, and bells. The outside of the skin drumhead is painted as shown in Photograph 10.

had no drums of their own. They reportedly used the drums belonging to the family in whose house the shamanistic performance took place.[78] The Koryak drum, called an *yyai*, was oval in shape and covered with reindeer-hide on one side. The drumstick was thick whalebone wider at the end with which the drum was struck. The contact end was covered with the skin of a wolf's tail.[79]

The frame of triangular and octagonal drums was made of cedar or birch pieces that were joined at the ends (see photograph 12). The timber for the frame was prepared where the tree was felled. The cut wood was taken to the shaman's home by a white ox. It was planed to the proper thickness and cut into even lengths, and the pieces were bound together with leather thongs.[80] The skin surface was "stitched" on the frame with leather strips. There are vertical protuberances attached to Huulas shaman drums. There were seven or nine "bumps" according to the shaman. These bumps were said to symbolize the "joints of the four limbs, hooves, ribs and tail of the *ongon's* mount."[81]

The drums used by Daur shaman (also spelled Daghor or Dagur to identify people living mainly in the northwest region of Inner Mongolia) were round. The skin was stretched over a frame of willow or elm and fastened at the back by leather thongs attached to an iron ring in the middle. The ring serves as a handle.[82] The skin covering was replaced when damaged or torn beyond use, but the frame was retained.

The oval drum of the Yukaghir, a Siberian people living east of the Lena River, was called a *yalgil*, which means "lake." The name signified the lake into which the shaman dove to descend into the shadow-world. The drum had hide on one side only and an iron cross near the inside centre that served as a handle. The ends of the cross were fastened with straps to the rim, to which four iron rattles were attached.[83] The Yukaghir and the Yakut drum were very similar. Not only were the rattles and cross the same material, there were also "protuberances on the outer surface of the rim, which according to the Yakut represented the horns of the shaman's spirits."[84] The drumstick was covered with the skin of a reindeer's leg. The drum without metallic additions is also found in Yukaghir tradition giving support to the notion that the practice of attaching the iron pieces was borrowed from the Yakut.

A similar concept about the drum and descending into the lower world of the goddess Sedna was found among the Eskimos. However, unlike the drums of the Yukaghir, the Eskimo drums were not large. They were either symmetrically

PHOTOGRAPH 12 — An octagonal Mongolian drum (*Henggereg*). The drum has a single cross member wrapped with silk that serves as a handle. Attached to the outer frame are jinglers (rattles) to give a metallic resonance to the drum. The frame is tied together with sinew strips, and the drum skin wraps around the entire frame and is attached to the wood with sinew.

oval or round, and a wooden handle was fastened to the rim.[85] John Murdoch[86] wrote in the *American Anthropologist* in 1888, that the Eskimo from Greenland to Siberia used such drums. The Eskimo and the Chukchee beat the lower part of the drum with the stick. The Koryak held the drum in a slanted position and struck it from below. Other Asiatic drums were most often struck in the centre. The indigenous peoples living south of the Eskimo used broad-rimmed drums for purposes of shamanism.[87]

The Yakut drum called a *tüngür*, *tünür*, or *dünür* was egg-shaped, and covered with the hide of a young bull. The drum's longest diameter was 21 inches, and the width of the rim is 4½ inches. The cross inside the back of the drum was attached to the rim by leather straps. Little bells, jingling trinkets, and other rattles of iron and bone were attached around the inside of the rim, especially in the places where the straps were fastened.[88]

> According to Mongolian legend, early shamans could use their drums to call back the souls of the dead. The Lord of the Dead, fearing that he would lose all his subjects, ordained that the shamans' drums, originally double-headed should have only a single head to reduce their power.[89]

The Karagas shaman (also called Tofalar, Karaga, or Tubalar, a Turkic-speaking people of southern Siberia) considered his or her drum as a symbolic horse that he rode during rituals,[90] whereas the Bön (in Tibet) shamans considered their drums to be vehicles to covey them through the air. The drum was an indispensable piece of equipment used by shamans in conducting séance or summoning spirits. Regardless of whether the drumming enabled the shaman to fly or dialogue with spirits, it aided concentration and promoted contact with the spiritual world through which the shaman was preparing to travel. "[B]oth the shell and the skin of the drum constitute magico-religious implements by virtue of which the shaman was able to undertake the ecstatic journey to the 'Center of the World.'"[91]

The drum symbolically represented the Neo-Siberians' philosophy of life. Even the Yakut blacksmith that helped in the adornment of the shaman's garment occupied a half-magical position. The blacksmiths were thought to have "peculiar fingers," and they possessed tools with "souls" that could make sounds of their own accord. The blacksmiths were those persons most closely associated with the shaman. It was believed that only a blacksmith with nine generations behind him could make a *ämägyat* without danger to himself from the spirits. An *ämägyat* was a copper plate with a drawing of a man in detail or an engraving in relief of a medallion with a man's figure in the middle.[92]

The *ämägyat* is in most cases was the soul of a departed shaman. W. L. Sieroszewski wrote in 1896, it was believe that the human body could not endure the continuous presence of a power equal to that of the great gods.[93] Therefore, the *ämägyat* as spirit-protector resided not within, but close beside the shaman. It (the *ämägyat*) was believed to come to his or her assistance at critical moments. The great shamans reportedly took their *ämägyat* with them when they died, and they were change into heavenly beings. If the *ämägyat* did not depart in this way, it eventually appeared on earth. When returned to the world of the living, the *ämägyat* might seek to re-embody itself in someone belonging to the same clan as the deceased.

The single-headed shaman's drum, sometime called a tambourine, with its narrow, round frame as found in many Asian societies was widely distributed. The square drums made in British Columbia in Canada, the state of Vera Cruz in Mexico, and Guatemala are more unusual. Other hide-covered drums are more localized. The Iroquois used a water drum made by stretching hide over a small, wooden keg partly filled with water. The same type of water drum also accompanies the incantations for the *Midewiwin* medicine rite.

The Ojibway shaman's drum was said to represent "the mythic cedar tree [that was] the cosmic axis that penetrated the mysterious regions and provided a path for the solicited healing power."[94] The notion of sacred center and power were connected to the cosmic tree or pole that united the cosmos from within. The roots of the sacred tree were said to extend to the depths of the earth and its branches reached to the gods. It joined the temporal and the eternal. The cosmic tree as described in the *Bhagavad-Gita* is an expression of the universe and man's condition in the world, and the Kabbalistic Sefirotic Tree is the arrangement of the Holy attributes according to the prime set of laws that govern existence.

Mircea Eliade wrote in *Images and Symbols: Studies in Religious Symbolism* (1991) that the future shamans of Siberia were believed "to approach the Cosmic Tree and to receive, from the hand of God himself, three branches of it, which were to serve as frames for his drums."[95] It was with the aid of the drum that the shaman attained an ecstatic state. Although it was commonly accepted that shaman of many regions, particularly Central Asia and Siberia employed drumming during ritual activities, not all shaman used drums. Claudia Müller-Ebeling writing in *Shamanism and Tantra in the Himalayas* (2002) states that "Drumming can be helpful—it can even be very helpful—but the doors to the shamanic cosmos are never opened by it."[96]

PLATE 25—Rewe, a sacred carved signpost of a female Araucanian shaman (*machi*) supported by bundle of branches. The name Araucanians designates a group of South American people that liven in south-central Chile along the Bio-Bio River in the north to the Toltén River in the south. The photograph is dated 1922.

Rattle: Shamans among traditional peoples in many locations use a drum or rattle to made "music," and to promote an altered state of consciousness. Where the drum was not used it was often replaced with a bell, gong, or shell. There was "always an instrument that, in one way or another, was able to establish contact with the 'world of the spirits.'"[97] The rattle was commonly used in South America. It was generally made of a gourd fitted with a wood handle that allows the shaman or dancer to produce a rhythmic sound to accompany his or her séance or ecstatic journey. "However, the use of drum and other instruments of magical music was not confined to séances. Many shamans also drum and sing for their own pleasure; yet the implications of these actions remained the same; that is, ascending to the sky or descending to the underworld to visit the dead.[98]

The concept of the rattle manifests itself in various forms. Rattles were made from a range of materials depending of the resources available to various cultures, and they were shaped and decorated according to the purpose of the instrument. The people of the North Pacific Coast carved wooden rattles in animal and bird shapes (see drawing 5.10), and Plains peoples of North America and South American Patagonian tribes make them of hide, in various shapes. Whereas, The deer dance rattles used by the Yaqui Indians of northern Mexico and southern Arizona included cocoons attached to the lower legs of the dancers and deer hoofs fastened above the knees. The momentum of the dances caused the cocoons and hoofs to work in opposition to the dance movements.

Gourd rattles such as those found in the southwestern North America and northern Mexico vary in shape and size and were used in both shamanistic and lay activities. They are as plain or decorated with beads, feathers, or carvings as the culture requires. The Papago shaman in the southwestern United States left the stem for a handle while other people insert a wooden handle into the gourd. Large rattles were those used in the *maso,* or deer dance of the Yaqui of northern Mexico, and the Iroquois eagle dancers used small ones. Between the two extremes there is a wide variety of shapes, sizes, and designs. There were also flat rattles made by the Hopi that were painted with symbolic designs and filled with maize kernels and squash seeds. The ancient Aztec rattles (*ayacachtli*) were small and round.

Among the Ojibwa (Chippewa) and Naskapi (Eastern Woodlands people) the shamans' *rattles look like* small drums, while the Iroquois made rattles from cow horns. The Yaqui *pascola* (clown dancer) shook a wood-and-metal *sena'asom,* a form of *sistrum,* rattle-like percussion instrument that can be traced to ancient Egypt and beyond. The horseshoe shaped *sistrum* was used in the cult of the goddess Hathor and later the practice spread throughout the Roman Empire. The *sustrum* existed by 2500 BCE in Sumer and early examples have found near Tbilisi, Georgia.[99]

The "jingler" attached to a dancer's clothing, is probably the oldest form of rattle. These sound producing ornaments were prominent in nomadic and hunting

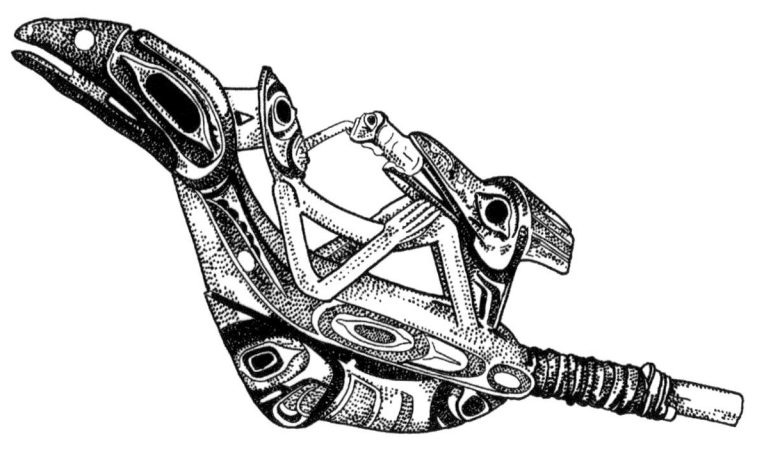

DRAWING 5.10—An elaborately shaped raven rattle used by a Tlingit shaman to call his or her guardian spirits. Carved from wood and painted, the rattle is in the form of a raven, a powerful shamanic figure, with a reclining man—possibly a shaman—reclining on its back. The shaman holds the tongue of his spirit helper (frog) in his mouth because the tongue was considered a conduit of power. The bird form holding the "frog" is identified as a kingfisher. A hawk or thunderbird-like face is carved and painted on the underside of the raven.

groups. The jinglers frequently consisted of animal hoofs, and Alaskan Eskimo dancers sometime used puffin beaks and belts with animal teeth. The peyote *(hikuli)* dancers of the Huichol, a people of northern Mexico wore similar rattles. Curing shamans or medicine men in northern Mexico to South America wore deer hoofs on the girdles and ankles, and the horny material covering the feet of deer, peccary, or tapir was worn on the legs or ankles of Brazilian people such as the Kamakán and Apinayé.[100]

Siberian shamans had iron, cone-shaped jinglers on their drums and clothing, because the iron was believed to confer power over demons. Aztec dancers fastened gold, copper, or shell bells to ankles or breast for much the same purpose. The Bororo of Brazilian and the Amazonian Jivero people used shells and dried nuts to produce the rattle sound. The Incas of ancient Peru used anklets of fruits shells or gold. Rattles were used in bison-calling rites conducted by shamans serving the Flathead people of the northern plains of North America. They were also used by Pacific coastal region Hupa dancing doctors (shamans), and by the Apache shaman-singer in puberty rite. The deer-hoof rattle was commonly associated with girls' puberty ceremonies in North and South America.[101]

The carapace of the turtle was a source for both worn and hand-held rattles. Turtle shells were worn behind the right knee of members of Hopi men's societies and often by Hopi *kachina* dancers. In the Great Lakes region Huron shamans shook a tortoise shell, filled with pebbles, near the ears of their patients. These rattles were often an accompaniment to the chant and the message conveyed by the shaman's chant that was the story of his or her journey into the spirit world and the return. "The tonal structures we call 'music' bear a close logical similarity to the forms of human feeling."[102]

Chants: "Shamanism devoid of some form of music is probably unknown, perhaps even unimaginable. Shamans throughout the world drum, rattle, whistle, pipe and blow on trumpets."[103] Similarly, the shaman's song (chant) can be a powerful instrument used for connecting with the spirit world. Australian aboriginal shamans sing songs they believe their ancestors sang in "Dreamtime"—the other world.[104] The songs offer a rhythmic cadence that may last for several minutes, and like the drumbeat, promote concentrate on the mission of the shaman. The monotonous sounds often accelerate as the shaman approaches his or her destination.

Ritually produced sounds were a socially recognized language. They disclosed intellectual and emotional meanings that were not always provided by objects and activities. For instance, the drum and drumming could be interpreted as symbols of social importance or elements of local custom. Either of those views could have substance, because the nature of an object or activities attached new value to the sound without removing or altering its perceived purpose or meaning. It was not only the sound of the drum that was important in the symbolism, but because it was believed to reference the mystic source of shamanic power. "During séance chanting, the shaman must build—by dint of his own song and the sound of the drum—a special vocal world; moreover, he has to attain an altered state of consciousness—the state of trance of ecstasy, or, at least, the borderline of this."[105]

Mouth Harps: Shamans in Siberia used two other musical instruments in addition to the drum. One was a stringed instrument similar to the balalaika and the other was an idiophone like that called a Jew's harp or Guimbarde. Among the Buryat a Mongol people living south and east of Lake Baikal, the harp was called *khur or huur*, in the local language and was used exclusively by the shamans.

Besides the drum, the mouth organ or huur was one of the most important instruments

5. Shamanism and Imaginative Representation 115

for Mongolian shamans.[106] They played the huur "by gripping it between the teeth and tapping its metal or bamboo tongue with the index finger while making a variety of sounds in the mouth and throat."[107] Shamans near Ulan-Ude in the Lake Baikal region used a similar instrument called a *khur*, which is used exclusively by shaman.

The Darhad and Huular shamans of Mongolia had three main uses for the huur: (1) It was considered to be the horse of the shaman who mounted it during his or her relay service for an *ongon*. (2) It was the horse of a shaman to use "during the trip between his or her firehearth and the Place (Dark World) of the *ongons*." (3) It was considered to be a guide and an interpreter for the shaman. These concepts view the harp (huur) as a means of transport

"When a Mongolian shaman performs his or her services using only the *huur*, the ritual that was called a 'Walking Shaman Ceremony;' whereas, a ritual using all the shaman's paraphernalia was considered an Armored Ceremony."[108]

Mirror: Unlike the auditory symbols produced by the drum, rattle, and chant, mirrors have a special visual reference that is found in many forms and locations. "Among some people, the shaman wears a metal disk, a 'shaman-mirror.'"[109] The mirror symbolized the passageway for communication between the underworld and the world of the living. According to Mircea Eliade,[110] the copper mirrors worn by shamans of northern Manchuria helped them to "see the world," and to "place the spirits." It was thought that the mirror reflected the needs of humanity. Mongol shamans were said to see the "white horse of the shamans" and the dead person's soul in the mirror. The Chinese believed that the mirror could light the eternal darkness of the tomb.

The mirror was an important tool for Siberian shamans. The most desirable mirrors were antiques that have been passed down for generations. Older mirrors were believed to have their own master spirits. "Shaman mirrors varied from five to fifteen centimeters in diameter and were made of brass, bronze, iron, silver or nephrite. Silver mirrors were usually small and were used mostly for

PLATE 2 — Standing male shaman with drum and drum stick. The shaman's costume was a manifestation of his familiars and was often described as "armor" to protect the shaman on his journeys into the spirit realm. The shaman costume was stored separately and must not be touched by laymen. After the death of a shaman his successor inherited the costume; sometime it was buried with the shaman.

Left: PHOTOGRAPH 13 — Back of bronze shaman's mirror showing Chinese characters. The mirror was originally made as a commemorative piece relating to the Chinese national examination, but was acquired by a shaman for ritual purposes. Mirrors with the signs of the zodiac on the back were especially useful for fortune telling. Although the face of the mirror was polished it was not used to reflect a specific image; instead, it was a void into which the shaman might look to see beyond the present.

Right: PHOTOGRAPH 14 — Back of shaman's mirror (*toli*) that originally had painted Chinese characters. A silk cloth is attached to a perforated center loop to provide a "handle" for the mirror during ritual activities. The surface of the brass mirror is smooth and reflective. Mirrors were frequently used in divination and fortune telling. The silk cloth attached to the mirror shows the traditional three over-hand knots used in shamanistic practice.

healing.

Mirrors were used in different ways and they did not have to be shiny to be useful. The shaman's mirror reflects everything, including the most secret thoughts. One of the mirror's tasks was to prevent the invisible attack of evil powers, and thereby to protect the shaman. The shaman's mirror was in the style of old Han-dynasty Chinese bronze mirrors that were traded all over central Asia during in the last centuries before the current era and the beginning of the current era. They were smooth on one side and perhaps polished. The reverse side was plain or ornamented with flower-tendrils, birds, figures, or Chinese characters (see photographs 13 and 14). Shamans in Mongolia (even those who abandoned the rest of their ceremonial dress) wore an apron that was a belt of leather hung with mirrors. The mirrors were called *toli* and this apron had several names: the "blue cloud-bee" and also *boge-yin kulug* the "mount of the shaman."[111]

The mirror reflected the interchange between two paths — the ethereal and the material worlds. It offered a view of reality that existed beyond the realm of normal understanding. This concept was a common theme that inhabited both popular and secret stories and myths. The mirror reflected images were also associated with the inner-life, truth, and power. It was also commonly used to diagnose disease. References to the "mirror" are found in many cultures and in different locations. It was this universal reflection that appealed to shamans and Buddhists. Other examples of the mirror as conduit to self-knowledge include the obsidian (smoke) mirrors of the Aztecs, mirror "eyes" of masks made in Mexico and West Africa, and the copper (bronze) mirrors of North Africa and the Middle-East. The image held within the mirror was removed from the mundane and transported to distant locations where it conversed with deities or demons.

The clothing of the shaman was often hung with mirrors that took the form of mystic doors through which the shaman might pass to the "other side." Ribbons or streamers were sewn along the edges of shirts, jackets, and skirts or trousers as contact with the spirit world.[112] Among the Chukchee people living in the northeastern part of Siberia the shaman cut slits in the sleeves of their coats through which they wove strips of fabric or leather to represent the Milky Way.[113] They often wore other personalized symbols made of wood or metal along with the mirrors.

PLATE 20 — Costume of Darchad head-shaman (*zajran*). Front view of robe showing the large nickel-plated mirror (*toli*) that protected the heart of the male shaman from evil spirits. The robe (caftan) is of cotton with a woven geometric pattern. Snakes of different color material are attached to the robe and headdress representing spirit helpers (familiars) that helped the shaman reach the other world.[j]

6

SHAMANIC RITUAL AND TRANSFORMATION

If humankind was to survive, the shaman, as a special person, had to enter a state of super consciousness that allowed access beyond the limitations of the natural order and into the world of spirits and ancestors. There the shaman could gather the symbols of ritual recognition that were believed to influence the physical conditions of the people.[1]

Ritual Validation of Shared Beliefs

The ritual is a symbolic action, and shamans try to reach the desired state of physical and emotional ecstasy by symbolic enactment. They made use of physical and emotional attributes to attain a transformative state often symbolized by "fire, water, and metal, all of which are associated with change."[2] Even so, some rituals were magical instead of propitiatory, that is, designed to win favor from the spirits. When the desired outcome was achieved, not by propitiating the favor of the spirits through sacrifice, prayer, and praise, but by ceremonies that were believed to influence the course of nature directly through a physical sympathy or resemblance between the ritual and the effect it is to produce.[3]

Couched in ideas about supernatural beings and forces, the myths and rituals of most magico-religions systems of belief are difficult to recognize as psychological knowledge. Consequently, the ritual was performed to establish a "working" relationship between the physical and metaphysical worlds. The shaman's role was to create conditions favorable for supernatural interaction, and to transport himself or herself into the lands of the spirits and gods. This transference of mind and spirit (and some would claim the body) emphasized the life-values of the group as determined by their traditions and beliefs. It was possible through ritual activities to observe the unseen, know the unknown, and discover the lost. The shaman interpreted, manipulated, and calmed the fears and anxieties of the socio-economic and cultural realities of daily life.

Rituals were those practices associated with the realm of belief, magic, sacrifice, and transformation. Certain rituals had "religious" context, and many were closely aligned with the activities of survival. Such pursuits were a bridge between the ordinary and the extraordinary. They were objective by nature, and the outcome of a ritual was expected to be beneficial to a particular person or group. Rituals also answered the need for verification of shared beliefs, and the greater part of ritual activities was often the repetition of acts attributed to mythical figures at the beginning of time. They influenced the lives of people, and were a recognized part of the life of in most societies. Early people (between 100,000 and 40,000 years ago) formed communities, established common objective, and endorsed practices based on mutually sanctioned beliefs. They recognized common gods and venerated those deities by various means including rituals. They had prescriptive burial practices that imply the existence of a system of complex and communally accepted beliefs. Rituals often included fasting and sun gazing, or consuming various stimulants, as well as group activities such as singing and dancing to achieve a transformational state. The body stayed behind while the spirit journeyed to where it was transformed and remained, or where it was rejected and returned to reunite with its material shell.

About 40,000 years ago "modern" humans either replaced or displaced the Neanderthals, and eventually, those people became the dominant creatures in most regions of the world. With these "new" inhabitants came more extensive attention to the supernatural world including shamanic practices. The reliance on spiritual intervention quite possibly reflected a higher level of insecurity and the anxiety about encountering the unknown. Consistent with that attitude early humans required a more developed method of supernatural alignment (see drawings 6.1, 2.6, 3.4, 3.5, 5.2, and 5.3).

It is likely that the struggle for existence was a part of all phases of human life, and that this effort influenced the activities of people since humankind first evolved. Early people created a protection system of distinctive observances to address those issues. Shamanism, as a cultural phenomenon, allowed groups of people to formulate a socialized protection system, and to believe that what they desired—success, safety, health, and wellbeing—was within reach. Shamanic practice offered a way for people to accept delusion when circumstances were too difficult or too uncompromising to achieve a desired outcome. Atypical circumstances were assigned to the influence of a particular deity, thus illness, drought, famine, as well as life and death were viewed as conditions requiring shamanic intervention. To intensify the power of intervention and to energize a force stronger than reality, rituals gave focus to societal needs.

[A]rchaic cosmologic myths in the religious creeds of

DRAWING 6.1—A painted bison figure with mask from Les Trois Frères, France. This figure is a masked male holding a magical bow. (The bow shape extending from the bison muzzle may represent the animal's spirit escaping from its nostrils—the breath of life.) The figure has the back, legs, and penis of a human and appears to be wrapped in the skin of a bison.

Siberian Turkic peoples, possible going back to beliefs of a substratum population of Siberia, became interwoven with more recent beliefs regarding the creator-deities. Thus, all Siberian Turkic peoples have preserved elements of the worship of the sky, sun, moon, stars, the Great Bear, Venus, and so on.[4]

The ritual as an event could have either shamanistic or non-shamanistic intentions depending on any number of elements. Ritual activities were a part of many social undertakings and not all had or were intended to have shamanistic connotations. Some ritual elements were compatible with different ideologies and sent different messages. Such comparable elements include sprinkling liquids, fumigating (with fire, smudge bundles, or candles); dabbing (with soot, blood, or ash); making offerings (with food, alcohol, or tokens); bowing, clapping, circumambulating, and affixing objects (ribbons, coins, effigies, notes or symbols). This practice has persisted to modern times.

When the primary purpose of ritual was to compel the spirits or deities to comply with the wishes of the shaman, the results were easily observed. If a person died, the shamanic intervention failed; or, if the crops or herds flourished then the ritual was a success. The process was self-fulfilling. People motivated by the need to vitalize success or resolve social insecurity relied on shamanic ritual as a way of deliverance from their predicaments. The intensified self-confidence produced by shamanic observance in the form of socially accepted ritual influenced daily existence. Any number of activities — natural or human — were attributed to shamanic success or failure.

The observances promulgated by rituals were closely connected to the sacred power epitomized in myth. The importance of these observances was that in the realm of the sacred all things had their place, and for humanity to thrive, they must correspond as closely as possible to the practices acknowledged and demonstrated by ritual activities. Different cultural traditions had different spiritual and philosophical formulations of the meaning of sacred, but it was an omnipresent concept. It might be an outward and visible sign of an inward and invisible energy, or an act that culminated at the end of a symbolic spiritual rebirth. In such instances, the action reinforced the relationship between the divine and secular worlds.

The shaman assumed the role of the mediator in the ritual event to maintain the "social/psychological equilibrium by symbolic mediation between worlds of ordinary and non-ordinary reality."[5] The shaman, to activate this potential, had an array of special symbols and practices that give him or her the power to modify or eliminate ordinary reality and thereby to access another state of consciousness. The beliefs of the Patagonian and Pampean people, of South America, are exemplified by the ceremonies for the transition of youth to adulthood. The people were required a gather in a common house where the shamans bled themselves and smeared the neophytes with blood.[6] The blood symbolically fed the spirits of the initiates and prepared them for entry into the adult community.

Shamans were believed to know the truths of this world by communication with other worlds. Sacred activities such as initiation rites symbolize the worldview of the participants and demonstrate the order of life as elucidated in myths. Life events were often explained as the outcome of supernatural manipulation, and the initiate was taught this secret and how to gain access to divine benefits. The initiate (new adult member of the group, society, or clan) was also taught the group (clan, tribe, or moiety) taboos and given an identifying mark, such as, a tattoo or scar to demonstrate that he or she was part of the group. The transformed initiate in some communities received a new name, learns a new language, and wore different clothing to denote his or her altered status.

6. Shamanic Ritual and Transformation

The activities related to a ritual combined two sacred functions; one generated new power or energy for the world, and the other purified the corrupted facets of human existence. Rituals were a socialized effort to return to a sacred time that came before the structured existence of contemporary humanity. Sacred events (rituals) provided the opportunity for profane time to be rejuvenated. The events were to make the people forget their past life and symbolically embrace the primordial chaos that existed before the beginning of the world and just as the world was created, so in the repetition of that time the present world was regenerated. The suspension of normal taboos expressed the unstructured, unconditioned nature of the sacred. "Every ritual drama has a myth that illustrates the supernatural origin of the ritual and also gives rules for its performance."[7]

Rituals declare the symbolic systems that acknowledge the worldview and society of a culture.[8] Such activities included dancing, singing, and drumming as techniques for stimulating the power of the shaman. The "Shaking Tent" séance exemplified that special power. This shamanic ritual was practiced by different Algonquian people of North America, and was found in South American and Southwest Asia. The Shaking Tent ritual was a classic example of a shamanic rite primarily concerned with intuitive intervention. In that ritual, the shaman was placed in a barrel-shaped tent to await a response from the spirits. When the tent began to shake and to fill the air with a loud noise the communicating spirit was present. Variations of this ritual are found in different locations (see photograph 15).

PHOTOGRAPH 15—Frame of peyote sweat lodge constructed of bent saplings that were covered with hides, vegetation, or canvas. During peyote rituals, the lodge was a source of shamanistic power. Edward Curtis took this photograph circa 1927.

Group identity was reinforced and traditional practices were redefined by ritual observances. The Ojibway had many ritual rules that were considered dangerous to break. There was the prohibition against incest, the prescribed treatment of the dead, and the correct handling of the killed game animal (the displacement of its bones and the elevation of the skull in a tree).[9] Although the ritual duties of a people had a presence in daily activities, individuals inadvertently broke a rule and fell mysteriously ill. The soul of the transgressor was thought to be separated from his or her body at that time, and the Shaking Tent séance was required for reunification.

The tent for the Shaking Tent séance (see drawing 6.2) was constructed of strong timbers formed in a narrow circle. The poles were thrust into the ground and the tips were lashed together. The poles were covered with canvas or animal skins to form a tall barrel-shaped chamber just large enough for the shaman to enter. Once inside the "tent" the shaman chanted and shook a rattle to call his spirit helpers. Those outside the tent assisted by singing and beating a drum. The tent swayed and shook as the summoned spirits converge. Unearthly voices were heard coming from the tent as forms were pressed against the canvas cover. The shaman emerged from the tent after a time to announce the success or failure of the séance.[10] The Shaking Tent event demonstrated the movement power (energy) in two directions — it concentrated it in one place, time, and occasion, and it released power into the everyday stream of events as the primal vibration reverberated throughout existence.

Shamans (*jessakid*), also called jugglers and conjurers by the Ojibway,[11] were practitioners of the Shaking Tent ritual. The object of the ritual is to determine the cause of the illness (divination), oversee the confession of the mistake that caused the offense, and thereby to initiate the healing process. Among the Menomini, a people who lived along the Menominee River, it was the *tshisaqka*, the most powerful shaman who conducted the shaking tent ritual. "The Menomini shaman also used the turtle spirit to diagnose [illness] during this ceremony."[12] The tent in which the ritual was performed shook from the energy released by the spirit summoned to diagnose the patient. Individual actions used in this ritual were given meanings that transcend their immediate purpose.

Similar shamanistic rituals among the Evenk (Tungus) people took place in "ordinary dwelling-tents or in a special structure, the shaman's tent."[13] Certain rituals such as the search for lost reindeer, the foretelling of the future or other similar activities were held in an ordinary tent; whereas, more important rituals were conducted in a special tent called a *shevenchedek* in the Evenk language.[14] An additional element was the "shamanistic tree, *turu*, that was an inseparable attribute in any shamanistic performance [ritual], whether it was held in an ordinary tent or in a special structure...."[15] The tree (usually a larch) was the symbolic guardian of the

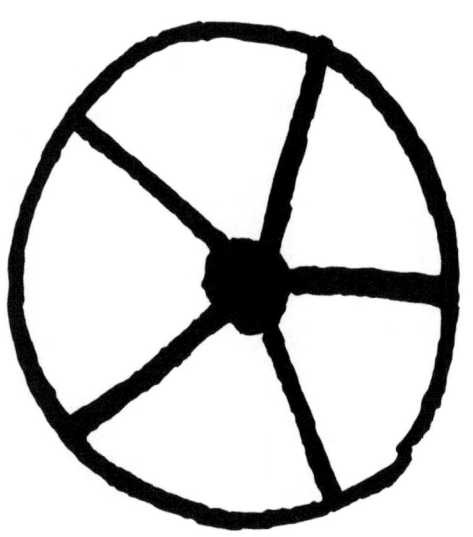

DRAWING 6.2— Drawing of a Malaysian dreaming inside the hut of a shaman. The center dot is the dreamer and the spokes radiating outward from the dot are the supports that form the roof of the hut and the spirits of the dreamer. The outside ring is the exterior of the hut and by extension the circumference of the world. The five sections of the circle represent the five aspects of the human soul.[k]

tent and a ladder for the shaman to climb to the Upperworld (see drawing 4.1). The association with the "world-tree" was essential. In the Evenk view, it was a "connection with the three shamanistic worlds — upper, middle, and lower — and was thought of as the shaman's road from one world to another."[16]

Manipulating the Senses

Shamanism, like other societal occurrences, was subject to development and change. The supernatural alignment differed at times because some shamanistic practices (and some cultures) required the spirit of the shaman to ascend to the ethereal plateau, and at other times, the spirits descended to interact with the earth-bound shaman. The power of shamanism was demonstrated in both transactions. Weather the spiritual interaction was a manifestation of psychic power is unclear; however, the shaman's role was primary in each encounter with the spirits. Rituals were in either process enabling events to facilitate spiritual encounters.

The historic record indicates that in times of high anxiety or celebration people in early cultures often ritually sacrificed humans to ensure the lives of others. A sacrifice or assassination was considered a primordial exchange that was re-enacted to promote the growth of subsistence crops or to ensure the renewal of life. The fatality of death was a means of assuring the continuity of life. The ceremonial activities associated with "remembering" or reconfirming the devotional act was ingrained in the cultural identity of the people. Over time the activity altered and animal victims replaced human sacrifice, grain and foodstuffs gradually replaced the animals, and eventually ceremonies offering symbolic sacrifices became the norm. However, most cultures continue to practice some form of the devotional activity to seek forgiveness for sins and societal transgressions.

The natural and supernatural events and circumstances of the world have the function of stabilizing human life. "Ritual language, with its powerful figures of speech, creates maps for transforming reality...."[17] Ritual activities address metaphysical questions about the relationship of mind and body and hold an essential position relevant to the concept of personal and group identity. When the parallel tracks of mind, body, history, and need converge, a heritage phenomenon emerges.

The family shaman had charge of the rituals that celebrated family festivals and sacrificial activities in much of Siberia. The family shaman was also responsible for the rituals associated with the domestic hearth and those activities involving use of the family charms, amulets, and incantations. In contrast, the person that organized ritual observances for a group of families was identified as a communal or professional shaman. This aspect of shamanism was often viewed as an extension of the family shaman's responsibilities.[18]

Professional shamans were those individuals who were not attached to a certain group of people. The more powerful they were, the wider the circle in which they practice their art. Among the Chukchee, the division into family and professional shamans was often supplemented by different categories of professional shamans. For example, ecstatic shamans communicated with "spirits," and shaman-prophets were responsible for divining, and incantation shamans produced incantations and cast spells. Though the duties of these shamans often merge, a certain specialization prevailed.

The Tungus-Manchu, a people living in fishing communities along the Pacific coast of Asia, had two types of shamans, the *bolongzi* and *wuwate*, and each type had specific duties within the population. The *bolongzi* (or bö) was the shaman of the clan, and his or her duties were to "direct and perform religious activities, the most important of which being the sacrifices to the dwelling place of the gods and to the ancestors."[19] The *bolongzi* as shaman/priest promoted the unity of the clan or community. The *wuwate* shaman activities, in contrast, were not limited to one clan or community. This shaman was a healer and he or she was capable of exorcising demons and warding off evil influences.[20] Whereas, among the Koryak, indigenous people of the Russian Far East, as among the other Paleo-Siberians (Chukchee, Itelmen [Kamchadal], Nivkh [Gilyak]. Yukaghir, and Ket, as well as the Koryak[21]), and most Neo-Siberian tribes routine ritual activities were the responsibility of both family and professional shamans.[22]

The relationship between the shaman and the spirit world was mutually beneficial. The group members (the community) were constantly reminded of the power of the spirits because of the activities of a shaman. It was common knowledge that life was fragile, and that it could be given or taken away. It was also understood that daily survival could be a success or a failure. The rains came or they did not. Environmental conditions changed due to unknown causes making living conditions more or less harsh and always tentative. These transformations were evidence of the supernatural, and in response to those conditions, people sought ways (rituals) to communicate with the spirits to regulate the natural world to which they were restricted. That attitude was a social response to relationships that were honored in all phases of human existence.

The division between cause and effect separated belief and outcome. It was the attempts to control the former that depended on the latter. There was often an inclination to divide the perceived world into separate events, whereas, ritual intervention proposed to influence the forces (cause) by demonstrating the desired outcome, and by connecting human activity with the environmental elements. The connection between ideology and outcome was true for the incidents prevailing at a particular moment. When the immediate needs of the participants were met, the link between cause and effect was replaced by new expectations that conformed to the attitudes in which those conditions occur. It was both the positive and negative aspects of human reality that were included in existing beliefs.

The supernatural was an extension of daily life, and as the central figure in ritualistic practices the shaman merged with the universe as a harmonious whole. Because the material and spiritual worlds were joined but different, and many physical realities were the result of spiritual causes, rituals located and consolidated supernatural influences. It was the shaman's role to facilitate the exchange between these two domains.

The shaman interacts with the spirit world in many ways. Two methods of travel to the world of spirits were in dreams and in an altered state of consciousness normally called a trance. Shamanic travel was associated with the sensation of flying or swimming. "In visiting the spirit-world, the shaman must be able to control his/her trance and possess a mental map or chart of the cosmos."[23] In an altered state of consciousness (trance), the shaman's soul was believed to travel in corporal or extra-corporal form to the upper and lower regions of the cosmos.[24]

Things tangible and intangible, real and imagined were often confusing. Conformity with ritual practice provided a sense of safety, whereas departure from the ritual sequence was often filled with anxiety and danger.[25] The imagined or believed became visible even to the inexperienced eye and to normal thinking. The shapes and meanings of familiar objects were transformed. The knowing and understanding processes became more complicated when belief reinforced by visual verification was a matter of personal importance. All rituals were intended to modify the viewer or participant's sense of space and time, reality and fantasy. "Siberian shamans performed rituals for success in hunting as well as to heal the sick, divine the future, and conduct offerings to local, family, and higher sprits."[26] Each of these "services" was a necessary part of community life.

Appearance of the Sacred

Shamanic instructions were often of a ritualistic kind. They referred to certain details of particular ceremonies that must be arranged in a precise manner to secure the desired result. In this specialized environment, charms, fetishes, and rituals were significant ingredients in the shamanistic process because shamanic power was often associated with prescriptive objects. Magic also had an affiliation with symbols, and although there was nothing particularly magical in most "magic activities," the psychological influence of pseudo-scientific manifestations had a tremendous impact upon receptive participants.

Beliefs and trust were manifested in individuals invested in sacred positions, such as priests, kings, and shamans, and in special places, such as rivers, the sun, mountains, or trees. The shaman was a special agent in the belief system, and his or her ritual activities represented the divine. Falicitas Goodman quotes the 1909 publication by Dutch social scientist Arnold van Gennep in which he proposed that "the multitude of rituals reported from around the would notwithstanding, they all could be ranged into three types: those of separation, of transition, and of incorporation."[27]

The shaman was the person that orchestrated and incorporated the social, and traditional dimensions of the ritual process, and had the knowledge, ability, and skill that permitted him or her to lead such activities. Shamanic rituals were practices associated with belief, magic, sacrifice, and transformation. Certain rituals had "religious" context, and most were closely aligned with the activities of daily life and group survival. Such pursuits were a bridge between the normal and the extraordinary, the real and the supernatural. The shamans' role in those activities was almost invariably intended to be health (life) promoting and they were generally subjective in that they were to be beneficial to a particular person or group. "The Forest Lapps of Finland, for instance, have cherished the belief that in a magic way the shaman may call the herds of wild reindeer to the hunting grounds of his own group."[28]

The sacred and the concept of the sacred appeared in myths, ritual activity, people, and natural objects. Through retelling the myth, the divine action that was performed in the beginning of time was repeated. The repetition of the sacred action symbolically duplicates the structure and power that established the world in the beginning. Thus, it was important to know and preserve the eternal structure through which humans received life, because it was the model and source of power in the present. The return to the past allowed the individual to be contemporary with the creation and live again in the initial satisfaction of well-being. It supported the notion of re-emerging or being born again. The return to the beginning was facilitated by the person's memory enhanced by ritual stimulation. As an example, in the healing process, the shaman recited the cosmogony myth causing the individual to relive each experience until the recovery was complete.

The Pomo, a Hokan-speaking people on the west coast of the North America, practiced a type of ceremonial religion that included esoteric dances, rituals, and impersonations of spirits. They are said to believe in a supreme being called *Marumda* and according to the myth, he "created the earth and then he made deer, birds, rabbits, women (out of four feathers) and men (out of his own hair)."[29] The myth tells that the first generation of men could fly, but because they were evil, and they were destroyed by a great flood. A few men survived the deluge and promised to do better In the future.[30] "Water is pre-eminent slayer; it dissolves, abolishes all form."[31] The myth was reconfirmed by ritual death and regeneration. Death provided the seeds for new life, and the means for both physical and spiritual transcendence.

Probably because death played such an important role in the spiritual activities of early people, a great deal of attention was given to making contact with the dead. Various rituals, both shamanistic and secular were employed to placate the gods of the underworld. Offerings (sacrifices) were made, prayers were offered, and promises were made to gain access to the spirit world. According to belief, the spirits were not happy with the "other world" location. Many believed that the departed had special knowledge of earthly affairs and they could be persuaded to share that knowledge provided the correct rituals were performed.[32]

"The recognition of death and the perpetuation of life were the two primary rituals observed by the peoples of the world."[33] These rituals symbolically communicated with supernatural powers through sacrifice, chants, dances, and other means, and a discrete spirit force energized each activity. Death in the form of human sacrifice was an example of cyclical thinking that was an essential elements of the death rituals practiced by the Aztecs. In other societies, the threat of death, humiliation, and pain was fundamental to the initiation or "purification" ceremony endured by persons enduring the "rites of passage."

The disposition of the soul after death was of extraordinary concern for many Siberian peoples. It was a fear that a living person's soul might be lost or "eaten" by demons, or the soul that descended to the land of the dead might be the one that caused illness by its departure. It was the shaman's role to "see" the soul/spirits and know where to find them. Only he or she might overtake the truant spirit, determine its nature, and return it to its body. Often soul retrieval involved sacrifice, and it was the shaman who decided if they were needed and what form they would take.[34]

The restitution of a patient's health was of primary concern, but was not the only cause for soul retrieval. The Yukaghir, an Arctic Siberian people, used shamanistic ritual to steal souls from the Kingdom of Shadows for the purpose of introduction into a woman's womb. The shaman attempted to convince the soul of a dead person to return to earth and to begin a new life. Sometimes when the living had forgotten to do its duties for the dead, the soul refused to return. When no soul returned voluntarily, the shaman went down to the Kingdom of Shadows, and stole a soul and forcibly introduced it into a woman's body, but in such cases the children did not live long. Their souls were in haste to return to the Kingdom of Shadows.[35]

It was believed that the Lapp shaman performed a unique ritual to "hire" a ghost from the realm of the dead to guard the reindeer herd. "[T]he dead person was sometimes persuaded — with the promise of sacrifices — to follow the shaman on his journey back to the living."[36] At other times, the dead refused to relinquish the chosen ghost, and the shaman was forced to fight the dead in an effort to steal the ghost. Once back in the middle world, the ghost was obliged to act as keeper of the reindeer for years or as long as he or she received regular offerings.[37]

The ritual practice of hiring or employing the dead was found in many cultures. The shaman in East African reportedly revived dead people to become their servants. It was believed that the corpse was dug from the grave the night after they were buried and were returned to a "reduced" form of life. They performed simple tasks during the nighttime hours and during daytime they remained seated in a darkened corner of the shaman's hut. The concept of the recovered dead, "zombie," was also found in voodoo. The disembodied soul of the dead person or the actual corpse was raised from the grave by magical means to perform menial labor.

The Eskimo shaman had three primary responsibilities: (1) to heal the sick (see drawing 6.3), (2) to ensure a plentiful supply of game by journeying to the undersea home of the Mother of the Sea Beasts, and (3) to help sterile women. Illnesses were often determined to be the result of a violated taboo or by the theft of the patient's soul by one of the dead. A confession was often adequate to cleanse the impurity of the violation, but the lost soul required an ecstatic journey to the sky or to the depths of the sea to confront the thief, recover the soul, and return it to the patient.[38] The soul recovery process could be very demanding and hazardous for the shaman.

The ritual activity frequently involved a transition period in which boundaries were broken and chaos ruled. During that phase of the process the shaman often acted erratically, run about, held conversations or shouting matches with spirits, and exert an amount of energy in song and dance. Eventually, the state of frenzy was overcome and order restored. The next phase normally included a conversation with the "supernatural" with the voices of "spirits" speaking through the medium of the shaman. The shaman's energies were outwardly oriented and "directed toward the community so the trance [visionary journey] served as a medium of communication between the supernatural or non-ordinary reality and the community of men."[39] The shaman and the audience were integral parts of the visionary journey, and the "ecstasy" ended if the connection was severed.

Ritual Practices

It is useful to make distinctions among the different types of rituals because of the complexities inherent in any discussion. Although typologies do not necessarily explain anything, they do help to identify rituals that resemble each other within and across cultures. For instance, imitative rituals were dependent upon an existing belief system from which to draw meaning. Similarly, many rituals were patterned after myths. Such rituals were imitative in that the ritualized activity repeats the myth or an aspect of the myth.[40] The creation myth, for example, had a prominent role in this type of ritual. Each time it was reenacted it called to mind the importance of the people and described their position among the elements of the universe. The creation myth and the associated ritual described the way it was "in the beginning."[41] It called to mind a time

DRAWING 6.3—Carved and painted Tlingit mask of an old woman's spirit probably worn by a shaman during a curing ceremony. The design on the mask represents the woman's crest affiliation.

without the challenges of daily existence. Life changed but was the same, thereby negating the variations in the everyday world.

The ritual world was essentially of its own making and governed by the needs and expectations of the community in which it evolved. It was a method of activating a group effort. Rituals brought group members together for a predetermined purpose and to achieve an anticipated result. The shaman was an element of continuity that activated the ritual process and subsequently carried the cares, concerns, and expectations of the participants to a higher authority. It was the shaman that connected the middle world with the upper or lower realms as needed to deliver the messages dictated by the community. The shaman in that role vacillated between being a member of the group and being a spirit in an environment of psychological uncertainty. The person and the deities were ritually united.[42]

The need for control of spirits and deities by mortals with special powers evolved in many locations. Most societies called upon the services of the shaman as oracle, healer, appeaser, and psychopomp, and each role required the performance of a specific ritual. Each ritual required various symbols, images, and symbolical actions in which a system of relationships between the shaman and his or her helping spirits was realized and continually renewed. Because rituals were defined in concepts involving relationships guided by the human psyche into different spheres of understanding, the ritual was altered as the shaman's role evolved. Although these changes were usually slight in any one generation, they were continual.

Rituals were nevertheless fixed by time and circumstances and ideologically configured as unchanging occurrences. They were thought to occupy an unambiguous role in the resident community that was projected through time. Such rituals practices were associated with beliefs, magic, sacrifice, and transformation. They could be described as a system of symbolic acts that were based on rules embraced by a certain group for certain reasons. The ritual process evolved within the culture fostering the activity and reflected both the myths and traditional practices of that society. Rituals were important because they strengthen the bonds that joined the believers to their gods, and at the same time, united the individual with the society of which he or she was a member.[43]

Shamanic rituals are found among the traditional practices of many people. According to Mircea Eliade the Greek legends that are the most comparable with shamanism are those related to Apollo. Although much admired by the Greeks, like many Hellenic gods, Apollo is believed to be of foreign origin possibly northwest Asia, perhaps Siberia.[44] Apollo was also called Lyceius because he protected the flocks from wolves (*lykoi*).[45] There is also the myth about Abaris who carried in his hand the golden arrow as proof of his Apolline origin. It is said "he passed through many lands dispelling sickness and pestilence by sacrifices of a magic kind, giving warning of earthquakes and other disasters."[46] The magic arrow, flight, and interaction with wolves are directly related to shamanistic practices.

The purpose and performance of many rituals, regardless of the location, were to reinforce stories of the past, that is, cultural activities of earlier times. Those heritage elements were transformed instead of transferred in their entirety, and were installed as a part of the daily life. They were granted mythological meaning, and incorporated into a value driven system of ideas that passed from generation to generation as points of socio-cultural reference. No human society has been found where such mythological motifs were not practiced in some form.[47]

Although shamanism required ritualization, it was only a part of shamanic practice. Rituals were composed of action elements that might be combined for different purposes and to meet specific needs. The ritual might be either a culturally prescribed response to a particular event or a personal request for assistance directed by a shaman. Such practices were established by custom and maintained by use. That concept of shamanic ritual was derived "directly from the ability to manifest in inspirational performances the energies perceived in 'nature' (*baigal*)."[48]

> To understand shamanism, one must explore the art and symbolism inherent in many shamanic ritual performances: an enactment of usually sincere belief in shamanic ability to be sacred intermediaries between human and supernatural worlds.[49]

The shaman in a state of induced trance performed rituals for curing the ill, guiding the soul of the dead to the netherworld, invoking a deity, or visiting the heavens. Elaborate costumes and ritual objects were used to give a dramatic and mystic demonstration of supernatural involvement. There were numerous types of rituals that involved shamanic activities, and the expectations of the audience were directly related to the purpose of the performance. Whether the ritual was to cure a patient or consult the oracle, those persons in attendance expected the ceremony to be an entertaining experience. Divination and healing were the activities that draw the most attention, and a range of practices and purposes were association with shamanic rituals. The motivation common to those rituals was service to the community in which the shaman lives.

The shaman's "spirit masters" were assigned to atmospheric phenomena (storm, rain, thunder, or lightning), as well as to trees, rocks, and other natural and human made formations. When assistance was required and the spirit masters were called upon to provide the requisite aid or to guide the shaman to the information source. The Korean shaman appealed to the *Bon-hyang-san-shin*, the Mountain spirit of his or her hometown, or that of her husband or father[50] for assistance in dealing with the impulses of nature or humanity.

A central ritual of Mongol shamanism was blood-sacrifice to the sky god *Tengri*. The shaman symbolically freed the spirit/soul of all horse to join the gods then the selected horse (usually white) was ritually killed, and its skin was hung on a high pole to show the gods the promised sacrifice had been performed. The sky — the land above the earthly region of humans was a location that related to most sacred entities. That belief played a role in the ritual activities of people in many regions of the world.

Rituals were performed by shamans and lay persons and they could be multifaceted or simple. People throw powder, dust, or pollen to ritually purify individuals and places. The Native American viewed the wind as an instrument of purification while the Australian aboriginal believe that the sounds of the wind in the trees are the voices of the dead speaking with one another or warning the living of what is to come. In some culture "the final purification of a person who has died, the final release of that person from this world, was in the form of ashes scattered into the wind."[51]

Shamanistic rituals often related to the lands, animals, and the conditions of daily life. In times of drought or famine, the need for beneficial assistance increased and shamans were called upon to deliver the appropriate message to the deities. The cosmological world was considered by many shamans to be as real as the world on earth with good and evil deities.[52] The Manchu of northern China believed the nine skies with their nine layers were filled with deities and spirits that were as numerous as the stars. The Manchu also believed in a nine-layered universe with three layers above, three layers in the middle level, and three layers below. The shaman was the messenger of the nine skies in this arrangement. He or she could "fly up to communicate with the deities or descend to the lowest layer to destroy the demons."[53]

As noted, the Han Dynasty organized an official state religion in the third century before the current era based on old traditions including the worship of nature gods and ancestral spirits. The "official" cult included the gods of the Five Direction — North, South, East, West, and Center.[54] Mongolian shamans also understood the universe in terms of "direction" and "color." The directions were divided into the "good" (west and south) and "bad" (east).[55] Professors Purev and Purvee suggest that the "main reason for our ancestors' [Mongols] conception of this [directional arrangement] may be due to the belief that blue represented Heaven worship and that white symbolized a kind heart and clean mind."[56] Black related to the invisible world of the afterlife. Therefore, the people imagined black as north, red as south, blue as east and white as west.[57] The Chinese and Tibetans represented south as red and north as black.

Belief in the cosmic directions is also a part of the religious practices of the people of northern Mexico. The Tarahumara observe the Four Direction — North, South, East, and West as part of their Eastertide feasting a ritual that includes the services of an *owirúame* or shaman.

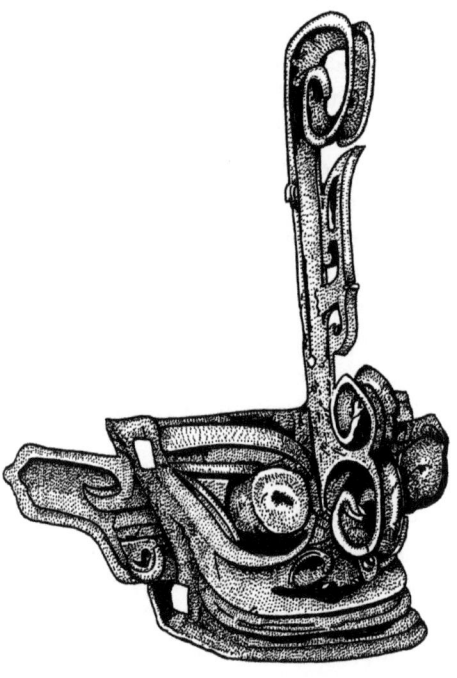

DRAWING 6.4 — Bronze mask found in Sanxingdui, China was made in the twelfth century before the current era. Shamans used these masks to communicate with the spirits of ancestors. The spirits having been brought back to the middle world by shamanic ritual were thought to settle in these objects. The masks were honored because of the spirits.

Ritual Paraphernalia

"From the earliest subsistence cultures up to and including our own civilization, [people have] attempted to establish order in [the] world by assigning various roles to unseen forces and divine powers."[58] Humans had contrived rituals and ceremonies that were performed as a form of reverential belief to influence those forces. Those activities, often included a shaman or shamaness that performed ritual dances and songs acquired from supernatural beings. Masks, headpieces, robes, and other forms of specially prepared raiment were worn during the performance of those ceremonial displays to reinforce the message and verify the presence of the supernatural (see drawing 6.4). However, a "ritual is not solely a homeostatic mechanism for bringing society into equilibrium through affirmation of its underlying values ... but also a cathartic outlet for irrational fears and desires reflecting primordial realities of life and death from which all carefully structured institutions offer imperfect shelter."[59]

Ritual observance was not limited to the living. The Egyptians reportedly prepared for the afterlife by placing a selection of objects including a mirror in the tomb. The mirror was made of bronze or copper, and the handle was often in the form of a shaft of papyrus. Other objects placed in the tomb ensured the deceased would be able to eat and perform the necessary rituals.

The shamanic ritual was a transformational link that joined the physical with the metaphysical. It was a mystical vehicle for the displacement of time and place and a means for creating or reestablishing psychic harmony within the community. The ritual reinforced belief and reaffirmed the power of both the shaman and the spirit/deity by magnifying the omnipresence of the spirit world. Rituals give people a chance to influence the fortunes and misfortunes of life.[60] In the ritual act, there was a commingling of the natural and supernatural worlds in ways that established empathy between the two spheres, and for the believers, reality and belief were joined.[61] Ritual paraphernalia was often a critical element in the psychic process, and as such, it was a means for focusing attention on ritual objectives.

Each shaman had ritual costumes and the associated paraphernalia that displayed regional variations, particularly in ornamentation. The Mongol shaman's costume was inherited from previous shamans and represented traditional attire. "Among all Tungus groups and Manchus, as well as their neighbors, shamanistic performances require a certain number of special things used only for this purpose. These things may be called by the general term 'shamanistic paraphernalia.'"[62] Among this ornamentation animals and birds were common, and metallic objects that were believed to possess a soul and therefore, did not rust, were important. The shaman was transformed by his or her costume into a super being.

The drum was used in ritual event as a divining tool as well as percussive instrument. Shaman also employed rattles, gongs, bells, and other sound making implements such as the harp (an idiophone) to call the spirits of the earth. As stated previously, the *huur* was an important instrument used by Mongolian shamans during ritual activities. Shaman sang, chanted, danced, and performed pantomimes to convey messages, demonstrate a trance-like state of consciousness, and to reveal the power granted to them by spirit helpers. When the Korean shamans danced, "they entered a trance, and their souls departed they body for the realm of the spirits."[63]

The ritual was a necessary part of social fidelity and a means for achieving and maintaining communal equilibrium. They verified the notion that people were constantly observed, assisted, restricted, and manipulated by the deities, and that the shamans could intercede on their behalf when the proper conditions were met. Different means were used to reinforce the consciousness (attentiveness) of the participants including visual and audible stimulants. Masks, clothing, and various accouterments provided the ocular stimulation, and chants, drums, rattles, and assorted other noises making apparatus fulfilled the acoustic role. Those elements fused to become a tangible expression of belief in the ritual process and a solicitous quest for supernatural intervention. Although, rituals might have been a gratuitous spiritual experience for some participants, they did influence the emotional and physical behavior of many individuals and verified the beliefs of the group as evidenced by their continued existence.

Costumes including masks used by shamans often represented ethereal beings, and evoked the presence of those spirits for the purposes of the ritual or ceremony (see drawing 6.5). The costumes of traditional design often included symbols of heroes and mythical being that were believed to be evidence that the ritual was being symbolically directed to the appropriate ancestral being. "A shaman's costume was an independently existing object, separated from its makers and even from its owner, having its own magical power."[64] The power of the costume was believed to originate in the spirit realm, and to reveal itself to the surface world occupied by humans.

"Mongolian shamans considered their garment as a spirit of a person and/or an animal such as a roe deer, whose original master departed to the Dark World."[65] According to Professor Purev, the Darhad shaman fabricated his or her gown (*böö deel*) to conform with the tribal customs of their mother. This tradition continued until the beginning of the twentieth century, and reportedly supported the belief that shamanism emerged during the matriarchal period.[66]

Both women and men made the Daur shaman's costume. The women created the coat or gown (*sumaski*), and men made the drum (*kuntur*) and drumstick (*gisur*). The metal objects attached to the gown including pendants, bells (*hwangoari*), and mirrors (*toli*) were purchased.[67] "A shaman's costume was an independently existing object, separated from its makers and even from its owner, having it own magical power."[68] Among the Daur people, the gown was the same whether for a male or female shaman.

Shamans in other locations wore special garments (described as armor by some Asian peoples) and associated paraphernalia for a ritual performance. The male shamans in Siberia reportedly wore the complete costume only on very important occasions, and for events of lesser importance they normally wore a woman's dress. The ritual use of masks was to achieve transformation of the shaman into a sacred animal, plant, or deity. Similarly, the mask and other pieces of shamanistic attire were, at times, an animal disguise that related to the helper spirit and included skins, masks, teeth, and claws. The resemblance was a reference to the past when there was commonality between humans and animals, as well as a connection with the practice of shape shifting. As an example of this practice, according to legend, the Dogon people of West Africa did not die in primordial times. They were transformed into serpents and lived eternally.[69] Consequently, the serpent form was incorporated into the "Great Mask" that was a primary element of the grand funeral ritual.

The Evenk contended that the "shaman's robe retained characteristic features of the female outer dress and the shamans imitated their women in many aspects of decoration...."[70] (see Plate No. 13). They maintained that the first shamans and the primogenitors of later shamans, were women, "mythical old women, the guardians of the road to the world of the dead...."[71] It was also noted that the "drawings on the shaman's robe and drum, with which the concepts of the act of being taken possession of by the shamanistic spirits and the animation of the shaman's paraphernalia are connected, [and] are as a rule executed by women."[72]

The Magar shamans of Nepal wore special clothing during ritual activities, and their "costumes" often included feathers of powerful birds. They struck drums and bells to create a hypnotic musical accompaniment to their "poetic language of spells and prayers."[73] The sounds and symbols were necessary trappings for moving the audience along with the

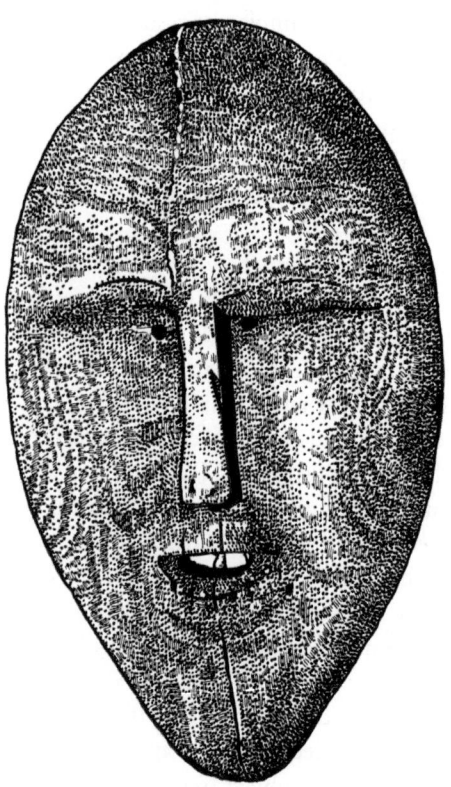

DRAWING 6.5—Evenks shaman's mask made in the early twentieth century of carved wood.

Left: PLATE 13—A 1910 portrait of Tolowa shaman and headman of Mestethlun Village dressed in a woman's dress. He wears a nose plug, dance apron fringed with jinglers, and a woven cap. Among certain cultural groups male shamans were known to undergo a change of sex. The shamans that received a command from the spirits exchanged their male clothing, behavior, and living arrangement for those of a woman.

Right: PHOTOGRAPH 16—Kwahwumhl—Koskimo dancer wearing raven mask with a coat of cormorant skins during the numhlim ceremony. Edward Curtis took this photograph circa 1914.

power of the performance. Yekaterina D. Prokofyeva wrote in *Studies in Siberian Shamanism* (1963) about the shamanistic songs of the Selkup people living in the northern Ob River basin. These songs, Prokofyeva explained, describe how and where the spirits fly. They explained that at the invitation of the shaman, "the principal spirit-bird, the eagle (or crane), arrived; behind it flew the lesser spirit-birds, a number of which entered the tent [of the shaman] through the smoke from the fireplace, and a number hid themselves under the wings of the large bird..."[74] (see photograph 16).

Writing in *Shamanism: Traditional and Contemporary Approaches to the Mastery of Spirits and Healing* (1999), Merete D. Jakobsen stated that, "the Tungus shaman dress was adorned with implements and thereby a symbolic representation of the powers of the spirits invoked."[75] Jakobsen also noted that the Korean *mansin* underwent transformation through dressing in different garments representing the invoked spirits, and "the Mongolian shaman was afraid of handing over his costume because the spirits inhabiting it might get out of control."[76] Those observations call to attention that dress and spirit manipulation were interconnected. However, the Greenlandic *angakkoq* (shaman) wore no special garment to conduct ritual activities, but was often semi-naked, with only a loincloth or belt.[77] Conversely, the Buryat shaman wore an iron helmet and a costume of furs.

Left: PLATE 15—Front view of shaman's costume from the Tungus. This costume dates from the second half of the eighteenth century. The costume includes a copper facemask, a Chinese mirror, several small copper fetishes, as well as iron figures of animals and humans, a doll-like figure, bells, coins, and a pouch from which protrudes a brass pipe.

Right: PLATE 16—Rear view of shaman's costume from the Tungus. This view of the costume shows a number of metal objects. The large brass or copper disk with a punched design protects the shaman's back from malevolent spirits. A second copper mask is partly visible under the right arm directly adjacent to the bell.

Siberian shamans and some sub–Arctic shamans wore distinctive clothing including coats, bibs, and head covers embellished with stripes of fur, amulets, bells, mirrors, and metal figures. The metal objects were essential, and some shamans wore as many symbolic helpers to be called upon as needed. Shamans also wore a head cover ornamented with small pieces of metal and bells, each of which was trimmed with little strips of cloth or leather that might represent a bird's feathers. Buryat shamans wore red head clothes, but at one time they wore masks, and Mongol shamans sometimes wore helmets with horns (see drawing 6.6).[78]

The costume of a Yakut shaman must have from 30 to 50 pounds (15 to 25 kilograms) of iron to have the necessary power to gain spiritual connection. The metal ornaments represented many things, but the object common to most Asian shamans was a metal mirror in which the shaman can see the souls of the dead.[79] The mirror was an important element of the shaman's costume because it reflected both the natural and supernatural environments.

The polished surface was a microcosm of the world that was believed to allow the shaman to see into the future and to understand the past. The only way of passing beyond the mirror was believed to be death.

The front and back of the Daur shaman's costume was often covered with small bronze mirrors (*toli*), "like overlapping plates or scales and there were said to represent fish and snake scales, armour, or an impregnable city wall."[80] The front of the costume might have eight large mirrors. "In front there was one further medium-sized mirror, called *neker-toli*, which was the heart protecting mirror."[81]

The mirror of the Daur Mongol shaman was believed to purify water. It could frighten away spirits; suppress or gather spirit manifestations; contain a soul or replace a soul; act as a symbolic wall or armor against spirits; and foretell a patient's recovery or death.[82] The mirror was usually polished on the face side and had signs and a loop on the back. The polished side was slightly convex, and the reverse was often recessed and rough. The signs on the back might include the twelve animals of the time cycle, Buddhist symbols, or Chinese symbols[83] (see photographs 13 and 14).

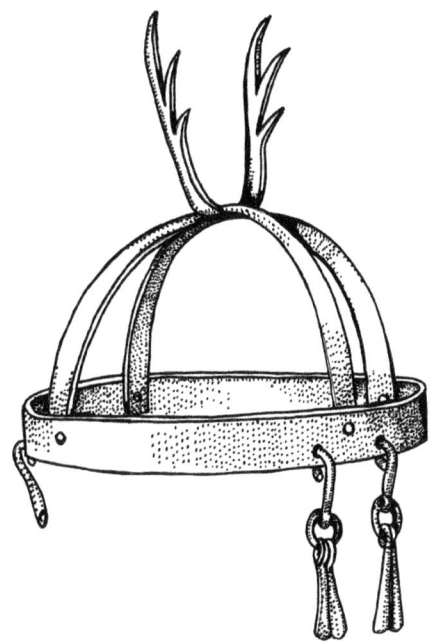

DRAWING 6.6—Iron headdress with horns and jingles. Mongol shamans sometimes wore headdresses of this type to emulate the power of the deer.

> As a shaman, the more mirrors you had, the more you became wise, majestic, and intelligent. And glamorous. Because you acquire all kinds of things through your mirrors—natural things, the sun, moon, and stars, all are absorbed into your body.[84]

Shaman used the paraphernalia to convey the appearance of power, cunning, speed, or dexterity of certain creatures and to perpetuate that popular belief. For instance, the shaman represented the dynamic and powerful nature of the beast by wearing the mask of the jaguar or wolf (see drawing 3.7) and a corresponding robe. The people believed that as a jaguar or wolf, the shaman could more successfully convey their wishes to the appropriate deity.

Masks worn as a part of ritual activities frequently represented spirit beings in the "power transformation strategy." The shaman's helping mask often combined anthropomorphic and zoomorphic images. The basic shape and look were human (anthropomorphic) with superimposed animal or bird (zoomorphic) forms. Those masks, common along the Northwestern Coast of North America[85] were transformation masks that combined an inner and outer image. One figure contained within another referred to the life and death process that influenced the survival of all living creatures. People in all cultures were the consumer or the consumed. Shamanistic transformation called on the power of the inner image to be given to the outer or more powerful spirit image (see drawing 6.7).

The concept of both physical and metaphysical transformation was found in ritual activities in different locations. As an example, the spirit qualities of bulls and jackals were common in Ancient Egypt. These part-human and part-animal transformation beings were represented in the nature of gods, and were associated with the dismemberment and rebirth of the Osiris. The Egyptians acknowledged the practice of trance employed by priests, and that these spirit journeys were believed to grant them knowledge like those afforded shamans. "The priests, *Kher heb* or *Kheru hebet*, were called the servants of the god."[86] These priest/shamans perform rituals for the Pharaohs and contribute to the general welfare of the people. "Ancient Egyptian hieroglyphic writing show a wide range of shamanistic functions of the *Kher heb* as official directors of religious and magic ceremonies."[87] According to Sir E. A. Wallis Budge, the *Kher heb* "knew how and when to recite spells, were able to draft incantations and magic formulae, could foretell the future, interpret dreams, reveal the causes of illness, and declare the name of the spirit of the dead who caused an illness."[88] The *Kher heb* also used their powers to pronounce oracles and to harm people by casting spells that caused sickness and misfortune.

The transformational activities of the Huichol revolved around rituals of compensation for the deer martyred by the wolf hunters in primordial time. For these northern Mexico people, the peyote hunting rituals and numerous other ceremonial traditions related to the creation myth and the appeasement of the souls of dead animals.[89] The Huichol, as the human counterparts of the predatory wolves, perform these rituals of gratitude to thank the deer for giving their lives as tribute to the agricultural deities for providing abundance. The shaman ritually pursued the deer, and it was transformed into the peyote cactus. The shamans' allegiance was to the supernatural dimension of the ritual that accommodated both placation and transformation.

Non-ordinary Psychic State

The words trance and ecstasy are often used indiscriminately.[90] According to Åke Hultkrantz in the chapter "Ecological and Phenomenological Aspects of Shamanism,"[91] "the trance cannot be compared with ordinary comatose state. In its genuine form it is a psychogenic, hysteroid mode of reaction forming itself according to the dictates of the mind."[92] The trance state often includes, "trembling, shuddering, goose-flesh, swooning, falling to the ground, yawning, lethargy, convulsions, foaming at the mouth, protruding eyes, insensitivity to heat, cold and pain, tics, loud breathing, a glassy stare...."[93]

In Daur shamanistic practice there was an expression "singing to frenzy."[94] That was thought to reference a range of behaviors such as "trembling, dancing, falling to the ground, croaking, [and] foaming at the mouth...."[95] However, that behavior did not represent contact with spirits or deities. Caroline Humphrey wrote in *Shamans and Elders* (1996) that "there

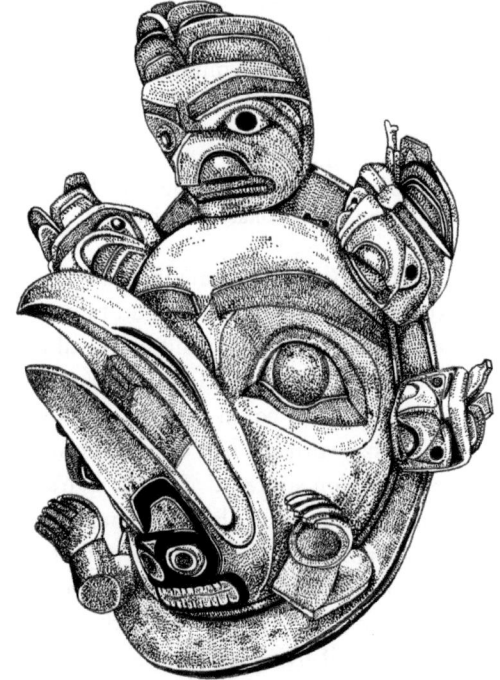

DRAWING 6.7—Northwest Coast mask made of carved wood and pigment. This piece is an example of the human/animal transformation role assigned to masks. The human face has a raven's beak and is surrounded by head-shapes that may represent other manifestations of the human/raven relationship.

is no psychological state that we can definitely identify with 'trance,' and it is impossible either to prove or to deny its presence."[96]

> Dance [was] central to much of the ritual in which direct contact with the spirit world [was] sought by means of altered states of consciousness, or trance. Dance [was] involved in the induction of trance, the central event of the ritual, and often the termination of trance as well.[97]

Shamans in some cultures used dance to attain an altered state of consciousness, and in that ecstatic condition, claimed their souls departed their bodies for the spirit realm. Such dance was often accompanied by sound to promote a state of ecstasy. The stupor associated with soul displacement might also come from dance enhanced by psychotropic drugs as found in the Amazonian regions of South America. It was this altered mental state and the related spiritual flight in search of information that characterized shamanistic practice.

The shaman in a trance-like state was reportedly possessed by a spirit and given the powers of healing and divining. To control and direct that energy, the shaman concentrated his or her imaginative powers into an intense mental image of an anticipated outcome. Yakut rituals to cure the sick, guide the soul of the dead to the Otherworld, invoke a deity, or visit the heavens were performed by a shaman in an altered state of consciousness induced some form of stimulant (see photograph 17). Elaborate costumes and special objects were used in the ceremony as dramatic expressions of spiritual connection and interaction. The shaman might employed ritual paraphernalia to assume an appearance thought to be agreeable to spiritual powers.

"The discourse of cosmological knowledge was communicated to the shaman through his spiritual connections when he [or she] was in trance...."[98] This special physical and mental alignment changed the shaman into a "specialist who could actively intervene in the world by taking responsibility for it."[99] Erika Bourguignon writing in *Shamanism: An Encyclopedia of World Beliefs, Practices, and Culture* (2004) noted that trance when used to describe an altered state of consciousness is referring to "a psychophysiological state other than that of the ordinary wakefulness of workaday life."[100] Bourguignon also stated that when, "[trance was] integrated into a system of religious rituals, its cultural meanings vary, but they fall into two broad groups: visionary experiences, which are remembered, as in the case of the shaman, and possession experiences, which are generally followed by amnesia."[101]

"Trance played an important role not just in the shaman's soul-journey to the spirits but in the shaman's actions as a performer. The theatre of shamanic ritual was critical."[102] For the community to believe in the effectiveness of the spirit-contact and to share in the shamanic experience, they had to have trust and confidence in the power of the shaman. Therefore, a display of power was a necessary part of the shamanic ritual. "Trance was central [to the shaman's performance] for it enables transformation, and the shaman had to be transformed in order to enter the spirit-dimension."[103] The mind in an altered state was thought transported from physical nature into the supernatural world that was opened by the idea of immortality, resurrection, and freedom of life after death.

The altered levels of consciousness often caused shamans in Siberia to dance, jump about, and sing in unknown languages. Shamans performed acrobatic twists, turns, and whirls with such intensity that the movements were difficult to control. However, the shaman's dance in the south Yakut (also written Sakha, a district in the Lana river basin of northeastern Siberia) was less frenzied. The black and white shamans of that region often gave up their drums to dance more unrestrainedly while in pursuit of good and evil spirits. The Yakut white shamans,

PHOTOGRAPH 17—The Tlingit shaman in this photograph is wearing a headdress that is reportedly in the Burke Memorial Washington State Museum. The shaman is ministering to a patient. He has a rattle in his right hand and a forehead mask that may represent a helper spirit. According to the notation in *Spirit and Ancestor* written by Bill Holm, this picture was made in 1889, and the shaman may be a Sitka, Alaska, man called Dr. Pete.[1]

DRAWING 6.8—Shang Dynasty ritual vessel (Yu) in the form of a bear or tiger consuming a man. These containers made of bronze were used to serve wine to priest/shamans during divination or healing ceremonies. The vessel may represent the spiritual, as well as physical, transformation of man into animal form.

called *aïy-oïuna* (or *ajy ojana*), took part in the spring festivals, marriage ceremonies, fertilization rites, and the curing of diseases.[104] Whereas black shamans, called *abasy ojuna,* were reported to have "hypnotic abilities and did extraordinary feats while in altered states of consciousness...."[105] Regardless of the purpose, the rituals performed were much the same.

Ritual, trance, and spirit possession were intermingled elements of shamanic activities. The expectations of the audience energized the shaman as a source for creating and performing the ritual. The activities associated with certain shamanic performance were intended to assuage the distress or pain of the persons who come for treatment by means of suggestion and hypnotism.[106] Songs, dances, and offerings of food and drink in special vessels accompanied Chinese ritual activities. According to Maurizio Scarpari writing in *Ancient China: Chinese Civilization from its Origins to the Tang Dynasty* (2006) "Wine was drunk by the shamans during the ceremonies to aid them in achieving the state of trance required for divination"[107] (see drawing 6.8). While on the other hand, shamans in the Malay Peninsula and Oceania danced to achieve an altered state of consciousness, and spirit "possession."

By attaining an altered state of consciousness the shaman could multiply his or her limited human capacity into a company of spirit helpers. He or she could penetrate the unseen elements of the sensible world with their guidance and support. Although, being a person of this world, the shaman could not see the unseen, his or her special "clear-sighted" spirit who always stays close by reported everything that happens.[108]

7

SHAMANIC DIVINATION AND CURING

> Illness could be caused by many factors, including taboo violations, theft of one's soul by a sorcerer, and the intrusion of sorcery powers or objects. Shamans treated physical, psychological, and spiritual conditions using a wide variety of techniques....[1]

The Origin of Disease

Shamans obtain much of their medical capabilities from the conceptual framework of their society, and the communally shared view of the treatment. This unanimity no doubt increased the efficacy of shamanistic treatment of functional psychiatric disorders. Although such treatments were basically magical, in that they were non-rational attempts to deal with non-rational forces, they often included elements of rational therapy.[2]

The earliest general belief, so far as we know, as to the cause of disease incidental to humanity was that it was due to the effect of unseen demons or evil-spirits that entered his body and were able to cause illness.[3] According to the Yoruba, one of the largest ethnic groups in Nigeria, sickness and illness were caused by both natural and supernatural causes. However, there was little distinction between the two, and traditional practice tended to assign sickness more to unnatural causes.[4] The Yoruba sought diagnosis, explanation, meaning, and treatment of disease through the insight of divination and spiritual intervention.

What was defined as illness, both mental and physical differed from culture to culture. Sickness and health often depended on benevolent deities and the successful intervention of a shaman. Many societies believed that disease was of supernatural origin; therefore, the basis for symbolic healing was to restructure the disorder, in a mythic world. Cultural myth positioned the general framework of a mythic world in which healing symbols were manipulated.[5] As an example, the Cherokee contended that disease was caused by animal spirits, and by "the little people ... ghosts, witches, dreams, neglected taboos,"[6] as well as power radiating from the sun and moon. Spirits entering the human body could cause both physical and mental disease or illness. As counter measures, the sucking method was traditionally used to extract offending spirits, whereas, chanting, yelling, and making threatening gestures were considered adequate for exorcisms in Central Asia and other locations.[7]

The shaman or medicine man, as they were called in different cultures, aligned disease with cultural beliefs in that superstition and anxiety gave meaning and reason to the patient's fears. The same beliefs provided a prescription for relief from illness thought to be the result of spiritual intervention. A part of the healing process often called upon the embedded mythological record of the culture to determine both the cause and effect of the malady. That societal reference offered the means for the shaman to identify with the offending person or spirit, and to discover the cause and solution for the psychological distress as well as the physiological condition. This process was similar to contemporary medical diagnosis in which cultural condition precipitates both mental and physical responses.

The Navaho believed that the causes for diseases fell into two categories — the definite and the undefinite.[8] They also considered excess in any activity as a possible cause for illness. Everything from weaving to sexual indulgence and from undue concentration to hoarding of property might promote suffering and physical distress. Ignoring ceremonial law was a major source of illness, and a person (shaman, priest, or elder) with special knowledge of such rules was required to determine the transgression and thereby the cause of the infirmity.[9]

The Ndembu of Zambia considered disease or illness to be a form of misfortune similar to "poor luck in hunting, reproductive disorders, physical attacks, and loss of property."[10] They also believed that disease was due to either a "disease-object" within a person or the temporary absence of the soul. The general belief was that neither of these circumstances could have taken place except through the direct action of another person.[11]

Although dealing with illness was often a part of the shaman responsibility the methods varied. Illness for some Siberian people was the result of their soul being stolen by evil spirits. Shamanic practice in such cases required searching the spirit world for the purloined souls and performing the appropriate ceremony to ensure their safe recovery. The malady in other cultures might be treated with more mundane methods drawing upon the shaman's knowledge of curative herbs or treatments. In both occurrences the shaman worked in partnership with spirits, but the method reflected cultural circumstance. Shamans used rituals to ask the gods for help with such matters as retrieving lost souls, locating and attracting game, controlling the weather, detecting broken taboos that brought misfortune, expelling harmful spirits, and for guiding the dead to the spirit world.

Group beliefs often foretold that illness, epilepsy, insanity, and soul loss were caused by spiritual or demonic possession. Although spirit intrusion was associated with shamanic trance, a condition deliberately sought for ritual purposes when "[s]hamans induced spirits to descend into their bodies temporarily...."[12] The trance was lifted at the conclusion of the ritual event, the spirits withdrawn, and the shaman suffered no ill effects. However, other forms of spirit possession were not desirable and often caused harm. Debilitating conditions of a physical or mental nature required the services of a shaman (medicine-man) to perform a curing ritual.

Dreams and visions as omens of future events foretold coming illness and, therefore, a person had to be vigilant to recognize the warnings. The Apache placed great belief in dreams and believe they prophesied the future. Dreams might predict illness and death as well as fire, flood, and other forms of personal difficulty. Thus, when the dreamer dreamed something bad, it was expected to occur unless he or she took the necessary precautions.[13]

> The first few dreams in which supernatural spirits appeared [could] be safely disregarded. But shortly, if the instructions received in the dream were not followed, it was necessary to call a shaman to doctor the patient. In the course of curing, the shaman told the patient to do as he had been told in his dreams. Then, if the summons was obeyed, recovery was assured.[14]

A Navaho who was sick could be the victim of bad dreams. When the dreams were of death, the dead, snakebite, tooth pulling, fire, or lighting they were bad. There were also good dreams about horses, sheep, cattle, and wealth. It was believed that these dreams brought good fortune. "To dream about killing was always bad and had to be counteracted in some way or other."[15] It was at those times that the dreamer sought help from the shaman.

Disease in central and northern Asia was attributed to the patient's soul having strayed or been stolen. Treatment in such cases was to find the soul, capture it, and return it to the patient. Illness, in many areas of the region, was considered to be due to the intrusion of a magical object into the person's body, or possession of the patient's soul by evil spirits.[16] It was the shaman's practice on occasions such as these to remove the harmful object by sucking, or to expel the spirits. The treatment was made more complicated because it was common for spirits to turn into objects and objects into spirits. In such extreme cases, the shaman was called upon to expunge the possessing spirit and to recover the dispossessed soul.

Contact with the dead was another cause for illness found in many locations, particularly in the southwestern region of North America. The Navaho, an Apachean-speaking people that migrated from Canada, were adverse to anything connected with the dead. The house in which a person died was often burned or a hole was cut in the north wall to allow the spirit to depart. It is alleged that a Navaho would rather freeze than to seek shelter in a house where someone died. There was no way of knowing the "real" cause of the person's death or what secret life the person might have had. According to superstition and belief, the dead could be dangerous. Nevertheless, it was one of the responsibilities of the shaman to journey into the beyond and report to the dead in the underworld. The shaman of the Salish, a people living in northwestern North America, had to cross the River of the Dead in his or her travels to recover the lost and stolen soul of a sick person or to accompany the soul of the dead[17] (see photograph 18).

PHOTOGRAPH 18 — Portrait of Sees-Yuse called Sampson, an Interior Sinkiuse Salish shaman in native dress. The identification of Interior Sinkiuse was to distinguish them from the Coast Salish of the Northwest Pacific Coast. Salish was formerly an alternative name for the Flathead; however, it is now often the broad name that is applied to a group of indigenous peoples living in British Columbia, northern Washington, Idaho, and western Montana in the upper basins of the Columbia and Fraser rivers.

Divination and Magic

When we take a patient's hand in order to feel their pulse, we enter into a connection of one heart to another where we are able to receive the first important information about a person whom we do not know.[18]

The shaman's paranormal powers reinforced his or her ability to regulate relations between the spirits and the community through rituals or transcendental activities. This interaction was to ensure the community's wellbeing. As a healer and diviner, it was often the shaman's role to provide such services to the resident community. These abilities were manifest in many forms, but two of the most common are curing (healing) and divination. The practice of divination (prophetic) focused on finding lost articles, identifying favorable or unfavorable persons and situations, telling the future, and predicting generally unknowable facts or information such as the cause of an illness or death. Curative shamanistic practices healed the natural or supernatural illnesses or maladies of humans and animals through special (magical) powers or incantations.[19] Both curing and divination were found in most early societies.

Undoubtedly the appeal of this concept has existed in the psyche of people since the beginning of time. It was inevitable that when a person feared spirits had abducted his or her soul, thus jeopardizing his or her physical and spiritual wellbeing, appropriate action had to be taken. The malevolent forces had to be driven out or by corrective action rendered inactive. In shamanistic practice, there was no distinction between shamans helping others and helping themselves. It was often the case that shamans had to heal their own maladies before they could be of assistance to others. The psychological evolution from sickness through self-cure was a multi-layered process in developing the ability to shamanize.

Similarly, people have always wanted to know the outcome of future events therefore, predictive techniques are very old. Early magicians believed that if a person swallowed "the heart of a mole freshly extracted and palpitating, he [or she] would at once become an expert in divination."[20] Devine communication delivered in response to a petitioner's request can be traced to ancient China. Thousands of oracle bones, an early divination tool were discovered in the Shang dynasty city of Yin near the current city of An-yang. The Shang palace stood on the site from 1384 to 1111 BCE. Elsewhere in Asia, the Mongolian *bagchi* (ritualist) was responsible for making sacrifices and offerings, consecrating horses to spirits, pronouncing spells, and making "divinations by reading the cracks in a sheep's shoulder blade heated on the fire."[21] The Kalmyk and the Kirgiz also practiced this divination process, and the coastal Koryak people used the shoulder blade of a seal to foretell the future.[22]

Half way around the world shaman/priests in the central region of the Western Hemisphere pursued ways to predict the future of individuals, civilizations, and the world. The Inca believed that life was controlled by unseen powers and to divine the requirement of the deities, the shaman/priests sought access to the supernatural through oracles. One accepted method of divination was studying the veins made visible by inflated lungs of a sacrificed white llama.[23]

Knowledge of the future allowed greater flexibility when people were required to adjust to change. The people in Southeast Asia domesticated pigs for of a practice called *haruspication*— the divining from the entrails of animals.[24] "The methods of divination from entrails of animals was carried on according to strict rules"[25] according to Ralph Linton. He states in *Tree of Culture* (1957) that, "Clay models of livers with the meanings of various anomalies written on them were used to instruct young diviners, and there was even reason to believe that the results of various predictions were noted down with a view to improving the method."[26] Animal bones and viscera symbolized the mystery of life and regeneration. Consequently, it incorporated in itself, everything pertaining to the past and future of life.

Divination was a form of communication in which supernatural powers gave or were coerced to give requested information. It was intended to discover the opinions of the spirits and thereby to foretell the future or discover lost or misplaced items. In many locations it was a practical process to achieve desired results or to avoid unwanted outcomes. Divination played a special role in human existence by filling the voids caused by the lack of knowledge of the forces that influence life, and provided a means for alleviating anxiety. As a part of life for many people, divination was not viewed as a disassociated attitude but as integrated into every aspect of survival. It was a part of the socio-religious belief system. Divination was used to select a building site for a new home and the burial site for a deceased family member. The shaman in the role of diviner was consulted for the best day to marry or go hunting, as well as the most favorable time for holding a ceremony or making a journey. Divination was a part of all facets of life from conception to the grave.

Annemarie de Waal Malefijt wrote about the nature of divination in her 1968 book, *Religion and Culture*. She stated that there were three major types of divination. In the first, the supernatural power initiates the process; in the second, man is the initiator; and in the third, there is a dialogue between man and the deity consulted.[27] In the latter exchange, the "man speaks directly to the gods in a face-to-face relationship, and the gods answer in words and sentences."[28] This interaction usually took place in a trance or in dreams. It was often the case that the divination process called upon elements of magic such as the use of objects, spells, or rituals to promote communication with the spirits.

Divination was a culturally accepted method of foretelling the future and also a way of knowing what was happening at a distance and in different places. Shamans in Siberia often forecast the future, found objects, and determined the source of illnesses by suspending an object by a thread. Questions were asked and the movement of the object was determined to agreement or disagreement with the inquiry. The shaman was able to find a solution to any problem by asking the right questions. The Dobu islanders of the Western Pacific used the same method to find acceptable answers to socio-cultural questions. Whereas, in the mountains of northwestern Laos and southwestern China, the Lolo (also called Yi or Wu-man) shamans performed a divination rite influenced by the Chinese and reading heat-caused cracks in cattle scapula or turtle plastrons.

Discovering the Unknown

The shaman was a link to primeval times and the creation. He or she was a life force—an energy—who could kill as well as cure. However, not all shamans were powerful. A fundamental form of shamanic activity could be viewed as simply "reading the signs." Many diseases were believed to be incomprehensible by normal methods of diagnosis because their origins were believed to exist on a supernatural level. No trance, ceremonial preparation, or mystical paraphernalia was required to gain insight into physical conditions that had obvious symptoms or signs and subsequently to predict an outcome. Cause and effect were calculated, rationalized, and determined and the corresponding remedies prescribed.

The shaman in Siberia dropped small stones or seeds on the head of a drum and observed the arrangement to divine the future. In Mexico shamans used beans and seeds in a similar way for prognostication. Such signs, and many others, were used to foretell the conditions or circumstances of particular maladies and thereby to aid the divination process. Nevertheless, finding disease and the cause of illness was sometimes very difficult. Often the spirits that cause physical or mental distress were illusive. They hide from detection by masking each other. When this subterfuge occurred the shaman gathered a force of "helpers" to assess the patient's condition and to assist in determining the nature and location of the offending spirit/object.

It is likely that instinct, rituals, and beliefs guided traditional behavior in many locations, and in early societies greater or lesser importance was placed on assistance granted by benevolent spirits. Although survival was a basic instinct, there was a progressive shift from instinct to learned behavior exemplified by rituals and ceremonies. Because divination was the process of obtaining information about future events or things otherwise unavailable to ordinary perception, that insight could only be achieved by consulting sources other than humans. The shaman had an important position within the social structure of most communities because of this special divining ability. He or she provided assistance to individuals that were experts in daily survival and normally self-sufficient, but required aid in assessing future events. Eventually, even traditional actions became less automatic as people relied on some form of supernatural help in making critical decisions.[29]

There were different methods for divination based on the social and cultural environment in which the diviner prognosticated. As an example, it was possible for the diviner (shaman) to provide the appropriate response to a situation based on his or her knowledge of the society in which the client/patient lives. The diviner might look into water, stare into the sun, or go into a trance, but the resulting prediction was information gleaned by the shaman or a helper prior to the séance. Another method used in the divination process was allowing the client/patient to verify the anticipated outcome of the session and through questioning guide the shaman to the desired conclusions. A less successful method was spontaneous predictions. The shaman followed the suggestions of the client/patient, but added his or her interpretation of the situation. This process depended on the shaman's ability to immediately analyze the issue being considered.

It was likely that an intuitive sense of social, cultural, and physical matters influenced divination activities. *A priori* knowledge, as well as, an inherent sensitivity to human nature was necessary elements of divination. It was equally likely that belief, faith, hope, and tradition reinforced the acceptability of predictions. The skilled shaman (diviner) might use all means for predicting an outcome. Odd or even numbers, heavy or light measures, and right or left movements could determine positive or negative responses. Even when the foretelling was incorrect the client/patient accepted the prediction assuming it was based on circumstances or conditions not yet encountered. It was also easy to blame the stars or malevolent spirits when the predictions were erroneous.

People have always searched for ways to address the uncertainties of their existence. They relied on instinct or learned response to acquire knowledge of pending success or failure, feast or famine, sickness or health. Foreknowledge influenced the wellbeing of the individual and the community. Critical decisions made without adequate information about the future could result in disaster. Decisions by individuals influenced the lives of one person or a family, whereas, the decisions of rulers impacted the lives of thousands of people. Therefore, rulers invested heavily in predictive techniques and skilled prognosticators (shaman/priests).

The shaman was believed to be able to see and know what others did not, therefore, they were expected to predict the future and explain the past. Peruvian shaman found predictions in omen from grains of corn or the excrement of animals.[30] Other Peruvian shaman (priests) made idols to speak, some divined by talking with the dead, and other consumed tobacco and coca (*Erythroxylum coca* a source of the drug cocaine) to made themselves receptive to spirit communication.[31] The shamans of the Caquetio and Jirajara peoples living in northwestern Venezuela consumed nicotine as a stimulant, and were said to practice divining with tobacco ash. "If the ash formed a curve, the enterprise would succeed, but if it remained straight, failure was certain."[32]

Object, Signs, and Techniques for Divination

All levels of society used omens and oracles to facilitate the divining process during the Ch'ing Dynasty (Pinyin Qing and also called Manchu Dynasty). The Qing almanac listed a variety of omens including twitching of the eyes, ringing in the ears, a dog barking, and a magpie chirping.[33] Such indications had to be considered according to time, direction, or location to gain the proper interpretation. Almanacs divided omen categories into twelve two-hours periods to facilitate interpretation. For instance, "A ringing in the left ear at the *zi* hour (11 PM to 1 AM) indicated that a loved one was thinking of you, while a ringing in the right ear during the same time period indicated that you would lose money."[34] Such divination was to obtain information about the future, so the believer might manipulate events by replacing uncertainty by certitude. Those systematized divination were generally available to the public without the benefit of shamanic interpretation.

Other cultures developed similar "guides" or "directives" for the lay population, as well as priests and shamans, to divine future events and circumstances. A Thai myth provided the source of rules that were applicable to daily activities. For instance, principle four states that, "a sleeping wife must not cross her feet."[35] This sleeping position was thought to be unlucky. On the matter of progeneration, the rules provide instructions on how to determine the gender of an unborn child. To know whether a boy or a girl was to be born, the diviner started with the mystic number 49, added the number of months since conception, and subtracted the age of the mother. From that total, the number one, then two, and so on up to nine, or as long as possible were subtracted. If the remind number was odd: the unborn child was a boy, if the number was even, it was a girl.[36]

There were numerous examples of magical practices for avoiding illness or promoting a cure. "The head of a buzzard tied round the neck could cure a headache, and the stomach of a cormorant tied at the waist was prescribed to relieve stomach pains."[37] It was also thought that a person died if they saw a falling star, stumbled near an open grave, or was cut by a razor that had shaved a corpse.[38] These situations, and hundreds more, often required the protective assistance of a shaman.

A para-shamanistic technique practiced by the Netsilik, a small group of Eskimos, was called *krilaq* (head lifting). John Middleton describes the practice in the book titled, *Magic, Witchcraft, and Curing* (1967). According to Middleton,[39] the *krilaq* was performed on the practitioner's wife. A hood was placed over the woman's head. A thong was tied around the hood and a helper spirit was called for assistance. The practitioner asked a series of question and in response the helping spirit gave the thong a tug. A gentle pull was a negative answer, and a stout pull was an affirmative. With the assistance of the helper spirit the curing was to determine which taboo had been broken allowing the evil spirits to cause mental or physical distress. Once the taboo was identified, amends could be made, and the spirits were to leave the body of the patient. Health was restored.

Various objects, signs, and activities were used to divine (determine) a client/patient's illness, resolve a dilemma, or predict the future. The method and the means of divination were cultural based and describing every scheme would be a complex undertaking. However, there were certain techniques that are indicative of the processes used. The role of bones in the divination processes in different cultures around the world is a good example. As noted above, the Chinese made use of the bovine scapula, whereas the Shona (a people living in eastern Zimbabwe) throw the "bones,"[40] and among the Balahis in central India the *janka* (medicine man or shaman) pulls the fingers of the patient to "pop the joints," and by the number of pops (snaps) identify the supernatural force causing an illness.[41]

Skulls played an important role in various manifestations of belief (see drawing 7.1). They were associated with the cult of the dead, ancestor worship, warfare, magic, and the rites of survival. The moss growing on a human skull was believed to be a significant curative, and other mystical references to the human head for both curing and divining were not restricted to one region or culture. The Persians consigned the top of the head to their deities, and early Germanic peoples preserved heads by fastening them to trees. The Celts hung the heads of slain enemies from house rafters to gain protection from the dead person's spirits, and Greeks, Jews, Semites, and Norsemen kept human heads so they might serve as oracles.[42]

The preeminent bone for divination and other mystic activities performed by shamans, medicine men, and seerers was the skull. The skull was an important part of the cultural belief system and for many societies it was associated with death, as well as foretelling the future. The Yukagir (a people living in Arctic Siberia east of the Lena River in Russia) undertook no activity without consulting the skulls of ancestral shamans. This divination method measured the weight of the selected skull to predict a positive or negative outcome of a particular event or activity. If the skull felt light to the diviner when he or she questioned it, the answer was "yes," if heavy, the answer was "no."[43] The oracle's pronouncement was obeyed.

Veneration of human skull began as early as the Early Paleolithic Period[44] and the practice of preserving the skull apart from the rest of the skeleton appears to have continued throughout history. The "skull-cult," as the socialized indication of skull veneration was closely connected with ancestor worship. Shamans used skulls, as symbols of recognition or power to emphasize the unity of the material and spiritual worlds (see drawing 7.2). This power association was of particular importance to the Evenk (formally Tungus), a people that from early time sacrificed the head of slain bears to their gods. The skeleton of the bear was buried to pacify the animal's soul, but the skull of the slaughtered animal was placed in a tree as a gift to their supreme god.[45]

DRAWING 7.1—Human skull with molded face made from a mixture of earth and fiber. This head came from the island of Toman that lies to the south of Malekula in the southwestern Pacific Ocean. The elongated (dolichocephalus) skull is painted with red and black colorants and has a fringe of hair.

In an interestingly similar practice, the Maori suspended the bodies of their dead from a tree so the flesh could decompose, and once the flesh was removed, the bones were cleaned, painted, and buried. Buddhists believed that the body after death was an empty shell and a formal ritual of disposal was not necessary. In other cultures, efforts were made to retard the decay processes as with mummification, so the body might be retained as long as possible.

Curatives and charms associated with skulls of humans and animals were used in different ways. People living in the Ukraine favored grass grown through the eyehole of a horse's skull for good luck.[46] The use of a human skull as a matrix to "reconstruct" an ancestral image (see drawing 7.3) with clay was common practice as was the configuring of a drinking cup out of the crown. "Skull cups" were made in different locations and associated with various beliefs. Tibetan Buddhists used skull cups, as did the Christians during the Middle Ages. The

Left: DRAWING 7.2 — Wooden Korwar-style skull reliquary made by a shaman for spiritual power. This late eighteenth century Melanesian piece was to preserve the soul of a distinguished person.
Right: DRAWING 7.3 — Human skull with a face modeled in clay and painted with designs to give an aesthetic quality to the remains of an ancestor. The eye sockets of this New Guinea ritual object were embedded with cowrie shells to give "life" to the face. The distinguishing facial marks are a reference to the deceased person.[m]

Scythians, Teutones, Bulgarians, and Australian aborigines used containers made from skulls as elements of rituals to transfer the life forces of the dead to the living. Skulls were also used to summon the spirit of the departed and to function as intermediaries with the spirit world.

The Chukchee shaman might be required to open the skull of the patient to replace an errant soul that was captured in the form of a fly. The soul may also be reinstalled through the mouth, finger, or great toe.[47] A hole might be made in the skull of the patient, to provide an afflicting disease (in the form of a malevolent spirit) with a means of escape from the patient's body. This practice called trepanning or trephining was used in prehistoric times in Britain, France, and other parts of Europe as well as in Peru.[48] Among the early Slavs trepanning was a process included in human sacrifices, along with evisceration and decapitation.[49]

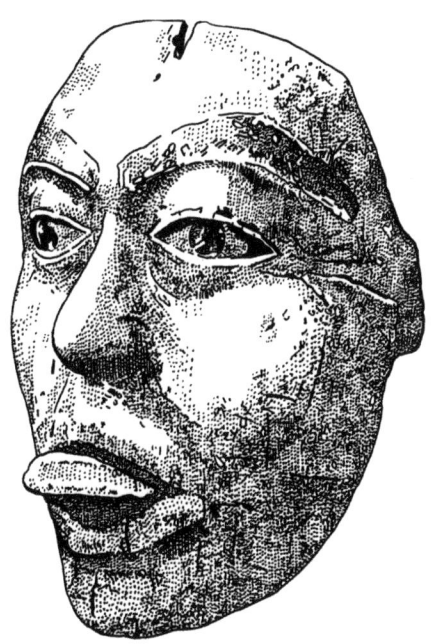

DRAWING 7.4—A Tlingit (Yakutat) shaman's facemask made of wood with traces of pigment. "[T]he greatest concentration of a shaman's spirit power resided in his mask."[n] When the shaman put on his mask, he became the manifestation of power. This mask, recovered from a site on the Akwe River forty miles down the coast from Yakutat Bay in the northwestern region of North America, represents the "spirit of a dead man."[o] The finely carved mask has a very human-like appearance that is made extraordinary by the intense expression of the eyes and the protruding tongue. The exact meaning of the tongue is unclear, but it may signify the man's spirit (soul). Tlingit shaman masks generally had no eyeholes.[p]

The Nazca culture located on the southern coast of Peru (c. 200 years before this era to 600 of the current era) preserved human heads. The skulls of ancestors or defeated enemies were displayed on ritual occasions. The skulls were believed by Nazca peoples to contain a powerful resource that could be utilized. It is possible that ritual headhunters, such as those in the Amazon region of Ecuador, collected skulls for the same reasons. The practice of preserving ancestral skulls and trophy heads with features made with clay was found among the sites on Kodiak Island and the Alaskan Peninsula occupied by the Kachemak peoples.[50] The skulls often had ivory "eyes" reflecting the tradition of other cultural groups in the same region. The eye plugs filled the ocular openings in the skull gave a vacant far-seeing expression and denied reentry to the spirit of the deceased.

The skull fulfilled a fundamental role as the reference source for symbols associated with death and funeral rites. It was also transformed into a mask such as one used by a shaman at the Hopewell site (200 BCE—550 CE) in Ohio.[51] The posterior portion of the cranium and the lower jaw were removed along with part of the nose cavity to form the mask. The remaining segment of the skull covered the eyes and forehead of the wearer (shaman). Altered in that way and adorned with hair and animal skin, the skull was a very effective death mask.[52] The shaman/priests of New Britain also used the anterior part of the skull modeled with clay as masks, and the Maya in Mesoamerica had a similar practice.

The Tsimshian people of the Northwest Coast carved portrait masks to honor deceased ancestors (see drawing 7.4). The upturned and half-closed eyes symbolized death. This form of veneration was less direct than the use of a skull; however, the masks were permanent reminders of the deceased and were believed to possess a certain power that could be activated by display.[53]

The skull was a link between the three worlds—lower, surface, and upper and the three cycles of life—past, present, and future. The fleshless bone was dehumanized by death and descended to the lower world, and it was used by the surface world in present time to connect with the spirits in the upper world for the purpose of predicting the future. The symbolic reference of the skull joined the spiritual and physical worlds in various physical and spiritual ways and emphasized the marginally definable different between life and death that reinforced shamanic practice.

Curing by Seeing the Unseen

> Shamanic ecstasy, like some religious traditions but unlike others, includes clairsentient phenomena such as visions and voices wherein directives or information is obtained for a healing or the spiritual heightening of solidarity in the community.[54]

Human anatomy has not changed significantly in thousands of years, and the motivations of daily life have remained equally constant. People have continued to measure their existence from birth to death by biological and sociological markers that are commonly held. An overriding factor in that accumulation of human concerns—infancy, maturity, sexuality, conjugality, and immortality—was the question of individual status in the limitless expanse of the universe. Possibly early people did not ponder philosophical or psychological issues in theoretical terms; however, common conditions and circumstances were believed to generate common responses across diverse cultures. Consequently, individual responses to sociological as well as physiological stimuli were generally dictated by tradition. Beyond daily survival questions about death and the disposition of the spirit after life ends figured prominently in the ritual activities of early people.

All peoples, regardless of their differing attitudes about the relationships between the natural and supernatural, had an abiding concern about physical debilitation. Illness, because of its mysterious nature, was feared because it deprived an individual of the ability to participate in activities necessary to sustain life. Death and injury from accidents or war, though often viewed as "bad luck" were understood, acknowledged, and sometimes honored. However, the avoidance of physical problems and the maintenance of good health were believed by most people to depend on observing social taboos and refraining from socially unacceptable practices. Shamans were granted the power to intercede on behalf of an offending individual to avoid calamity, and thereby to relieve this practice of societal unacceptability.

"The basis for symbolic healing was a restructuring of a disorder, modeled in a mythic world. Cultural myth sets the general framework of a mythic world in which healing symbols were manipulated."[55] The shaman, healer, medicine man (or medicine woman), or sometimes "singers" were believed to have powers that exceeded those of normal individual. Those especially enabled individuals worked within the established system to cure diseases caused by culturally identified spirits and demons. Therefore, "[o]nce a part of cultural myth had been designated as applicable, the healer and patient worked together to adapt it to the patient's problem."[56] Healing and belief were overlapping concepts.

The determination that spirit caused illness and the accompanying expunging techniques is quite ancient. Early medical documents dating from about 2500 years before the current era included incantations to induce evil spirits to depart from their victims, and the casting out of such spirits persisted in Europe well into the nineteenth century. This practice was associated with traditional attitudes, and Biblical accounts of demonic possession and the driving out of adverse spirits (exorcism) reinforced this concept. It is reported, however, that physical and mental illness challenged the understanding of most early people, and the need to assign fault was a common practice. Shamans, sorcerers, and witches were believed to cast evil spells, as well as to provide the requisite remedies. Evil eye, bad dreams, curses, evil spells, and exposure to moon light were culturally acceptable explanations for various maladies. The unknown was explained as the unseen — spirits, demons, and curses.

It is probable that early people were consumed by the conditions of daily existence. Life was precarious. Consequently, the assistance of one or more deities was often required for relatively common activities. Hunting, travel, building a house, and other forms of individual or group interaction required supernatural concurrence, and without that support, the activities were avoided or delayed. The power behind almost all events often rested with the supernatural — a force both omnipresent and omnipotent. It was normal to ask for additional assistance from the supernatural in times of physical, mental, and social distress. The shaman in a supportive belief system served as the ceremonial guide for instituting connection with the spirit world. The shaman as the leader of the ritual event dramatized a personal meeting with the spirits and announced that encounter with symbols from the natural world, so the people could be certain their messages were being heard.

It was a commonly held idea that spirits entering the human body accounted for both physical and mental illness. It was a belief in may cultures that the soul that departed the body or came into existence after death was in need of a psychopomp to escort it to the other world. It was also believed that the soul of a person who died a heroic or violent death went to the Upperworld, but the soul of a person, who dies from disease, especially when an evil spirit causes death, went to the Underworld. The shaman in the role of a psychopomp had the responsibility for conducting the soul to its final location.[57]

For many societies, the shaman was the only hope for curing certain types of illness, especially those associated with sorcery, spirit attack, and soul loss.[58] This special skill came from beyond the visual world where shamans were taught certain practices and gestures for use in ritual activities. The rituals provided a curing energy for the community. The shaman was also concerned about the nature of the disease — its origin and condition. This information was necessary to determine whether the patient's soul/spirit had left his or her body and been captured by the dead. The curing skills of the shaman along with his or her other social activities were constant reminder of the power of the spirit world.

Rites performed by shamans in Korea, were purported to cure illness. People believed only shamans could cure or control illnesses caused by spirits. Consequently, they assumed that the houses of the shamans were "safe from the spirits causing illness, so when epidemics spread, they took refuge at their houses."[59] The Korean royal court sought assistance from shamans during times when disease became dangerous, and private individuals had shamanic performances to chase away "fearful conditions."[60]

The Malay shaman treated "'sickness of the soul'" with ceremony, singing, and dancing. In a trance he or she became the voice of disembodied spirits.[61] The shaman invited the spirit (*minduk*) to the séance and told the story of the "Creation — a double creation, of the universe and of humanity, the universe in microcosm."[62]

Not all Malay healers were shamans and some treatments involved herbs, dietary changes, and massages to treat illnesses. The causes for illness for the Malay were not separated into natural or supernatural but a more common alignment of usual and unusual sicknesses.[63] Usual illnesses were caused by a physiological (humoral) imbalance, whereas unusual illnesses might be attributed to incursions from the spirit world. The "humors" related to air, bile, and phlegm. The characteristics of these three elements were used to determine the personality type and subsequently the source of the patient's condition. The imbalance might be physical or mental. Mental disorders were assuaged by spiritual practice (shaman), and a balancing of the three humors relieved the physical problems. That balance was achieved with herbal remedies and adjustments in lifestyle and diet.

Though the shaman was an archetype healer (psychotherapist) whose powers were believed to come from the supernatural, he or she did not act in his or her own name. A higher force was believed to be behind the shaman. It was not the shaman who healed but a spiritual power that was greater than humankind. The patient's belief in the shaman and faith in the healing process activated, or made real the healing process. The shaman called upon his or her spirits (helpers) to correct the imbalance and to restore order.

The Shamanic Power to Cure

Shamanism is one of the oldest divinatory practices to promote healing. The shaman often fulfilled his or her healing function by performing rituals to expel or conciliate spirits causing the illness by using cosmology to recreate a meaningful world and thereby reintegrating the patient into his or her society.[64]

According to the Siberian communities in which they lived, shamans were individuals who by submission to the will of the spirits had been cured of a grievous illness and had acquired by that means great supernatural power.[65] They were transformed. Shamanism was an attitude of mind and a psychological anomaly. It was, in addition, a cultural, historical, and ethnological phenomenon, but its psychological side must not be overlooked.[66]

The power of shamanism drew from the belief that the universe existed on, above, on, and below ground, and the authority of the shaman lay in his or her conviction that he or she could communicate with the spirits on all three levels. The shaman was considered to have the power to make contact with the pervasive forces of the macrocosm, and that paranormal ability came as a calling from beyond the realm of the visual world. It was from that calling that the shaman learned ritual practices to transmit healing energy. "In this other world the shaman [was] taught certain symbolic gestures that [were] used later in ritual activities to impart a sustaining or healing energy to individuals or the community."[67]

The shaman was believed to be a healer and psychopomp because he or she commands the techniques of ecstasy. In an altered state of consciousness the shaman's soul was thought to safely leave his or her body and to travel great distances penetrating the underworld or rising to the sky.[68] That extraordinary ability gave access to insights not available to ordinary individuals. It was in that paranormal realm that healing and diagnostic powers were conveyed. Before curing was possible, a first step in the process was diagnosing the malady and determining its source. Divinatory practices played a significant role in that procedure (see drawings 7.5. and 7.6).

The belief in the transfer of disease was common among many peoples, and it was a curing technique favored by many Siberian shamans. When the evil spirit of disease from the

7. Shamanic Divination and Curing 153

Left: DRAWING 7.5 — Bowls are often used in African divination activities. The Yoruba place sixteen sacred palm nuts in the bowl and through this medium the Ifa priests communicate with the deities to obtain insight into an individual's future. In this example, the kneeling female figures with the bowl resting on their heads and outstretched arms is a form of respect or prayer of gratitude to the divine. Most divination bowls are made of wood and have a special place in the ceremonial life of the community.

Right: DRAWING 7.6 — Luba (Congo-Kinshasa) *Kabila*, seated woman with vessel used for divination. The piece is carved from black wood. The figure with the bowl is sometimes called a "beggar-woman." The bowls are used for various purposes. Magicians are believed to use the bowls as containers for magic elixirs used to treat illness. The bowls are also placed outside the hut of a pregnant woman so passers-by can leave a gift.[9]

Lower World attached itself to a human, the shaman performed a séance to "transfer the spirit of the disease into a pair of wooden birds."[69] According to the former shaman S. S. Krivoshapkin as quoted in *Shamanic Worlds* (1997), "the birds were loons or hawks [and] as the result of the séance, the shaman made the birds fly to the celestial world, having previously transferred the evil spirit of disease into them."[70] It was believed that if the birds disappeared, the sick person would recover and that by dividing the spirit of disease into two parts it could not return. In a similar West African ritual, the sickness was transferred to two fowls (chickens) and the birds were subsequently sacrificed to *Elegba*, protector of families.[71]

In a less dramatic method although equally effective way to restore the patient's health, the Navaho medicine man (shaman or singer) used chants. Chantway ceremonies often lasted for days and included numerous chant and occasional hundreds of associated songs. Donald Sandner reports in *Navaho Symbols of Healing* (1979) that one Nightway Chant included a total of 324 songs[72] (see drawing 7.7). The songs were accompanied by dram and rattle. The sound was said to make the patient's body "come to life," and also "symbolizes pounding evil out of the patient's body."[73]

The Iban shaman (indigenous people of Brunei, a sultanate on the northern coast of Borneo) undertook treatment of disease in different ways "of which the ecstatic journey to recover a patient's departed soul was the most potent."[74] In that curing ritual the shaman traveled over water to the land of the dead in search of the patient's soul that he retrieved while in a trance, and returned it to the sick person.[75] When the Iban shaman was unsuccessful in the soul quest, the patient could seek a personal encounter with the spirits to whom "he offered food and sacrificed a cock on a solitary hillside in a graveyard."[76]

The Malay shaman cured with the help of spirits and sometimes used quartz crystals. The shaman might change into a tiger and call forth the tiger's spirit to assist in the healing process. Malay shamans dance to achieve a trance (*lupa*) during which the spirits took possession of him or her to aid in the performance of healing or divination tasks.[77] Such spirit contact was characteristic of shamanism in Sumatra, Borneo, and Celebes.[78]

The curing process among the South American forest peoples required the shaman to remove the object causing the sickness. The offending object might be a small stone, a leaf, an insect, or any substance that was sent through the black magic of an evildoer. The curing generally consisted of massages, suction, blowing, and fumigation.[79] In extreme situations where the illness resulted from loss of the patient's soul, the shaman visited the upper and lower worlds to find and recover the aberrant soul. The shaman often required the assistance of one or more auxiliary spirits to accomplish the patient's recovery, especially if the process encountered a malevolent spirit.

DRAWING 7.7—Nightway masks (*ye'-i bichai*) used in the Navajo nine-day healing process were cut and sown during a Nightway ceremonial and used at a subsequent ceremony. The buckskin masks were either head or face masks, and had to be made in a public ceremony but could not be "induced" until the following ceremonial gathering. The singer who was to use them sewed the buckskin. The Nightway ceremonial included 14 different masks representing 24 different gods. The masks were painted white, blue, red, or black according to the deity represented.

The Pueblo people of southwestern North America believed that witches cause disease, and that they could kill a person by stealing their heart, or they can send sharp objects into a person's body.[80] Pueblos had curing or medicine societies instead of a single shaman for the sick to provide relief from these threats. Pueblo communities frequently had several curing societies with each having responsibility for a different set of ailments. They treated each illness using various methods such as, bloodletting, massage, and sweating. Most curing societies received their power through the invocation of particular "beast gods," of which the bear was the most powerful.[81]

A difficulty encountered in the curing process was that Pueblo witch might be a man or a woman who instigated sickness through the performance of rituals somewhat similar to the curing rituals.[82] A Pueblo member with a life-threatening illness that resists conventional treatment might give his or her "life" to a curing society to counter this paranormal situation. The patient sought the protection of the beast god to gain relief from the malady by promising to become an active member of the society if cured. The induction of recovered patients was the primary way the societies are perpetuated.[83]

Animals also played a role in the curing process. The bear and the badger were important animal spirits in the transfer of curing and divining power among many North American peoples.[84] The Apache, however, found the ability to diagnose and cure illness in many sources. Sometimes the invisible curing power served good purposes and breathed vitality and life into things, and other times the same power was responsible for disease and death.

The Apache healing (curing) ceremony generally involved pollen "representing the life-force, fertility, and beauty. In the healing ceremony, it represented health, the condition that the patient sought to recapture."[85] The curing process required a series of activities including marking the patient and the shaman with pollen, the extraction of poison from the patient by sucking (the poison was supposedly planted in the patient by an evil shaman), imposition of dietary restriction, dancing, drumming, and feasting with the patient's family. The pollen used in these curing activities is called "*hoddentin*."[86] It is from the tulle—*Scirpus californicus Scirpus acutus*—a type of bulrush found in California and southwestern North America. The curing ceremony often lasted for three or four nights. On the second or third night the shaman checked the curing progress by pressing a mollusk shell to the patient's forehead. If the shell stuck, the patient was recovering. If the shell did not stick, the patient was likely to have a prolonged illness.[87]

The Hmong (also called Miao) shaman living in northern areas of Laos and Thailand was a roving healer. He (it was usually a male) made house calls. The shaman went wherever he found patients and his technique were usually direct and uncomplicated. He built an altar on arrival at the patient's home and began the curing process by summoning his spirit helpers. According to Jacques Lemoine in the paper titled, "The Diagnosis of Disease as a 'Shamanic Equation' among the Hmong of Laos and Thailand,"[88] the shaman always operated in an altered state of consciousness, but used no hallucinogenic drugs. The altered state was achieved by the sound of a gong being struck by an assistant and the ring-bell and rattle-sword he held. The shaman chanted in cadence with the percussion from the beginning to the end of the process as the main support to the trance.[89]

The Hmong shaman focused his attention on the diagnostic process. The explanation for that approach was based on the belief that relief followed a good diagnosis and if the relief was achieved the same shaman was called upon again to perform curing. Being in a trance was a necessary part of the curing performance, which was a reenactment of the performance the shaman employed to successfully identify the cause of the illness.[90]

PLATE 6—Portrait of the shaman "Shippin" (Always Riding), a Ute shaman, in native dress, with pouch, knife, and hairpipe choker. The photograph was taken in 1868. The Ute are a Shoshonean-speaking people of western Colorado and eastern Utah. The date of this photograph is significant because the Indian Wars were fought between 1864 and 1870. After that time most of the Colorado Ute were placed on a reservation in southwestern Colorado.

As previously noted, shamans often acquire the power to cure by having a mystical interaction with supernatural forces. Australian aboriginals believed that the healer gained the power through relations with the spirits of the dead, and that the magical rituals were exclusively "owned" by the individual and could not be used by others. In contrast, a Cheyenne might learn curing lore from an elder after having a unique dream experience, and a Shoshone shaman (also spelled Shoshoni and sometimes called Snake) obtained his or her curing power from special dreams or visions.[91] The Cheyenne placed primary importance on visions or dreams in which an animal spirit adopted the individual and granted him or her special powers.

Pursuing a practice common to other cultural groups, the Arunta, an aboriginal people of Australia, also believed the shaman accomplished the curing of illness by extracting the foreign object that was the cause of the affliction. The removal process required the shaman to suck the object from the ailing individual. The object causing the illness was believed planted in the patient's body by a magical process initiated by a vengeful shaman or witch, and should the curing shaman fail to accomplish a cure, it was assumed that the person causing the illness had greater power or stronger magic. This type of malicious affliction might require the activation of other services available to some shamans, those being the use of sorcery (black shamanism) to harm another person or to determine who was responsible for a death or illness.[92]

As beneficial as shamanistic practices might have been, not all individuals sought a healing vision or possession by the curing spirit. Writing in *Navaho Symbols of Healing* (1997), Donald Sandner states, "When a Plains Indian was visited by powerful supernaturals, he was forced to obey their dictates."[93] Sandner gives the example that when an animal occurred in the dream of a Sioux, and gave the dreamer a special song to cure certain illnesses, the dreamer had no choice but to use the song to heal.[94] Similar experiences are found in other cultures.

Visions received while in an altered state of consciousness are commonly associated with the shamanic experience; however, the Parintintin, a tropical forest culture of the western Amazon region of Brazil, believed that many of the shaman's (*ipaji*) influences on the world were only achievable through dreams. This remnant population of the Kawaib people (also called Kagwahiv) contended that shamanic empowerment was acquired through dreaming, and that the ability to communication with the supernatural world was only possible by that means. The *ipaji*, "one possessed of power" (shaman) could inflict vengeance on an enemy, cure an illness, or cause a woman to conceive a child by including the event in dreams.[95]

The Iroquois people of North America also had a strong reliance on dreams, and they carefully followed the guidance received through dreams. Whatever they did in their dreams they felt obliged to do during their waking time.[96] Mircea Eliade writes about dreams as methods for spiritual contact as practice by the Chukchee of Siberia. He states that the Chukchee shaman once woke from sound sleep "with the patient's soul in his hand and at once proceeded to restore it to its place in the body."[97]

The idea that dreams influenced life activities supported a similar belief to that of sympathetic magic. The dream was believed to act upon events from a distance through a secret sympathy with the impulse being transmitted from the dreamer to the event by spiritual intervention. Similar results were anticipated when the shaman pantomimed an action or event that was to be duplicated by a person, animal, or spirit being. It was believed that an adequate amount of passion, devotion, and belief could cause the act or event to be achieved.

Responses to Spiritual Intrusions

In response to debilitating "spirit intrusions" the shamanic healing technique involved the ability to visit the spirit world, and to negotiate a cure or recovery. This belief reflected the attitude that "[d]iseases came into the world when negative energies gained the upper hand,"[98] and that it was the shaman's role to regain control by promoting positive energy. There are contravening indications that suggest the ecstasies and trances of shamans were largely culturally influenced and carefully organized performances to achieve the desired effect. Nevertheless, to be successful shamanic healing required the ability to give form and structure to feelings emanating from events in the unseen world.

An extraordinary example of psychological intervention and an important manifestation of the shaman ability was "fertility magic." According to Andreas Lommel[99] shamans performed a special rite requesting the spirits of the earth to "fill the women with *jalyn*, the energy of the sexual urge."[100] This rite was also called "the taking of sexual passion from the spirit of the earth for men and beasts" or "the bringing down of the power of procreation."[101] The procreation of certain peoples was dramatically inhibited by psychological stress and anxiety. Biological productivity was dependent upon the mental state of individuals. The ritual conducted by the shaman was to direct the subconscious toward a positive outcome. Although the process described by Lommel identifies with Siberian people, similar conditions were found in other parts of the world. As a related example, the procreation of the Australian aborigines was said to diminish or cease altogether when their mental life was disturbed. They were said to explain this situation by saying, "We cannot dream any more children."[102]

Shaman as Intercessor

> Throughout much of the world, the capacity to heal was traditionally seen as resulting either from power or office, as by priests or king or by a sacred commission or special gift. Both of these traditions were combined in the role of shaman....[103]

The significance of shamanistic activity in a particular group requires a comparative assessment that views the culture in broad terms. Cultural identity can be described as those attributes that express the singularity of the "group," and what restricts or disallows their uniformity of thought and practice. This approach demonstrates the uniqueness of the group's heritage including beliefs, practices, and traditions. The verification of cultural values explains the societal placement within the worldview context. A group, for example, that places emphasis on the treatment by non-medical means of physical or spiritual ailments that are regarded as manifestations of evil are often categorized as "healing cults." Such cults fall into one of three types: "those centered on certain shrines or holy places, those centered on certain organizations, and those centered on particular persons."[104] In those societies where shaman existed he or she was the "center, the brain, and the soul of such a community."[105]

Methods for removing or extracting unwanted evil spirits include different shamanistic practices. One method that had extensive application was suction. The shaman identified the location the invading spirit by carefully examining the patient's body. The examination might occur in a dream, trance, or by actual physical investigation, and once the location was identified, the object was extracted by suction. The shaman "sucked out" the illness in the form of bug, pebble, thorn, small animals, or similar object, and showed it to the patient to demonstrate the success of the removal. The shaman might suck the patient's skin directly or use a hollow bone or reed. The suction process was similar to the ritual transfer of illness or wrong doing from one person to another. In some locations the intruding spirit was transferred to the shaman who then must expunge it from his or her body. The purging activity might include sweating, regurgitation, or ritual bathing.

The ideas, beliefs, and practices regarding the curing practices and spirit intrusion were generally know to the entire community, and each person of the shaman's "group" was well informed on the details of shamanic rites. The suction process, for example, might required the shaman to "spit blood" to symbolically demonstrate the severity of the removal process, whereas, in other locations the display of the invasive spirit was adequate reassurance.

The Ojibway medicine man (shaman) used the suction method to activate the curing process. He swallowed a number of small hollow bones and used a similar bone to suck the diseased object from the patient's body. He subsequently vomited all the bones into a basin of water along with a small feather, or other object such as a worm. The regurgitated objects representing the disease were visible to the patient and to bystanders.[106] The Ojibway shaman (*jessakid*) might also use a hollow bone to blow on an injured area, whereas the Zulu shaman (South Africa) used a cow-horn to blow on the injury. Shamans were also thought to recover lost souls and return them by blowing them into the patient's mouth. The more difficult curing process required the shaman to blow smoke on the patient, massage him or her, sing healing spirit songs, and try to suck out the hidden object. The rubbing that proceeded sucking was a form of massage and the sucking was symbolic bleeding or bloodletting.

The Arapaho medicine man was thought capable of sucking ghost arrows from the patient's body and swallowing them. He was believed to increase his power by retaining the objects he extracts from the patient. However, according to Åke Hultkrantz in his book *Shamanic Healing and Ritual Drama* (1997), the supernatural power of the medicine man was made evident by his ability to produce various objects by vomiting.[107]

Forms of locally applied heat as well as sucking, blowing, massage, and vapor baths while devoted to magico-religious purposes might also successfully relieve stress or anxiety. The peoples of the central plains of North America made extensive use of sweat lodges for purification (see photograph 15). In addition, medicine men and women (shamans) used pharmacopoeias, including infusions, decoctions, salves, ointments, inhalations, and enemas for pharmacologically and physiologically reasons throughout the world.[108] Some treatments were to induce a euphoric state while others addressed more basic needs.

The Cherokee, a people living in southeastern North America, believed that spiritual power was held in many physical objects. The medicine men (shamans) use a range of mystically endowed items including quartz crystals. Natural objects could be invested with mystical power in different ways such as contact with thunder, being struck by lightning or exposure to the smoke of a sacred fire.[109] There was a belief among many Lower Mississippi cultures that the spirits of animals killed in the hunt caused disease and plants could cure. Shamanic practices were closely connected with the magical and mystical worlds, but often included practical procedures such as sweating, bathing, bloodletting, blowing, sucking, vomiting, and the use of medicinal herbs.

The shaman's connection with the "other-world" was motivated by the illness of a patient or a need for information.[110] The transcendent journey to locate that information often took place in the world of dreams and visions. The shamanic quest for knowledge generally required the assistance of spirits and sacrificing was at times ordered by supernatural powers to produce the vision. Culturally endorsed practices for addressing physiological issues were not the sole responsibility of shamans. Many cultural groups had parallel positions occupied by practitioners endowed with special abilities to diagnose and treat illness. There were also tradition and myth based procedure (rituals) that endorsed the behavior of human beings. These practices were meaningful and therefore ordered.

Examples of traditional practices to address perceived physiological needs was the bleeding of genitals by Arapesh, Kwoma, and Busana youth of the central highlands of New Guinea.[111] It was believed that woman stayed healthy because of their menstruation, and that men could stimulate growth and health by bleeding. This practice was also viewed as a curative for illness. In the Amazon area of South America the Barasana claimed that women, because of the menstruation, were semi-immortal. They compared ability to menstruate to the ability to change one's skin.[112] Conversely, Gururumba youth also living in the central highland of New Guinea practiced nose bleeding and vomiting to rid them of menstrual blood and fluids thought to be sources of female pollution.[113]

> The Maya shaman-kings, scribes, artists, and others opened [pierced] their ears in order to hear the gods' oracles and revelations. They opened [pierced] their tongues to be able to speak what they had heard. And they opened [pierced] their penises in order to participate in the divine procreation of the cosmos....[114]

8

SPIRITS, DREAMS, AND ECSTASY

Rituals celebrated for and prayers to the spirits of family and place reinforced loyalty to communal virtues and authority of the elders in defending ancient beliefs and practices. In return for these prayers and rituals, the spirits offered their adherents protection from misfortune, adjudications, and divination through seers or shamans.[1]

The Soul and the Spirit

The human body was thought to live and act of its own inhabiting spirit-soul, so the activities of the world were believed to be the responsibility of other spirits. Consequently, the primordial world was believed populated by a profusion of spirits, and their presence was reflected in every aspect of human existence. Those spirit beings declared themselves in different ways. Some spirits made possible a productive domestic life and granted success in the hunt or warfare. Other spirits concerned themselves with the power and magic assigned to shamans for the practices of survival. There were also spirits that occupied rock, trees, rivers, and forests. They inhabited the sacred mountain and the cosmic tree that were common element of Siberian shamanism. Thus, it is reasonable to assume that unconsciousness, sickness, and derangement were due to the loss of the soul, and it was a regular part of the shaman's role to retrieve lost souls and to return them to their rightful owners.

Spirits were of the same nature as souls, only separated from bodies. Some physically liberated souls became demons while others acted in a different ways as tutelary guardians. Some souls lingered near the tomb or were incorporated into certain objects. They appeared to humans in the form of vapor, or as visages retaining a likeness to the bodily shape. People feared the influence of souls, so they tried to control that influence by propitiation and magic (see drawings 4.9 and 5.8).

The Chukchee, a reindeer herding people of Siberia, believed that spirits inhabits the entire universe. They contend that spirits were invisible but can easily change their appearance, size, and location. The life of the spirit was thought to be similar to that of humans. They owned reindeer, lived in encampments, hunted, and quarreled among themselves.[2] The Chukchee believed that evil spirits hunted human souls that they captured, dismembered, and consumed. Consequently a person's illness and death was the direct result of a stolen soul.

The Chukchee resorted to various amulets, incantations and rituals to counteract the difficulties imposed by spirits, and for protection against illness and misfortunes.[3]

The Chukchee reserved special place for sacred objects connected with spirit protection. Objects given particular attention were the wooden tools for making fire, the family protectors (amulets), and the family tambourine (drum).[4] The fire-making tool had a unique position in the hierarchy of sacred objects. It was a board with hollows into which the bow-drill was twisted. The hollows were considered the "eyes of the board and sound of the drill its voice."[5] Fire made by the board was believed to be sacred, and one member of the family was given protective care of the tool. There were family rituals associated with fire and care of the hearth. "According to Mongolian shamanist considerations, any fire, a family-hearth (in Mongolian *Gal golomt*) in particular, was sacred and revered as a symbol and source of good things."[6]

Each culture had a method for acknowledging the importance of fire. The Buryat believed that fire ensured a celestial destiny after death. This concept was confirmed by the belief that the soul/spirit of those persons struck by lightning flew up to the sky.[7] The domestic fire was the symbol of continuity in all North Asia. It was "kept alight if at all possible and to say, 'may your hearth fire be extinguished was the worst curse.'"[8] The hearth fire (among the Manchu was an old woman spirit) was also the agent of purification for any tainted objects.[9]

Every family had a tambourine (drum) that was used during times of festivals and special ceremonies (see photographs 19 and 20). At the time of the autumn slaughter when reindeers were killed as sacrifice, family members took turns striking the tambourine for most of the day. It was also at these special times that the shaman was actively involved in rituals to gain the protection of spirits for the forthcoming year.

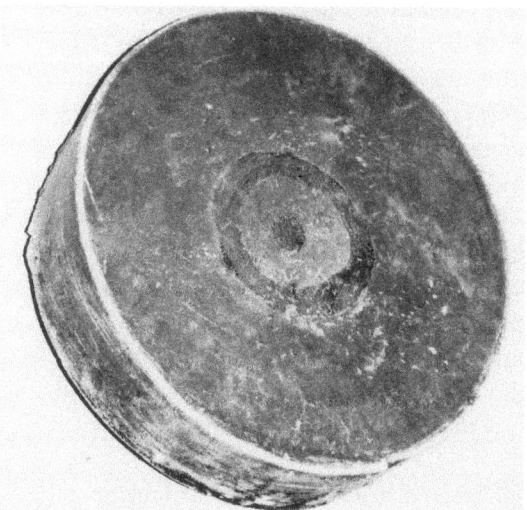 

Left: PHOTOGRAPH 19—Drum used by a female shaman. The flesh, blood, fat, and bones of animals were represented on the surface of a Sharnuud and Hullar shaman's drum by white circles and red spots.[r] This representation acknowledged that the animal should be strong and fat to become a permanent and reliable mount of a shaman's *ongon*.

Right: PHOTOGRAPH 20—The back of a drum used by a female shaman showing the cross supports used as a handle. Above the center point of the supports is a wire with rattles and bells. The outside of the drumhead is painted as shown in Photograph 19.

In Korea it was said that, "spirits occupied every quarter of heaven and every foot of earth. They lay in wait for a man along the wayside, in the trees, on the rocks, in the mountains, valleys, and streams. They kept him under a constant espionage day and night."[10] The shaman (*mudang*) was called upon to perform the appropriate ritual to support "the human will trying to maintain itself as an eternal being."[11]

In Africa, the Kamba (Amba), a Bantu-speaking people of Kenya, included a full range of supernatural spirits in their world, as well as an abundance of human spirits. It was believed that the number of spirits exceeded that of the living. Therefore, "it was difficult to systematize the beliefs of the Amba concerning this other world (supernatural) and the ritual means with which they dealt with it."[12] They resolved the soul/spirit conundrum by a lack of rigidity in their belief system. They drew no distinction within the supernatural world and referred to all such (spirit/soul) entities as *balimu*. No list of deities could be given, although there were some that were well known as those personifying "natural phenomena such as the sun, the moon, the rainbow, fire and storms, there [were] countless other spirits and new ones seemed to be constantly invented."[13] The spirits influenced every activity and object of daily life.

Among the Amba there were two types of persons involved with ritual activity. One was a male who was a ritual specialist. He was self-selected (it is not a hereditary position nor was the incumbent selected by the spirits), and a generalist with the exception of those male practitioners who were in charge of linage shrines.[14] (A similar practice was found among peoples in Siberia. Among the Daur Mongols, the ritualist was called *bagchi*.[15]) The second group involved with rituals was women that had been "caught" by the spirits. Those individuals were usually "caught" when they were outside their homes doing domestic activities. It was believed that when a woman came into contact with the spirits she became ill. She fainted or had a feeling of dizziness, and in some instances visions and a trance-like state occurred. A "priestess" (healer) was called to "heal the patient" by "putting the god on her head" and "bringing it into the home."[16] That set of circumstances was not unlike that of Eurasian peoples and the selection of shamans. Illness and recovery (resurrection) were common initiatory themes.

The concept of the soul and of helping spirits in the worldview of shamanism contributed to the close relationship of the shaman with death.[17] The rituals practiced by most cultures related to the continuation of life in all its manifestations. The observances identified a concern for the prolongation and renewal of the people, animals, and lands. Closely associated with renewal was resurrection as a way of renouncing the discontinuation of life due to death. There was a dynamic contradiction in terms of death and life, and in the mysteries associated with the opposites of darkness and light or good and evil. Mystics in all cultures sought physical and mental balance through reconciliation to accommodate the connections between opposites. The opposing forces were by necessity given an equitable measure of importance to establish and maintain stability.

"According to the *Popol Vuh* [a document that was a source of ancient Mayan mythology and culture], the soul had five enemies — disease, death, stupidity, arrogance, and fear. Of the first two, one was only marginally under human control while the other was completely beyond it. The third, fourth and fifth were not."[18] Douglas Gillette wrote in *The Shaman's Secret: The Lost Resurrection Teachings of the Ancient Maya* (1997) that, "the Maya believed that disease was the whisper of death, its first hint."[19] They also considered disease to be "an invitation from the Lords of Life to engage in the miracle of turning death into resurrection, of changing non-being into Being."[20]

The humanized manifestation of the soul/spirit often assumed the form of a "ghost" that was identifiable and associated with pending disaster. The images were a contrast with life or the living (see drawing 8.1), and were a reminder to the collective memory of the people, that illness and death were conditions against which constant vigilance was required. That image was an element of socio-cultural expression and it had to be in harmony with the other parts (myths, legends, and beliefs) of the host environment (see drawing 8.2).

The Nyoro people of western Uganda considered a ghost as the disembodied spirit/soul of someone who had recently died. It was believed that the ghost might appear in dreams in the form of the dead person whose ghost it was, and subsequently the ghost made its presence known by causing the visited person to become ill.[21] A diviner (*muraguzi*) or a doctor-diviner (*mufumu*) — shaman — who was able to treat as well as diagnose the illness was needed to identify the malady caused by a ghost.[22] Adding to the complexity of that situation was the notion that the difficulty might be the result of sorcery instead of ghostly intervention. The proper treatment for ghosts was to trap or capture them and thereby to allay the power of their deleterious influence. "Different *mufumu* had different techniques for inducing ghosts

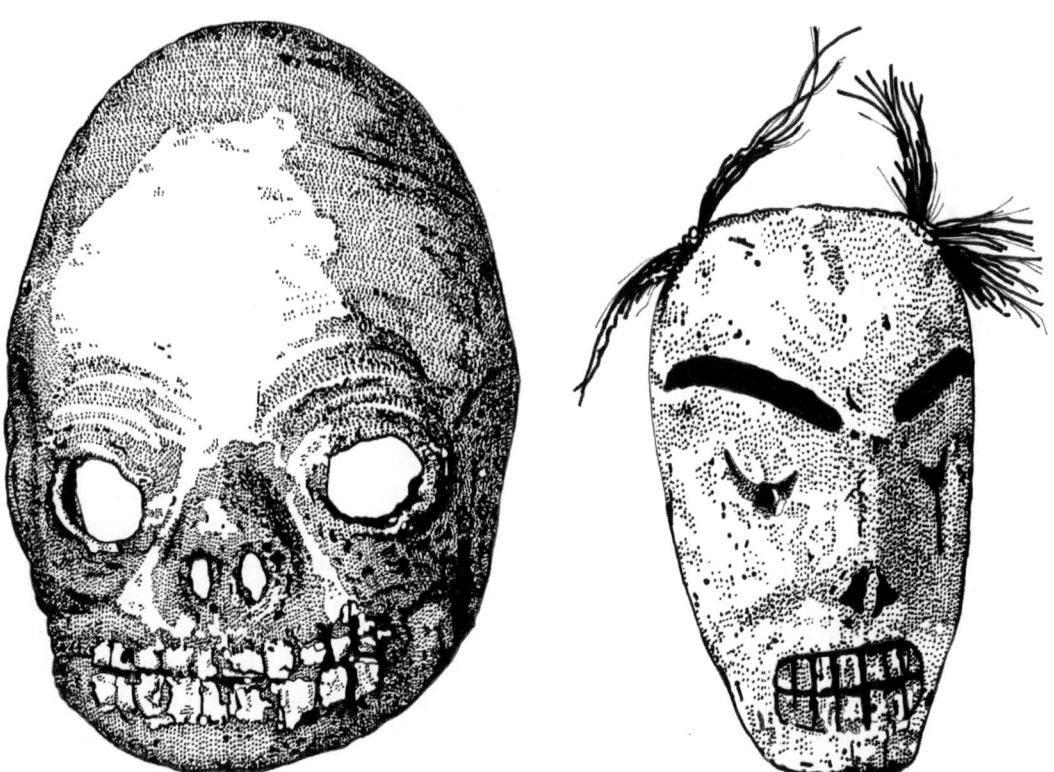

Left: DRAWING 8.1— A skull mask from Bolivia with a simple realism that was both humorous and frightening. The dead were buried with masks of gold or silver to protect them from the devil's "insidious watch,"[s] while the living wore masks representing the bones of their ancestors. Skull masks were often viewed as sacred objects through which it was possible to communicate with the dead.

Right: DRAWING 8.2— Kwakiutl ghost dancer's mask from New Vancouver Village. The mask made of carved wood with horsehair was used in association with the ***Winalagalis*** war spirit ritual. These masks had symbolic meaning to the Hamatsa secret society and their annual "Cannibal Dance."

to mount into the heads of their clients, but always the use of medicines, singing special ghost songs, and the rhythmical shaking of gourd rattles formed part of the ceremony."[23]

The soul was a complex element of human existence and belief. It was equally complicated to determine exactly how and when souls were transformed to spirits. The Tungus (Evenk or Evenki) people of Manchuria contend that the first soul was easily observed with the onset of unconsciousness. This condition might also include "traveling in dreams, communicating at a distance, and intrusion of the soul into other people, etc."[24] The movement of the first soul did not result in death unless it failed to return to its human host. The second soul was more complicated and less visible. It might be seen but only indirectly. It was believed that the soul might be seen in a mirror such as the copper disks worn by shamans. The shiny surface was thought to reflect not only the proper image of the soul but the future as it related to that soul.

The second soul was considered by the Tungus to be the principal soul, and without it the body could not be revived. Traces of this soul could be seen as it left the body on the seventh day after death.[25] "On that day at night, the Tungus put some ashes or sand on the threshold or in the entrance of [the] wigwam [sic] and see what kind of foot prints were left by the soul."[26] The footprints, if recovered, might be those of "a man, a horse, a roe-deer, a chicken, or other animal."[27] The existence of the second soul was verified by a certain minimal interaction (communication) with the living.

It was the third soul that remained with the body at death. The Tungus believed that soul remained with the body until it decomposed. The soul left the rotting carcass, but remained with the family for up to one year. At the end of that time the mourning period officially ended and the life could return to "normalcy." The surviving spouse could remarry, and the name of the dead could be spoken without fear of attracting vengeful spirits/soul. The shaman was ritually involved in all phases of dealing with the three souls. The shaman might recover souls one and two as they wander, and escort souls two and three to the lower or upper world when they left the middle world. When a Tungus died there was certain proficiency required to send the soul to the world of dead people. It was at that time that the shaman was called upon to perform a role as psychopomp and to conduct the spirits/soul to the other world.

The Ob-Ugrians, a people living mainly in the Ob River basin of central Russia believed a person consisted of a body and souls. A man had five souls and a woman four.[28] The reason for the different number of souls was not totally clear, but the fifth soul might have related to strength. One of the souls was known as the "shadow soul." It was "thought to be the most material soul and the concept of it was connected with the visible shadow cast by every object."[29] That soul, according to Ob-Ugrian belief, was "plainly visible."[30] It attached itself to a person and never left that individual. At death the shadow-soul followed the person to the grave.

Souls that did not reach the lower world became spirits (*arenk'i*) according to Tungus beliefs. Those spirits lived in rotten and hollow trees and sometimes they inhabited rocks. It was believed that they were more frequently encountered around graves and that during stormy weather their activity was greatly increased. *Arenk'i* whistled and produced echoes. They were not generally harmful to humans but were often mischievous. They sometimes threw rocks and twigs at people especially when they were alone. Those spirits were described as miserable beings. They were believed to have only skin and eyes; they were thought to have no tobacco or meat, and were always hungry. Because of their miserable conditions, the *Arenk'i* stole.³¹ Intervention by shamans was required to alleviate or counteract the activities of these aggravating spirits/soul.

The belief that the soul as spirit was quasi-physical and could exist outside the body in dreams and visions, could be transferred from one body to another, and persisted after the death and decomposition of the body was reassuring. Beliefs and deities were compressed and incorporated into forms that could be used as the need arose in the process of spiritual consolidation. Dreams and visions, apparitions in sleep and at death, revealed that the human soul was distinct from the body, and this belief was transferred to other objects. That transference/transformation made the belief system more stable as it was collectively maintained, and in that permutation, it was formalized with a hierarchical structure, systematic rituals, and predictable practices.

Concern about the unknown aspects of existence was a consuming human condition, and a great fear was that no conscious experience exists after death. Death was for many early people an archetypal metaphor or symbol for an unimaginable transformation that penetrated the barriers of the rational mind. It was a symbol for the end of one part of life and the beginning of a new life. People sought assistance from the supernatural to deal with these concerns and to provide a measure of protection against the dangerous forces of spiritual intervention. They found a measure of that aid in the forces that existed beyond the limitations of the biological body. The logic of engaging the unknown to combat the unknown seemed totally rational. It was a strategy based on belief that could only be confirmed by survival. Spirits brought either safety or calamity.

However, the spiritual pursuits of early people required no external justification or validation. As Alan Carter Covell writes in *Shamanist Folk Painting: Korea's Eternal Spirits* (1984), "the shamanist spirits in Korea should not be considered as actively good or bad, as the Western dialectic system of reasoning promulgated by Aristotle demands, but more ambivalent in nature. Spirits, who might persecute, could also help."³² It was to be expected that the spirits unless properly placated, would cause undue stress or allow disease to enter the house, but they could also be of assistance. Here again, the shaman performed the rituals to connect the natural world with the supernatural. The shaman, in that role, guided the minds of the living to an attitude of reconciliation with the unknown.

Group myths, such as those relating to spirits, were symbolic narratives, usually of unknown origin and at least partly traditional, that allegedly related actual events, and that were associated with an identified belief system. Myths were specific accounts of spirits, deities, or superhuman beings involved in extraordinary events or circumstances in a time that was unspecified but was understood as existing apart from ordinary human experience. The loss of spirits or spiritual endorsement for activities often reflected a disregard for a particular myth (practice or totem) and the results could have a strong negative effect on the people. Consequently, shamans of the Turkic people of Siberia perform rituals associated with many aspects of human life and activity. These important rituals were described as séances (*kamlanie*).³³

The Inner Regions of the Spirit World

The concept of "spirit" can be defined in different ways. The word in many cultures reflected the principle of life as associated with breath and air. Early peoples often associated

Left: PLATE 10 — Front view of an Uryankhaisk (Uryankhai) shaman in costume. The Uryankhaisk are a sub-division of the Soyot, or Tuvinian, people of south-central Russia. These Turkic-speaking people with Mongol influences lived along the headwaters of the Yenisey River. Their traditional social structure was based on a system of clans, and their traditional religion combined shamanism and elements of Tibetan Buddhism. The photograph was taken circa 1917.

Right: PLATE 11 — Rear view of an Uryankhaisk (Uryankhai) shaman in costume circa 1917. Front of costume shown in Plate 10.

the idea of breath with life. The cessation of breath was view as the loss of soul and an indication of death. The soul was also synonymous with spirit. Mircea Eliade wrote in *Shamanism: Archaic Techniques of Ecstasy* (1974) that "Several volumes would be needed for an adequate study of all the problems that arise in connection with the mere idea of 'spirits' and of their possible relations with human beings...."[34] Eliade continues by stating that "a 'spirit' can equally well be the soul of a dead person, a 'nature spirit,' a mythical animal, and so on."[35] The Dorset people, an ancient culture of Greenland and the Canadian eastern Arctic, believed animals had souls that became ghosts, and could manifest themselves as spirit beings.[36]

Shamanic thinking in most Arctic cultures evolved from a similar heritage that identified "a distant past when there was no difference between humans and animals, when they could talk to one another and even transform themselves from animal to human form at will."[37] It was also likely that because the beliefs of these ancient nomads were similar to other shamanic peoples, they believed that the personal powers of an individual could be augmented by the strength and energy of "helper spirits"[38] (see photograph 21).

The relationship between the idea of the shaman's spirit or helper spirit and the concept of soul was complex. The helper spirit, often in animal form, communicated with the shaman in a secret language, and the shaman might be transformed by mask, dance, or action into an incarnation of the helping spirit to demonstrate his or her relinquishing of the human condition. "The helper spirits in animal form played an important role in the preliminaries to the shamanic séance, that is, in the preparation for the ecstatic journey to the sky and the underworld."[39] The helper spirit was a necessary part of the shaman's entourage. It enabled the shaman to emotionally and spiritually transform himself or herself into an "animal form," or as Mircea Eliade stated, the alter ego "soul in animal form."[40]

The Guarani, a people living in eastern Paraguay and adjacent areas in Brazil and Argentina, believed that man had an animal soul that governed his temperament and his instincts and he also had a second, spiritual soul, sent by a divinity at the moment of conception. It was the second soul that allowed humans to speak, think, and have noble sentiments. After death the spiritual soul returned to live among the gods, while the animal soul wandered the earth as a ghost intent on menacing the living.[41]

"Seeing a spirit, either in dream or awake, was a certain sign that one had in some sort obtained a 'spiritual connection,' that is, that one had transcended the profane condition of humanity."[42] The importance of this spiritual interaction was found in most locations. The Lapp shaman could "only travel to the world of the dead with the assistance of his spirit helpers and there the supernatural animals, the bird and fish (in some accounts a snake) played an important role. In their shape, or in their company, his free-soul undertook the perilous journey." The vision quest performed by Native American peoples was but one example of this search for a supernatural connection. In Greenland the "possibility of becoming a fully recognized *angakkoq* [shaman] was dependent on an ability to interact with the spirits."[43] The *angakkoq* had to "go through fearsome encounters with several spirits [to be successful] and, through those encounters, be able to transform his interaction with them from that of possession to that of mastery."[44] The spirits mastered by shamans were called by different names in the Northern Tungus dialects and those terms may come from the common stem, *seva*; whereas, the Manchu used the term *vocko*.[45] Among the Goldi (also in Siberia) the word applied to such spirits was *seon*.

PHOTOGRAPH 21— Tokou Indian doctor (medicine man/shaman) in traditional dress. The individual has a bear mask suspended from his right shoulder (a possible helper spirit figure) and is holding a raven rattle in his right hand. He has a necklace of metal pieces and on his left shoulder is a row of metal jinglers. This photograph was taken in Alaska in 1899.

Spirits had different manifestations to comply with cultural beliefs. For instance, Orlando Figes wrote in *Natasha's Dance* (2002) that the Komi, a Permic-speaking

8. Spirits, Dreams, and Ecstasy

PLATE 9—A Goldi shaman and his assistant. One of the most important tasks for the Goldi shaman (Amar River region in Siberia) was to direct the memorial ceremonies for the dead and to conduct the soul/spirit of the deceased to the final location. As in the soul-loss therapy, the shaman dispatched his free soul to accompany the dead person.

people living between the Pechora and Vychegda rivers in the northern regions of Russia, believed in a forest monster called "Vörsa." These ogres had a "living" soul called an "*ort*" that shadowed people through their lives and appeared before them at the moment of their death.[46] This expression of spiritual presence was an element that reinforced the cultural identity of the Komi, and a verification of their heritage.

Mircea Eliade described spiritual activity in Malay where shamanism had distinctive characteristics that included "the evocation of the tiger spirit and obtaining the condition of *lupa*—a state of unconsciousness into which the shaman fell and during which the spirits descend on him...."[47] The Malayan shaman (*poyang*) attained an state of unconsciousness and was possessed by spirits that spoke through his or her mouth. The features of the Malayan *séance* included the evocation of the tiger; otherwise, they resemble those of the Mongol shaman. The beating of a tambourine (one-sided drum), singing (chanting), speaking and hearing the voices of spirits, and the return to consciousness oblivious of what had occurred were focal elements of the Malayan séance. The performance took place inside a round hut or magic circle (similar to the Native American practice), and the shaman wore a wreath of leaves on his or her head, and carried a branch of leaves. The "ritual" hut was darkened, and the invocations were chanted to the sound of bamboo poles knocked against logs.

The Malay *séance* like its Siberian counterpart was to cure illness, discover the locations of lost or stolen property, or predict the future. The curing ritual required the shaman to stroke the evil spirit out of a patient with the branch of leaves and shout to drive it into a cage where it was imprisoned by magic. The mythical tiger spirit was often evoked to summon and secure the assistance of the mythical ancestor, the first Great Shaman for other more complex or demanding shamanic routines.[48]

Belief in the existence of a secure environment surrounded by a dangerous world and safe from outside intrusions was symbolically represented in many cultures. The circle defined the symbolic center of the human—the soul. It also marked the ritualistic center of social order—the safe zone. The consecrated circle has been traced to ancient Assyria,[49] but it was present in many belief systems from the indigenous peoples of North American and Australia, to the inhabitants of Tibet, India, China, Mexico, Egypt, the Middle East, part of Africa, and other locations. The microcosmic, magic circle or "cosmic center" was exemplified in the sacred places of the Eastern and Western worlds (see drawing 6.2). Those locations were commonly viewed as sacrosanct and isolated from the hazard of the secular world. The sacred grove, circle of stones, wedding band, and halo were symbols of continuity, renewal, and self-containment that were a part of many societies. The circle, among the various indigenous peoples of the southwestern United States, was symbolically related to the universe and an opening was made in the design as a passageway for the human spirit to emerge, as from the womb.

People living in the Arctic region considered the sky to be a circular tent or an immense roof that covered the earth. They believed the sky was pierced with holes through which it was possible to glimpse the universe.[50] "The Yakuts [also called Sakha, one of the major peoples of eastern Siberia] believed the sky to be fashioned from an infinite number of tautly stretched skins."[51]

It was in an altered state of consciousness that the shaman had a range of powers that he or she did not possess in ordinary reality. The shaman saw spirits and souls and communicated with them, and made magical flights to the Upperworld where he or she was an intermediary between the deities and the people. The shaman also descended to the land of the dead. Those activities were believed accomplished while riding a mythical horse, traveling in a spirit boat, or being transformed into a bird. It was also commonly believed that "entering the circle" enhanced the mystical experience of being united with the gods. The circle as a universally accepted image of perfection and isolated from its surroundings, was thought to consolidate energy and provide a focus for ritual activity. "It is the most general shape, possessing the fewest individual features but serving at the same time as the matrix of all possible shapes."[52] The power of the center was a crucial source of energy employed by many peoples (see drawing 6.2 and photograph 15).

Spirit Assisted Supernatural Powers

> Journeys of the soul outside the body necessitates the cooperation of supernatural beings, therefore such voyages were carried out by professional shamans.[53]

The retrieval of the lost or stolen soul often involved complex techniques and the services of a shaman. The essence of most shamanistic recovery activities required psychic transformation powers to catch a lost soul and to reintroduce it into the owner's body. An example of this psychic transposition was the supernatural world of the people of the Sepik region in New Guinea. Their beliefs reflected a two-part mythological foundation. One part dealt with spirits living in specific locations such as water, land, and vegetation. Those spirits appeared in either human or animal form and were responsible for a number of "natural" phenomena such as storms, fast currents, and other environmental variables. The second part, the supernatural element, was associated with ancestors. Those myths relate to the creation process of which the most recent generation was the latest manifestation.[54] The former category of myths was recognized and revered while the latter is perpetuated by social interaction and exchange. The two elements were combined to form the mythological foundation for the people that established both a historical validity and a process for continuation of traditional values. Most societies depended on the two very basic concepts regardless of their status within the sociological continuum. It was when one of the elements was lost or disregarded that social order was disrupted. The validity of that assessment is confirmed by contemporary society.

The shaman's spirit, as well as spirit helpers, played a major role in the social wellbeing of the endorsing (host) community. Traditional wisdom alleged that the shaman's spirit, as well as spirit assistance, departed with his or her breath. "At birth, we inhale for the first time, at death, we exhale for the last."[55] The association of life and breath (vapor) was indisputable, therefore, many cultures believe the human "spirit" was located in the head and resided in the breath. Probably for that reason the mouth, the opening through which the breath passed, was considered in many cultures as the exit opening of the spirit/soul.

The breath had important social implication in some cultures. The Maori believe that the breath of the chief had the power to kill. Consequently, the chief did not blow on a fire. It was assumed that his breath would communicate its sanctity to the fire, which would pass it on to the pot on the fire. It followed that the breath would be passed to the meat in the pot and eventually to the individual who ate the meat. The expected outcome was that the consumer of the meat, infected by the chief's breath conveyed through the intermediaries, would die.[56]

An accepted belief was that if the spirit (breath) left the body or could be drawn from the body the person would die. A technique used to harm a person was to steal their breath —

to take their spirit away. That act of malevolence was performed in different ways. Sorcerers (and sometime shamans) in the Pacific Northwest used a long pole with cedar bark wrapped around the end. The pole was held below the victim's nose at night, and the bark captured the person's breath (spirit). It was then only a question of time before the person expired. That this technique actually produced the desired results is not verified; however, it is certain that the power of the imagination working through superstitious terrors is by no means unknown.

Spirits and shamanism were believed joined in functional as well as traditional ways. The shamans in the Andaman Islands, in the Bay of Bengal, were believed to get their power from contact with spirits, and the most common method to attain that power was for the neophyte to die and return to life. This sequence of physical alteration was similar to the death and resurrection process experienced by the shaman in Siberia and Mongolia. In addition, "...the Siberian shaman had his 'helping spirits' that may be also the spirits of his dead ancestors."[57] He or she wore on his or her coat, symbols that were to be understood as skeletons. It is also generally known that spirits were not always benevolent. When they enter people who could not master them, those individuals might lose their minds completely and parish.[58] It was thought "spirits carried on continuous war and minor quarrels between themselves and with the other spirits, which might greatly affect the people."[59] It was also alleged such wars "sometimes continued during several generations and thus the people lived under conditions of uncertainly expecting at any moment to be affected by this war."[60]

Because of the complexities of daily existence, the Koryak people of the Russian Far East relied on both professional and family shamans to meet their survival needs. The Koryak also believed the world was inhabited by a multitude of harmful being called *nin'vit's*. The *nin'vit's* were invisible most times, but they could assume anthropomorphic forms with "huge ears, burning eyes (sometimes with one eye, sometimes with three), with long sharp teeth and a body covered with thick black fur."[61] The Koryaks made sacrifices to the *nin'vit's* to placate them. The dead were believed to become *nin'vit's*, and for that reason wooden images were made to honor ancestors. Those figures were crudely shaped with no nose, two shallow indentations for eyes, and a rather large opening to represent the mouth. The mouth-hole was filled with fat or fat meat during family celebrations.

The Koryaks believed that the shaman had power over *nin'vit's*. The shaman communicated with *nin'vit's* in total darkness, and often in a state of intoxication brought about by the consumption of "prophetic fly-agarics" (the mushrooms, *Amanita Muscaria*). The shaman struck his tambourine, cried out fragmentary words and phrases, danced, and sang.[62]

The shaman of the Evenk (Evenki also called Tungus), a people living west of the Koryaks in north central Russia on the Central Siberian Plateau) uses helper spirits to protect the members of his or her clan from the evil spirits of other clans.[63] The assistant spirits were closely associated with the shaman, and after his or her death they (the spirits) departed with the shaman's soul. Occasionally, under the correct circumstances, the spirits could be "passed on" to a person identified by the shaman in a dream. It was believed that a sick person had a dream in which the shaman came and ordered him or her to become a shaman. This gift of spirit assistants could be passed to the next generation from both males and females.[64]

The Yakut people of northeastern Siberia believed that the souls of future shamans were nurtured in nests attached at different levels in an Upper World (or Cosmic) tree. Whereas for the Quechua in South America, the spirit beings selected shaman candidates and became their guides (familiars). The selection process for the Quechua could be fatal because it required the candidate to be struck by lightning three times. It was believed that the first strike killed the aspirant, the second reduced his or her body to small pieces, and the third strike reassembled the shattered body.[65] Such a ritualistic selection process involving death and resurrection was common among the peoples of Central Asia, Siberia, and parts of Africa. Alternatively, shamans (*tamararamaw*) among the Puyuma people of southeastern Taiwan receive their position (calling) from the spirits of their ancestors, and according to Josiane Cauquelin writing in *Shamans and Culture* (1993), they had no choice about being called to serve their guardian spirit (*kinitalian*).[66]

The Lapp shaman had the assistance of anthropomorphic guardian spirits called "supernatural men" and "holy-mountain men" that lived in sacred mountains awaiting the call into service. When the shaman wanted their aid, he sent for them using a bird spirit[67] (see drawing 2.10). A female spirit called the "supernatural virgin" was responsible to give the shaman water when during his calling he suffered from spirit attacks, and when his *saiva sarva* [supernatural bird] fought in a way that exhausted his power.[68]

The anthropomorphization of spirits was a common and persistent practice among early people. The deities were more approachable as well as more understandable when assigned human characteristics. However, the transformation or transmogrification was seldom complete. Often only the body was humanoid while the head was that of an animal, and in other manifestations the combination was reversed (see drawings 4.10 and 4.11). The entire persona was one of a human/animal amalgamation. This transformation was not necessarily based on the belief that the spirit being had the physical appearance of an animal, but that they embodied the characteristic of particular zoomorphic or anthropomorphic entities.

The Place of Spirits and Ancestors

> For most Indian people, sacred traditions are based on cosmologies which include certain lands, the waters, the sky above, and all the creatures inhabiting these places. So for them taking and destroying the land means destroying what is sacred.[69]

Individuals in different societies attained an altered state of consciousness (trance or non-ordinary reality) to gain direct contact with the supernatural, whether to interact with deities or spirits, or to merge the "individual soul with the Universal Soul."[70] They sought possession by a spirit or a deity or transcendence of their soul (spirit) to the land of the ancestors. In Japan, the transcendent soul was found in the practice of ancestor worship along with belief in a future life. Opposites alternately generated and succeed each other. Death followed life and out of death life was created.

As previously noted, in many early cultures supernatural practices were reserved for the designated practitioner such as the shaman, and that person attained his or her status by natural endowment, inspiration, training, or initiation. The shaman often practice healing rituals, performed divination rites, and conducted important cultural ceremonies; however, seldom were they considered to be priests in the usual sense of the term (an exception to this generality was the shaman/priests of the Maya). However, among some peoples, the shaman had a position that directly influenced the activities of the group.

It was believed that as early as Paleolithic times "shamans were thinking in broader and more abstract terms"[71] than simply giving hunters' confidence in their hunting endeavors. It was certainly possible that "shamanism was thus the oldest form of ritual activity, and was the earliest indication we have of human communities developing a sense of non-material existence and an awareness of their place in a broader environment...."[72] Among those early hunting and gathering people, daily interactions with their natural environment formed a unique world-view, and created the theoretical starting point for not only humans, but all the animate and inanimate things of the world that had souls. Consequently, shamanism is often described as a form of animism. Indigenous peoples, early hunter/gatherers, were generally animist to whom every animal, plant, and objects in nature contained a spirit to be appeased or feared.

The belief in spirits emerged from within the concept of animism and the notion that animals, plants, and inanimate things had souls/spirits. It was because spirits were feared that the shaman sought to control their influence with rituals and other forms of appeasement. Shamans endorsed a type of spiritual reverence as a means of addressing the moral (the concept of correct and incorrect acts) and social issues they encountered. Masks and other elements of shamanistic paraphernalia were interrelated elements of spirit veneration because they portrayed "spirit beings" and were often intended to represent real as well as imagined creatures (see drawing 8.3).

There was no real distinction between the animate and the inanimate to early people. Nature was alive, and an independent spirit guided every object. Spirits inhabited almost everything, and consequently, almost every object had a sacred essence to be worshiped. The mystic association of animals, plants, and natural phenomena to peoples was often on the basis of analogies or myths (decisive events in the group's past beyond the horizon of actual experience). A traditional Australian aboriginal group (clan) named for its totem divided the male members into "lodges." Each lodge was responsible for certain myths, rituals, sites, and symbols associated with one or more animals or plants as well as ancestral heroes. The myths and rituals constitute "the Dreaming" or "Dreamtime," signifying continuity of life unlimited by space and time.[73] Life for many aboriginal peoples was conceived in a circular instead of linear patter. The conditions of existence were constantly revolving around tradition and myth. There was no beginning and no end.

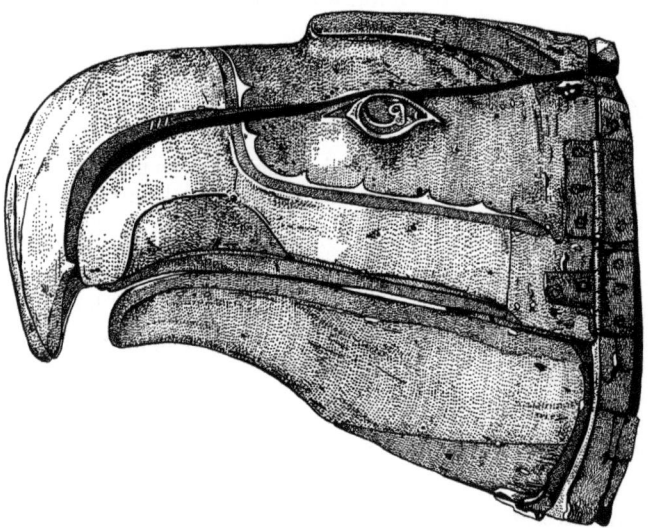

DRAWING 8.3— Kwakiutl eagle-human mask made of painted wood from the Bella Bella culture. The mask opened to expose the human face inside. It is a transformation mask probably related to the legend that the sun flew to the earth in the shape of a bird, assumed human form, and took a Kwakiutl bride. The mythological concept of creatures changing from animal (or bird) to human form was closely related to Siberian shamanism. Among most Siberian peoples, the creature that gave power to the first shaman was the eagle from the sun. The eagle was called *Aiy* (the creator).[t]

The Mongols' world was also envisaged as a circle "not only in the three dimensions of space but also in time."[74] Everything moved in a circular pattern. Belief was an ascending spiral that grew smaller at the top. It included a range of issues at the surface level and became more focused (concentrated) as it moved upward.

Shaman in a supporting environment carried messages to the deities and at other times spirits took possession of the shaman. For example, in Sumatra, Borneo, and Celebes shamanism included different forms of mediumistic practice. The spirits reportedly possessed the shaman during the trance, and in his (normally a male) persona replied to questions asked by the audience. Possession by gods or spirits was a peculiarity of Polynesian ecstaticism. The frequency of spirit possession in that region helped to generate a wide range of healers. Priests, inspired persons, medicine men, and sorcerers performed magical cures. It is not possible, for that reason, to speak of shamanism in a strict sense in Polynesia.

Shamanism was pervasive on the Malay Peninsula and in other regions of Oceania. Indo-Malayan beliefs were present throughout the region. The shaman/medicine man in the Andaman Islands ("*oko-jumu*, literally 'dreamer' or 'one who speaks from dreams'"[75]) got power from the spirits. It was common practice for the shaman to "die" and return to life. He was thereafter an *oko-jumu*.[76] The spirits were normally encountered in dreams or while in the jungle. During the séance the Malayan shamans called upon the tiger's spirit to achieve an altered state of consciousness (*lupa*).[77] The *oko-jumu* gained their reputations by "their acts of healing and their meteorological magic (they were thought to bring on storms).[78]

The shaman was a special person granted unusual abilities, however, among the Maori every warrior was considered a shaman. There was no regular shamans' caste in Samoa, but in other Polynesian groups, the shaman was the exclusive privilege of a hereditary class of nobles. Elsewhere, the gift of shamanism among the Yakuts (in Siberia) was not hereditary, but the protecting spirit of a shaman that died was reincarnated in a member of the same family. The Yakut shaman's *āmāgāt* (spirit-protector/teacher) was derived from the soul of a dead shaman and was an indispensable attribute. The shaman also acquired an *ie-kyla* (animal protector) that granted power. (The weakest *ie-kyla* is a dog, and the most powerful is a bull or an eagle.) Every person was thought to have a spirit-protector, but that of the shaman had special attributes.

The guardian spirit recognized by the Native American, from whom the novice (neophyte shaman or medicine man) derived aid, was more generally secured from the hosts of animal spirits. The guardian could also be obtained from the local spirits, spirits of natural phenomena, from the ghosts of the dead, or from a greater deity (see photograph 22).

The shaman was generally believed capable of using his or her powers to shield people and to provide a kind of protection that rendered evil spirits inactive or ineffective. The shaman's role was that of guardian to ordinary people. The Eskimos and other native people believed that all the affairs of life were under the control of hateful spirits, and that those spirits were subject to a great spirit called by some northern people *Tung-Ak,* a name for "Death." This contentious "Great Spirit" was thought to harass the living to gain control of their spirits/souls. It was also generally believed, among the northern peoples, that the shaman was the only person capable of dealing with *Tung-Ak*.

Across a range of early cultures, death and illness were understood to be the result of a loss of power that left the individual unprotected and vulnerable. Impending death might be communicated to the person so preparations should be made, never the less, the dead or the state of being dead was a constant cause for concern. Help was always needed to counteract the probability of physical debilitation.

The Lapps of Northern Europe spoke of the dead as "*jamegeh* or *jabmek*,"[79] and described them as living in the underground where they were "ruled over by a powerful old woman [named] *Jabmieakka*."[80] This realm was also where the shamans retrieved the lost souls of sick person, or things belonging to sick persons, in order to restore their health. Still, death was inevitable, and for protection against vengeful spirits, the Karo Batak shamans of Sumatra wore large anthropomorphic funeral masks with piercing eyes, darkened faces, and grinning mouths with carved teeth to transmit a symbolic message to the living as well as the dead. A similar practice existed among other societies in Polynesia. The principal participants wore "mortuary costumes" including masks during funeral ceremonies. The shaman acknowledged the passing of the spirit and the need to encourage a safe but complete transfer of the deceased to the Underworld.

Spirits were ubiquitous, and Polynesian islanders attempted to accommodate the unfriendly spirits that influenced their daily existence with the proper rituals and ceremonies. Recognition and appeasement ensured a peaceful coexistence with the most demanding spirits. The Maori were harassed by demons that were ever watchful to inflict evil, and in Kamchatka, a province in far eastern Russia, every aspect of the world was believed occupied of dreadful spirits. The Navajo, Ojibwa, and Dakota peoples, and many others in North America, contended with numerous spirits, both evil and good, that fill all space. The influence of the spirits could be counteracted only by powerful spells and charms, that could only be made after due preparation by the persons (shamans) who had power to do so.

Dreams as Divine Intervention

The conception of the human soul formed from dreams and visions served as an exemplar on which early peoples framed their ideas of other souls and of spiritual beings. Accord to J. S. Lincoln writing in *The Dream in Primitive Culture* (1935), "...dreams always fall into two very different categories. In the first category are spontaneous dreams during sleep—dreams that are thus unsought and which are called individual dreams."[81]

PHOTOGRAPH 22—Bear Bull of the Blackfoot people. The hairstyle is a sign that Bear Bull was a shaman and Medicine Pipe owner. The Blackfoot (sometimes called the Northern Blackfoot) are Algonquian-speaking people living in Alberta, Canada, and Montana. They were among the first Algonquian in the westward movement. The exaggerated topknot of twisted hair is found among a number of northern peoples. The Atsina (an offshoot of the Algonkian-speaking Arapaho), as well as Hunkpapa and Ogallala Sioux, and Blackfoot shaman were identifiable by this hairstyle. Edward Curtis took this photograph of Bear Bull in 1899.

The second category of dreams identified by Lincoln is "the sought or induced 'culture pattern' dreams of special tribal [group] significance that are called traditional dreams."[82] Also according to Lincoln, "cultural pattern dreams in each tribe conform to a definite stereotyped pattern laid down by the culture."[83] The shaman's dreams might follow either pattern. The initiatory dream might be unsought but fell within the category that could be called traditional. Dreams that focused on the activities and events of the people might be sought or spontaneous. The issue is not the correctness of Lincoln's assessment, instead it is the difficulty of attempting to strictly categorize socio-cultural phenomenon. The dream patterns of a culture appear to be consistent only when there is no outside influence.

There is, nevertheless, something mysterious in sleep that, from the earliest times, impressed humans and aroused their curiosity. Cultural beliefs about sleep came to be considered as the effect of divine intervention and as something sacred and mystical. It is likely that the mystery of sleeping was enhanced by the dreams that accompanied it. Early people were apparently unable to explain the

PLATE 14—This photograph is of "Washie," a female shaman at Fort Wingate. The Navajo woman shown in the photograph taken in 1883 is reported to be 106 years old. She is wearing a blanket and moccasins and holding what appears to be a cane. In a companion photograph of "Washie" standing, she is using the shaft and a walking cane.

concept of dreaming or to discover the causes for sleep. They observed that when awake a person could control his or her thoughts, yet when asleep they were incapable of dreaming as they wished or of controlling those dreams that offered themselves to his or her faculties. They, therefore, attributed dreams to supernatural beings invested with the power to influence the lives of humankind. It was thought that spirits could communicate with humans through dreams. Hence, the belief evolved that individuals favored by frequent dreams were sacred and chosen intermediaries between the gods and humans.[84] The perspective of dreams and dreaming includes the concept of dreams as "intentional messages, i.e. culturally defined means of communication," or as cultural systems composed of interconnected symbols.[85]

Dreams allowed the individual to transcend time and space, as well as the limits of the body and rational logic, and thereby to gain access to the supernatural. The Maya believed that the "dreaming places" were where shaman/kings and shaman/priests were transformed into their "*uayob* or animal spirits."[86] Dreams also affected the mind by identifying a location where the shaman/priests were believed to have extraordinary perception and special relationships with supernatural forces. The Mayan supposed that the shaman/priests could enter the "Black Dreaming Place" through a portal in the head (mind) of the humanlike (anthropomorphized) god.[87]

Dreaming, a hallucinatory experience that occurred during sleep has "since the dawn of human history given rise to myriad of beliefs, fears, and conjectures, both imaginative and experimental, regarding its mysterious nature."[88] For instance, when a Dyak, an indigenous peoples of southern and western Borneo, dreamed of falling into the water, "he supposed that this accident had really befallen his spirit, and he sent for a wizard [shaman], who fished for the spirit with a hand-net in a basin of water till he caught it and restored it to its owner."[89] As a further example of the great concern attached to sleep and dreams, the *Minangkabau* of Sumatra believe that it was dangerous to "blacken or dirty the face of a sleeper, lest the absent soul should shrink from reentering a body thus disfigured."[90]

> Dreams thus appear to be the continuation of life under another form, on a plane that makes possible communications and contacts with distant invisible beings, with those beings, that is who purse their life in a changed form or in other abodes.[91]

"The experiences of people in dreams were regarded as proof of the existence of spirits."[92] There is an ancient belief that dreams predict the future, and a person may be severely punished for awakening a sleeping person in some cultures. The Eskimo of Hudson Bay believed that during sleep the "soul" left the body to live in a special dream world. They considered it dangerous to wake someone for fear that his or her "soul" would be lost. The Macusi people of Guyana believed that dream events were identical with reality, and in Borneo if a man dreamed that his wife was an adulteress, her father must take her back. Kurdish people were traditionally expected to take a thing of value after dreaming of it, and Kamchatka man (in eastern Russia) need only an intimate dream of a girl for her to owe him her sexual favors.[93] On the other hand, when an Asante (people of south-central Ghana) had an adulterous dream, it could lead to an adultery fine.[94]

The "festival of dreams" was an Iroquois celebration to acknowledge the new year. The people wore disguises and went from home to home smashing whatever they found. It was a time of general license when everyone was "out of their senses" and not responsible for their actions. The people were seemingly allowed to do anything that had entered their dreams and the only way to avoid the mayhem was to guess the dreams. The festival included a general confession of sins (dreamed or real), as a means of expelling evil influence and removing the burden of guilt.[95]

The interpretation of dreams was probably one of the oldest and most widespread forms of divination.[96] Envisioning dreams as curative energy was a very ancient practice dating at least to Egypt of the second millennium before the current era. The prophetic dreams in early Middle Eastern cultures were often combined with activities such as animal sacrifice to heal the ill and dying. "Dreams were the object of religious incubation, the practice of sleeping within the precincts of a temple in order to receive a vision from a god who would reveal a remedy for an illness or give an oracular response."[97] This procedure was open to all persons except those subject to pollution taboos. Dreams were directly associated with healing in classical Greece, and ailing people came to dream in temples where priests explained the cures dreams were thought to provide. There were more than 600 temples to the gods of medicine where suffering petitioners performed rites or sacrifices to dream the appropriate dream and thereby to be granted a divine cure.[98]

The Maori of New Zealand also assigned great importance to dreams. They believed that the spirits lived an independent existence in a dream world that was regarded as real.[99] Among many peoples the dream was given a status of reality but that did not necessarily imply that the two were indistinguishable. The dream, in some instances, might be differentiated from reality, but dreams often gave special status to the activities of daily existence. The Ainu people of Hokkaido, Sakhalin, and the Kuril Islands of Japan considered dreams to be manifestations of the sacred. They believed that dreams were essential to determine the course of activities in general and especially for matters relating to subsistence.[100] The most inspiring dreams were thought to be "true" dreams that carry an important message. What the dreamer believed was envisioned and what was seen was believed. A similar condition existed for the *Chepang* people of Nepal. Dreams played an important role in the practices of the Chepang shaman (*pande*) who did not recognize any form of earthly instruction. Their teaching was provided by supernatural beings and transmitted through dreams.[101]

Dream divination so influenced the daily life of pre–Islamic peoples that the practice was forbidden by Muhammad (c. 570–632). The most confidence in so-called message dreams is found in ancient literature. A deity might appear to the dreamer (shaman/diviner) in times of crisis to transmit a message. The meaning of the message conveyed in those dreams was sometimes obvious and unmistakable, as when the circumstances were plainly revealed. Those dreams often foretold some coming event. However, the meanings of other dreams were unclear, because they were presented as symbolic encounters narrated by enigmatic utterances. The significance of dream in those instances depended on the interpretation, and the meaning and importance attributed often varied. In cultures where dreaming was important, the task of interpreting was associated with diviners, wizard, or shamans because many dreams provided no clear message.

The Eastern Woodlands shamans of North American had a power to cure that was conveyed in a vision or dream. Dreams indicated not only the causes of illness and the means to cure, but also the ways of maintaining good fortune in different aspects of life. So much attention was given to dreams that, among some indigenous peoples, the children were asked in the morning if they had dreams the previous night. Dreams were to be cultivated as a way of understanding and of bringing to consciousness knowledge stored in the unconscious, including knowledge as to where one's greatest abilities lay. Dreams were thought to indicate whether an individual had special capacity in warfare, hunting, or other necessary skill.

Dreams That Predict the Future

Dreaming was, for many early people, the real experience of the soul while the body slept. Self-introduction of spirits was a common phenomenon among the Tungus.[102] According to Sergei Shirokogoroff writing in the book *Psychomental Complex of the Tungus* (1935), "the self-introduction of spirits was based upon the firm conviction of the Tungus that (1) the spirits existed; (2) the spirit might enter the body; (3) the spirit might act when introduced."[103]

The Evenk shaman's dreams were interpreted and communicated to his or her animal-double or ancestor-spirits described as "mythical beings of a dual nature—half-animal, half-human...."[104] The interpretation of the shaman's dreams often defined the construction of the "shaman's tent" (*shevenchedek*) used in ritual activities (see drawings 4.1 and 6.2).

The Australian aboriginal believe that what was given by the gods could not be changed and that the past existed in an eternal present. It was the past that related the individual and the landscape to the continuing spiritual influence of "the Dreaming." The Aboriginal people also believed that the mythological past was a time when the existing natural environment was shaped and humanized by ancestral beings. Faith of that nature meant a steadfastness of belief. It also defined faithfulness, whether of the spirits toward humanity or of humanity toward the supernatural. As signifying people's attitude towards the spirit world, faith was construed to mean, "to believe." It was therefore reasonable to conclude that faith was analogous with the concept of belief, because humans tended to put "trust" in a person's (shaman's) activities based on previous claims to such confidence.

For the indigenous people of southwest North America, objects, places, and events radiated a power that affected the mind and promoted an understanding that certain emotional responses like beauty and happiness were synonymous. Traditional Pueblo ceremonialism reinforced that belief through its preoccupation with maintaining harmony in the universe. Everything was significant and everything significant was alive. All things combined into a rhythmic and interlocking web,[105] and as a part of that ordering, there was a commonly held belief that there was more to the universe than was seen or known. That conviction emanated in the distant past and was not limited by time or circumstances (see drawing 8.4).

Dreams may occurr in a random fashion or were guided by emotional response and subconscious thoughts; however, symbolic activity was believed to be a central influ-

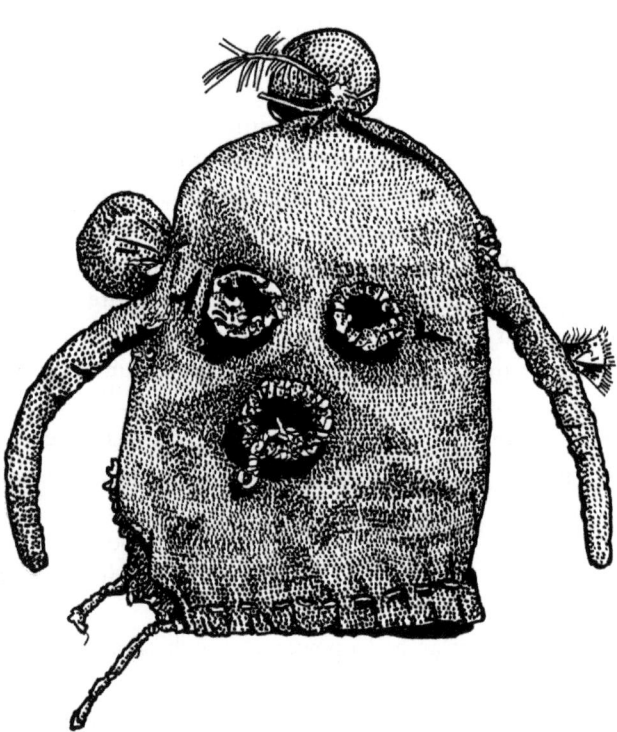

DRAWING 8.4— There are more than 500 divine ancestral spirits to act as intermediaries between humans and gods in Pueblo Indian beliefs. Each culture (tribe) had distinct forms of veneration. Ball-on-head (*Koyemshi* or Mud head) masks were made with bags filled of dirt scooped from the streets. Dancers wore them during ritual events. The bodies of the ten *Koyemshi* performers were coated with mud or clay that gave them an "other" world appearance. Reportedly, the first *Koyemshis* were the result of an incestuous relationship between the son and daughter of the Sun Father. The first progeny of this union was reported to be normal and is considered the ancestor of makers of rain. The following nine siblings were believed to be insane and deformed. They "eat filth," have ritualistic intercourse, or beg for food. These activities were viewed as the fruitful process of nature.

ence. Regardless of the initiating authority, people assigned creditability to the psychic activity. However determining the place of that activity in a personal system of waking behavior was too difficult for most individuals. Fantasy and perceptions were not indistinguishable, and although there were cases of such confusion, both were of equivalent value and both were regarded as forms of objective reality.[106] To say "a dream has broken" summarized a complex set of circumstances that were for the people of Nepal impossible to untangle.[107]

Ecstasy and Psychic-Transformation Powers

> In Okinawa, spirits notify the future shaman through visions and dreams; most of the recipients who are "called" try to ignore their summons, but eventually succumb to the spirits' directions.[108]

The shaman's task in many cultures, from the holistic perspective, was to open the way to the supernatural powers through the medium of ecstasy.[109] The shaman's power as a mediator was based on the belief that he or she alone was equipped to serve the interests of society on an ecstatic level. The Yakut had many supernatural spirits that were both benevolent and malevolent. They believed that black shamans dealt with evil spirits and could be harmless or harmful, whereas, white shamans were concerned with spiritual intercession on behalf of humanity.[110] The ecstatic capacities of Eskimo shamans enable them to take spirit journeys to any region of the cosmos. The shaman always had his or her feet, or feet and hands, bound with strong rope before the journey to ensure they travel in spirit only. Should they travel in body as well as spirit, they might be carried into the sky and vanish forever.[111] "Securely tied, and sometimes separated from the rest of those present by a curtain, they began [their journey] by invoking their familiar spirits; with their help they left the earth and reached the moon or entered the depths of the earth of the sea."[112]

A primary purpose of shamanism was "to establish means of contact with the supernatural world by the ecstatic experience of a professional and inspired intermediary, the shaman."[113] The Lapp shaman was reportedly able to enter into a state of ecstasy at will. This capacity was said to be his specific endowment.[114] The ecstasy (altered state of consciousness) was an important but highly varied element of shamanizing. Ecstatic behavior, however, might exist on different conceptual levels, because of the diverse means for initiating the altered state of intellectual and emotional consciousness. Shamanic ecstasy was at times regarded as "a symptom of a pathological state and at [other] times as 'cold-blooded' playacting."[115] One of the difficulties with understanding or verifying an "altered state of consciousness" was the varied forms it might take. Some forms of ecstasy could be explained as physical-psychic changes while other manifestations were more closely aligned with concepts emerging from the host culture or social order.

Shamans employed different techniques to serve the people, however, ecstasy — union with the divine — was believed to be an essential element of their repertoire. Various and often unique means were used to achieve ecstasy. Some shamans danced to achieve a desired state of mental expansiveness. The whirling dervishes, a Muslim Sufi sect attained a hypnotic state and ecstatic trance through ritual recitation and such physical exertion as whirling and dancing.[116] Other shamans depended on drugs such as peyote, mescaline, hashish, and similar stimulants or sedatives to achieve a state of ecstasy. The *Mudang*, Korean shamaness, sang and danced to gain access to the spirits.

"The Lapp's ecstasy transplanted him [the shaman] into the world of the supernatural

... the deeper the ecstasy, the further was the shaman's penetration of this other world."[117] It might be that the shaman's trance was proof that the Lapps considered their gods, spirits, and ghosts as belonging to a supernatural world. However, Bäckman and Hultkrantz wrote in *Studies in Lapp Shamanism* (1978), "many actions of the shaman had apparently nothing to do with ecstasy at all."[118] According the Bäckman and Hultkrantz the Lapp shaman performed many functions in a normal state of mind depending on his (normally a male) knowledge, skill, and authority.[119]

Songs and chants were often elements of the ecstatic experience, and a part of the ritual process whether a healing rite or a request for a successful hunt. Navaho songs and chants told stories about mythological characters including heroes and heroines from the distant past. The "singers" also told about when men and animals spoke the same language and shared the same land. The narratives were frequently accompanied by the drum and rattle. The rattle, made of gourds or animal hides, was a distinguishing feature of the [Navaho] chantways. Drumming was done on an inverted basket that commemorated the drums used by the supernatural.[120]

The ceremonial singers (*abisuas*) of Cuna people living in Panama performed rituals that included healing song to aid a person that was physically or mentally ill or when a woman was having difficulty giving birth. The healing songs were complex and difficult to master. "The shortest healing song lasted about one hour, the longest — the song of the dead — took about fourteen hours to perform...."[121] The Cuna gave great attention to preventing disease. When a dream was determined to be a premonition of sickness, the shaman might recommend medicinal baths. "Fifty spears carved from black palm trees were placed in a water-filled canoe for this ritual. In addition powdered wood was placed in the bath to cleanse the dreamer's eyes."[122]

By falling into ecstasy, the shaman communicated directly with the spirits and displayed supernatural strength and knowledge as their mouthpiece. The shaman played the role of an intermediary between man and the supernatural, speaking for the humans to deliver their wishes and for the spirits to reveal their will.[123]

A shaman was believed to have immediate interaction with gods and spirits. He or she saw them, talked with them, prayed with them, and implored them — but the shaman did not 'control' more than a limited number of them.[124] The Sami shaman

PLATE 21— Shaman's drum from the Lapps. The painting on the drum is divided into the three levels: upper, middle, and underworld representing the spiritual realms of the shaman. The illustrative design includes animals as well as humans in all three levels of existence.

(*noaide*) had the authority to control his ancestor companion (*gaddse*) and his power-animal (*salvo*) while those without shamanic power served as a medium that passively received messages from the spirits that in many instances were ancestor spirits from the kingdom of death.[125]

I. M. Lewis wrote in *Ecstatic Religion: A Study of Shamanism and Spirit Possession* (1989) that, "shamanism and spirit-possession regularly occur together."[126] However, the shaman imitated the spirits in a trance of varying depth during shamanistic activities, and sometime exerted a hypnotic influence on the audience, suggesting their acceptance of spirit possession. Those alleged possessions might have been nothing more than genial imitation, nevertheless, in some cases, the step between imitation and experienced possession was very slight, and the latter took place. As with most aspects of shamanistic practice belief in spirit possession had to be endorsed by both the shaman and the audience (community) to be effective and socially fulfilling.

9

TRANSFORMATION AND SHAPE-SHIFTING

Belief in transformation was associated with the practice of journeying into the land of the spirits. That transitory act did not presume that the person became a spirit/deity, but that they passed beyond the mirror (the barrier between worlds) and entered the space occupied by spirits.[1]

Just as certain persons are consecrated, specific places are designated as the "gate of heaven." The transformed shaman were, in traditional societies, not simply an individual granted certain responsibilities; they were reflections of the sacred essence of life, and their actions and pronouncements were believed to be communications from the divine sphere. In this context, shamans were granted their special powers.

Much of communal life was about transformation, and celebrations were held to mark the changing of the seasons, major events in the lives of the people, and the beginning or ending of a cycle. Similarly, the human body was stretched, painted, pierced, and mutilated to mark the transformation from one status or condition to another. Self-mutilation was a form of transformation intended to enhance people's lives by "altering the contours of nature." Some methods of alteration including distention were common to many cultural groups. The practice of physical modification included piercing ear lobes and other parts of the body and the attachment of all types of ornaments. Lips, breasts, and buttocks were increased or reduced to accommodate fashion. Male circumcision is the most pervasive form of self-mutilation in the world. Belief and tradition dictated the requirement for physical modification and adornment. Often the expectations of a particular cultural conformity were spiritually motivated and non-compliance was thought to promote disastrous retribution.

The world, from the beginning, was thought inhabited by a profusion of spirits, and their presence was reflected in every aspect of human existence. Those omnipresent spirit beings declared themselves in different ways. Some made possible a happy and productive life. Others granted success in the hunt or warfare, and others concerned themselves with the power and magic assigned to shamans for the practices of communication and survival. Everything that resided in the natural world occupied by humankind possessed some form of associated power that emanated from the supernatural. The shaman was the intermediary to deal with the complex interaction between those distinct yet closely joined aspects of the natural and supernatural worlds.

Belief in the paranormal is considered to be as old as humankind. It offered an acceptable explanation for unpredictable occurrences that were beyond human control and comprehension. Although the materialistic values of an evolving society were formulated on systematic rationale, belief in the supernatural had a far greater influence on the lives of humans. No other force was even remotely equivalent to the impact upon the existence of individuals and communities as that generated by endorsement of the transcendental world. The supernatural could be both astonishing and terrifying because it supported the notion that life as a transcendental concept, not just material embodiment, had meaning.

Belief in the supernatural is one of the greatest of human institutions. As previously stated, no societies have been encountered that did not include some form of expression dedicated to belief in the supernatural. It occupied a central role in the beliefs of people from the earliest limits of history. How far back into time such beliefs may go is a matter of speculation, but evidence indicates that as early as c. 10,000 years before the current era, ritual activities were a part of human culture.[2] Research supports the opinion that 100,000 years ago ritual references suggest a concern for the afterlife of the dead — a conscious recognition of the supernatural.

Transformation as the "Rites of Passage"

One of the most significant occurrences in a group's (tribe, clan, extended family) communal life was the birth of a child. The continuation of life and the perpetuation of group tradition often depended on the successful birth of the next generation. Magical and shamanic activities had for that reason an important role in the birth and the well being of the child and mother. As an example, the expectant mother in British Columbia inserted an eel or other slippery object under her garment at the neckline, permitting it to slide to the ground to symbolically ensure a quick and successful childbirth.[3] Shamans in Southeast Asia and Indonesia dressed as women to simulate successful delivery.

Shinto rites of passage in Japan require the newborn child to visit the tutelary *kami* (spirit/deity including the forces of nature) in 30 to 100 days after birth to initiate the baby as a new adherent. That event was reinforced by the *Shichi-go-san* (Seven-Five-Three) festival, the occasion for boys of five years and girls of three and seven years of age to visit the shrine and to give thanks for the *kami's* protection.[4] The *shintai* is the "god-body" in Shinto religion and the manifestation of the *kami*, its symbol, or an object in which it resides such as a mirror. Although not defined as shamanistic, the practice has obvious symbolic connections with the early shamanic practice that traveled south from Siberia and Mongolia to China and Korea and subsequently to Japan. The *kami* are similar to the Masters of various natural elements, both animate and inanimate, as found in Siberian shamanism.

"The idea that life falls into a fixed number of distinctive periods — infancy, childhood, adolescence, young and old adulthood, senescence, and finally death — is far from obvious."[5] The ritual transition between life stages was critical to humans but was not a practice found in other creatures. Conversely, "no reliable observer has ever described a human society that did not have some ceremonial ways of making such transitions."[6] The movement between life stages seems routine, but for early peoples, each step in the process involved a special challenge that had to be anticipated and overcome. The shaman often had a role in such transformations of status.

The transition from youth to adult and adult to old age has a complexity that is difficult to explain, as are other aspects of human existence. Life to death and life after death are transformational issues that occupy the thinking of contemporary society much as they did in ancient times. The transformation of a living and active member of the community into a dead body has mystical implications that require explanation. The birth of a child is the transformation of a seed planted within the body of a woman into a living person. It was a process that required special knowledge, and the shaman was called upon to provide mystical and cultural understanding at critical times in the life of individuals as well as the community. Transitional or transformational events change the lives of people thereby altering the present and the future of the family and group.

The rites of passage are frequently viewed as being divided into three separate and distinct phases: separation (removal from a fixed place or time in the social structure), transition (a position between the past and the future and a position of vulnerability often associated with death or the darkness of the womb), and reincorporation (emerging into the light of a new life often with a new name, an altered appearance, and a new role in the community). Such changes caused group instability. Therefore, the primary sociological function of rites of passage was to foster a new state of equilibrium, to restore social order and thereby to confirm the society as a system of harmonious parts.[7]

The "rites of passage" (a phrase coined by French anthropologist Arnold van Gennep in 1909) had an important role in symbolically and psychologically reinforcing social continuity and allaying personal anxiety. The rites assured the successful intervention of humans in the activities of the universe. The shaman reinforced the transitional process by performing the proper ritual to remove the transgressions of the people, conveyed the dead to the other world, and ensured the birth and successful maturation of a child. Shamanism and magic were recurrent elements in the ritual events that assured the successful outcome of the sociological exercise. Those communally necessary activities were to relieve stress and the anxiety associated with times of transition or transformation. Prayer is used in orthodox religion to request the assistance of the supernatural in similar events, and it is common to "promise" forms of self-sacrifice for a granted request — applied magic and superstition.

A person reaching a transitional time such as moving from childhood to adulthood might receive a new life by the death of his or her earlier self after a series of ordeals designated an initiation ceremony. The neophyte in transition was neither living nor dead from one perspective and both living and dead from another. The transitional beings had nothing "no status, property, insignia, secular kinship, clothing, rank or position...."[8] The transitional ritual often included severe conditions to demark the end of one "state of being" and the beginning of another (see drawing 9.1). The ritualization of this process often involved secret ceremonies. Antagonists, wearing masks or other forms of ritual paraphernalia frequently tormented the neophyte with threats of symbolic death. The rebirth following a series of demoralizing acts was analogous to the hero's successful fight against cruel or evil beings. The initiation ritual frequently followed the mythic narration of group or clan predecessors. Group members with zoomorphic attire reminded the initiates of his or her true beginning, as opposed to the apparent biological origin.

In all societies, preliterate and literate, there were recurrent rites of passage (transformation) that were connected with the critical events of in the human life cycle — birth, attainment of physical maturity, mating and reproduction, and death.[9] In many locations the "disembodied spirit" of the person was also an essential element in the communal ritual practice. Countless stories (myths) exist about the origin and transformation of animals, plants, humans, and other elements of the world. The shamanic activities were often considered in terms of transformation. During "possession" ecstasy the shaman's body was possessed by the spirit — he or she was transformed into an agent of the spirit; whereas, in "wandering" ecstasy the shaman's soul departed to travel into the realm of the spirits. The body of the shaman was transformed in both of these ecstatic states. The changes might be visual in the form of quivering, raging, struggling, and falling unconscious, or the shaman's body function might decrease to an abnormal level — a near death experience.

Animal and plant transformations played a significant role in locations where the social order was temporarily altered or revised, such as during the rites of passage. Transformation, in that time of social revision, exemplified both positive and negative energy and the presence of spiritual power. Prominent in transformation tradition was the Greek god Dionysus, who could assume vegetable, animal, or human forms at will. He was a god of dramatic manifestations and whose devotees, through orgiastic rituals, advocated the vitality and fecundity of primordial chaos.

Transformation and Transference as Belief

"Shamanic thought postulates a distant past when there was no difference between humans and animals, when they could talk to one another and even transform themselves from human to animal form at will."[10] Robert McGhee writing in *Ancient Peoples of the Arctic* (1996) states that, "The transformations and communications are thought to occur in the present under special circumstances, such as in a dream or when a human soul journeys to one of the other planes of existence, where the animals live as humans do in the mid-world."[11]

Shamans in many early cultures were believed to be "healers, seers, and visionaries who mastered death."[12] The shaman often interacted with the supernatural in an animal guise to fulfill their unique role in an increasingly complex cultural setting. Along the Northwest Coast of North America, animal and bird masks symbolize the transformation of humans to animal forms. These masks, as symbolic references to the duality of the human subconscious, often opened to reveal the human face inside — the coupling of two life forms (see drawing 9.2). Other articles of shamanistic regalia included animal headed human figures (see drawing 2.8), and a variety of creatively and at

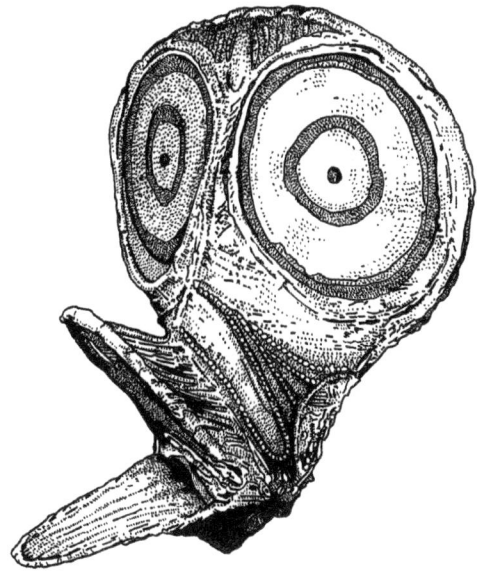

DRAWING 9.1— Bird-form mask from New Britain made by stretching bark cloth over a palm-wood form. These masks were used for social and secular occasions but most likely were originally used for strictly religious (spiritual) purposes. They represented supernatural spirits and often had bizarre and asymmetrical shapes. The large eyes were said to represent those of an owl.[13]

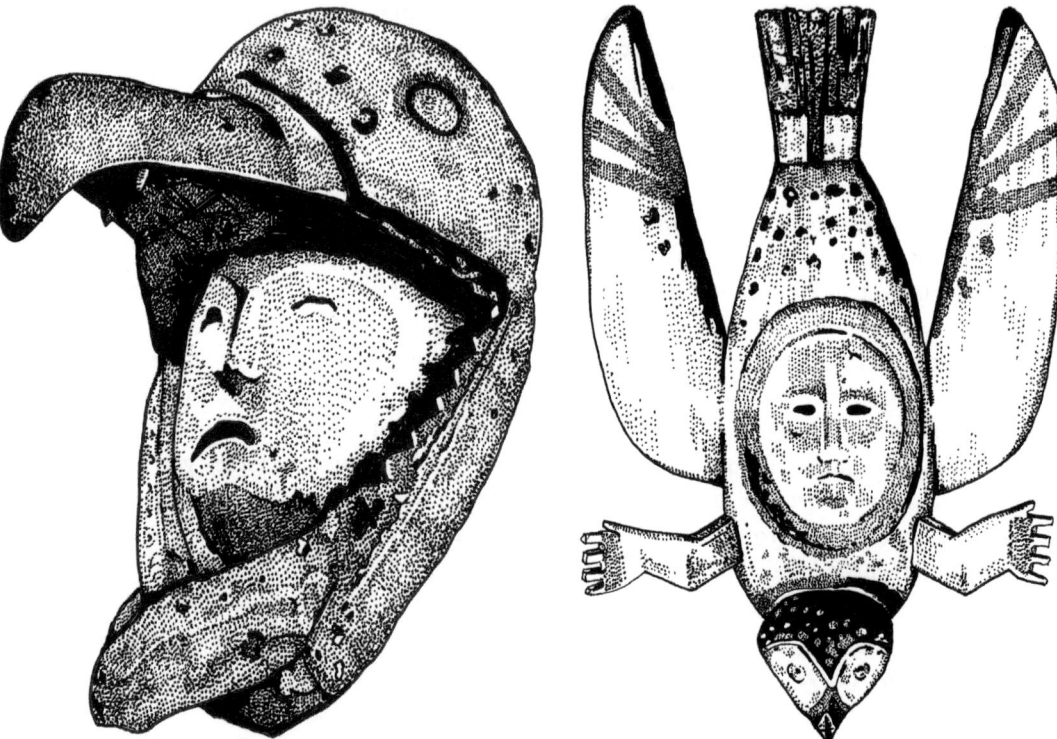

Left: DRAWING 9.2— Carved and painted mask of a supernatural bird with a human face visible through the open red-painted beak. Shaman masks similar to this were popular from Cape Prince of Wales to the Aleutian Islands. The spirit (human) peering from the bird's mouth emphasizes the transformational abilities of the shaman.

Right: DRAWING 9.3— Carved wood mask from Kashunuk, a village site at the mouth of the Kashunuk River. The mask (*yua*) represents an owl with its human spirit mask on its back.

time grotesquely joined animal and human elements. This joining of human and animal forms was more that a combining of images (see drawing 9.3). It represented a spiritual commingling of natural and supernatural elements. It emphasized the certainty that in shamanism spiritually bolstered ideas of the "real" world acquired a unique character. Many of those objects were derived from supernatural experiences as helper or totem beings and had meanings known only to their owner.

At an early time when humanity was at the mercy of the extraordinary powers of nature, shamanism sought to divide the paranormal forces into matter and spirit. Thus, external challenges were encountered on a psychological level instead of on an intellectual one. Transformation and transference were interrelated parts of the process of subversion because they included the involvement of "mythical or spiritual beings" that were believed to verify the heritage of the people.

The shaman's transformation was sometimes made more vivid by the use of paraphernalia to represent his or her familiar or to alter his or her persona. Such transformational practices were common elements in myths, rituals, and beliefs, as well as shamanistic behavior. The real and the imagined, invisible and visible, mundane and spiritual were but examples of the transformational elements that give substance to myth and group tradition. References to life transformed by death and dismemberment, transformation of male to female (and vice versa), and the changing roles of the sexes were common to many cultures. The processes of change found in the context of natural and human activities fascinated all people (see drawing 9.4). Tentative issues, the uncertain and vague, influenced the existence of all people regardless of their social, economic, or intellectual development.

The shaman might transform his or her physical appearance with the use of masks, animal skins, and related paraphernalia that included claws, teeth, and an array of symbols. This form of transformation was illustrated in the cave paintings at AltaMira (see drawings 2.6, 5.3, and 6.1), and other locations. Those practices possibly gave credibility to many ritual activities. A similar transformational practice occurred among the people of the Northwestern Coast of the North America where masks were worn that opened and closed to reveal or cancel the human image within the animal guise. The ploy was obvious but effective in delivering the requisite message to the audience (see drawing 9.3).

Gender was an issue of transformational complexity. Men in New Guinea social groups were anxious that they might become pregnant and thereby becoming feminine. This concern was based on myth and the persistent issue of procreation. Whereas the Mambai of East Timor are said to believe that semen is responsible for the bones in fetal development and also the source of breast milk.[13] This belief called to attention the need to preserve seminal output to ensure strong well-nourished prodigy. There was also a myth held by the Arapesh, a Sepik River people in New Guinea, that man taught women how to have babies by vaginal delivery. The myth explained that until the instruction provided by man the only way to deliver was by slitting open the abdomen of the woman.[14] Humans feared what they do not understand, and were particularly concerned about those activities or events that transform one circumstance or condition into another.

Although these attitudes did not specifically call upon the powers of the shaman to regulate either the beliefs or the practices, they demonstrate the diverse forms of uncertainty that influenced the lives of early peoples. The physiological and psychological complexities associated with daily existence challenged traditional existential practices adding uncertainty and insecurity. Transformation of the ordinary — mundane — into the extraordinary gave greater importance to socio-cultural activities and supported the creation of ritual events that could be controlled by designated intermediaries (shamans).

A form of transformation that had critical shamanistic orientation was the opening of

DRAWING 9.4—"*Tullukarokaak Kinakut*" (imitation raven mask) made of wood with raven feet attached to the forehead and a raven's head sticking out of the mouth. Raven, the Creator, was known throughout Alaska, but the Yup'ik infrequently made raven masks. This mask is an interesting combination of human-formed and modified natural objects.

the mind to know things not known to others. This transformational practice demonstrated that similar trends of thought have influenced communities so diverse that they might belong to different worlds. Opening the mind to greater understanding or knowledge—enlightenment—was an inherent element in many belief systems. The mystical concept of transformation provided the means for humans, plants, and animals to share and exchange information and thereby gain access to critical survival knowledge.

Different practices were devised to deal with various comprehendible and incomprehensible situations and to address the inconsistencies of daily life. The belief that souls were quasi-physical and could exist outside the body in dreams and visions and that they could be transferred from one body to another and persisted after the death of the body as ghosts or by reincarnation[15] were dominant postulations of early times. In the process of spiritual consolidation, beliefs and deities were compressed and incorporated into forms that were more prescriptive. That transformation made the belief system more stable as it was collectively maintained, and in that permutation, it was formalized with a hierarchical structure, systematic rituals, and predictable practices. That transition was a gradual evolution that moved the people out of an age of acknowledged fear and apprehension into a time of presumed understanding based on unifying beliefs.

> The interplay of life- and death-giving functions in a divinity is particularly characteristic of dominant goddesses. The Life and Birth Giver can turn into a frightening image of death. She is a stiff nude or a mere bone with a supernatural pubic triangle where the transformation from death to life begins.[16]

Mythical and Ritual Transformation

There is a large amount of folklore about transformation and transmogrification including stories about werewolves, vampires, or leopard men that verify the wide utilization of this theme. Humans were believed transformed into mammal, bird, fish, insect, reptile, amphibian, or plant. There were transformations in which animals or humans were normal by day but reversed characteristics at night. There were also types of transformation that involved the dead who by means of magic rejoined the living in animal and human forms. These restless souls of the dead were said to wander among the living awaiting some extraordinary form of demise so they could find eternal rest. Every variation and combination of the transformational concept was explored.

Within many cultures there were shamans who were believed to journey to the Upperworld or the

DRAWING 9.5—Papier mâché mask of Yama (*gShin rje*), the bull-headed Lord of Death and ruler of the nether world. This masked figure was central to most sacred dances of the Gelugpa and appears in both the Tibetan and Mongolian pantheon. Yama is comparable with Erleg Khan, a shamanistic lord of the underworld,[v] and it was he or one of "his stag-headed messengers who ceremonially kills the *lingka*, a figure that embodies demonic force."[w] In some dances four minor Yamas appear to denote the cardinal points.[x] The Yama also appears as an ancient Hindu god of death who is generally portrayed as a placid figure riding a buffalo.[y]

9. *Transformation and Shape-Shifting*   191

Left: PLATE 17— Front view of female shaman's robe, a "bird costume" type. It is a relatively simple Chinese style, cotton garment that has few pendants, but has long fringes on the hem and sleeves to aid in voyages to the Upperworld. The multi-color "snakes" are manifestations of friendly spirits.

Right: PLATE 18— Back view of female shaman's robe illustrating the "bird costume." On each shoulder (scapula) is a tuft of feathers representing wings. The center panel is the tail that is to help guide the shaman's spirit as she flies into the upper region. The profusion of "snakes" demonstrates the array of helpers the shaman has accumulated.

Underworld, and to mingle with both the deities and the dead (see drawing 9.5). The shamanic travels occurred through magical flight (often in the form of a bird) accompanied by animal guardians or by ascending the sacred tree that connected heaven and earth. The shaman might also be transformed into zoomorphic form with the attributes of the particular animal. An exemplar transformational occurrence was believed to take place in Africa within the leopard societies. The principal practitioner in those secret groups was believed able to transform himself into an animal considered to be his second identity.

The feline transformation concept is also found at *Huaca de los Reyes* on the Peruvian coast (*huaca* is also spelled *wak'a* meaning a state of being after death or tomb — place of spirits). At that location there is a clay head that has a wide nose, pendant irises, and a fanged mouth. "The themes of shamanic transformation and the iconographic tradition of the jawless lower mouth, wide feline nose, claws, and entwined serpents are early precursors to a later art style known as Chavín."[17] The fanged shaman is found in many images attributed to the Inca (see drawing 9.6).

Transformation also had an important role in myths, and the power to exceed physical limitation, for purposes of good or evil often depended on the traditions of a particular culture. Transformation of a person without their consent was in the majority of instances the result of evil magical powers, and most such myths concluded with the subject's release from the evil power, and his or her return to original form. In contrast, many of the instances of self-transformation were for the positive purpose of transcendence (the ability to exist above and apart from the material world). The Netsilik (Central Eskimo) believed that there was once a "great shaman who wanted to see what it was like to live as an animal, so he let himself be reborn as all kinds of beasts."[18] When the shaman returned to his human form, he was well acquainted with the behavior of animals, and it was from him that humans learned the habits of various animals.

The shaman transformational role was often represented as trans-species. A shaman in a trance state might experience transmogrification from human to animal form.[19] To cross the boundaries of the natural and supernatural worlds, shaman changed their form and state of being. The ability of a shaman to alter his or her physical shape was commonly believed throughout much of the world. The mythology of most people included stories about were-animals

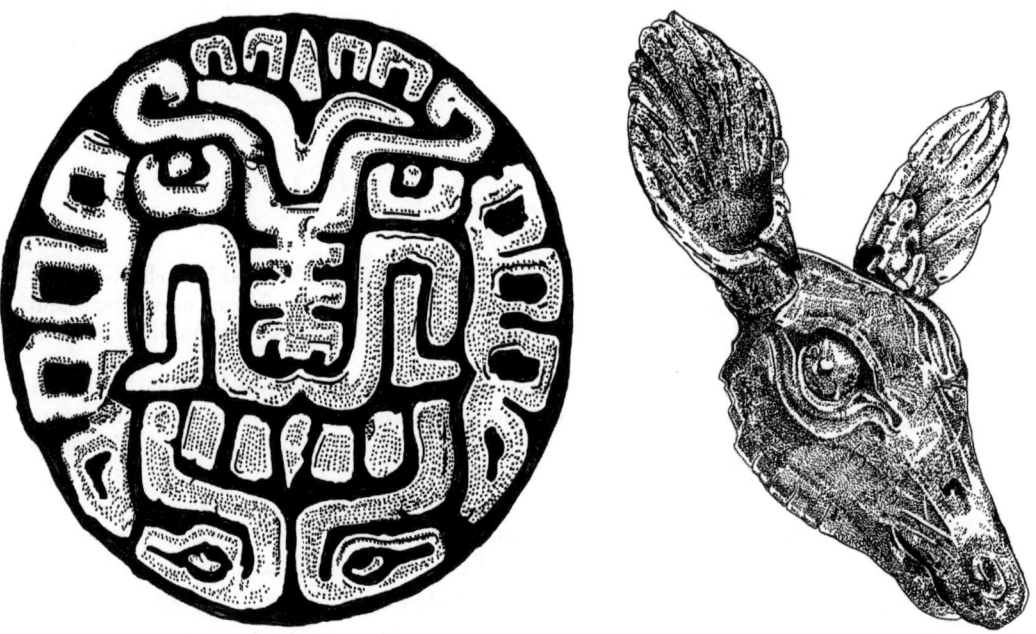

Left: DRAWING 9.6 — This drawing is the center of a gorget in classic Chavín style showing a figure with a feline nose, piecing eyes, and fanged mouth. The image conforms to the shamanic transformation tradition of the northern Andean highlands. Although the Chavín style derives it name from the ruins of Chavín de Huántar it is not known whether this site was the actual origin of the culture and artistic style. The principal motifs of the Chavín style are human, feline, and crocodilian or serpentine figures. The figures are often combined in highly complex and fantastic images.[z]

Right: DRAWING 9.7 — Calusa deer mask uncovered near Key Marco, Florida. This small fifteenth century mask is considered one of the most unique archaeological finds relating to this extinct indigenous culture. It was probably worn on the crown of the head and attached with leather thongs. As the dancer moved, the ears could move, giving a feeling of the grace of a deer. Originally the mask was painted and probably had shell-inlaid eyes.[aa]

and the ability of humans to assume the shape and characteristics of real and imaginary beasts.

The zoomorphic symbolism of the shaman's costume was a reference to the cosmic arena in which he or she was active. Cultural acknowledgement of particular symbols informed the audience of the shaman's activities. For instance, the bear was a link to the Underworld while a bird referred to the Upperworld. The symbol of the deer might refer to either realm and to the world between (see drawing 9.7).[20] Shamans reinforced the symbolic references by sound and movement in addition to objects attached to their costumes. In some instances, as in ancient China, the costume was the skin of a bear, or among the people of the northwestern part of North America, the shaman wore a mask to symbolically represent the animal spirit.

To understand the development of the shaman and shamanistic masks as elements in the traditional transformational practices, it is necessary to consider the survival strategies of early humans. The historic record indicates that the first peoples were primarily hunters dependent on opportunistic encounters to provide their primary food source. The hunter sought the available products of nature and seized them as a way of surviving. Eventually, a more stable order was established and people developed a planter culture that involved planning and rudimentary technology. That calculated form of existence was the basis of modern civilization.

The hunter culture adjusted its activities to find compatibility with the forces of nature and adopted an attitude of sharing rather than domination. In contrast, the planter culture endeavored to develop methods for regulating the forces of nature and the environment (see drawing 9.8). Productivity was a concern as was the accumulation of tangible property. In both of those "sophisticated" activities, chance and reliance on the forces of the natural world were factors that required constant attention.

The hunter needed a harmonious relationship with the various elements of nature. To sustain that relationship and meet the communal survival requirements, a scheme had to be developed to satisfy the seeming contradictory aspects of daily existence, the killing, and consuming of creatures emanating from the natural environment. Early humans conceived the notion of immortality to address the conflicting attitudes of reverence and destruction. Therefore, living creatures were endowed with a spirit to ameliorate that contradiction, and the spirit survived when the body was destroyed. In addition, the spirits of slain animals might be appeased by proper appreciation and caused to return as a food source for future generations. Those practices of appeasement required the development of rituals and similar magico-religious acts of spirit recognition.

Because all creatures (human and animal)

DRAWING 9.8—Hudo' (or Hudoq) dance mask from Kayan, East Kalimantan, made of wood, pigment and fiber. The mask represents the wild boar and was worn by dancers in agricultural rites intended to ensure a good rice crop. Shamans (*balian* in Borneo) also wore Hudo' masks in the curing ritual for constituents afflicted with various diseases.[bb]

were composed of two parts, one physical and one spiritual it was possible for the two to be separated. That idea accepted the death of the physical body while the spirit/soul survived. It also provided a method for humans to gain superiority over a stronger adversary through spiritual domination. It was a way for humans to achieve a measure of control over the environment and especially over the animals on which their lives depended.

The significance of a transformational state of spiritual being was reflected in the many animal masks used in ritual activities and the shamanistic practice of "talking with the animals." The power of the myth reminded people of the paradise lost (purgatory) due to human indiscretion, and the importance of regaining a state of cosmic wholeness — a return to the beginning when all creatures lived in complete harmony. The human/animal kinship was a strong element in the mythical history of most cultures and a major element of shamanic paraphernalia.

The shaman often relied on his or her ability to transform his or her appearance (physically or metaphysically) into that of an animal. The Huichol shamans of Mexico preferred to be transformed into the wolf and the jaguar (puma) was favored in South America. The connection to the particular animal form was often drawn from the distant past of the people. The Huichol believed that in early times man was part wolf. "They came out of the darkness and into the sun, which gave them the option of choosing to become either wolves or human beings."[21] Wolves were believed to be the mythical ancestors of the Huichol.

DRAWING 9.9—Ceramic figure from the Colima culture of western Mexico holding peyote cactus in each hand. The peyote cactus (species *Lophophora williamsii*) was used for its hallucinogenic effects. Peyote figured prominently in shamanistic rituals of some North American peoples, as well as the people living in the northern and northwestern areas of Mexico. There is no clear understanding of the role peyote played in the spiritual activities of the Colima culture. However, the Huichol living in the Sierra Madre Occidental continue to use peyote as a ritual substance. "In the founding myth of the Huichol peyote ritual, a party of divine ancestors — the ancestral gods — set out to search for the peyote cactus under the leadership of their shaman, the old fire god himself."[cc] The Huichol called peyote *hikuri*, the plant of eternal life.

> At the dawn of Huichol history ... the first people were half human, half wolf. Before the Great Flood, and for a time after these wolf-people lived in darkness, in the coastal region near San Blas, Nayarit, which is the homeland of the Wolf People, the Kamuketai, as the wolves of myth are called.[22]

The myth explained that the early "wolf shamans" used lizard and grasshopper blood to anoint their offerings because they did not hunt deer and did not know the power of deer blood.[23] Later the deer in human form came and was hunted by the wolf people, and as the deer was being eaten by the wolves it was magically transformed into peyote (*hikuri*). The wolf people gained great wisdom by eating the deer/peyote (see drawing 9.9). "Once the wolf people learned about deer hunting, rain making, healing, and all the infinite knowledge of the peyote given to Kamukemai [Father of the Wolves] by his cohort Kauyumári, they moved out of the darkness and into the light."[24]

PLATE 3— The Mongol shaman, Ostria Böö from Bajangol wearing a ritual coat (robe) and holding a drum. The robe has the distinctive array of "snakes" down the back and the head cover is fitted with feathers. There is what appears to be an antler-form extending from the far side of the head covering. The upper end of the cross-shaped handle of the drum has the image of a spirit helper. Sakari Pälsi took this photograph in 1909.

Shamans in South America are believed to be able to transform themselves into jaguars. "The jaguar represents the sun, fertility, and the energy contained in nature. It is the protector of the forest and because of its color is often associated with fire, its roar being likened to thunder."[25] The Paéz and Kogi people of Columbia called themselves "children of the jaguar," and their shamans consumed hallucinogenic substances to facilitate the transformation into the jungle feline.[26] Shaman in Ecuador wore cloth masks with rods to connect to the spirit world. These masks were said to symbolically represent jaguars or pumas (see drawing 4.7). An important element of certain masks was an array of small shapes, figures, and amulets representing the shaman's spirit helpers. Other masks had strings, rods, or animal tails attached to them. The strings and rods (called snakes by some shamans) were connecting elements for attracting and joining with spirits, and the animal tails were another reference to the dual nature of human/animal spirituality.

Critical factors in the early foundation of shamanism were the "anthropomorphization of former zoomorphic images of the spirits, personifying not only natural but also societal forces, and the transition from feminine to masculine personifications and the appearance of many new cults...."[27] The theme of human-animal transformation was found in the Andean highlands during the pre–Incan period. There were images of insects with human heads and what is "possibly a shaman in hallucinogenic transformation."[28]

By anthropomorphizing the spirits, they could be caused to serve society in a positive way by promises of sacrifices or threats of rejection. That approach followed the belief that an objective could be achieved by a consciously abnormal concentration of will power. A small-scale imitation of the desired act or action was performed to supplement the concentrated effort. Wearing an animal mask and making the movements of the represented animal to guarantee its accessibility to hunters, or the sprinkling of water to attract rain exemplified that type of activity. It was believed there was a sympathetic or corresponding relationship between like activities in the spirit world and those in the terrestrial domain.

Acknowledging the essential nature of transformational practices, traditional cultures recognized various deities endowed with the power to assume different forms. Some deities came into the world of humans as animals and they were afterwards associated with those creatures. Masks and other forms of shamanic paraphernalia representing the particular deities often drew upon those animal images for symbolic reference. If a deity was born of a cow or took the form of a water snake, those likenesses found their way into the costume symbology for shamanistic representation or mythical reference.

The influence of animal transformation in the shamans' rituals was significant in Oceania, as well as, along the Northwest Coast of North America. In those areas, the shaman's mask was often used to express the dual nature of humans—part animal and part human. That duality was also found in areas of West Africa.[29] Those masks exposed the inner presence of the twin beings (human and animal), or they illustrated the physical union with one half of the face showing a human likeness and the other half animal. It was believed that those masks recalled the past and referred to the time when humans could change their appearance.

Masks worn as a part of shamanistic activity represented spirit beings in the "power transformation strategy." Due to the personal nature of those masks, they were normally placed in the shaman's grave or funeral house at the time of his or her death. The shaman's helping mask combined anthropomorphic and zoomorphic images to give full consideration to the transformation process. The basic shape and look were human (anthropomorphic) with superimposed animal or bird (zoomorphic) forms. These masks, common along the Northwestern Coastal region of North America[30] were similar to the transformation masks that combined an inner and outer image (see drawing 9.4). One figure contained within another referred to the life and death process that influenced the survival of all living creatures. Humans were the consumer or the consumed. The transformation called on the power of the inner image to be given to the outer or more powerful spirit image (see drawing 9.2).

The foundation of shamanism was closely related to the interaction of humans and nature. "Shamanism seem[ed] to occur in almost every area where an early hunting economy...."[31] Once the supernatural connection was established between the material and spiritual worlds, an agreement was initiated that allowed the shaman to call upon the spirits and convinced them to perform services for the good of the group. It was the capacity of shamans to communicate directly with nature that established and confirmed their creditability.

A characteristic of shamanism in ancient Egypt was associated with an animal totem. The Egyptian shamans wore special garments made of animal skins to denote rank or position. The leopard skin was worn by several categories of priests, and it was believed that the attire related to shamanistic rituals. According to Geraldine Pinch writing in *Magic in Ancient Egypt* (1994), "Real or artificial leopard skins were worn by *sem* priests when they officiated at funerals and by the High Priest of Ra at Heliopolis, whose title was 'The Seer.'"[32] Leopard or panther images appear on some of the earliest ritual objects in ancient Egypt. The leopard (*panthera pardus*), a nocturnal hunter, was associated with the starry night sky and the realm of the dead.[33]

Secret Traditions of Shamanic Transformation

Humans, from the earliest times, divided the world into two realms, the sacred and the secular, and in many societies that division was clearly defined and separated. However, the two spheres were more closely aligned in other cultures. Despite the divisions or perhaps because of that separation, the supernatural played an important role in the lives of individuals as well as the community. Shaman, priest, sorcerers, and magicians were essential elements of society for promoting an understanding of how humans related to the supernatural world. That sentiment of cosmic affiliation had both intellectual and emotional content, and in most societies, the two elements melded into one consciousness. The people accepted and endorsed the concept of the supernatural to give added meaning to life values.

A form of shamanic transformation found among some cultural groups was, in practice, the change of gender. Chukchee male shamans were known to "undergo a change of sex."[34] Shamans that received a command from the spirits exchanged their male clothing, behavior, and living arrangement for those of a woman. They dressed as women and some married men. It was reported that the Chukchee viewed the shamanistic calling as being "doomed to inspiration," and "when the command of the spirits demand[ed] a change of sex, the youthful novices were purported to express themselves as preferring death."[35]

A similar "calling" occurred among the young men of the Omaha people, a North American indigenous group. They went into the wilderness to fast, pray, and seek a vision. If they dream that they receive "a woman's burden-strap, they felt compelled to dress and live thereafter in every way as women. Such men are known as *mixuga*."[36]

The Ngadju-Dayak in Borneo had a special class of shamans called *basirs* who dressed and acted like women. According to Mircea Eliade,[37] these men were hermaphrodites and incapable of procreation. The *basirs* (as they were called) were intermediaries between heaven and earth because they united in their own person the feminine element of the earth and the masculine element of the heavens. This duality was not unique to Southeast Asia. Male shamans in Siberia were known to dress in women's clothing, take husbands, and conduct their activities as a woman (see Plate 13).

The so-called "change of sex" among Siberian shamans was found chiefly among Paleo-Siberians, namely the Chukchee, Koryak, Kamchatka, and Asiatic Eskimo.[38] This form of ritual transformation was also found in Indonesia, South America, and among some North American peoples (Arapaho, Cheyenne, and Ute). Ritual transformation of male into female might relate to early matriarchal practices, but in most cultures it did not appear to reference any priority of women in early shamanism.[39] The transvestite shamans found among the *Tsist-sistas* (Cheyenne) were called *hemaneh* (half-man, half-woman). These individuals symbolically represented the union of the blue sky and the deep earth, and were said to be famous physicians.[40]

The Inuit, Arctic peoples of Canada and Greenland, identified shamanism as a third androgynous gender — neither male nor female but having both masculine and feminine traits. This classification was both a developmental consideration linking the asexual fetus to the shamanic capacity to change sex, and a sociological one related to the presence in Inuit society of significant numbers of transvestites and *sipiniit* (people considered to have changed sex at birth).[41] The manifestation of elements of both genders was considered critical to the shaman's ability to accommodate both male and female concerns.

The Chukchee called the male that changed of his sexual orientation "soft-man-being," *yirka-laul-vairgin* or "soft man" (*yirka-laul*) meaning a man transformed into a being of the weaker sex. "A man who had 'changed his sex' was also called 'similar to a woman' (*ne uchica*), and a woman in like condition 'similar to a man' (*qa cikcheca*). These latter transformations are much rarer."[42]

The mystical change of a male shaman into a female and vice versa was a curious phenomenon. That sexual transformation, especially as it concerns powerful shamans, could not be explained on a purely physical basis. Several motivations for such cultural practice appeared among different peoples, but it did not stand to reason that every pathological individual was the subject of shamanic intervention. The transformed shaman was described in most cases as a normal individual that only later, by inspiration of spirits, changed his (most often a male) sex. Some outwardly transformed persons secretly had normal relations with a person of the opposite sex, and some of them may actually become sexless.[43]

The sexually transformed shamans (transvestites) were sometime regarded as curiosities and, at times, ridiculed because they dressed and behaved like the opposite sex, but more often they were accorded respect. It was believed that stress or some form of psychological disturbance caused a mental state that distorted memory, embraced fantasy, and confused objective experience resulting in a psychological and emotional change of sex.

> It is an old, old story, difficult to understand. They say that the world collapsed, the earth was destroyed, that great showers of rain flooded the land. All the animals died, and there were only two men left. They lived together. They married, as there was nobody else, and at last one of them became with child. They were great shamans, and when the one was going to bear a child they made his penis over again so that he became a woman, and she had a child. They say it is from that shaman that women came.[44]

M. A. Czaplicka postulates that the first shamans were women. She writes, "Among the Palaeo-Siberians, women received the gift of shamanizing more often than men. The woman is by nature a shaman...."[45] Nevertheless, there is no clear pattern to trace the evolution of the shaman from female to male. Different theories about the origin of shamanism influence the notion that shamans were originally female. Czaplicka supports her theory by noting that nearly all Neo-Siberians had a common name for female shamans, while each of those tribes had a special name for the male shamans. "The Yakut call him *ayun*; the Mongols, *buge*; the Buryat, *buge* and *bo*; the Tungus, *samman* or *khamman*; the Tartars, *kam*; the Altaians, *kam* and *gam*; the Kirgis, *baksy*; and the Samoyed, *tadibey*."[46] Whereas, the Mongols, Buryat, Yakut, Altaians, Turgout, and Kirgis used similar names for the female shaman, "*utagan, udagan, ubakan, utygan, utügun, iduan*, and *duana*. These words come from a root the meaning of which has not been certainly determined."[47]

The concept of morphological transformation is ancient regardless of the cause for this orientation among the Siberian peoples. Transformational endorsement is believed to extend into the earliest time of human existence. Ritual activities and communal beliefs were often based on the idea of duality and the physiological and psychological ability to change — to be transformed. The traditions of most peoples confirm the inclusive identity of all beings great and small. It was this "sameness" that allow shamans to cross the physical boundaries that separated humans, animals, spirits, and in some instances, gender.

Honored deities embodying male and female capacities were found among many peoples. They were the duel elements — the two halves of the whole — necessary to create life. The power in humans to generate life was a shield against death. The act of procreation was for that reason a natural foundation for early belief systems, and symbols of regeneration were found in most cultures. The concept of the primordial couples of Africa, the phallic monuments and emblems of China, India, Japan, Korea, and many other parts of the world, and the fertility dramas of ancient Europe, North Africa, and the Middle East were of particular significance.

The union of opposites was symbolized by the joining of the sun and the moon and by the male and female principles. It was also identified by the "androgyny" (or hermaphrodite); the being that united the masculine and feminine principles within a single embodiment. The androgyny symbolically watched over the beginning and end of every magical process.[48] The hermaphrodite was also described as the "cosmic figure," as well as the beginning and the completion of the evolutionary cycle. The androgyny might represent to the shaman that time before the sexes were separated, as well as the decomposition and combination of the elements — death, dismemberment, and resurrection.

Androgynous beings are a part of many creation myths. The Dogon of West Africa, the Tahitians, Japanese, and Chinese have myths about the cosmic egg and the creation of androgynous beings. Other cultures had deities that embody male and female capacities. The androgynous being personified the duel elements — the two halves of the whole — necessary to create life. There was Osiris and Isis in Egyptian mythology; the Greeks had a pantheon of mythical pairs including Dionysus and Demeter, Zeus and Hera, and Uranus and Gaia; and in Tibet the duel nature of regeneration was embodied in Yab and Yum.[49]

Myths about the androgynous nature of god and goddesses fulfilled important functions in society; they expressed, classified, and in many ways validated beliefs. Those beliefs reenforced a concept of morality, and in some cultural settings they provided explanations to verified traditional beliefs and customs. For instance, early Christian belief endorsed "the ancient Asian concept of the combined male/female deity, the Primal Androgyny."[50] The Jewish mystical tradition includes the belief that the original Jehovah was an androgyny, and that his/her name was "composed of Jeh (*jod*) and the pre–Hebraic name of Eve, Havah or Hawah, rendered *he-vau-he* in Hebrew letters."[51] These four letters form the "Sacred Tetragrammaton, *YHWH*, the secret name of God."[52]

The creation of Eve from the rib of Adam draws upon the conjoined nature of the male and female elements. A further aspect of this associations is that when "Eve was still in Adam, death did not exist. When she was separated from him death came into being. If he again became complete and attained his former self, death will be no more."[53] However, the most commonly held androgynous myth that came to modern time from the ancient past is that the Christ child was born of a virgin Mother. It was the belief of certain elements (Ophites) of the Christian Gnostics, a movement prominent in the Greco-Roman world during the second century and beyond of the current era, that the "true divine revelation could only come from an androgynous Christ, who was hermaphroditically united in heaven with the Goddess Sophia, 'Mother of All.'"[54]

There are many traditional beliefs that call to attention the relationships between the female and male elements. They provide the foundation for social, sexual, and religious beliefs. Those practices are exemplified by the male domination of the secrets of some Australian aboriginal peoples. According to one account, it was believed that if the women were allowed to know the secrets of the society, the entire race must be exterminated.[55] That belief was used to explain why only males were initiated into the secret societies, and why only they were granted access to the traditions, myths, and rituals that were the means for cultural continuation.

Transformation beliefs emanating from the distant past generally were held to be psychologically true because they conveyed a history of social acceptance. The concepts associated with those beliefs were often represented by symbols, and they were transmitted by traditional methods. Those cultural markers were primary elements of the transmission process, and over time they became more idealized and less directly influenced by the originating beliefs. However, they generally retained significant elements of the traditional meaning as exemplified by the androgynous god or goddess.

The primary reference for gender determination in many locations was the physical characteristics of the genitalia. However, some societies "constructed multiple nonstigmatized gender statuses for individuals by separating gender tasks and social roles from sexual morphology."[56] This issue became important when the transgender behavior was regarded as abnormal and many societies regarded any form of homosexuality or transvestitism as aberrant. However, there was no form of sexual behavior or attitude that had a universal social or psychological value for good or evil — the whole meaning and value of any expression of sexuality was determined by the social context within which it occurred.

"Many Amerindian cultures ... traditionally recognized, and in some cases still recognize, four genders: woman, man, woman-man, and man-woman."[57] It was reported by Ruth Benedict in *Patterns of Culture* (1959) that homosexuals and transvestites were regarded as good healers for certain diseases, but considered with some embarrassment.[58] Among the Siberian Koryaks "transformed" shamans were also considered very powerful. The people were said to believe that since the change of sex was in obedience to the commands of spirits it enhanced the shaman's curing or divining abilities.

The Bambara and Dogon peoples of Mali believed that human spiritual principles were sexed like the body, and that circumcision was an aid in "terminating boys' identity with the female role."[59] The male was thought feminine in his foreskin, and the female masculine in her clitoris. The sexuality of the individual was defined by the removal of the contrasting element. Conversely, "the subincision, practiced by some Australian aborigines, might be directly motivated by an envy of women, because it greatly increases the resemblance of the male genitals to those of the female."[60]

Male activities seen as transgender might be the cultural response to envy of the females' ability to reproduce. The power of reproduction was a process given considerable attention in myth, and shamans were often called upon to perform fertility rites to ensure new life. In response to this societal need, spirits were petitioned to blow the breath of life into the womb — the insertion of a spirit child. Myths also verified that men taught women how to have babies, and that at one time men "followed the cycle of the moon" (menstruation). There were also myths about male pregnancy, lactation, and defecation.[61] However, early males also associated the female with the devil and often represented her genitalia as the "mouth of hell" to call to attention her participation in the "original sin."[62]

Although "change of sex" practices occurred among cultures in Central Asia and among the Amerindians, it was not necessarily unique to any group of people or to any time in the history of shamanism. The conversion of men into women was often related to the priesthood in that transvestitism was thought to relate to the societal transition from a matriarchal to patriarchal configuration. It was during that societal realignment that priestly functions became available to man.[63] The concept of spiritual "oneness," and the inclusion of both aspects of gender in one being also corresponded with Hermetic teaching. The same concept was included in numerous myths that featured a hero/heroine capable of exchanging identity (and gender) according to the circumstances.

Masking activities often accommodated transvestitism with male dancers or actors portraying women. That sexual transformation can be found in cultures of West Africa, South America, China, and Japan where tradition defined a clear separation of gender-related activities (see drawing 9.10). The appropriately designed transformational mask allowed the performer (shaman) to be either male or female without endorsing either gender. The mask was also a means for crossing the gap between humans and spirits. It presented both an implied identity and a sense of ambiguity.

Although the shamans (*temararamaw*) of the Puyuma in Taiwan were predominately women, they maintain that Samguan, a transvestite man, was the first *temararamaw*. Before him there were reportedly no shamans only *miapali*, those with a third eye[64] (perhaps referring to believers in the Buddhist deity *San Po-lo* or the Hindu Lord Who is Half Woman, *Ardhanarisvara*). Other stories say that Udekaw was the first real Puyuma shaman and that the memory of her has "gone with the wind."[65] Nevertheless, Samguan continues to be honored today as the ancestor-spirit of senior *temararamaw*.

It was believed that the change in the habits (of one sex) was demonstrated when the man "throws away the rifle and the lance, the lasso of the reindeer herdsman, and the harpoon of the seal-hunter, and takes to the needle and the skin-scraper."[66] Reportedly transgender male learned the use of these implements quickly, because the "spirits" helped

DRAWING 9.10 — White Maiden (*mmwo*) mask made by the Ibo people of Nigeria. This carved and painted wood mask depicted the ideal of Ibo beauty. Male masqueraders wore these masks in the annual "fame of maidens" festival. The masks were to represent adolescent girls and embodied the ideals of feminine beauty including a pale complexion, slender nose, and delicate mouth.[dd]

him. Even his pattern of speech and pronunciation changed from masculine to feminine. It was also said that the transformed shaman's body lost its masculine appearance, and he became shy.

Socially, the shaman did not belong either to the class of males or to that of females, but to a third class, that of shamans. Sexually, he or she was sexless or had homosexual inclinations, but it was equally possible that he or she was heterosexual. Shamans were simply (and professionally) a special class. They had special taboos including both male and female characters. Their shamanizing costume also combined elements peculiar of both sexes (see Plates Number 16 through 20).

Shamans moved between worlds and display multiple natures that were often displayed in gender or species that vacillation between human and animals. The androgynous nature of shamans in some cultures also exemplified the "two-spirits" that crossed the gender division. "Among the Chukchee, whose eastern Siberian territory extends from the Bering Strait to the Kolyma River valley, a woman may only become a shaman at or after the menopause, because reproductive capacity is seen to inhibit shamanistic power."[67] Shamans of both sexes were active among the Yakut and Buryat. However, in many Siberian communities a woman shaman was not allowed to touch the drum. The shamanesses were believed especially capable at foretelling the future, looking for things that were lost, and curing mental diseases. Nevertheless shamanesses among the Yakut were considered less capable than the males, and the people asked their help only when no shaman (male) was available.

Social structures were often configured to promote both male and female sexual activity and fertility. It was one of the social functions of the shaman to resolve issues such as impotency and infertility. As an extension of the propagation obsession, men wanted to more fully participate in the reproduction process by assigning and assuming feminine roles. The use of masks, dress, dance, and in some cultures vocabulary were elements of that pseudo-physiological transfiguration. It was not just the shaman that represented the transgender practice in those circumstances. The males of the group participated in a role-playing event so they might know themselves better. The male element wanted to be a whole being — the male and the female (see drawing 9.10). As a further example of this role-playing, the males in some cultures ceremonially lacerated their penises to symbolically represent the production of menstrual discharge and to gain a closer connection with the primal progenitor. The joining of emotions stimulated by spirits and traditions promoted ritual activity.

There are numerous references to male shamans wearing female clothing. As an example, the shamans of the Araucanian, a people living in south-central Chili, were said to be female but in earlier times it was the prerogative of "inverts."[68] Among the Iban also called Sea Dayak of Sarawak (southwest Borneo) the shaman (*manang*) puts on women's clothing at the conclusion of the shamanistic initiation and continued to wear that form of attire the rest of his life.[69] The early practices of the Hausa people of Nigeria and Niger included belief in spirits (*bori*), and the *bori* ritual was a ritual of inversion. Homosexuality among the Hausa was considered an "inversion" of appropriate male heterosexuality.[70] Such practices were not found in all cultures, however, transvestitism, with all the challenges that it involved, was considered obligatory after the supernatural command came three times in dreams. It was believed that to refuse that call would be to seek death.[71]

Traditional practices allowed the shaman to cross the socially and biologically defined line of masculinity and femininity. Shamans "often work with both masculine and feminine forms of energy, sometime even shape-shifting into beings of the opposite gender."[72] The transgender practice might be related to the "marriage" between a shaman and a spirit. This concept of mystical or holy marriage between a person and a spirit is found in religious orders that advocated celibacy. It was likely, however, that the adaptation of female attire by male shaman or the masculine mannerisms assumed by female shamans was a symbolic gesture to accommodate social and cultural expectations. As a demonstration of that practice, some male Eskimo shamans had breasts represented on their garments to symbolically demonstrate their inner feminine side — the side associated with their connection to the spirit world.

The balance of male and female principles is identified in numerous myths relating to creation of the world and the first people. Principle of the myths represented the symbolic union of upper world, the human plane, and the lower world: fire, water, and wind, male, female, and hermaphrodite.[73] The twin symbols of the phallus and pudendum muliebre (*lingam* and *yoni*) represented the union of the male and female elements. They symbolize creative energy and the continuance of human and natural forces. Those symbols were a part of the belief systems of many cultures in both the ancient and modern worlds. That sexual reference occurred in ancient Egypt, India, Syria, Babylon, Persia, Greece, Italy, Spain, Germany, and Scandinavia.

Shape-Shifting and Ecstatic Journeys

> The world was populated by great numbers of spirits, some animal, who might appear in either their own or human form, some human with similar shape-changing abilities, while still other, among the most powerful and dangerous, were monsters with partly human, partly animal attributes.[74]

The belief that a shaman could alter his or her physical shape was commonly held throughout the world. There are numerous stories about shamans that took the form of spirit animals with which they had developed a special "shape-shifting" relationship. To demonstrate that connection and to embrace the essence of the spirit being, putting on a mask was an act of mind-altering importance for the shaman. That transformation set aside the mundane world and offered a way for joining with the supernatural. To cross the boundaries of the two worlds, shaman were thought to be "shape-shifters,"[75] and that transformation allowed them to change their physical form and state of being. Were-animals as transmogrified shaman walked the earth, flew in the sky, and occupied the waters. They were messengers of good and evil.

Becoming an animal while in a trance state was an important part of the shaman's experience. The shaman's guardian spirits often assume the form of animals, and they were a necessary element in the shamanic ritual for dealing with hostile spirits. The impression was that by shape-shifting, the shaman was above both man and beast and moved in a superior order of beings that communicated directly with the spirits.[76] Shape-shifting or transmogrification from human to animal form while in a trance state was an important part of shamanic ritual (see drawing 9.11). Shamans promoted the notion of theriomorphic — being in the form of an animal, or thought of as being in animal form — by adding animal pelts, feathers, or antlers to their ritual attire. The use of masks that depicted mythical beings or animals implanted the necessary image to guide the viewers' imagination, and the imitative disguise and symbolic gestures reinforce the transformational impression. Belief became all the more powerful when augmented by sight, sound, and scent.

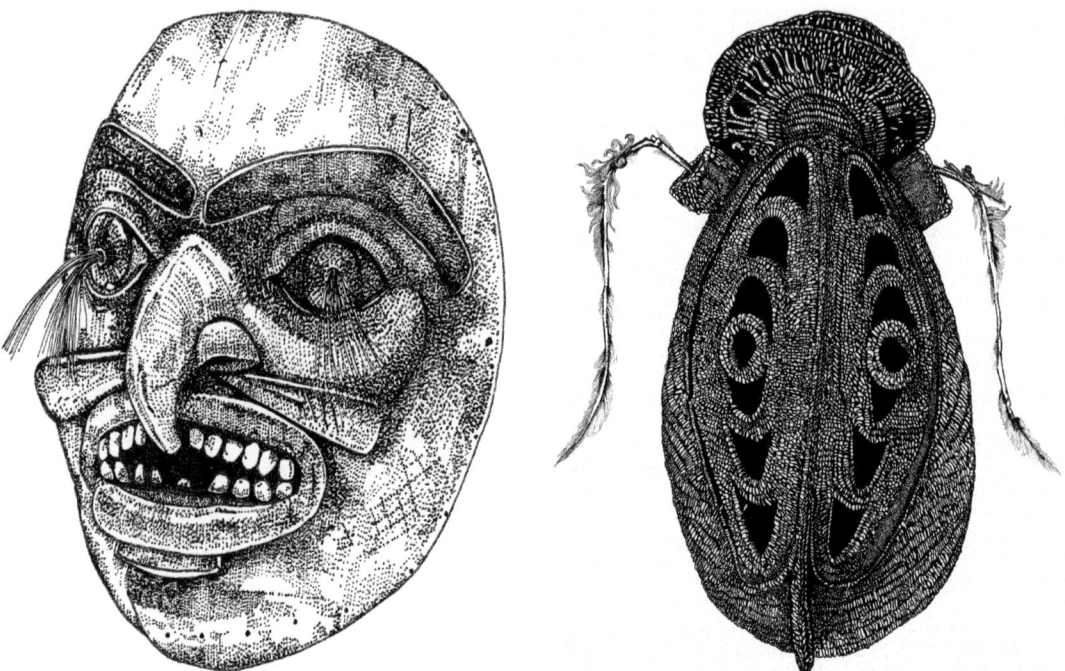

Left: DRAWING 9.11—A carved and painted Tlingit shaman mask from the Northwest Coast of North America. Most Tlingit shaman masks have closed eyes perhaps representing death or the transitional period between life and death. This mask has two distinct features that make it unique. The exaggerated nose probably represents the female salmon spirit, but the tufts of hair emanating from the eyes have no established purpose. The hair may suggest vision or light that goes beyond earthly perception.[cc]

Right: DRAWING 9.12—"*Baba*" mask of woven fiber made in the Sepik River area, Papua, New Guinea. The plaited mask covered the head of the dancer and was remade for each use. The dancer's body was covered with a wrapping of leaf strips. The *Baba* masks represented a pig-like spirit being that mediated between the living and the dead. These masks were to personify the intrusion of the supernatural world into the natural world.[ff]

The influence of transformation in the shamans' rituals was significant in Oceania, as well as, along the Northwest Coast of North America. Ritual activities in those areas expressed the dual nature of humans—part animal and part human (see drawing 9.12). That duality was also found in areas of West Africa.[77] The dual nature of this primal creature was expressed in masks that exposed the inner presence of the twin beings (human and animal), or they illustrated the physical union with one half of the face showing a human likeness and the other half animal. As already mentioned, masks often recalled the past and referred to the time when humans could change their appearance.

Shamanic transformation into different forms was fairly common and well documented. The reasons for that transmogrification often depend on the cultural influences that dictated the practices and expectations of resident shamans. The shaman might view his or her soul as a bird that flew to the Upperworld or a fish that swam to the bottom of the sea to establish contact with the Underworld. These journeys could not be achieved without transformation.

The shaman might also assume the shape and demeanor of the spirit from which his or her power emanates. That practice usually reflected the historical origin of the people with whom the shaman was associated. Such belief in many locations was based on the assumption of close association between humans and animals "in the beginning." Although it was thought that humans and animals shared common beliefs and practices, that connection ceased in the distant past. Nevertheless, that connection was not forgotten. Consequently, many early people embraced the notion of totemism — the belief that humans had a kinship or mystical relationship with a particular animal or other object. Among some peoples the totem was thought to mean the guardian spirit of the individual (shaman).

A form of individual totemism found in southeast Australia involved the relationship between a sorcerer or shaman and a certain animal species. Normally the subject animal was a reptile.[78] A similar relationship took place between shamans and vision encountered animal protector spirits among the indigenous peoples of the central plains of North America. The vision animal had a totem-like relationship with the particular individual. The animal was in some instances an assistant to the shaman as a beneficial agent and a messenger. "A shaman was part of the sky and wild animals were cousins of the sky, so a shaman and animals were relatives."[79]

Although the concept of totemism has been called "anthropopsychic," that is, granting souls to animals and plants and giving them unique qualities, the totem was a symbol of the kinship group and a sociological link for an individual. It was common for the social alignment with a particular totem to be expressed outwardly in taboos, symbols, and rituals. The totem with its restrictions was believed to grant special power to a person (shaman) and it was that mystical relationship that influenced social beliefs and subsequently shamanism.

Quasi-totemic animals associated with transformation and transmogrification differs according to the society in which the reported act took place. In Europe the animal "of choice" for transformation was the wolf (timber or gray wolf), and in many locations masks were used to promote the *Canis lupus* identification. The jackal's mask (*Canis mesomelas*) fulfilled a similar role of deception as employed by the ancient Egyptians in the humanized form of Anubis (also called Anpu the Egyptian god of the dead and inventor of embalming during the Early Dynastic period). The jackal-masked figure was associated with the cult of Isis (see drawing 9.13).

DRAWING 9.13— Mask representing the jackal-headed god of embalming, Anubis. The embalmer (priest/shaman) known as "he who controls the mysteries" (*hery seshta*) wore a jackal mask during the rituals that accompanied the embalming process.[gg]

The shaman's costume often included the symbols of the animal spirit from which he or she, as well as, the entire clan or cultural group descended. The Siberian shaman's costume most commonly carried the markings of the reindeer (caribou), bear, bird, or deer;[80] whereas, among the Huichol Indians of Mexico the wolf was the animal of cultural endorsement.[81] The preferred animal in other areas was the jaguar, panther, eagle, raven, bat, fox, crocodile, or various snakes, and fish. The relationship between humans and wolves was, however, nearly as universal in "traditional" societies as the belief in magical healing.

An omnipresent animal transformation belief closely associated with shamanism was that of were-animals. Moreover, while superstitions and myths dealt with were-animals in different ways, from the hysterical to heroic, there were certain universal correlations. The belief that unknown forces could assume a form that played on existing fears or associations was common. As one example, the belief in werewolves was most common in regions where wolves were routinely encountered. Cultural myths that include transformation were intended as regulatory measures to control or direct social behavior. Although in this example, people were warned against wandering about at night least they meet a were animal on the prowl, travel of the group often required shamanistic insight.

Belief in ability to be transformed (to change shapes) was related with the practice of voyaging into the land of the spirits. That brief did not presume that the shaman actually became a spirit, but that he or she passed beyond the mystical barrier between worlds and entered the realm occupied by spirits. A number of methods were used to attain a transformational state including group activities such as singing and dancing, ritualistic ceremonies involving fasting and sun gazing, or consuming various kinds of stimulants or hallucinates. (Ancient Persians were believed to drink a hashish-based concoction, and various South American tribal groups consumed vast amounts of tobacco to achieve a shamanistic trance.) However, the only way of actually passing beyond the limits of terrestrial space—the middle ground was spiritual or physical death. The corpse, in that culminating act, stayed behind while the spirit journeyed to where it was transformed and remained, or where it was rejected and returned to reunite with its material body.

The practice of transformational release served many objectives including the purging of sins and maladies that were conveyed to either animate or inanimate objects. The weaknesses of the body could be transferred to a stone, stick, plant, or effigy, and casting the object away eliminated fatigue or pain. Alternatively, social misconduct, misfortune, illness, and sin could be transferred to other humans or animals. The shaman performed in the presence of the errant person and accepted the malady or sin to facilitate the exculpation process. Immediately following the transposition, the shaman adjourned to a traditional burial place and reclined on a brier or the ground as though dead. The act of symbolic death exorcised the negative spirits leaving both the patient and the shaman free from the malady.[82]

The supernatural was an extension of daily life, and as the central figure in ritualistic practices the shaman lost individuality and merged with the universe as a harmonious whole. Because the material and spiritual worlds were joined but different and many physical realities were the result of spiritual causes, rituals served to locate and consolidate supernatural influences. The shaman facilitated the exchange between the two domains.[83]

10

LIFE, DEATH, AND SACRIFICE

For the Hopis, death was part of the recurring cycle of life — another emergence from one world into the next — and the ceremonies that accompanied it were the simplest of all the Hopi rituals. A man's body was wrapped in a deerskin, a woman's in her marriage costume and a cotton mask, symbol of the rain cloud, was laid over the face.[1]

The Connections of Life and Life-Giving Worlds

Shamanism was the connection between the living and life-giving worlds. The material and spiritual realms in that arrangement were viewed as inter-relational instead of being distinct from one another.[2] The dynamic paradox of life and death was not easy for people to understand or explain. However, examples of natural transformation were abundant in their lives as some organisms were consumed so others could live. Reasons to believe in renewed life could be found in natural cycles that appeared to be inspired by shamanistic ritual and spiritual intervention. Seasons changed, crops returned, the sun reappeared, the ill recovered, and the complex process of childbearing for humans and animals were phenomena most easily explained by the intervention of spirits and the notion of death and rebirth by spirit transfer.

The shaman had a primary role in three life events: birth, marriage, and death. The shaman of the Goldi-Ude (also called Nanai, people from the Amur region of northeastern Asia) had a ritual to perform when a child was born, and when a woman could bear no children the shaman ascends to the heavens to acquire an embryo soul to ensure conception. Among the Buryet (people living south and east of Lake Baikal), the shaman performed a special ceremony after a child was born to keep the infant from crying. In addition, the Goldi-Ude shaman had the responsibility for catching the soul of the dead and escorting it to the Yonder World for possible return as a newly born member of the clan. The shaman also encouraged the transient soul to prevent illness.

Life and death were linked in many ways. The Yukaghir (also spelled Yukagir or Jukagir, a people living in Arctic Siberia east of the Lena River in Russia) traced their origin to a primordial shaman. In ritual acknowledgement of that ancestry, they retained the skulls of deceased shamans and no action was undertaken without consulting those skulls.[3] The Yukaghir believed that humans have three souls and at the time of death, they separate. One soul "remains with the corpse, the second went to the Kingdom of Shadows, and the third ascend to the sky."[4] According to the writing of Mircea Eliade,[5] the important soul was the one that became a shadow, because in the Kingdom of Shadows, the person continued to lead the same life as he or she had known on earth.

Displacement of the corpse reflected social attitudes about the dead. The northern Yukaghir placed the dead on platforms raised on poles. However, the southern Yukaghir of the Kolyma district distributed the flesh and bones of the deceased among the relatives, who dried the portions they received and place them in leather bags.[6] These "scraps" were used as amulets, called "Grandfathers," and were considered very effective in sympathetic magic.[7]

Among the Koryak, a people of the Russian Far East, an individual was declared dead when breathing ceased. The final exhalation was believed to signify that the chief soul (*uyicit*), was being attacked by the *kalau* (evil spirits corresponding to the Chukchee *kelet*), and it had deserted the body (although death can also be sent as a punishment from the Supreme Beings).[8] "There was, however, another soul called 'breath' (*wuyivi*), and still another called 'shadow' (*wuyil-wuyil*)."[9]

The Khanty and Mansi, people of western Siberia, also connected the moment of death with the last breath. A stick was placed in the dying person's mouth as death approached to prevent him from clenching his teeth and hindering the fourth soul from leaving the body. (The reference material described the procedure for males.) After death preparations were made immediately for sending the deceased on his last journey. His hair was carefully cut and someone, not a close relative, cut one lock for the subsequent preparation of his image. A mask made of "reindeer skin or cloth onto which opposite the ears, nose, mouth, and especially eyes, copper buttons or disks are sewn"[10] was placed on the face of the dead. Before the coffin was closed a copper disc or a stone was placed on the corpse over the heart. In cases where there was particular fear of the dead, a rock was also placed on the mouth. These precautions were to prevent the deceased from wandering and disturbing the living.[11]

The Maya shaman believed that "death attacks us in the forms of suffering and cruelty"[12] before its final approach. They said, "[d]eath comes to the body as disease, disfiguring, handicaps, reduced resources of energy and concentration, growing aches and pains — failing biological and mental systems."[13] The Maya also believed that because death was inevitable individuals should be judged on how they prepared for that finality. "According to the shamans, all ecstatic experiences of the sacred were brushed with the eternal life that awaited prepared souls in the timeless realm of death-life."[14]

> When the souls [the "body soul" and the "life soul"] of the deceased leave the body, they take the shape of birds, and fly towards the north, where the realm of the dead is to be found according to [Finno-Ugric] legends.[15]

Two beliefs exerted great influence on the concept of death. The first was belief in the death and resurrection of an enduring being who could confer the gift of immortality on others. That belief in an afterlife was first sought by the kings and priests and subsequently by ordinary people. The second important influence was belief in a postmortem judgment in which the quality of the deceased's life influenced his or her ultimate fate. As an example, the ancient Egyptians spent much of their time thinking of death and making provisions for their afterlife. The vast size, awe-inspiring character, and the number of funerary monuments bear testimony to this obsession.

"The universality of man's faith in the survival of the soul after death [was] attested partly by the universality of the belief in ghosts, and the uniform practice of placing food in the tombs of the departed."[16] Life changed and was renewed. The notion of new life and salvation existed among virtually all people in all times. Life and death in many cultures were the same; only the physical state of the body changed. The Tibetan Buddhists believed there was a short interval between death, the departure of the spirit, and the beginning of a new cycle of life. The spirit, during that interlude, was thought to dwell in the intermediate world and experienced many strange and unusual encounters.

Life and death were an inseparable cycle that imposed a temporal state of being on all creatures. As a permanent metamorphosis, death was an acknowledged separation from the world of the living and a transformation that included the relocation of energy from one source to another. "The spirit went out of the body when it died, but it could go into some strange-shaped stone or a piece of carving. Such a thing had power."[17] The confirmation of this belief was assigned to shamans, and their power-aligned role varied in different cultures or ethnic groups. However, in most places, shamans were involved with the activities of daily life, and their authority reflected their personal experience.

> The dwellers of the upper world were regarded as the owners of the souls (kut) of humans and animals. They were viewed as deities capable of providing humans with happiness and prosperity and of defense from sickness and misfortune, if they so desired.[18]

Power in its various manifestations was central to shamanism wherever it was found. It was power as an expression of existence and nonexistence (death) that was essential to all animate and inanimate objects.[19] The quest for spiritual power was inherent in most early cultures, and one way to gain that power was to kill other human beings.[20] Members of headhunting societies took heads as trophies to mark their prowess and to assure a measure of mystical power because the head was believed to be the spirit home.

Belief in death as a phenomenal state of being was structuralized in some cultures. The cult of the dead was based on fear of ghosts or the spirits of the deceased. It was naive fear of a primal nature. Measures had to be taken to prevent the return of spirits and to ensure that they did no harm to the living. Precautions consisted of breaking the bones of the corpse, so the ghost (soul/spirit) could not move, transporting the body to its grave by a circuitous route so the soul could not retrace the path, or removing the body from the dwelling place through an opening made for that purpose in the side of the structure. Among Bushmen and Bantus in South Africa, the entire village moved after the death of one of its members.[21]

The shaman, as psychopomp, was responsible for escorting the "souls of the dead to their new realm in the other life."[22] This was an important task in many cultures, for instance, among the Goldi at the Amur River in Russia, the shaman also directed the memorial ceremonies for the dead. The shaman was believed to dispatch his free soul to accompany the dead person to his or her final location. In the Khumbu and Pharak regions of Nepal, "one of the important functions of the shaman [was] to determine how many days the body of a deceased person should remain unburied. It was supposed that the spirit did not leave the body immediately after death...."[23] The people of those regions also believed that the dead person had absorbed the spirits of others in the community, and that if they were not recovered by the power of the shaman, they would accompany the dead man's spirit on his long journey "up the river," to the village of the dead.[24]

The shaman responsibility was to recover the purloined souls or the owners would die. To fulfill this task, the shaman stood by the body of the deceased and gave it a slight blow with the hand to initiate the recovery process. The blow presumably dislodged an absorbed spirit that was subsequently kept in a safe place for a few days until it was returned to its owner.[25] The soul recovery alleviated communal concerns about the uncertainty of life after death, and reestablished an acceptable balance between the living and the dead.

The Tungus believed that during shamanizing, especially when the shaman went to visit the lower world, the death of the shaman might suddenly occur. The Tungus explained that the shaman died because his soul could not return. It was assumed that the soul was stopped on the way back by other spirits and even by other shamans. Therefore, special measures were taken for calling back the shaman's soul.[26] Death in that case might also be caused by overexertion or self-deprivation, or the shaman might be convinced that his or her soul was captured and in response reduced the normal functioning of the heart and breathing causing death. Among the Reindeer Tungus in the Lake Baikal region, soul recoveries from the lower world were believed to be so dangerous that few shamans accepted the request.[27] It was for that reason that Tungus shamans rarely descended into the lower world.

Various forms of "voluntary" death were known among ethnic groups. The Australian aborigines might decide that death was inevitable because of a violated taboo, and will their passing. Among the Chukchee self-determined death was a regular occurrence. Death might be the result of deep sorrow for the demise of a relative, for a quarrel, or sometime because of a feeling of depression. Another more prevalent form of voluntary death among the Chukchee was (traditional) suicide. "Mature or old people were killed by some near relative at their own request."[28] The killing of old people also existed among the Koryak,[29] and it was considered lawful for a Central Eskimo man to kill his aging parents.[30] It was generally believed that old people were killed because they preferred death to the hard conditions of life as invalids. The Chukchee believed that "[a] voluntary death [was] not only better than a natural one, but [was] considered praiseworthy, since people who die this kind of death had the best abodes in the future life."[31]

When people realized that life was the expression of death and death was the expression of life, and that continuity could not exist without interruption, then there was no longer a need to cling to one and fear the other.[32]

For some northern (Arctic) peoples there was a contradiction of attitudes about death and the dead — a further manifestation of the dichotomy of opposites. The Eskimo identified three dwelling places for the dead: "the sky, the underworld immediately below the earth's surface, and another deep underground."[33] It was believed that the dead had a happy and prosperous existence in the sky and the deep underground. The great difference between living in those locations and life on earth was the seasons were always reversed. When it was winter for terrestrial beings, it was summer in the sky and underground.[34] It was also believed that "the shamans had perfect knowledge of all these regions, and when a dead person, fearing to take the road to the beyond alone, abducted the soul of a living person, the *angakok* [shaman] knew where to go to look for it."[35]

Egyptians had a pervasive belief in a future life. Consequently, preservation of the body was for the Egyptians central to all concerns about an afterlife, and the notion of a disembodied existence after death was unacceptable. They provided provisions for the spirits of the departed, preformed elaborate funeral ceremonies, and developed mummification (preservation) of the bodies into a ritual practice. Those activities were witness to the strength of the Egyptians' convictions of the reality of the next life. It was alleged that an individual's body (*khat*) had a double (*ka*) endowed with all the person's qualities. It was uncertain where the *ka* dwelled during an individual's life, but to go to one's *ka* was a euphemism for death. The *ka* was believed to have power, and the after the person's death, it had to be cared for and fed. The maintenance of the *ka* was the responsibility of a specific group of priests (shamans). The *ka* gave comfort and protection to the deceased as illustrated by its hieroglyphic sign that shows two outstretched arms in an attitude of embrace.[36]

Sanctification with Blood

The difficulties that humanity endured were often prefigured on the adventures of mystic heroes, and the alternation between production and destruction — life and death — was a primary theme in many myths. The Dogon, an ethnic group on the central plateau region of Mali, were followers of traditional practice that included the spiritual leader called a *hogon*. The Dogon expressed issues of life and death in terms of ascent and descent, and their difficulty was whether to attribute the division of life forces to *Amma* (above) or *Jackal* (below).[37] The question reflected the traditional struggle between good and evil. *Amma* (the creator) was androgynous and considered perfect, whereas, Jackal (the created and subject to hunger and death) had no second self and was, therefore, imperfect and sinful.[38] The myth included the need to make the appropriate sacrifices with blood to sanctify and fertilize the ground.

Fear and respect of death were real consideration, and for most people the possibility of dying whether real or imagined caused concern about issues that might have otherwise gone unattended. The dead, in many early societies, was considered a primary threat whether they were an ancestor, enemy, or beast. Consequently, the ethereal world was occupied by a variety of potentially harmful spirits that had to be pacified. The shaman had a special role in dealing with the potentially dangerous spirits. It was his or her ability to intercept or divert the harmful intent of malevolent spirits that was critical to the wellbeing of community members. Because of the secretive powers they possessed the spirits of the dead were feared. Their dynamic force could provoke any number of calamities from sickness and infertility to bad luck and privation. A combination of activities and spirit evoking devices were required to circumvent the powers of the dead. Weather the need to control these spirits was real in the sense of power or mental in the way of ego/potency was uncertain; nevertheless, the shaman's role was very important in the ongoing struggle.

Acknowledging the relationship between shamanism and life was to recognize the "ecstatic oneness with the gods,"[39] and to be aware of the shaman's need to sacrifice his or her physical and spiritual wellbeing to become mediators of daily existence. The attribution of a spirit presence to all objects including clothing and tools, environmental features, and natural conditions such as storms and illness was part of the inclusive shamanic tradition. "For example, smallpox was considered by the Nganasan [people of the Yenisey River valley in central Russia] to be a Russian spirit."[40] In life situations people sought to befriend good spirits and fought against evil ones by those means available to the particular society (see drawing 10.1). Such means included taboos regarding eating, hunting, rituals, and sexual intercourse. Shaman as the keepers of tradition mediated between the many spirits and the people. They defined the taboos, performed the necessary rituals, validated the hunt, and often confirmed the proper time for procreation.

The Maya, a Mesoamerican people, viewed death as the "great black wall against which all life shattered. It was the end toward which each of us was racing with our achievements,

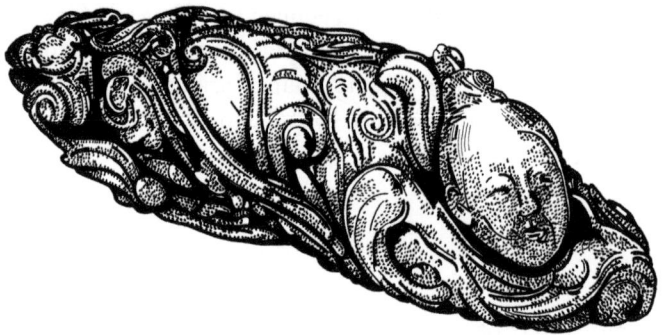

DRAWING 10.1— Carved jade *Apsaras* (heavenly nymphs/spirit beings) made in the Tang Dynasty (eighth to tenth century of the current era). The image is associated with Chinese shamanism or Daoism.

our hopes and disappointments, our loves and hates, our cherished identities"[41] According to Douglas Gillete, writing in *The Shaman's Secret* (1997), the Maya were "fascinated by the darkness. But their morbidity, like that of the ascetics, warriors, and sages of other religions, had a purpose. It helped them to stay awake to death."[42] Belief in the inevitability of death was a real part of Maya life, but when it came near, belief contended it could be overcome. "Seeing in this way helped the Maya shamans unmask death's crafty, tricksterish ways and expose its life-imitating pretensions."[43]

People in many cultures were guided by spiritual beliefs and practices that evolved from earlier times. Indigenous tradition defined accepted practices. As an example, the Yanomamö of South America believed that all deaths other than those caused by human or animal intervention were attributed to harmful magic.[44] In contrast, the Navaho of southwestern North America were believed to place little importance on death and the afterlife. Unlike other indigenous people in the area, Navaho mythology has few references to the subject. Sorcery, fear of the dead, and ignorance are characteristics of the underworld and considered to be separate from Middle World activities. The first experiences of death are appropriately assigned to an early world and a part of the natural order.[45]

It is generally alleged that indigenous peoples of North American were unperturbed by the possibility of death. Their survival activities often included individual or group conflict, and bravery shown in the face of the enemy was a mark of honor. That is not to say that the Native American did not appreciate life or strive to provide for and protect his or her life and those of their families and clansmen. However, warriors often gave more attention to their behavior when threatened by death than to their hopes for life on the other side.[46] The uncertainty of the other world-afterlife was reflected in the fact that most Native peoples isolate the land of the dead from the world of the gods. It was said that the place of the dead was ruled by a spiritual personality that "might be the brother of the mythic culture hero or the first man."[47]

The Zuni were reportedly unafraid of death partly from a fatalistic attitude and partly due to the belief that after death existence was a continuation of the better aspects of life. Nevertheless, there were specific fears about death and the dead that might entice the living to join them. It was believed that a Zuni witch might bury a prayer-stick for a deceased member of a family and asked him or her to draw to himself or herself the one who caused the death.[48] It was not death, but the dead that was often a cause for concern. A deceased person was never mentioned by name to avoid contact with the dead. At Zuni a person that recalled the dead, dreamed, or fell sick soon after assisting at a burial inhaled smoke from piñon gum (copal) for protection. Frightened members of a household inhaled smoke from a lock of hair cut from the head of the deceased to avoid possible encounter with the spirit of the dead.[49]

The journey of the American Indian from the land of the living to the world of ghosts was recounted in numerous legends and myths. It was the medicine man/shaman who attended the living and escorted the souls of the dead. The transformation process was arduous, and it was often told that the deceased person started to the other world before physical death. The "free-soul" left the body for the land of the dead and when it had safely arrived, the "body-soul" that granted the body life and motion also left. "Sometimes there were four days spent between death and burial, considered to be the time the soul needed to make its way to the land of the dead."[50]

Death for the Shona, a people living in the eastern half of Zimbabwe, north of the Lundi River, was natural only for the aged, when it was believed to be an act of *Mwari*, the creator-god. The death of an old person was not a surprise, because it was a part of life that everyone should die. "Otherwise [death] was perpetuated by a witch (*muroi*) or sometime by the anger of a dead person whose spirit (*mudzimu*) was offended and had elected to punish the family in that way."[51] The afflicted person and his or her family consulted the village diviner (shaman) to learn the reason for the illness that eventually resulted in death; otherwise, the anger of the departed relative or the malice of the witch would continue and more illness and death would be visited upon the family. A major part of the shaman's (*nganga*, literally "medicine man or witch-doctor"[52]) duties was concerned with the determination of the source of the malevolence, because illness as a physiological manifestation of mental or physical disorder was a threat to group survival.

It was generally believed that witches cause all manner of illness and disaster. Some cultures believed that young women practiced sorcery and as old women they became witches that used nefarious methods to obtain their malicious objectives. Witch's used plants and animals in their ritual activities similar to the methods of shaman's, but for the opposite purpose. The Navajo believed that witches congregate at night, wore nothing except masks, sat among baskets of corpses, and had intercourse with the dead. In some African cultures, witches were believed to assemble in cannibal covens and feast on the blood of their victims.[53] Villages in Bali had a temple of death dedicated to witches and witchcraft (see drawing 10.2)

Throughout history the dead has been given special consideration, because the idea of some form of afterlife was an important aspect of early belief. Such thinking usually pertained to phenomena beyond the ordinary experience of the natural world. A number of deities governed different natural phenomena and various aspects of human life in the shamanistic world. It was common within that cumulative arrangement to have a special ritual to acknowledge death. The inclusion of such an activity in a group environment was not necessarily the same as the glorification of death. However, in practice the initiation of different rituals and tradition varied according to a number of factors including geography, politics, and the influence of other beliefs.

Traditional responses to death were an important part of humanity and central to many societal systems. In most cultures, the body underwent some form of ritual disposal normally either by cremation or interment in a tomb, crypt, or cave and accompanied by ritualized observances. Another method of corpse disposal used in Tibet was sky burial. This practice involved placing the body of the deceased on high ground and leaving it for birds of prey. Some native peoples of North America practiced a similar disposal process by placing the dead on a raised platform in a secluded location. That disposal process generally related to a traditional view that birds were carriers of the soul to the Upperworld.

It might have been a lack of knowledge about death and the physical limitations of the

DRAWING 10.2—A Rangda mask made in Bali. This mask of wood and leather represents the angry widow, a primary performer in the *Calonarang* drama. This drama was first performed in the fourteenth century in Java and gained popularity in Bali during the last century. In the dramatization the Rangda represented Dawi Durga, the "Queen of Witches," an expert in black magic and a symbol of evil. She challenged the local witches to match her ability during the performance. Although the "temple of death" in each village was dedicated to this character, the drama also tells a story about the history of the Indonesian people.

human body that influenced early beliefs about the metaphysical and ultimately resulted in the adoration of ancestors. Consequently, the mummification of ancestors was a common practice in the Andes. In the Peruvian highlands community ancestors were "spirit beings" that were consulted for many everyday activities such as travel outside the community as well as transitional events like naming and marriage ceremonies. The mummified ancestors often participated in those community-wide events. "They were dressed up in new clothing and offered food and drink."[54] Community members narrated the stories of their ancestral origins.

The ancient Egyptians had elaborate mummification practices and a fascination for the Underworld. Their Book of the Dead carefully guided mortuary practices including the disposition of the seven souls (*ba*) of the deceased at the time of death. The soul is represented in Egyptian hieroglyphics as the human-headed bird (see drawing 10.3). The soul in bird form was linked to the ancient belief about ancestral divinities in avian shapes. It was believed to have a sentimental attachment to the deceased, and could not survive without the preserved body.[55] Tombs were often constructed with a small opening or passage to allow visits by the *ba* after death. The shaman/priests were thought to have consulted birds—the souls of the dead—"throughout Greece, Rome and northern Europe because of the belief that all birds once lived on earth in human form and gave omens to those presently living on earth [that] were able to understand them."[56] The death ritual for the Shona also gave attention to the soul of the deceased; however, the process followed a different sequence of events. The first phase of the ritual was the burial (*kuriga*), the second was the determination of the cause of the death (*gata*), and the third was the settling of the spirit (*kurova guva*).[57] The shaman was a participant in all three phases of the burial ritual.

Many cultures incorporated a deity of death into their mythology or beliefs. Death, along with birth, was one of the major aspects of the life cycle, and the related deities were often among the most important in the particular culture. In some location where belief was resident with a single powerful deity, a hostile deity against whom the primary deity struggled represented death. For certain, all deaths might have been attributed to sorcery or witchcraft, but it was often only the "important" individuals that were singled out for special attention. Even so, the Yakut of Siberia believed that the good and bad went to the sky where the souls (kut) of the deceased took the form of "soul-birds" that perched on the branches of the World Tree.[58]

Shamans in communities in the Brazilian Amazon provided ideas, information, and ritual resources to address the crisis of death. They helped individuals and groups to cope with psychological trauma, social disruption, and cosmological imbalance.[59] In a comparable way, the funerary practice of the Lolo of western China required the shaman (*pimo*) to accompany the coffin of the deceased to the grave while describing the "ritual of the road." That ritual described the places through which the deceased must pass between his home and the grave, and continued by naming the cities, mountains, and rivers the soul must cross before reaching the original home of the Lolo people.[60] It was a final rite of passage.

DRAWING 10.3— The ancient Egyptians represented air (soul) as a human-headed bird that was thought to accompany the dead to the Underworld. The Egyptian goddess Maat first appeared as an egg and later changed to more conventional form.

The ancient Chinese envisioned the universe as being constantly reshaped and transformed out of primordial chaos, whereas, other peoples relied on the past to predict the future. The cycle of life and death was endless. The Jivero, a South American people living on the eastern slopes of the Andes in Ecuador and Peru believed that the real world and the determinants of life and death were only visible with the aid of hallucinogenic drugs. They considered all commonly described "normal" aspects of life to be false, and that truth could only be found by entering the supernatural world or what they considered the "real" world.[61]

Mystical Conjectures of Life and Death

Life and death were but one of the pairs of cyclical phases. Life and death for some cultures were not opposites but two aspects of the same reality. Nevertheless, death was very disruptive for communities, and for some peoples, it was such a catastrophe that mentioning it to those bereaved was regarded as a curse. It was thought that the dead were equally sensitive about their loss of life and resented being separated from the community.[62] Among some peoples the name of the deceased was not spoken, nor was direct reference made to the dead. The Apache, a militant people, had an abhorrence of death. Scalps taken in battle had to be purified in smoke to make them safe. When a member of the kin-group (band) died, he or she was quickly buried and his or her belongs (dwelling and possessions) burned.[63] In contrast, the Tlingit dressed their dead chief or his wife in ceremonial robes and seated the corpse against the back wall of the house where it remained for several days. During this time of mourning, "close relatives cut their hair short and blackened their faces."[64]

The natural and supernatural were intertwined in life and death. There was an inexorable flow of energy between the critical elements of human existence. The Andean Mapuche living in central Chile consider the corpse of the recently deceased dangerous to touch until after the wake and the burial process were underway.[65] In earlier times, the Mapuche smoked the body of an important person to dry and preserve them. It was the shaman's responsibility to perform an "autopsy" for the purpose of determining the cause of death and to prepare the corpse for the smoking process.[66]

Life and death for the early Chinese were contained in the eternal transformation from Non-Being into Being and back to Non-Being, the underlying primordial unity was never lost.[67] It was the acceptance of physical transformation that confirmed death as the ultimate transitional state of being. It was regarded as an occurrence of great significance in most early Chinese societies, and shamans had a primary role in the ritual-related activities associated with the transition. However, because the boundary between life and death lacked clear delineation many early peoples viewed death as simply a condition of "non-life." Among populations that recognized death as a conclusive physical condition, the cessation of life was seen as a release from the current cycle of existence and the beginning of another. Death could be viewed as an opportunity for renewed life through the transferal of guilt, sin, and other social transgressions, a concept reflecting the mingling of the material and spiritual worlds.[68]

Life after death was one of the earliest mystical conjectures and it had direct influence on the development of shamanistic practices. The socially recognized fear of death was the disclosure of a subconscious instinct common to humans. They did not want to believe their existence would end, and found it difficult to accept the idea of the complete cessation of being. It was likely from this perspective that belief in spiritual existence—immortality—evolved as a way to reassure people of life after death. However, with the sense of personal salvation came the discomforting hazard of the malevolent spirits of enemies and ancestors. If the good survived, so might the evil. The hopes and fears associated with life after death offered many opportunities for shamanic séance and the reassurances of spiritual intervention.

Possibly because death was a primary concern for early peoples, death's counterpart—the regeneration of life—was a primary focus for celebration. The foremost symbolic reference to the mystical practices of early people, and therefore of shamanistic importance, related to death and rebirth. In almost all cultures when a person passed from one level of existence to another—from birth to death—the transmigration of the inner being followed a culturally defined process. A person in Australia might become a medicine man (shaman) through a ritual of initiatory death, followed by a resurrection to a new and superhuman condition. The initiatory death, like that of the Siberian shaman, included steps or phases not found elsewhere: first, operations were performed on the candidate's body including opening the abdomen, removing the organs, washing and drying of the bones, inserting magical substances; second, an ascent to heaven. This activity was sometimes followed by ecstatic journeys into the other world. The secret techniques of the shaman were obtained in a non-ordinary psychic state (trance), dream, or in the waking state before, during, or after the initiatory ritual.[69]

The Aztecs gave considerable attention to the disposition of the human soul after death. They conceived different categories of death and therefore different location for the final resting place of the disembodied soul. Warriors who died on the battlefield or on the sacrificial stone could expect to become "companions of the sun" or "Eagle People." A similar fate awaited merchants who were killed while traveling in distant places and women who died in childbirth. The last of these were called "Divine Women." Other persons were sent to a purgatory under the northern deserts to be tormented by the skeleton-faced god of death (see drawing 10.4). The souls of the damned traveled for four years until they arrived at the ninth level of hell, and there they disappeared.[70] As expected, the shaman/priest as psychopomp guided the souls of the dead and were believed to have direct contact with the transcendent world.

Belief in renewal or reincarnation was a commonly held notion in many locations. The earth confirmed the renewal process as it brought forth new life after consuming the bodies of the dead. Accordingly, it was the responsibility of the shaman to intercept and placate the "passing souls." The transmigration of the soul offered endless opportunities for renewal but was equally invested with the possibilities of harm for the living. Ceremonies were arranged and séances held to evade the vengeful spirits. There was a psycho-physical need for the shaman, as psychopomp, to conduct the soul to its predestined location. The shamanistic rituals were to facilitate the safe movement of the soul from the physical confines of the corpse and where appropriate to aid in its recovery and return.

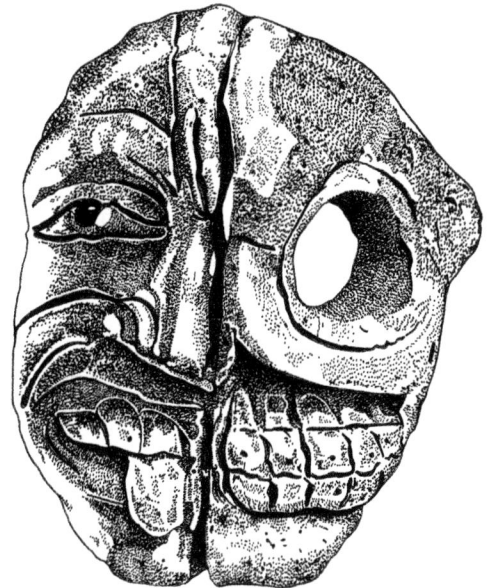

DRAWING 10.4 — Life and death mask made of clay from the middle preclassic culture of Mexico (circa 900–300 BCE). This mask exemplifies the concept of duality that was a central part of the indigenous cultures of Mexico. The two elements are combined to make a single statement. They represent the dual aspects of existence — good and bad, creator and destroyer.

The power in humans to generate life was a shield against death. The act of procreation was for that reason the natural foundation for early beliefs, and the symbols of regeneration were found in most cultures. Because the concept of rebirth was fundamental to most cultures, acceptance of the act of renewal or reemergence was a necessary aspect of perpetuating the social order of a people and a form of individual "spirit quest." It was a future oriented belief that marked the physical and psychological transformation of the participants. The Medicine Dance of the Winnebago was a ritual portrayal of rebirth that confirmed belief in life and death.[71] The participants in the ceremony experienced symbolic death and were reborn on a higher level (reincarnated). Those activities reaffirmed faith in the existing social order, evoked a sense of shared experience, and helped to formulate answers to questions about the destiny of the group.

Death and resurrection were a recurring theme in myth and superstition — the concept of transformation. Heroes or villains overcame the powers of death to return to the world of the living. Symbolic death and rebirth were aspects of the recognition process for many mythical heroes and heroines, as well as other lesser beings. "...[T]here [was] a dynamic paradox of death and life in all the mysteries associated with the opposites of night and day, darkness and light, above and below...."[72] Shamans sought physical and mental balance through reconciliation to accommodate the connections between opposites.

Death also altered the physical life of shamans, but unlike most Tlingit people that were cremated at death, Tlingit shamans were enclosed in a small funeral house. Reincarnation beliefs were strong among the Tlingit as was the opinion that the departed person continued to exist in the supernatural realm.[73] However, most other North American Native peoples did not deem the departed souls of their dead coexisted with the gods. A notable exception to this general situation was the Pueblo dead that were believed to become *kachina*—"spiritual beings that may live in the clouds and give rain and fertility...."[74] The souls of the deceased were believed by most Native people to travel to the world of ghosts, and to accommodate that repositioning, there was often a delay between death and burial to allow time for the soul to make its way to the land of the dead.

Ritual Death (Sacrifice) to Give Life

Both life and death required ritual recognition that often involved the shaman. The Daur Mongols called upon the bird spirit during the annual ritual of renewal to express their happiness and reconfirm the power of the shaman by raising his soul energy. The last night of the event (*ominan*) was reportedly devoted to "blood drinking." A calf was slaughtered (sacrificed), and the blood was collected in a bowl where it was mixed with milk.[75] Those persons present shrieked in a bird's voice to stimulate the shaman and announced the coming of the bird spirit. The shaman reportedly drank from the bowl of blood and milk until the spirits had satisfied their thirst and the shaman had renewed his life form. The shaman ended the ceremony by blowing blood over images of spirits hung in the trees.[76]

Sacrifice, such as the one just described, may have originated with traditional belief, because history shows that scarcely a single organized belief structure existed without some form of sacrifice. A belief tradition completely without sacrifice might not be impossible, but it was unnatural. Veneration and placation require some form of compensation, and the natural response was to sacrifice something to which value was assigned.

Sacrifice fulfilled a rational need in most culture. As an example, the hunter required a harmonious relationship with the various elements of nature. To sustain that relationship and at the same time meet the communal survival requirements, a way had to be developed to satisfy the seeming contradictory aspects of daily existence. The hunter killed and consumed the living products of nature; consequently, early humans constructed the idea of immortality to address the dichotomy of reverence and destruction. It was understood that living creatures were endowed with a soul that survived when the body was destroyed, and under the correct circumstances, the soul of slain animals could be appeased and caused to return. Sacrifice as a form of ritual appeasement was at the core of that practice, and once the belief in the supernatural connection was established, a bond between humans and the spirits was to be maintained. The shaman was a connection between the survival driven environment of humans and the supernatural.

The shaman of the Buryat, a Mongol people living south and east of Lake Baikal, was said to know the will of the gods, and so declared to the people what sacrifices and ceremonies were to be held. (The shaman was an expert in ceremonials and prayers.) Sacrifice for the Buryat was generally limited to animals especially horses and reindeer. In a somewhat comparable way, the Bushmen (San or Saan) indigenous people in South Africa were guided by the myth of Kaggen and the first eland. The San established and maintained communication with their god through the eland. "...[T]he mythological eland sacrifice, of which every hunting kill was a duplication, was the inexhaustible vessel out of which the bounty of the great god's world proceeded."[77] It was through the eland that the eternal cycle of sacrificing life to conserve and promote life was expressed.

Ritual sacrifice often required special preparation to ensure the acceptability of the offering. In *Shamanic Worlds* (1997), Marjorie Mandelstam Balzer wrote, "The Altaians [a Turkic speaking people living between the middle Volga and southern Urals in Russia] did not cut the animals intended for the spirits, but strangled them."[78] The author states that if "an animal were killed in the ordinary manner, the *siur* [the inner essence/soul] would escape through its mouth and the sacrifice would not achieve its purpose."[79]

Ritual sacrifice was a commonly used method for accessing the sacred, and the central element in all sacrifices was the victim or substitute that served as a mediator between the sacred and profane worlds. The sacrifice allowed the profane world access to the sacred without being destroyed; instead, the victim was destroyed in serving as a channel between the two realms. It was important to duplicate the original (divine) act in sacrificial rites; and because creation was variously conceived in different traditions, different means of imitation were preserved. As examples, the corn mother was burned or crushed, a white horse or bear slaughtered, or the blood of a shaman/priest spilled.[80] Sacrifice had validity only so long as it fulfilled the spiritual needs of the community in which it took place. The Native American willingly sacrificed a finger to confirm his belief, whereas self-mutilation in that form was repugnant to other cultural groups.

The rituals of sacrifices embodied the custom of propitiating the gods. Animals, fowls, and humans were sacrificed to secure bountiful harvests and success in the hunt, as well as the blessings and protection from the deities.[81] The Aztecs priests removed the hearts of the humans with flint knives to serve their gods. They held the still-beating hearts aloft, and then placed them in a ceremonial receptacle. Subsequent to the ritual sacrifice, the bodies were dismembered and eaten as an act of ritual cannibalism. Although the sacrifice of human life was fairly common in many cultures, blood sacrifices by shamans in Siberia were usually limited to reindeers, horses, or dogs.

The Daur Mongols made a clear distinction between "sacrifice" and "propitiation." According to Caroline Humphrey, sacrifice involved the "mystical giving-up of the life of the animal in return for a transcendental energy, which infused the social group with *keshi* (blessing, good fortune, luck)."[82] Whereas the act of propitiation "exchanged the animal's flesh for a variety of defined returns, such as the spirit agreeing to stay away or remove a disease."[83] In both rituals the Daur ate most of the meat once the proper observances had been made.

The Daur shaman did not participate in sacrifices. It was the *bagchi* or the "old man"[84] that directed that group activity. Sacrifice was viewed as an "intervention in the processes of the world and the indeterminate blessing it brought was essentially simply the good fortune that the cyclical current of harmonic world processes should be maintained."[85] When the processes of renewal were disrupted by natural or human actions other forms of propitiation were offered to the sky, mountains, or forest.

PLATE 7—Tatar shaman. The Tatar (also spelled Tartar) refers to several Turkic-speaking peoples that lived mainly in west-central Russia and western Siberia. Many Tatars were converted to Sunnite Islam in the fourteenth century but the influence of shamanism continued until the Russian Revolution in 1917. J. G. Granö took this photograph in 1914.

Sacrificial Transcendence

[T]he behavior of human beings is — except in cases of extreme insanity — meaningful and therefore ordered.[86]

Death was an essential part of the mystery of transcendence, and humans could enter the altered emotional state of blood-ecstasy.[87] As members of society, individuals believed what they were conditioned to believe when they learned the traditions of their people. Death as a consistent element of traditional practice inspired imaginative speculations about what happens to departed spirits. Nevertheless, it (death) was unyielding as a destructive force and its arrival meant that a man or a woman had his or her existence extinguished.

The occurrences of human sacrifice were widespread. The purpose of these activities varied from participation in a form of divine existence, to expiation, and the promotion of the earth's fertility. Ritual sacrifice included self-inflicted bloodletting as a means of offering the human life force. The bleeding of ears, tongues, and genital organs was a daily ritual occurrence for the shaman/priests of Mesoamerica, and sometimes the flow of blood reaching ghastly proportions.[88] However, "...the most sacred form of sacrifice was surely the offering of human life, for that offering involved the sacrifice of life to life...."[89] It is believed that the priests (shamans) viewed the sacrificial act as transferring a god to the gods. "A vital part of the sacrificial ritual, therefore, involved a symbolic transformation of the sacrificial victim into a god, a transformation metaphorically possible because man was both spirit and matter and could, through ritual 'become' spirit."[90]

Human sacrifice was often required to satisfy ritual events. "The Pawnee and the Sioux in North America, the Bagados of Mindanao in the Philippine Islands, the Gonds of Dravidian India, and the Incas of Peru, among others, all practiced human sacrifice to ensure the fertility of crops."[91] The belief that the fertility of the earth was linked to blood, and particularly, the blood from human sacrifice can be traced to creation myths. The "creators" of the world often were killed and dismembered. The elements for sustaining life emerged from their cadavers.

There are numerous reference of divine sacrifices recounted in mythology. For example, Osiris, Dionysis, and Attis were dismembered in sacrifice for rebirth. Offerings to the deities had to be untainted to assure the maximum response. "...[C]reation [could] not take place except from a living being who is immolated — a primordial androgynous giant, or a cosmic Male, a Mother Goddess or a mythic Young Woman."[92] The process remained the same in all circumstances. Nothing could be created without sacrifice. Myths told the people how their world was created out of the body of a primordial deity and other myths told how the human race came into being. Always it was from an ancestor or sacred being that was sacrificed, dismemberment, and in most culture resurrected as a deity in human form. Myth captured emotional truths that people perpetuated in life.

Human sacrifice is an example of cyclical thinking that was an essence of rituals involving death. In Aztec mythology, "There is no better single example of the fundamental idea that life [comes] from death, that sacrifice release[s] the life force, than the flayed god ... Xipe Totec.... By donning the skin of a sacrificial victim who had been flayed, the priest became the god."[93] In another form of sacrifice to Xipe Totec — the creator of god — the victim was tie to a scaffold and executed by being shot with arrows. In a less violent practice, shaman among the Aleutian Eskimos wore death masks made of wood to transform themselves into spirits.[94] The person behind the mask was generally well known to the audience, but the ritualized transformation stirred the imagination and called to attention the inevitability of death (see drawing 10.5).

Sacrifices of infants or adults were found among the Timucua of Florida (an extinct people), the Natchez of Mississippi, the Pawnee of the plains, and some aboriginal peoples of California and the northwest coast. Placation and appeasement required traditionally defined observances. Elsewhere, animals were offered as ritual nourishment for the spirits of deceased ancestors.[95] The sacrifice often was accompanied by requests for aid to overcome family difficulties such as infertility, sickness, or general misfortune. The sacrifice was, in that way, a part of a healing ritual and frequently it was the blood from the offering that had the most sacred (restorative) significance. In China, it was the responsibility of the head of household to make sacrificial offerings to the dead as a part of traditional ancestor worship. In early times those observances might have included blood sacrifice, but such offerings were replaced by foodstuffs and sanctified objects.

Blood sacrifices had special significance and in different cultures a range of animals served as offerings. This practice was exemplified by the deer as a part of the harvest cerebration of the Gurang people of Nepal or the bear sacrificed by the Ainu. A wild deer was captured and after a series of ritual events the shaman escorts the animal to the sacred grove where it was killed and its heart removed. The heart was offered to the ancestor deities and the Upperworld. The deer and the bird have important roles in the supernatural legacy of the Gurang. The Ainu captured a bear cub, raised it in the village, and killed it as a sacrifice to ensure successful hunting. The ritual included the "wearing of the fresh bearskin by a young villager who reenacted the bear's behavior during the ritualized hunt."[96]

Along with the sacrificial effusion of blood, burning was one of the most widespread ways of making an oblation available to sacred beings. The prior death of the victim (human or animal) was often incidental in sacrifice by burning. The act of human and animal sacrifice was viewed as a tribute to the continuity of life, and although the sacrificial method (burning) differed, the objective was the same. It was a ritual by which death entered into matter by "dividing the endless play of the elements in such a way as paradoxically to bring life into the world."[97]

The three levels of the universe for the ancient Maya — the Underworld, earth plane, and Overworld — were "like a fertilized egg dividing immediately [to] form themselves into first four, then eight vertical partitions, so that the cosmos took on the appearance of a seg-

DRAWING 10.5 — Magemut mask made of carved wood with goggles and large labrets. Bering Sea Eskimo men wore these masks in religious and dramatic presentations. Goggles symbolically informed the viewer that the identity of the figure was concealed. The labrets extending from both sides of the lower lip gave the mask a tusk-like appearance associated with the walrus. The belief that men could change into animals and animals into men was a central element of western Eskimo belief.[hh] The idea of transformational reality was pervasive among the people of that area.

mented sphere."⁹⁸ The Mayan system of beliefs included *Itzam-Yeh*— the "Bringer of Magic" and the arbiter of life and death, creation and destruction.⁹⁹ The shaman/priest gave "instructions for preserving the essence of the human spirit after death and then resurrecting it into eternal life."¹⁰⁰ Later Aztec culture also included the cyclic drama of death and regeneration. The drama as a social and cultural declaration confirmed that life and death were inexorably linked.

The notion of death for life was also manifest in cannibalism (anthropophagy), head hunting, and consuming the first produce of the fields. Ritual murders for purposes of cannibalism in which the human body or part of the body was consumed were often related to sorcery and witchcraft. However, among the aborigines of Australia, ritual cannibalism was an act of respect. Although the extremes of the activities seem great, the practices reflected survival strategies embedded in the particular cultures. The purpose was shared, but the methods of veneration differed.

Death might be a void, the cession of intelligent life, or "something immovable like the axle around which the wheel of circulation turns, whichever we choose, we have a notion that is definable only in terms of its opposite." The essential idea was that life could only take birth from another life that was sacrificed. Life and death were the opposite sides of the same spirituality (see drawing 10.6).

DRAWING 10.6— Press-mold made clay figure of a priest or shaman holding a head from the Tuaco-La Tolita culture circa 300 BCE to 300 years into the current era. The early culture was located on the southwest coastal region of Colombia and northwest coastal area of Ecuador. Human skulls were retained for divination purposes in many locations.

Life as an Imperfect State of Being

Death was the ultimate transformation from a life of activity to one of inactivity. However, it was also a process of physical change that correlated with other events that were elements of the life cycle. The symbolic enactment of death and the corresponding act of rebirth were significant aspects of the physiological metamorphosis of a person. Many societies endorsed the belief of rebirth in which the soul was transferred to another being. The migrating soul, in some belief systems, sought a higher manifestation that did not require a corporeal presence. This transcendental belief sanctioned a spiritual reality for the dead that relinquished earthly presence for a sustained existence in a state of perpetual ecstasy. The concept of paradise was, for others, viewed as simply an intermediate resting place for righteous souls awaiting resurrection. Death was an imperfect state of being for all people.

Sometime the land of the dead was a place not so far from the living and the attraction to cross the invisible line was great. The Maya shamans believed that soul-death was so seductive and diabolically clever that, without our knowledge or conscious consent, it often gained our fullest cooperation. It uses our personal weaknesses to attack our souls and those of the people around us.[101] The shaman in that unstable environment was thought to move back and forth across the division between the living and the dead as he or she carried out their interactions with the supernatural.

Nevertheless, people normally viewed death and the land of the dead from the perspective of the living. Myth and belief foretold that there were differences between regions of the dead, therefore, the method of death and the adherence to social codes and values (taboos) were important factors to consider. People tended to believe that a properly conducted life would ensure a greater degree of satisfaction in the afterlife, but in some cultures protecting against the invisible forces was a complicated process. Socially acknowledged spirits made their presence known at every opportunity.

Life offered numerous challenges, and there was a profusion of forces that threaten the Navajos including the Holy People—powerful spirits that "travel on the wind and on sunbeams, on rainbows, thunderbolts, and lightening flashes."[103] Those spirits used their power against the people unless rituals and offerings were made to placate them. It was only Changing Woman, the Earth Mother, who was always benevolent. The others spirits were often capricious. There were also lesser but equally threatening spirits such as "Big Fly, Corn Beetle, Gila Monster, Big Snake Man, and Brooked Snake People, Wind People, Thunder People, Cloud People, and Coyote, the trickster."[104] Each of those spirits had power and an energy that could cause sickness and death. There were, in addition, the ghosts of Earth Surface dead (*chinde*) that attacked travelers at night and inflicted the deadly "ghost sickness."

Navajo shamans concerned themselves with treating ailments caused by the spells of witches, ghosts, Holy People, and the effects of contact with non–Navajo people.[105] The process to exorcize the evil magic that caused sickness required the shaman to conduct an elaborate ceremony involving the construction of dry paintings (designs) made of ground materials or vegetable matter. Each painting solicited the help of a different deity depending on the diagnosis of the ailment. Once the painting was completed the "patient" was blessed by the shaman and receives the energy from the spirit depicted. The painting was destroyed to end the ceremony.

> When you bury a dead body you shouldn't leave tracks. Sweat shouldn't be dropped on the burial place. If you scratch yourself on a rock, blood shouldn't fall on this place. Also you shouldn't talk at the burial. When a person dies, only two people should wash and dress the body. They wear only moccasins and are covered with ashes. If you don't follow these rules there is sickness later, and you know it is because something was done wrong at the burial.[102]

Every culture had beliefs relating to the dead and their influences on those persons remaining on the land between the upper and lower worlds. Among the Chukchee the funeral rite included a series of protective magical ceremonies to guard against the evil influences of the dead.[106] According to Waldemar Bogoras writing in *The Chukchee* (1907) and quoted in M. A. Czaplicka's *Aboriginal Siberia* (1914), "The most dangerous were the double dead, the completely dead. They live on the very border of the country of the deceased people...."[107] The double dead were beyond the possibility of being reborn into the world therefore they became evil spirits. They were known to disrupt funeral activities. To avoid such disruption and to safely prepare the body, the clothing of the deceased was removed and the corpse placed between two skins with care taken to cover the face and the genitals. The body was watched for twenty-four hours to be certain the deceased did not return to life. People called "followers" cleaned and dressed the body, and after three days, the body was either burned or placed in a lonely spot exposed to the elements.[108] During the funeral

PLATE 12 — **Navajo Medicine Man.** The Navajo medicine man (shaman) served his community as a chanter (singer) of healing songs or by recitation of a cosmogony including the creation myth as a magical incantation. Healing the sick among the Navajo often involved purification rites including dry sand painting, fire jumping, sweating, and vomiting.

ceremony, the corpse was asked about the preferred means of burial and the disposition of property.

The Chukchee funerary ritual generally included sacrificing a reindeer and breaking the sledge used to transport the body. The bones of the reindeer and the remnants of the objects used in the ceremony were placed in a pile. "The 'followers' then transformed themselves into ravens or foxes, making appropriate noises...."[109] The leather straps that held the body to the sledge were torn to pieces, and the clothes torn off and placed beside the body, which was covered with pieces of reindeer flesh.[110] Then the nearest relative proceeded to "rip up" the body with a long knife. The throat was cut and the heart and liver removed. The process of disemboweling the corpse allowed inspection of the remains to establish the cause of death — often determined to be an evil spell.

A lingering spirit such as the double dead had a potency that was mobile and illusive. It could take other forms, and was capable of injuring a person. It was possible to guard against the attack of a living enemy, but defense against the malingering spirit of the dead required the assistance of the shaman. Special means had to be developed to regulate the activities of the dead and to prevent unwanted interaction with malicious spirits. People might influence the actions of spirits by using the proper charms, actions, and substances.[111]

Shamanism maintained that the soul of one who died a heroic or violent death ascended to the heavens, but the soul of a person who died from disease, which was caused by an evil spirit, went to the underworld. The role of a psychopomp, or conductor of souls to the netherworld was, therefore, an important responsibility performed for the shaman. The shaman guided the soul to its destination while narrating details of its journey to his audience. In cultures such as the Lolo, or Yi, in the mountains of southwestern China, the souls of all the dead were led by the shaman to the underworld; while in others locations, such as that of the Tungus, a subarctic forest people of eastern Siberia, the shaman was only called upon to act as psychopomp if the soul of the deceased continued to haunt his residence.

The adaptation of the psychopompic role of the shaman into Tibetan Buddhism resulted in the recitation of the *Tibetan Book of the Dead* to the corpse. That book described in detail the frightening apparitions the deceased encounters day after day while in the 49-day interval between death and rebirth, and its reading was analogous to the shaman's narration of his journey to the underworld.[112]

The Uncertainty of Psycho-Physical Beings

It may be considered that the Shaman religion was founded and developed as a combination of the understanding of "totems" or "sacred Heaven." This involved worshipping various natural beings and phenomena such as animals, plants, stones, wind and other beings or forces.[113]

People believed that the earth and sky were full of all types of deities or spirits. The Evenks imagined the upper world or *ugu buga* to be similar to the land inhabited by people. "According to their mythological concepts about this, the life of the sky-dwellers was conceived of as analogous to that of the Evenks."[114] Shamanic writing described the cosmological world as being like the world on earth, with good and evil deities with emotions and personalities similar to humans. Also, the division of labor of the human world was reflected in the upper world—men and women, young and old.

The Daur Mongols gave special veneration to natural objects such as the sky or mountains. Nonetheless, in rituals the various practices associated with natural elements were also made to substitute symbolically for social acts and activities. The tangible and intangible in ritual practice were given equal value and many qualities were interchanged. For instance, Mongols of the central steppes deified the sky and gave a name meaning "eternal."[115] Natural elements were personified, as were animals.

In "psychological terminology, shamanism consists of animistic and pre-animistic conceptions...."[116] According to Mariko Walter and Eva Jane Fridman, "shamanism was based in animism, the belief in spirit entities."[117] K. V. Vyatkina writing about the Buryat, a Mongolic people of southern Siberia, also noted that shamanistic practices among the people of Siberia, were based on animistic beliefs.[118] This concept follows the traditional theory of animism that endowed everything with a soul. Walter and Fridman note that animism "involved attributing human mental, personal, and social qualities to the unknown and natural phenomena."[119] Animism assigned spiritual life to all things; consequently, there was no distinction between the animate and inanimate. However, shamanism as a form of animistic belief as it originated in Asia differed from the animistic beliefs of other parts of the world. "Because of the animistic worldview, the boundaries between the material, vegetal, animal, and human worlds and between earth, heaven, and the land of the dead were not seen as absolute."[120]

Animism was common among ethnic population in South and Southeast Asia, as exemplified by the Ainu of Hokkaido. They believed that gods or their incarnations were found in every phenomenon or object. A similar belief was found in parts of Africa particularly among the Voltaic peoples, the Malinke, and the Bambara.[121] Across an expansive cultural horizon, humanity responded to unexplained events and beliefs by configuring a coherent cognitive matrix that addressed psychological needs. However, humans tend to draw boundaries, both conceptually and practically. One of the primary resources used in adjusting those limitations was myth including the legendary relationship with animals and plants (see drawing 10.7).

Animism was associated with magic, superstition, and the personification of nature in which inanimate and animate objects were viewed as active powers. The Yupik shaman of southwestern Alaska believed that "all living creatures and important natural phenomena (like storms, wind, rain), and landmarks (river mouths, hot springs, mountains) had souls and personalities and led their lives concealed in the background."[122] Those elements of the environment were thought to communicate directly with shaman/priest as though they heard and understood words. It was believed that discussion with the responsible spirits would ensure favorable conditions for community events and activities.

Some objects and rituals were considered more powerful than others. That attitude acknowledged

DRAWING 10.7—Tsimshian (also spelled Chimmesyan) painting representing a bear. The animal is "unfolded" to give a flat appearance. The two halves are joined along the centerline running from the top of the head to the rump. The front paws have a distinctively avian form. The bear had important symbolic and spiritual meaning throughout much of Northwestern North America and eastern Siberia. This image was probably a clan crest.

social order and promoted respect for certain animals and plants, thereby contributing to totemism, a system in which humans believed they had a special kinship with a totem. The term "totem" was derived from *ototeman* in the language of the Algonquian people of the Ojibwa. It originally meant "his brother-sister kin."[123] The root of the word signified the blood relationship between siblings but was incorrectly translated to refer to a belief that it referenced to the guardian spirit of an individual that appeared in animal form.[124] In general, totemistic beliefs were based on the psychological behavior of early peoples that ascribed to nature and natural beings a soul. The things of nature were given anthropomorphic essence often with superhuman qualities. The special relationship between social groups and natural elements established a feeling of unity that was promoted and enhanced by shamanistic rites.

In the regions occupied by the Finno-Ugric people the societal order was connected to animistic and totemic concepts. The oldest system of Finno-Ugric belief was thought to be ancestor worship and the practice was believed to include shamanistic participation. It was thought that the word for "shaman" was known in the Proto-Finno-Ugric era perhaps 3,000 years ago.[125] The shaman "thanks to the knowledge acquired by his double, or 'free soul' in his extracorporeal journey, maintained humanity in harmony with the mysterious forces of nature and animals, elevated to the level of spirits."[126] Totems, particularly those conceived as animals, bestowed a level of self-esteem on group members. Animals were thought endowed with qualities superior to humans.

"The Chukchee believed it useful to appeal to their departed ancestors for advice in difficult situations. The shaman, reaching ecstasy, would summon an ancestor spirit and ask it questions."[127] Ancestor worship as practiced in China was distinct from the worship of deities and there is no reference to an ancestor becoming a god. Belief in the soul or spirit presence in objects was not the same as ancestor-worship, and many people had belief systems that included reconciling the souls of the dead where ancestor-worship was unknown. The objective was often to get rid of the soul/spirit by conducting it to the Underworld, or sending it to the Upperworld, where it would not trouble the survivors.

> A limited number of people were inspired by stronger spirit powers than others. These were the shamans. They formed an elite since the numbers of men and women with shamanistic abilities were very small, and they were sometimes considered as outsiders to the community.[128]

The shaman's special ability within the group was to make personal contact with the supernatural by use of a sacred language. It was a privileged form of communication that separated the shaman from other members of the community.[129] The Yakut (also called Sakha) in the seventeenth century included a social stratum of shamans (*oiuun*) and shamanesses (*udagan*) as officiants of "religious" ceremonies.[130] The shaman employed many tricks and stratagems that were performed with the involvement of his or her helping spirits. The Yakut shaman was believed to be able to "blight" people and livestock—send sickness or death.[131] They were believed to possess the ability to be transformed into animals, and there were myths concerning the ability of Yakut shamans to "eat" a human soul—*kut* (life force).[132] There was an association between those possessing the gift of shamanism and evil spirits.

The act of "blighting" an individual used a mental process to disorient, oppress, and render a person powerless. The procedure called by Nikolai Alekseevich Alekseev "antipsychotherapy" resulted in psychological isolation of the individual causing him or her to be given over entirely to the power of the spirits summoned by the shaman.[133]

The shaman's activities were located between the land of human beings and the world of deities and spirits. Belief in the psychological and spiritual processes of re-creating the cosmos and turning death into life were noticeable influences in every aspect of ancient Maya life. Whereas "the Ogalala Sioux *yuwipi* man or shaman referred to himself as *iyeska*, 'interpreter' or 'medium' because one of his chief functions [was] to interpret the meaning of the visions of others."[134] The shaman's duties depended on the communities he or she served. Among these northern plains people, a shaman sang a chant to Buffalo Woman at the time of a girl's first menstruation and instructed her in her womanly duties. The shaman fastens a symbolic eagle feather to her hair to show her new status.

Siberian peoples generally acknowledged that one shaman could take the power of another. The more powerful shaman might destroy the weaker shaman and thereby eliminate his or her ability to shamanize. The shamans might battle for power in the community, for possession of a protector spirit, or for revenge of a past insult. "[T]he legends about shamanic combat reflected a continual testing of the 'powers' of the shamans by the faithful."[135] The supposed mortal combat between shamans was often a "performance" enacted as part of the process of healing a patient or gaining the safe return of a lost soul. According to Paul Radin writing in *Primitive Religion: Its Nature and Origin*, a book first published in 1937, "the initial and primary task of the shaman-priest was to emphasize and magnify the obstacles that stood between man and his natural and realistic adjustment to the outside world."[136]

11

TRANSCENDENTAL SHAMANISM

It is well known that shamanism can be found in every human culture at particular stages of development. During the evolution of humanity the functions of shamans as medicine men, magicians, mythmakers, and spirit connections, etc., were distributed among other social figures.[1]

There was probably never a time in the history of humankind when shamanism or a similar concept was not employed to meet the needs of the people and to promote community unity. Shamanistic activities included a practice of ritualization characterized by references to the past. It was probable that the extant community had little recollection (*a priori* knowledge) of the spiritual resource being endorsed, but the illusion of having already experienced something actually being experienced for the first time was a necessary part of shamanistic practice. Recollection (memory) and repetitive ritual reinforced acceptance.

"It is evident that shamanism is deeply anchored in the old hunting cultures with their individualism, animal-spirit beliefs, and hunting symbolism. In one or another form the shamanistic practices occur in all recent marginal hunting cultures...."[2] Related practices are less well adapted to agrarian cultures and cultures with "a higher level of technological and social complexity."[3] Although shamanism may be regarded as a continuous historical complex there is no clear evidence of its beginning as a socio-cultural phenomenon. Nevertheless, an early belief system based on interaction with spirits supported by rituals and ceremonies was very likely regardless of the designation. Shamanism provided relatively simple answers to complex questions about the circumstance that regulated the wellbeing of humans, animals, and the environment.

People at different cultural plateaus separated their social conditions into subsections and arranged those elements into an order of preference. In that configuration, emotion and passion were usually tempered by basic experience and reason, and individual reaction was moderated by group requirements.[4] Possibly the physical and mental equilibrium of early humans was compromised when confronted by events and circumstances that were previously unknown. Beset by such survival challenges, it was natural to imagine such conditions concealed evil and danger. Therefore, endorsement of the supernatural was an important way of maintaining the basic qualities of life because it preserved the values accepted by the people.

Shamanism in its earliest manifestations likely evolved from belief sanctioned comprehension of the relationship between the living and life-giving worlds. The material and spiritual realms were interrelated instead of distinct from one another.[5] Consequently, the ultimate shamanistic process was to bring the people into contact with the supernatural and natural worlds, and to enable them to live in harmony with those elements in all their extremes.

It may be assumed that the physiological and emotional needs of early people exceeded the limits of normal understanding and required supernatural intervention to find culturally acceptable solutions. It was a primary task of the shaman, therefore, to open a connection with the supernatural powers through the medium of ecstasy and thereby to control physical nature. Friendly spirits assisted the shaman to establish contact with the supernatural realm, but it was the helper spirit (familiar) that facilitated the beginning of the non-ordinary psychic state. That practice reinforced various methods by which the spirits could be brought near or driven away. It was also that transcendental practice that ranged beyond commonplace experience and allowed emotional interpretation to ameliorate an imperfect reality. The acceptability of that practice on both the physical and mental levels was continually modified to accommodate group tradition and experience. A sympathetic understanding had to exist between all elements of the transformational process to be effective.

Transcendental Aspects of the Material World

"Really great truths are invisible, and the realms of knowledge are a few scattered islands in a boundless and uncharted sea of ignorance."[6] In pursuit of essential knowledge, generations of humans have endeavored to reach into the regions of spirituality to understand the forces that influenced the tangible environment. Objects in nature, including the sky, humans, sticks and stones, the wind and human-made artifacts were assigned their own form of causal force or energy. Natural objects — plants or animals — had an identity that existed externally (outside their physical structure), and in that reality (the natural and spiritual life) represented a universal meaning for a particular culture.[7] Such symbols in favorable circumstances were a combination of form and content. It was a union of image and idea. Sometimes, especially in ritual contexts, people anthropomorphized those energies and gave them human characteristics, such as intention or consciousness.[8] Belief (psychological continuity) in those transcendental practices was an important ingredient in the notion of shamanism.

Shamanism is commonly described by reference to the elements of which it was comprised and its general motivations. In other words, there is a central idea and a series of symbols that expressed it. The central idea of shamanism was to establish contact with the supernatural world by the ecstatic or non-ordinary psychic state of an inspired intermediary—the shaman.[9] According to Louise Bäckman and Åke Hultkrantz writing in *Studies in Lapp Shamanism* (1977), there were four important component of shamanism: "the ideological premise, or the supernatural world and the contacts with it; the shaman as an actor on behalf of a human group; the inspiration granted him by his helping spirits; and the extraordinary, ecstatic experiences of the shaman." Those aspects of shamanism placed it on a different—elevated—level of cognition.

Making a distinction between natural and supernatural circumstances and conditions often challenged the most perceptive individuals. It is therefore possible that the real and the imaginary worlds were inseparable for many peoples, and the ideological combination was reinforced by hope and belief. Within that emotive paradigm the imagination, although defined by a variety of terms, was a field for psychic conjecture allowing various spirit beings to be present in a self-defining and protective environment. The important thing, however, was not so much the nature of the spirit world, but how, through that accepted structure, contact was possible between shaman and spirits.

Therefore, shamanism should not be considered just by the principles that applied to reality and everyday life, but by the standards that identified with the transcendental world of belief and tradition. Shamanistic practice interpreted the natural and supernatural influences people encountered as a form of truth that was indispensable to the environment in which early peoples lived. Because all natural objects had an existence that extended beyond human knowledge, they possessed universal importance no matter how small that universe might have been. Perfect perception and complete understanding of shamanism were not always possible in that setting. The stimulants of belief, hope, and anxiety were often only transcendental aspects of the material world. (Those ingredients might elevate expectations without generating an equivalent response.) Awareness of the possibilities inherent in shamanism had to find its way into the psyche of people through their sensibilities, and the most effective mechanism for assimilation was often a visual (physical) manifestation — the shaman's performance.

PHOTOGRAPH 23 — Taku (Tlingit) shaman from the Alexander Archipelago located off the coast of southeastern Alaska. The Archipelago was once the exclusive home of Tlingit and Haida people. The Tlingit potlatch was used to mark a cycle of rituals mourning for the death of a chief. It was also a time for other socio-cultural (shamanistic) activities such as the initiation of young men into a ceremonial society that included distinctive masked enactments of totemic spirits.

A commonly recognized symbol associated with Neo-Siberian shamanism was the shaman's dress — the coat, the mask, the cap, and the copper or iron plate (mirror). A cloth might be tied over the eyes in some locations as a substitute for the mask, so the shaman could penetrate into the spirit-world by his or her inner sight. Regardless of certain elements, the paraphernalia was unmistakably identified with shamanic practice. In other locations the shaman might have no special attire but used ritually enhanced and recognized objects (see photograph 23). The paraphernalia was of importance, because the spirits were thought not to hear the voice of the shaman unless the right dress and implements were used. Each people had some particular object that played an important part in the shamanistic ceremony. As a result of that affinity and because of their contact with a supernatural and often dangerous power, the objects were thought to be sacred.

It was generally believed that the shaman communicated directly with the supernatural world, and that connection was thought to give the shaman power to make impossible things happen. It gave him or her control over the forces of nature. Belief in the supernatural acknowledged an energy that addressed fundamental but challenging questions regarding existence that were unanswerable in other ways. The shaman in that facilitating posture had a primary role in attracting or exorcising spirits. The performance of duties and rituals based on traditional beliefs and myths concerned with supernatural powers were the shaman's tools, and since myths were not confined to physical limits, their creditability was unimportant.

It may be assumed that many shamanic activities were in support of practical matters such as determining where to hunt or fish, and how to survive a group-threatening situation. While these purposes may seem basic by contemporary standards, they were nevertheless essential to the survival of individuals and communities. There was no denying that demanding circumstances existed or that environmental and sociological conditions influenced the daily lives of people. Relief from extremes of whether, famine, warfare, or sickness was not only beneficial but necessary. Seeking reprieve from calamity could be viewed as a realistic approach to life-altering situations.

Shamanistic belief expressed a sense of elevated values and an ultimate reality that exceeded the mundane. The experience was understood as reaching into the realm of spirits as a quest for concentrated power to address a predetermined need. Although this ritualistic process may have been little more than a projection of the shaman's persona, or some type of illusion, it was nevertheless considered in many cultures as an initiating process that could alter human existence and promote survival. In support of this notion it was assumed that people sought to achieve consistency between their beliefs and their actions or between one belief and another. The shaman articulated and protected that union of ideology and practice.

As practitioners of spiritual intervention, shamans were transcendental (metaphysical) beings in that they were thought to move between worlds in an extra-corporal form and had multiple natures. They might therefore possess a dual persona, sometimes with opposed identities, which displayed ambiguities in species and where there may be oscillation between human and animal forms.[10] "Shamans were [considered] experts in the movements of the human soul, because they not only controlled the ecstasy of their own souls but specialized in the knowledge and care for other's souls, as well."[11]

According to most traditions, the shaman was also a doctor, and in some locations medical and spiritual practices were closely interwoven. In Kelantan (a state in northeastern West Malaysia) *séance* formed part of the ritual used to appease the spirits of a particular location or to banish evil spirits from the community or an individual (see drawing 11.1). The object of *séance* for the sick was to expel or coax an evil spirit out of the sufferer's body (or the community), sometimes into the shaman's own but usually onto a receptacle containing food. Subsequent to the ritual, the food was discarded along with the malevolent spirit.

Existence of the spirit/soul was an important element

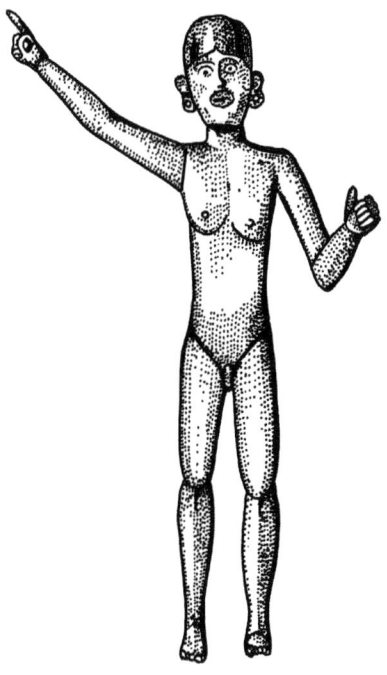

DRAWING 11.1—Spirit-scaring effigy figure from Southeast Asia used to cure disease believed to be caused by evil spirits.

in the development of shamanism and a common factor found in different locations. This belief gave reason to the notion of life after death including the possibility of resurrection. "Thus the concept of the continuation of life beyond physical death was consolidated and the idea of the coexistence of two souls in one body or in different places, although both souls belonged to the same individual was formed."[12] As wrtten in the *Popol Vuh*, Mayan chronicle of ancient mythology and culture, "the soul had five enemies — disease, death, stupidity, arrogance, and fear. Of the first two, one was only marginally under human control while the other was completely beyond it. The third, fourth and fifth were not."[13] Douglas Gillette wrote in *The Shaman's Secret: The Lost Resurrection Teachings of the Ancient Maya* (1997) that the "Maya believed that disease was the whisper of death, its first hint. But it was also an invitation from the Lords of Life to engage in the miracle of turning death into resurrection, of changing non-being into Being."[14] This concept was echoed across the plateau of human existence.

Shamanism as Memory of a Culture

The people gained a better understanding of the past by participating in ritual activities relating to tradition and by generating from that experience an understanding that had a strong instructional, as well as emotional component. Ritual activities stabilized the people's sense of who they were. Traditional events give a permanent shape to heritage of the people that otherwise would dissolve in the flux of consciousness.[15] Shamanism reacted to the sociocultural environment around it, because it stimulated its own understanding, as well as the formulation of directional messages and their use. The shaman worked in a setting that required a demonstrable knowledge of group practices and beliefs to promote community investment. The shamanic performances afforded a level of associational reference and consequential validation in addition to a level of spiritual elucidation.

Shamanism, because of its communal role, was often considered a unique feature in the evolution of human culture, and as Margaret Mead wrote in the preface of Ruth Benedict's book *Patterns of Culture* (1954), the word "culture" referred to the "systematic body of learned behavior which is transmitted from parents to children."[16] That collective memory of culture is of peculiar importance. It incorporates the history of a people and a record of past practices. Subsumed under the notion of culture are intangible elements that evade direct observation, including forms of spirit intervention (magic and mysticism). People in early societal units acted according to the examples given to them by their history and the characteristics of their communal order. This perceptual investment was true for their ritual, ceremonies, and beliefs. This concept related to all humans and all locations equally. Consequently, it is generally believed that time and place were necessary factors for determining the basis for such events.

Shamanistic belief had greater meaning than the symbols that assigned a historical reference to that practice. However, the representative values of shamanic activities were often subordinate to symbolic or mnemonic allusions. The shamanic heritage in most circumstances was verified through time as individuals or groups confirmed the importance of certain rituals and ceremonies. Examples of ceremonies confirmed by Native North American peoples were the Sun Dance of the Plains Indians (highly developed by the Arapaho, Cheyenne, and Ogallala Sioux), the Snake Dance of the Hopi, and the Salmon Dance of the Columbia tribes

(Sahaptian-speaking people living along the Columbia, Yakima, and Wenatchee rivers). Each of these people held within their traditions a body of beliefs and lore that confirmed their ritual activities.

Ceremonial activities were seldom separated into strictly social and spiritual events. Shamanic rituals included an element of the "popular performance," and most social gatherings had a measure of spiritual gratitude. The potlatch ceremony as practiced by the southern Kwakiutl people of the Pacific Northwest Coast was an example of that unification of social and spiritual activities. Potlatches were held to celebrate major life events as well as to address breaches of ceremonial taboos. Often the latter celebration required an amount of restitution to gain absolution. Those events often included dance performances that dramatized ancestral experiences with supernatural beings.[17] The Shamans' Society was a secret dancing society and the Hamatsa or cannibal-dances were a part of that group (see photograph 24).

The purpose behind every early belief system, including shamanism was to fortify group cohesion or integration. That process encouraged communal sustainability while delineating acceptable human behavior. When a group had that relationship there was an innate notion of identity, and with that identity the related tradition had validity. Real or imagined shamanic manifestations were likely viewed as elements of group continuity.

Memory of traditions was stimulated by two separate but interconnected systems. One mnemonic stimulus was verbal reminders associated with myths and legends delivered in abstract symbolic terms. This process included shaman guided ceremonies and rituals involving a learned and often evocative language. The other means was the use of imagery that incorporated symbols and various forms of perceptual information as represented by the objects associated with shamanistic paraphernalia (as in the example of the shaman's attire already mentioned). The concept of physical

PHOTOGRAPH 24 — Hamatsa novice preparing for the rite of purification. The hemlock boughs on his head and wrist show that he has been held in the woods as a prisoner of evil spirits. The Kwakiutl Dancing Societies were sometimes secret societies, each of which had a number of fixed dancing positions ranked in order of importance. Membership in the Shamans' Society was not restricted to shamans, but connected with an array of fearsome and violent supernatural figures. The cannibal-dancer, or Hamatsa, was the most prestigious character. Only a member of a chiefly lineage could occupy that position.

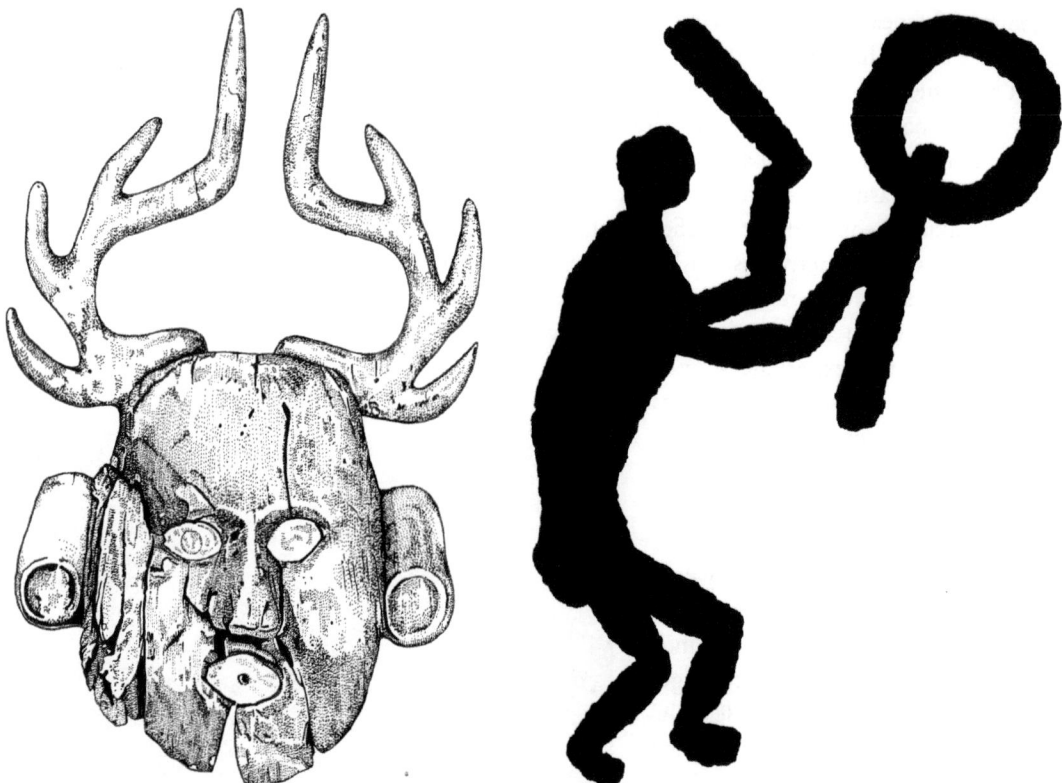

Left: Drawing 11.2—A transformation mask with antlers uncovered at the Spiro Mound, Le Flore County, Oklahoma (1200 to 1450 CE). The mask was made of wood with shell inlays for eyes and mouth. It was originally painted. This mask is an example of a symbolic representation of man and animal, probably used in the deer dance to ensure good hunting. An earlier example of antlers was found in sites related to the Hopewell period (ca. 200 BCE to 400 CE). People of status were buried during that time with copper and wood replicas of deer antlers. The deer, as a magical creature, was found in many cultures. Indigenous peoples in the Western world prized the deer as a prototype horned god, and in the East, Buddha began teaching in a Deer Park.

Right: Drawing 11.3—Shaman playing a drum.

transformation added both a vocal and visual reminder that traced its origin to "the beginning of time"—the primordial (see drawings 11.2. and 11.3).

Shamanism as a society-defining element had the function of stabilizing human life. It addressed the metaphysical question about the relationship of mind and body and held an essential position to the concept of personal and group identity. However as a social phenomenon, shamanism was often difficult to explain without overlapping into fields of behavioral science and psychology. There were, however, certain considerations to be pondered particularly the apparent contradiction between the finality of information dissemination and the abstract character generally associated with shamanic investigation.

A complicating element in the study of shamanism is that each cultural group developed its own beliefs, customs, and values that the incumbent population continually recreated. The physical world in which a people existed was composed of various circumstances that were continually mingled and transformed. It was a world regulated by organic laws that maintained the unity of substances in all their forms. Human interaction with the physical world was tempered by physical and psychic prowess that manifested itself as spirits. Human understanding was extended into that concoction through sensation, knowledge, judgment, and will. The spirit world in its various permutations embodied both physical and psychological elements, and was believed to be the source of all life.

Although the beliefs of a society were formulated at its inception, most people have limited recall due to the selective nature of generational transfer. In dealing with conditions beyond the normal bounds of human experience, people sought assistance from ethereal beings. To convey that aid the shaman used symbolic elements that were products of the past, although the producers were not always easily identified. That practice allowed spirits to manifest themselves in various ways and to be perceived as fulfilling different functions. They were a source of power — real or imagined.

Shamanistic practice had extraordinary (powerful) emotional appeal since it evoked a feeling of stability based on an established relationship with the spirit world. Shamanism helped to promote an environment where the people: (1) acquired awareness of the continuity that verified human existence, (2) glimpsed a past that they received with admiration and gratitude, and (3) projected a future that provided an acceptable level of hope.

The symbols and symbolic references were derived from human convention as products of unique cultural environments. The ideas behind specific shamanic performances had clearly assigned activities to validate their intentions. Typically the value of shamanism was predicated on its practicality to the host community. Such practices had elements that were recognized for their symbolic reference as well as their application to ensure acceptability. Practices that lacked symbolic reference were viewed as activities that sought to modify certain values and norms by repetition. However, because the relationship between idea and representation was an abstract notion, the amount of information transferred or the change realized might be limited.

As stated, primary element of ritual symbolism was the drum. It was the most important of the shaman's tools (symbols) in cultural groups across Siberia and most regions of Northwestern Asia. The shamans of the Turks of Central Asia perform ceremonies in which the drum (*tiungur*) plays an important role,[18] and the Tlingit people living along the Alaskan coast also relied on drums for ritual purposes. Drum making was a part of the initiating period, and drumming was a primary element of the ecstatic technique. The drum was made from special wood that symbolized the cosmic tree in the belief system of the Siberian shamans. It is possible to establish exactly which ethnic group made the drum by its form, because it was a traditional instrument and belonged to the class of sacred objects, therefore its form conserves both tradition and belief (see plate 21 and photographs 10, 11, 19, and 20).[19] Shamans outside Siberia and surrounding regions were less likely to use the drum to induce trance. Across North America and Northern Mexico, drums were used for ceremonial purposes, but shamans most often relied on rattles, whistles, and chants to enhance ritual activities (see drawing 11.4).

Masks were another symbolic vehicles designed to communicate a pre-established message or series of messages. In that interchange, they had an artificial presence interposed between the person behind the mask and the audience. The communication emanating from the masked activity often was complex and evolved on multiple levels. A special message was sent to persons in the presenting or competing social organizations. Viewers of the opposite gender to the performers were given a different message, and persons of an older or younger age cohort received a completely different signal. All the messages were included in the masking activity, and all were calculated to have the optimum impact upon the audience — old or young, male or female, initiated or uninitiated (see drawings 11.5).

Masks reflected "vision quests" to identify particular bird or animal to serve as a spirit helper or "friendly." Connection with the appropriate helper facilitated access to powerful and important supernatural beings that were visited through dreams and visions. Those visionary images were also the principal source of inspiration for masks for numerous cultures.

Certain ritual masks by their implicit rigidity were associated symbolically with the face of the dead and spiritual transcendence. They encouraged a psychological as well as a ritual relationship between the living and the dead.[20] This relational concept is illustrated by the legends of the Dogon people of Western Africa, They believed that in primordial times people did not die, they were transformed into serpents and lived eternally.[21] Consequently, in that region, the serpent form was incorporated into the "Great Mask" that was a primary element of the grand funeral ritual.

Shaman as Life Force of the People

Life from death as a part of the shamanistic transformation extended to the notion of rebirth. The myth of the devouring spirits that ate evildoers and subsequently returned them to life existed among the Bushmen of South Africa, the Greeks, the Hindus of India, and others. Zeus was swallowed and disgorged. *Indra* once entered the body of a cow and a deity of the African Bushman, *Cagn*, entered the body of an elephant before emerging to assist the people.[22] Reemergence was a part of the transformation process. In South America the shaman must died that he or she might receive the teachings of the dead, because the dead were believed to know everything.[23]

Left: DRAWING 11.4—Tlingit salmon rattle containing an effigy figure of a shaman. The Northwest Coast people believed salmon were supernatural beings that voluntarily became fish to sacrifice themselves for the benefit of humanity. Once taken, the spirits of the salmon returned to their home beneath the sea where they were reincarnated provided their bones were returned to the water. If, however, the salmon spirits were offended, they would refuse to return to the river. Therefore, there were many prohibitions on acts believed to offend them and observances were designed to placate them. The salmon ceremony was the primary means for honoring the salmon.
Right: DRAWING 11.5—Devil (Diablo) mask worn during celebrations in Mexico. This mask was carved from wood and has a leather tongue and ears. The antlers are from a deer. Masks of this type incorporated human and animal elements to create a visually thought-provoking image. Devil-masked individuals play the part of tricksters. They draw attention to local issues and by receiving problems and concerns from the people they performed a curative function.

Those life-altering mythological experiences were the source of distinctive practices that perpetuated cultural traditions. Control of life and death was an issue of considerable importance among most early peoples.

The shaman as possessor of supernatural power represented the life (and death) force of the group (tribe or clan) in which secular and spiritual spheres were not distinguished. The magical power of the community was often concentrated in the shaman, and his or her authority was based solely on the possession and exercise of that supernatural energy. The impact and comprehensiveness of such power often reached into all aspects of communal life.[24]

The shaman, wearing a special coat (see plates 10, 11, and 15 through 20), was believed to receive supernatural power that allows him or her to go to the Upperworld and Underworld to meet spirits and deal with them. However, this concept did not acknowledge the complete significance of the relation of shamanic paraphernalia to the spiritual world. Such objects (large and small) were of great importance, for the spirits did not hear the voice of the shaman unless the right dress and implements were used, and the drum beaten; they are sacred because of their contact with a supernatural and often dangerous power.

Seeking power was a demanding process and visions were said to appear before the shaman "as in a dream." The force of the vision and the sense of reality could be so great that "the shaman could even die during the séance, if the dangerous journey to the spirit world beyond lead to an encounter with a powerful enemy, who according to the beliefs of the people, could capture the shaman's soul and kill him."[25] Spirit unification was represented "physically in a cultural repertoire of shuddering, 'falling unconscious,' making inarticulate noises, foaming at the mouth, etc., but there were also established shamanic routines of contact with spirits that did not involve such 'ecstatic' behavior."[26] Interaction with spirits in dreams or awake was a determining sign of shamanistic vocation, whether spontaneous or voluntary (see drawing 11.6).[27]

It is said that the shaman performs his or her activities in a trance or non-ordinary psychic state, and that the altered plane of consciousness was achieved by means of monotonous sound including chanting and drumming or dancing. Some shaman used both sound and motion and others use neither; however, a primary aspect of shamanic performance was audience participation. The transcendent state had to be transmitted to the audience to be completely successful.

Considered from the practical point of view, shamanism acquired greater meaning when assessed from the perspective of its host environment. As an example, the role of the Sibundoy shaman (from the Upper Patumayo in Colombia) was to "cure illness and other misfortunes believed to be mystically caused."[28] The shaman was the only person believed capable of curing diseases originating from mystical causes. The practice of the shaman was inseparable

DRAWING 11.6—Metal (probably copper) shaman's helper mask, possibly Evenki. Masks of this type were not worn but were placed by the shaman during ritual activities.

from *yagé* (*Banisteriopsis sp.*) a hallucinogenic plant. "When a Sibundoy shaman discusses his conceptions of the world, he affirmed that they were learned only under the effects of *yagé*. *Yagé* leads to a transcendental experience of comprehension of the world's essence."[29]

> *Yagé* is a force that has power, will, and knowledge, with it we can reach the stars, enter the spirit of other people, know their desire to do good or bad; we can foresee the future of ours and others' lives, see illnesses and cure them, and with it we can travel to heaven or hell.[30]

In the Andean highlands of South America the shamans also used powerful mind-altering drugs to transcend the profane and to attain a transtemporal perspective. "Thus shamans are frequent travelers across the threshold between life and death and, beginning with the initiatory 'dismemberment' and contemplation of their own 'death,' they 'die' repeatedly in the course of their praxis."[31] "The ingestion of entheogens [vision-producing drugs that figure in shamanic or religious rites] made the celebrant consubstantial with the deity, providing a communion and shared existence mediating between the human and the Divine."[32] The use of "medicinal plants has been traced to early burial sites associated with shaman, and it is likely that shamanic [beliefs] and ritual structures developed "around chemically altered states of consciousness."[33]

The Sacred Realm of Myths

> All things have emotions which are subject to influence. In a cosmos that is essentially as unpredictable as the human realm, the shaman's tapping into power allows for the possible reversal of death, the transformation of form, and the transcendence of time and space.[34]

The issues relating to shamanism and belief were complex. Archaic society had a limited number of ways for addressing important issues such as the origin of people, animals, and other elements of the physical and spiritual world and for determining the meaning and purpose of life, death, and the afterlife.[35] It is possible that the essential elements of early reverential activities were practice and repetition, instead of belief. Such activities were associated with natural or physiological phenomena and therefore became the accepted routine in a particular circumstance. A belief common to that early environment was the separation of the physical elements of the human being and the inner self — the spirit or soul.

The shaman was believed to enter a liminal realm during séance in which the reality of the temporal, mundane world was simultaneously juxtaposed to and fused with the timeless world of the spirit.[36] The concept behind many such shamanistic activities emphasized the idea of spiritual and/or physical transformation and evoked the act of symbolic death and rebirth. It might also portray the losing and regaining of personal identity. Such performances were magico-religious actions that transmitted a message of transcendence and renewal.

Belief in the supernatural that existed apart from the material world was an important element in the development of the human psyche. All early societies included some form of expression dedicated to belief in the supernatural. Cultural endorsement of faith as a psychologically fulfilling concept occupied a central role in the beliefs of peoples from the beginning of known history. The supernatural also allows for those times when humanity needed "liberation from any state of being that was too immature, too fixed or final. In other words, they concern man's release from — or transcendence of— any confining pattern of existence, as he moved toward a superior or more mature state in his development."[37]

Shamanism in most manifestations was not a conglomeration of haphazardly combined elements, but a fusion of culturally endorsed activities and beliefs in a state of perpetual change. The abilities of early humans allowed some of them to use their natural abilities to explain the reasons for phenomena such as sky, sun, moon, and fire. According to their beliefs they created links between humans and nature that enabled them to live amicably.[38] Caroline Humphrey wrote, "The shaman was like a sounding-board of the world...."[39]

Concern for the unknown aspects of existence was a consuming human condition, and one great fear was that no conscious experience existed after death. To address those concerns and to provide a measure of protection against the forces that constituted those dangers humans sought comfort in the supernatural.

It is possible that early people lived in a profane (not initiated in mystical rites) state of being that was ameliorated by the endorsement of a mythically sacred realm. That environment allowed a distinction to be made between the sacred and the profane, and it was only the acceptance of that separation that allowed the difference between the supernatural and the natural to be acknowledged. Consistent with that recognition, shamanism was created by society for social purposes. The rituals, ceremonies, taboos, and modes of thought, were common property, developed as needed. Succeeding generations inherited that belief system and passed it on to the next. For a time, that system joined the spiritual energies of humans, not just for themselves, but also for humanity in general. It helped to bind communities (peoples, tribes, or clans) together, and to strengthen and direct their common action.

> Shamanism was a natural religion, and the degree of its transformation into societal religion among various peoples is what defines its character. Even among the most advanced peoples of Central and Northern Asia, it remained an idolization of the forces of nature and preserved ritual as its major, but no only component.[40]

Shamanism has undoubtedly undergone many changes since its inception. Placing it in a world context shows that it, like competing religious movements was a combination of elements that were in a state of perpetual change. Different belief systems evolve to express the fears and expectations of different people. Each system was satisfactory to those who were taught its values. Life in most societies depended on the ability of the people to adapt to their surroundings and their aptness in coping with unknown forces. Beliefs arose about the causes and effects of natural occurrences out of those survival practices. In turn, those beliefs prompt discrete ceremonies and rituals to assure a level of security in uncertain times.

Shamanism persisted among the people of the world because the influence of the shamans was not purely illusory. The hunters continued to find game, many of the sick recovered, and arduous journeys were safely completed. The shaman performed his or her rituals according to time honored practices to ensure the desired outcome.

Åke Hultkrantz states, "Shamanism, as defined in this opus [*Studies in Lapp Shamanism*] is a meaningful and clearly designated concept. It has been a world-wide phenomenon, but [probably] reached its peak in Northern Eurasia and bordering area, Central Asia and northern North America."[41]

> All true wisdom is only to be found far from men, out in the great solitude, and it can only be acquired by suffering. Privations and sufferings are the only things that can open a man's mind to that which is hidden from others.[42]

NOTES TO THE CAPTIONS

a. Heissig, W. and D. Dumas. *The Mongols Die Mongolen*, An exhibition catalog (Innsbruck: Pinguin-Verlag and Frankfurt/Main: Umschau-Verlag, 1995), p. 78.

b. Campbell, J. *The Way of the Animal Powers: Historical Atlas of World Mythology*, Vol. 1, Alfred Van Der Marck Editions (San Francisco: Harper & Row, 1983), p. 250

c. "Dragon" Encyclopaedia Britannica Library, from *Encyclopaedia Britannica* 2005 Deluxe Edition CD-ROM. Copyright © 1994–2003 Encyclopaedia Britannica, Inc. (accessed July 8, 2007).

d. Edson, G. *Masks and Masking: Faces of Tradition and Belief Worldwide* (Jefferson, NC and London: McFarland, 2005), p. 151.

e. Exhibition catalog "Ancestors' Spirits in the Sound of the Tambourine," The collection of the Shaman Cult Accessories of Peoples of Siberia and North-east Asia (Irkutsk: Regional Studies Museum, nd), p. 4.

f. Hartmann, G. *Masken südamerikanischer Naturvölker* (Berlin: Veröffentlichunger des Museums für Völkerkundt, 1967), p. 42.

g. Urban, G., and J. W. Hendricks. "Signal Functions of Masking in Amerindian Brazil," in: *Semiotics* 47–1/4 (Austin: University of Texas at Austin, 1983), 181–218.

h. Edson, *Masks and Masking*, p. 169.

i. Heissig, W. and D. Dumas. *The Mongols*, an Exhibition Catalogue published by the Staatliches Museum für Völkerkunde München [1989] (Innsbruck: Pinguin-Verlag and Frankfurt/Main: Umschau-Verlag, 1995), p. 78.

j. Heissig, W. and D. Dumas. *The Mongols Die Mongolen*, An exhibition catalog (Innsbruck: Pinguin-Verlag and Frankfurt/Main: Umschau-Verlag, 1995), p. 74.

k. Laing J., and D. Wire. *The Encyclopedia of Signs and Symbols* (London: Studio Editions, 1993), p. 240.

l. Holm, B. *Spirit and Ancestor: A Century of Northwest Coast Indian Art at the Burke Museum* (Seattle and London: University of Washington Press, 1987), p. 238.

m. Edson, *Masks and Masking*, p. 130.

n. Holm, J., and J. Bowker, ed. *Myth and History* (London and New York: Pinter, 1989), p.232.

o. Campbell, *Historical Atlas of World Mythology*, Vol.1, p. 202.

p. Edson, *Masks and Masking*, p. 167.

q Wassing, R. S. *African Art: Its Background and Traditions* (Alpine Fine Arts Collection [U.K.] London, 1968), p. 207.

r. Purev, O. and G. Purvee. *Mongolian Shamanism*, Vols. I & II (Ulaanbaatar: Purvee, 2007), p. 217.

s. McFarren, P. ed. *Mascaras de los Andes Bolivianos* (La Paz, Bolivia: Editorial Quipus/Banco Mercantil S. A., 1993), p. 36.

t. Waite, A.: In Fraser, D. ed. *The Many Faces of Primitive Art* (Englewood Cliffs, NJ: Prentice-Hall, 1966).

u. Edson, *Masks and Masking*, p. 24.

v. Berger, P. "Buddhist Festivals in Mongolia," in: Berger, P. and T. T. Bartholomew, ed. Mongolia: The Legacy of Chinggis Khan (London: Thames and Hudson, 1995), p. 150.

w. *Ibid.*, p. 168.

x. Nebesky-Wojkowitz, R. *Tibetan Religious Dances* (The Hague: Mouton, 1976), p. 77.

y. Pal, P. *Art of Tibet* (Berkeley and London: University of California Press, 1983), p. 171.

z. "Chavín," Encyclopaedia Britannica Library, from *Encyclopaedia Britannica* 2005 Deluxe Edition CD-ROM. Copyright © 1994–2003 Encyclopaedia Britannica, Inc. July 19, 2007.

aa. Edson, G. *Masks and Masking: Faces of Tradition and Belief Worldwide* (Jefferson, NC and London: McFarland, 2005), p. 55.

bb. *Ibid.*, p. 57.

cc. Gardner, J. L., ed. *Mysteries of the Ancient Americans: The New World before Columbus.* (Pleasantville, NY and Montreal: The Reader's Digest Association, 1986), p. 303

dd. Edson, *Masks and Masking*, p. 89.

ee. *Ibid.*, p. 100.

ff. *Ibid.*, p. 73.

gg. Oakes, L. and L. Gahlin. *Ancient Egypt* (New York: Barnes and Noble, 2006:397.

hh. Fitzhugh, W. W., and Kaplan, S. *Inua: Spirit World of the Bering Sea Eskimo* (Washington, DC and London: Smithsonian Institution Press, 1982), p. 187.

NOTES TO THE TEXT

Chapter 1

1. Langdon, E. J. "Shamanism as the History of Anthropology," in: M. Hoppál and O. van Sadovszky. *Shamanism Past and Present*, Part 1 (Budapest: ethnographic Institute, Hungarian Academy of Sciences and Los Angeles/Fullerton: International Society for Trans-Oceanic Research, 1989), p, 53.
2. Winkelman, M. "Cross-cultural Perspectives on Shamans" in: Walter, M. N. and E. J. N Fridman eds. *Shamanism: An Encyclopedia of World Beliefs, Practices, and Culture*, Vol. 1, pp. 61–70 (Santa Barbara, CA and Oxford: ABC CLIO, 2004), p. 63.
3. Bäckman, L. and Å. Hultkrantz. *Studies in Lapp Shamanism* (Stockholm: Almqvist & Wiksell International, 1978), p. 11.
4. Baumer, C. *Bön: Tibet's Ancient Religion,* Translated by Michael Kohn (Trumball, CT: Weatherhill, Inc., 2002), p. 27.
5. Bäckman, L. and Å. Hultkrantz. *Studies in Lapp Shamanism*, p. 11.
6. Webster, H. *Magic: A Sociological Study* (Stanford, CA: Stanford University Press, 1948), p. 39.
7. Macgowan K., and H. Rosse. *Masks and Demons* (London: Martin Hopkinson and Company, Ltd., 1924), p. viii.
8. de Waal Malefijt, A. *Religion and Culture: An Introduction to Anthropology of Religion* (New York: The Macmillan Company, 1968), p. 11.
9. Müller-Ebeling, C., C. Rätsch, and S. B. Shahi. *Shamanism and Tantra in the Himalayas* (London: Thames & Hudson, 2002), p. 31.
10. Krippner, S. "Profiles of three Contemporary Central American Shamans," in: R-I Heinze, ed. *Proceedings of the Ninth International Conference on the Study of Shamanism and Alternate Modes of Healing* (Berkeley: University of California, 1992), p. 149.
11. Stone, P. G. and Molyneaux, B. eds. *The Presented Past* (London and New York, Routledge, 1994), p. 2.
12. Halbwachs, M. *The Collective Memory*, Translated by Francis J. Ditter, Jr. and Vida Yazdi Ditter (New York: Harper Colophon Books, 1980), p. 49.
13. *Ibid.*, p. 50.
14. Campbell, J. "The Historical Development of Mythology," in: H. A. Murray ed. *Myth and Mythmaking* (New York: George Braziller, 1960), p. 20.
15. Lommel, A. *World of the Early Hunters*, Translated by M. Bullock (London: Paul Hamlyn, 1967), pp. 26–27.
16. Siikala, A-L. *The Rite Technique of the Siberian Shaman*, FF Communications, Vol. 93. No. 220, Suomalainen Tiedeakatemia, (Helsinki: Academia Scientiarum Fennica, 1978.), p. 11.
17. Odgaard, U. "Palaeo-Eskimoic Shamanism," in: T. Vestergaard, ed. *North Atlantic Studies*, Vol. 4 No. 1+2 (Højbjerg, Denmark: Aarhus University Press, 2001), p. 25.
18. Mikhailov, T. M. "Buryat Shamanism: History, Structure, and Social Functions," in: M. M. Balzer. ed. *Shamanism: Soviet Studies of Traditional Religion in Siberia and Central Asia* (Armonk, NY and London: M. E. Sharpe, Inc., 1990), p. 117.
19. *Ibid.*
20. Driscoll, J. T. "Shamanism," Transcribed by Douglas J. Potter, in: *The Catholic Encyclopedia*, Vol. XIII. (New York: Robert Appleton Company, 1912) p. 750.
21. *Ibid.*
22. Balzer, M. M. ed. *Shamanic Worlds*. (New York and London: North Castle Books, 1997). p. xvii.
23. Birket-Smith, K. *The Paths of Culture*, Translated by Karin Fennow (Madison and Milwaukee: The University of Wisconsin Press, 1965), p. 375.
24. "Shamanism" *Encyclopaedia Britannica*, from Encyclopaedia Britannica Deluxe Edition 2005 CD. Copyright © 1994–2004 Encyclopaedia Britannica, Inc. (accessed May, 30, 2004).
25. Lommel, *The World of the Early Hunter*, pp. 8–11.
26. Peters, L. *Ecstasy and Healing in Nepal* (Malibu, CA: Undena Publications, 1981), p. 13.
27. Krippner, "Profiles of Three Contemporary Central American Shamans.," p. 148.
28. *Ibid.*
29. *Ibid.*, pp. 148–149.
30. Gillette, D. *Shaman's Secret* (New York and London: Bantam Books, 1997), p. 117.
31. Webster, *Magic*, p. 213.
32. Krippner, "Profiles of Three Contemporary Central American Shamans.," p. 149.
33. Hultkrantz, Å. "Ecological and Phenomenological Aspects of Shamanism," in: Diószegi, V. and M. Hoppál, ed. *Shamanism in Siberia,* Selected Reprints, Translated by S. Simon (Budapest: Akadémiai Kiadó, 1996), p. 12.
34. *Ibid.*, p. 14.
35. Krader, L. "Buryat Religion and Society," in: J.

Middleton ed. *Gods and Rituals* (Garden City, NY: The Natural History Press, 1967), p. 117.
36. *Ibid.*, pp. 117–119.
37. Clottes, J. and Lewis-Williams, D. *Shamans of Prehistory*, translated by Sophie Hawkes (New York, Harry N. Abrams, Inc., Publishers, 1996), p. 19.
38. Eliade, M. *Shamanism: Archaic Techniques of Ecstasy*, translated by Willard Trask (Bollingen Series LXXVI, Princeton, NJ: Princeton University Press, 1974), p. 4.
39. Balzer, *Shamanic Worlds*, p. xvi.
40. *Ibid.*
41. Wilson, F. A. ed. *Art as Revelation* (Fontwell Sussex: Centaur Press Ltd., 1981), p. 16.
42. Balzer, *Shamanic Worlds*, p. 77.
43. Krippner, S. "Shamans: The First Healers," in: Doore, G. ed. *Shaman's Path*, pp. 101–114. (Boston and London: Shambhala, 1988), p. 101.
44. *Ibid.*
45. Walter, M. N. and Fridman, E. J. N. eds. *Shamanism: An Encyclopedia of World Beliefs, Practices, and Culture*, vol. I (Santa Barbara, CA and Oxford: ABC CLIO, 2004), p. xi.
46. Vitebsky, P. *The Shaman* (New York and London: Little, Brown and Company, 1995), p. 10.
47. Balzer, *Shamanic Worlds*, p. xiv.
48. Benedict, R. Patterns of Culture (Boston: Houghton-Mifflin 1934), p. 96.
49. d'Aquili, E. G., C. D. Laughlin, and J. McManus. *The Spectrum of Ritual: A Biogenetic Structural Analysis* (New York: Columbia University Press, 1979), p. 161
50. Wallis, R. J. *Shamans/neo-Shamans: Ecstasy, Alternative Archaeologies and Contemporary Pagans* (London: Routledge, 2003), in: Walter, M. N. and E. J. N. Fridman, eds. *Shamanism: An Encyclopedia of World Beliefs, Practices, and Culture* (Santa Barbara, CA and Oxford: ABC CLIO, 2004), p. 22.
51. Maddox, J. L. *Medicine Man: A Sociological Study of the Character and Evolution of Shamanism* (New York: The Macmillan Company, 1923), p. 42.
52. "Shamanism" Encyclopaedia Britannica, From Encyclopaedia Britannica Deluxe Edition 2005 CD. Copyright © 1994–2004 Encyclopaedia Britannica, Inc. (accessed May 30, 2006).
53. Dow, J. *The Shaman's Touch: Otomi Indian Symbolic Healing* (Salt Lake City: University of Utah Press, 1986), pp. 7–8
54. Balzer, *Shamanic Worlds*, p. 3.
55. *Ibid.*, p. 4.
56. Clottes and Lewis-Williams, *The Shamans of Prehistory*, p. 22.
57. *Ibid.*
58. Wallis, W. D. *Religion in Primitive Society* (New York: F. S. Crofts & Co., 1939).
59. Van Deusen, Kira. 2004. Singing Story, Healing Drum. Montreal & Kingston and London: McGill-Queen's University Press.
60. Balzer, *Shamanic*, p. xvi.
61. Lommel, *Early Hunters*, p. 10.
62. Leakey, R. *The Origin of Humankind* (New York: Basic Books, A Division of HarperCollins Publishers, Inc., 1994), p. 139.
63. McMillan D. W. *Emotion Rituals* (New York and London: Routledge, 2006), p. 79.
64. Radin, P. *The World of Primitive Man* (New York: Grove Press, Inc., 1953), p. 143.
65. MacGowan, K. and H. Rosse. *Masks and Demons* (London: Martin Hopinson and Company Ltd., 1924), p. viii.
66. Middleton, J. ed. *Gods and Rituals* (American Museum Sourcebooks in Anthropology published for the American Museum of Natural History, Garden City, NY: Natural History Press, 1967), pp. ix–x.
67. Durkheim, É. *Elementary Forms of the Religious Life*, trans. by Joseph Swain (Glencoe, IL: The Free Press, 1947 [1915]), p. 224.
68. *Ibid.*, p. 226.
69. Walker, J. R. *Lakota Belief and Ritual*, eds. R. J. DeMallie and E. A. Jahner (Lincoln and London: University of Nebraska Press, 1991), p. 122.
70. Walter, and Friedman, *Shamanism*, p. xi.
71. Hayden, B. *Shamans, Sorcerers, and Saints* (Washington: Smithsonian Books, 2003), p. 48.
72. Purev, O. and G. Purvee. *Mongolian Shamanism*, Translated by G. Purvee (Ulaanbaatar: Purvee, 2007), p. 69.
73. *Ibid.*, p. 70.
74. Manuscript 1279, Smithsonian Institution National Anthropological Archive
75. Maddox, *Medicine Man*, p. 42.
76. Purev, O. and G. Purvee *Mongolian Shamanism*, pp. 230–231.
77. Sharon, D. *Wizard of the Four Winds: A Shaman's Story* (New York: The
Free Press, A Division of Macmillan Publishing Co., Inc., 1978), p. 77.
78. *Ibid.*
79. "Shamanism" *Korean Heritage Series*, No. 15 (Seoul, ROK: Korean Overseas Information Service, 1995), p. 9.
80. *Ibid.*, p. 3.
81. *Ibid.*, p. 5.
82. *Ibid.*, pp. 7–8.
83. Humphrey, C. and Urgunge, O. Shamans and Elders: Experience, Knowledge, and Power among the Daur Mongols (Oxford: Clarendon Press, 1996), p. 315.

Chapter 2

1. de Waal Malefijt, A. *Religion and Culture: An Introduction to Anthropology of Religion* (New York: The Macmillan Company 1968), p. 153.
2. Kim Tae-kon *Korean Shamanism—Muism*, Translated and edited by Chang Soo-Kyung (Seoul: Jimoondang Publishing Company, 1998), p. 162.
3. Fontenrose, J. "The Ritual Theory of Myth," in: *Folklore Studies* (vol. 18), Berkeley and Los Angeles: University of California Press, (1966). Pp. 50–60.
4. Dow, J. *The Shaman's Touch: Otomi Indian Symbolic Healing* (Salt Lake City: University of Utah Press, 1986), p. 7.
5. Kehoe, A. B. *Shamans and Religion* (Prospect Heights, IL: Waveland Press, Inc., 2000), pp. 15–16.
6. Humphrey, C. and U. Onon. Shamans and Elders: Experience, Knowledge, and Power Among the Daur Mongols. Oxford: Clarendon Press, 1996), p. 48.
7. Howells, W. *The Heathens: Primitive Man and His Religion* (Garden City, NY: Doubleday & Company, Inc., 1948), p. 18.
8. Hultkrantz, Å. "The Place of Shamanism in the History of Religions," in: M. Hoppál and O. van Sadovszky. *Shamanism Past and Present*, Part 1 (Budapest: ethnographic Institute, Hungarian Academy of Sciences and Los Angeles/Fullerton: International Society for Trans-Oceanic Research, 1989), p, 43.
9. Gillette, D. *The Shaman's Secret* (New York and London: Bantam Books, 1997), p. 108.
10. Oman, J. *The Natural & the Supernatural* (New York: The Macmillan Company, 1931), p. 377.
11. Oman, *The Natural & the Supernatural*, p. 377.
12. Barton, G. A. *The Religions of the World*, 4th edition. (Chicago: The University of Chicago Press, 1937), pp. 3–4.

13. Turner, V. *The Forest of Symbols: Aspects of Ndembu Ritual* (Ithaca and London: Cornell University Press, 1967) p. 45.
14. Lommel, A. *The World of the Early Hunters* (London: Evelyn, Adams & MacKay, 1967), pp. 26–27.
15. Child, A. and Child, I. Religion and Magic, p. 70.
16. Lewis, I. M. *Ecstatic Religion: A Study of Shamanism and Spirit Possession*. 2nd ed. (New York and London: Routledge, 1989), p. 43.
17. Lommel, *World of the Early Hunters*, p. 27; also see, Peters, L. *Ecstasy and Healing in Nepal* (Malibu, CA: Undena Publications, 1981), p. 7.
18. Torrance, R. M. 1994. *The Spiritual Quest: Transcendence in Myth, Religion, and Science* (Berkeley, Los Angeles, and London: University of California Press, 1994), p. 39–40.
19. Markman, R. H. and P. T. Markman. *The Flayed God: The Mesoamerican Mythological Tradition* (New York: HarperCollins Publishers, 1992), p. 6.
20. Ryan, R. E. *Shamanism and the Psychology of C. G. Jung*. (London: Vega, 2002), pp. 88–89.
21. Lommel, A., *Masks: Their Meaning and Function* (New York and Toronto: McGraw-Hill Book Company, 1972), p. 117.
22. Lommel, A., World of the Early Hunter, p. 16.
23. Kitagawa, J. M. *Religion in Japanese History* (New York and London: Columbia University Press, 1966), p. 5.
24. *Ibid.*, p. 13.
25. *Ibid.*, p. 14.
26. *Ibid.*
27. *Ibid.*, p. 20.
28. *Ibid.*, p. 5.
29. *Ibid.*, p. 20.
30. Kehoe, A. B. *Shamans and Religion: An Anthropological Exploration in Critical Thinking* (Prospect Heights, IL: Waveland Press, Inc., 2000), p. 14.
31. Lommel, *World of the Early Hunters*, pp. 8–11.
32. Peters, L. *Ecstasy and Healing in Nepal* (Malibu, CA: Undena Publications, 1981), p. 13.
33. Halifax, J. *Shamanic Voices* (New York: E. P. Dutton, 1979), p. 5.
34. *Ibid.*, p. 3.
35. Lommel, *World of the Early Hunter*, p. 8.
36. Burland, C. A. *The Magical Arts: A Short History* (London: Arthur Barker Limited, 1966), p. 74.
37. Halifax, J. *Shaman: The Wounded Healer* (London: Thames and Hudson, 1982), p. 5.
38. Lewis, *Ecstatic Religion*, p. 5.
39. Vitebsky, P. *The Shaman: Voyages of the Soul Trance, Ecstasy, and Healing from Siberia to the Amazon* (New York and London: Brown, Little and Company, 1995) p. 8.
40. Young, D. *Origins of the Sacred: The Ecstasies of Love and War* (New York: St. Martin's Press, 1991), p. 162.
41. Kehoe, *Shamans and Religion*, p. 14.
42. Ryan, *Shamanism and the Psychology of C.G. Jung*, p. 88.
43. Frazer, J. G. *The Fear of the Dead in Primitive Religion*, Vol. III (London: Macmillan, 1936), p. 54.
44. *Ibid.*
45. Edson, G. *Masks and Masking: Faces of Tradition and Belief Worldwide* (Jefferson, NC and London: McFarland & Company, Inc., Publishers, 2005), p. 95.
46. Burland, *Magical Arts*, p. 7.
47. Jensen, A. E. *Myth and Cult Among Primitive Peoples* (Chicago: University of Chicago Press, 1963 [1951]), p. 225.
48. Mumford, S. R. *Himalayan Dialogue: Tibetan Lamas and Gurung Shamans in Nepal* (Madison: University of Wisconsin Press, 1989), p. 8.
49. *Ibid.*
50. *Ibid.*
51. Peters, *Ecstasy and Healing*, p. 18.
52. Lommel, World of the Early Hunters, p. 15.
53. Halifax, Shaman: Wounded Healer, p. 5.
54. Benedict, R. *Patterns of Culture*, 2nd ed. (Boston: Houghton Mifflin Company, 1959 [1934]), p. 96.
55. *Ibid.*, p. 96.
56. Halifax, Shaman: The Wounded Healer, p. 5.
57. Eliade, M. *Shamanism: Archaic Techniques of Ecstasy* (Bollingen Series LXXVI, Princeton NJ: Princeton University Press, 1964), pp. 4 and 495
58. Grim, J. A. *The Shaman: Patterns of Siberian and Ojibway Healing* (Norman: University of Oklahoma Press, 1983), p. 15.
59. *Ibid.*, p. 16.
60. Vitebsky, *Shaman*, p. 10.
61. Doore, G. ed. Shaman's Path: Healing, Personal Growth, and Empowerment. (Boston: Shambhala, 1988), p. 7.
62. Lommel, *Early Hunters*, p. 25.
63. Howell, *Heathens*, p. 142.
64. Humphrey and Onon. Shamans and Elders, p. 31.
65. Forsyth, J. A *History of the Peoples of Siberia: Russia's North Asian Colony 1581–1990* (Cambridge: Cambridge University Press, 1992), p. 85.
66. Basilov, V. N. "Chosen by the Spirits," in: Balzer, M. M. (ed.) *Shamanic Worlds: Ritual and Lore of Siberia and Central Asia*. Armonk (New York and London: North Castle Books, 1997), p. 3.
67. Balzer, M. M. (ed.) *Shamanic Worlds: Ritual and Lore of Siberia and Central Asia*. Armonk (New York and London: North Castle Books, 1997), p. xv.
68. Forsyth, History of the People of Siberia, pp. 51–52.
69. *Ibid.*, p. 52.
70. Bancroft-Hunt, N. *People of the Totem* (New York: G. P. Putnam's Sons, 1979), p. 76.
71. Forsyth, History of the People of Siberia, p. 20–21.
72. Hansen, H. H. *Mongol Costumes*, The Carlsberg Foundation's Nomad Research Project (London: Thames and Hudson, 1993), p. 154.
73. *Ibid.*
74. *Ibid.*
75. *Ibid.*, p. 155.
76. *Ibid.*
77. Kehoe, Shamans and Religion, p. 12.
78. Eliade, M. *Shamanism,* p. 6.
79. Forty, J. *Mythology: A Visual Encyclopedia* (London: PRC Publishing Ltd., 1999), p. 186.
80. Purev, O and Purvee, G. *Mongolian Shamanism* (Ulaanbaatar: Purvee, 2007), p. 179.
81. *Ibid.*
82. *Ibid.*
83. Editors. *The Spirit World*, Alexandria, (VA: Time-Life Books, 1992), p. 77.
84. *Ibid.*, p. 77.
85. Walter, M. N. and Friedman, E.J.N. (eds.) *Shamanism: An Encyclopedia of World Beliefs, Practices, and Culture*. Vols. 1 & 2 (Santa Barbara, CA & Oxford: ABC CLIO, 2004), p. 257.
86. Encyclopaedia Britannica Library, from *Encyclopaedia Britannica* 2005 Deluxe Edition CD-ROM. Copyright © 1994–2003 Encyclopaedia Britannica, Inc. (accessed March, 25, 2007).
87. Mikhailov, T. M. "Buryat Shamanism: History, Structure, and Social Functions," in: M.M. Balzer. *Shamanism: Soviet Studies of Traditional Religion in Siberia and Central Asia* (Armonk, NY and London: M. E. Sharpe, Inc., 1990), p. 110.
88. Service, E. R. *Profiles in Ethnology*. New York and London: Harper & Row, Publishers, 1963), p. 58.
89. Halifax, *Shamanic Voices*, p. 5.

90. Norbeck, E. *Religion in Primitive Society* (New York: Harper & Row, Publishers, 1961), p. 110.

Chapter 3

1. Kramer, S. N. *Mythologies of the Ancient World* (Chicago: Quadrangle Books, Inc., 1961), p. 390.
2. Bäckman, L. and Å. Hultkrantz *Studies in Lapp Shamanism* (Stockholm: Almqvist & Wiksell, 1978), p. 57.
3. Benedict, R. *Patterns of Culture* (Boston: Houghton Mifflin Company, 1934) p. 268.
4. Maddox, J. L. *The Medicine Man: A Sociological Study of the Character and Evolution of Shamanism* (New York: the Macmillan Company, 1923), p. 141.
5. Melody, M. E. *The Apache* (New York and Philadelphia: Chelsea House Publishers, 1989), p. 34.
6. Müller, K. E., U. Ritz-Müller, and H. Christoph. *Soul of Africa: Magical Rites and Traditions* (Cologne: Könemann Verlagsgesellshaft mbH, 2000), p. 142.
7. Müller, Ritz-Müller, and H. Christoph. *Soul of Africa*, p. 142.
8. Bancroft-Hunt, N. and W. Forman. *People of the Totem* (New York: G. P. Putnam's Sons, 1979), p. 69.
9. Webster, H. *Magic: A Sociological Study* (Stanford, CA: Sanford University Press, 1948), p. 39.
10. "Shamanism," Encyclopaedia Britannica Library, from *Encyclopaedia Britannica* 2005 Deluxe Edition CD-ROM. Copyright © 1994–2003 Encyclopaedia Britannica, Inc. (accessed May 19, 2007).
11. Park, W. Z. *Shamanism in Western North America* (Evanston and Chicago: Northwestern University, 1938), pp. 26–27.
12. Humphrey, C. with O. Urgunge. *Shamans and Elders: Experience, Knowledge and Power among the Daur Mongols* (Oxford: Clarendon Press, 1996), p. 76.
13. Peters, L. Ecstasy and healing in Nepal: an ethnopsychiatric study of Tamang shamanism (Malibu, CA: Undena Publications, 1981) pp. 8–9.
14. *Ibid.*, p. 10.
15. Manuscript 4832, Smithsonian Institution National Anthropological Archive.
16. Arendt, H. *Human Condition* (Chicago: University of Chicago Press, 1958), p. 137.
17. Csikszentmihalyi, Mihaly, "Why We Need Things," in: Lubar, S. and W. D. Kingery (eds.) *History from Things: Essays on Material Culture*. (Washington and London: Smithsonian Institution Press, 1993), p. 23.
18. Halifax, J. *Shaman: The wounded healer* (London: Thames and Hudson, 1982), p. 9.
19. Bancroft-Hunt, *People of the Totem*, p. 76.
20. Nooter, M. H. *Secrecy: African Art That Conceals and Reveals*. Munich: Prestel, 1993), p. 114
21. de Waal Malefijt, A. *Religion and Culture* (New York: Macmillan Company, 1968). p. 205.
22. Kiev, A. Magic, *Faith, and Healing* (London: The Free Press of Glencoe, a Division of Collier-Macmillan Limited, 1964), p. 395.
23. *Ibid.*, p. 396.
24. de Waal Malefijt, A. *Religion and Culture*. (New York: Macmillan Company, 1968), p. 230.
25. Park, *Shamanism in Western North America*, p. 76.
26. *Ibid.*, p. 79.
27. *Ibid.*, p. 80.
28. *Ibid.*, p. 78.
29. Gillette, D. *Shaman's Secret* (New York and London: Bantam Books, 1997), p. 39.
30. Figes, O. *Natasha's Dance* (New York: Metropolitan Books, 2002), p. 360.
31. *Ibid.*
32. Webster, *Magic: A Sociological Study*, p. 213.
33. Fontenrose, J. "The Ritual Theory of Myth," in: *Folklore Studies*, vol. 18 (Berkeley and Los Angeles: University of California Press, 1966), pp. 50–60.
34. Schafer, E. H. and Editors of Time-Life Books. *Ancient China* (New York: Time-Life Books, 1967), p. 59.
35. *Ibid.*
36. *Ibid.*, p. 60.
37. *Ibid.*
38. *Ibid.*, p. 61.
39. Walker, D. G. *The Woman's Dictionary of Symbols and Sacred Objects* (Edison, NJ: Castle Books, 1988), p. 50.
40. Thomas, K. *Religion and the Decline of Magic* (Oxford and New York: Oxford University Press, 1971), p. 178.
41. Eliade, M. *Shamanism: Archaic Techniques of Ecstasy*, Translated by Willard R. Trask, (Bollingen Series LXXVI, Princeton: Princeton University Press, 1974), p. 88.
42. Service, E. R. *Profiles in Ethnology* (New York and London: Harper and Row, 1963), pp. 23–24.
43. Macgowan K., and H. Rosse. *Masks and Demons* (London: Martin Hopkinson and Company, Ltd., 1923), p. ix.
44. Webster, *Magic: A Sociological Study* Press, p, 39.
45. *Ibid.*, p. 2.
46. Vetter, G. B. *Magic and Religion: Their Psychological Nature, Origin, and Function* (New York: Philosophical Library, 1973), p. 146.
47. *Ibid.*
48. Webster, *Magic: A Sociological Study*, p, 39.
49. O'Keefe, D. L. *Stolen Lightening: The Social Theory of Magic* (New York: Continuum, 1982), p. 29.
50. Webster, *Magic: A Sociological Study*, p. 407.
51. Sullivan. L. E. *Icanchu's Drum: An Orientation to Meaning in South American Religion* (New York: Macmillan Publishing Company, 1988), p. 458.
52. Lommel, A. *The World of the Early Hunters: Medicine-men, Shamans, and Artists* (London: Evelyn, Adams & Mackay, 1967), p. 126.
53. Radin, P. *Primitive Religion: Its Nature and Origin*, 2d ed. (New York: Dover Publications, 1957), p. 60.
54. Webster. H. *Primitive Secret Societies: A Study of Early Politics and Religion*, 2d ed. (New York: Macmillan Company, 1932), p. 170.
55. Birket-Smith, K. *Paths of Culture*, Translated by Karin Fennow (Madison and Milwaukee: The University of Wisconsin Press, 1965), p. 373.
56. *Ibid.*
57. Pinch, G. *Magic in Ancient Egypt* (Austin: University of Texas Press, 1994), p. 76.
58. Levin, M.G. and L.P. Potapov, eds. *The Peoples of Siberia*, Translated by Scripta Technica, Inc., English translation edited by Stephen Dunn (Chicago and London: The University of Chicago Press, 1956), p. 823.
59. Hultkrantz, Å. "Shamanism: A Religious Phenomenon?" in: G. Doore ed. *Shaman's Path: Healing, Personal Growth and Empowerment*, pp. 33–42. (Boston and London: Shambhala, 1988), p. 35.
60. Read, C. *Man and His Superstitions* (London: Senate, an imprint of Studio Editions Ltd., 1995 [1925]), p. 147.
61. Humphrey with Urgunge. *Shamans and Elders*, p. 36.
62. Freidel, D., L. Schele, and J. Parker. *Maya Cosmos: Three Thousand Years on the Shaman's Path* (New York: William Morrow and Company, Inc., 1993), p. 39.
63. *Ibid.*
64. Keesing, R. M. *Kwaio Religion: The Living and the Dead in a Solomon Island Society* (New York: Columbia University Press, 1982), p. 52.

65. *Ibid.*, p. 54.
66. Seligmann, K. *The History of Magic* (New York: Pantheon Books, Ltd., 1948), p. 61.
67. *Ibid.*
68. *Ibid.*
69. Levin, and Potapov, *The Peoples of Siberia*, p. 821.
70. *Ibid.*
71. Kluckhohn, C. "Recurrent Themes in Myths and Mythmaking," in: H. A. Murray, *Myth and Mythmaking*, pp. 46–60. (New York: George Braziller, 1960), pp. 48–49.
72. Ennemoser, J. *History of Magic*, vol. II, Translated by William Howitt (New Hyde Park, NY: University Books, Inc., 1970), p. 122.
73. *Ibid.*
74. Middleton, J. ed. *Magic, Witchcraft, and Curing* (Austin: University of Texas Press, 1982 [1967]), p. ix.
75. Müller-Ebeling, C., C. Rätsch, and S. B. Shahi. *Shamanism and Tantra in the Himalayas* (London: Thames & Hudson, 2002), p. 24.
76. Maxwell, J. A. ed. *America's Fascinating Indian Heritage* (Pleasantville, NY and Montreal: The Reader's Digest Association, Inc., 1978), p. 240.
77. *Ibid.*, p. 308.
78. Mair, L. *Witchcraft* (New York and Toronto: McGraw-Hill Book Company, 1971), p. 200.
79. Hultkrantz, Å. *Shamanic Healing and Ritual Drama: Health and Medicine in Native North American Religious Traditions* (New York: The Crossroad Publishing Company, 1997), p. 53.
80. *Ibid.*, pp. 65–66.
81. Keesing, R. M. *Kwaio Religion: The Living and the Dead in a Solomon Island Society* (New York: Columbia University Press, 1982), p. 50.
82. *Ibid.*, p. 51.
83. Evans-Pritchard, E. E. *Witchcraft, Oracles, and Magic Among the Azande* (Oxford, Clarendon Press, 1937), p. 21.
84. Reynolds, B. *Magic, Divination and Witchcraft Among the Barotes of Northern Rhodesia* (Berkeley and Los Angeles: University of California Press, 1963), p. 16.
85. *Ibid.*, p. 29.
86. Lieban R. W. *Cebuano Sorcery: Malign Magic in the Philippines* (Berkeley and Los Angeles, 1967), p. 67.
87. *Ibid.*, p. 68.
88. *Ibid.*
89. *Ibid.*, p. 68.

Chapter 4

1. "Relation of religious symbolism and iconography to other aspects of religion and culture." *Encyclopaedia Britannica Library*, from Encyclopaedia Britannica 2005 Deluxe Edition CD-ROM. Copyright © 1994–2003 Encyclopaedia Britannica, Inc. (accessed March 25, 2007).
2. Eliade, M. *Images and Symbols: Studies in Religious Symbolism*, Translated by Philip Maier (Princeton, NJ: Princeton University Press, 1991), p. 12.
3. Eliade, M. *Symbolism, the Sacred, and the Arts*, edited by Diane Apostolos-Cappadona (New York: Continuum, 1992), p. 18.
4. Eliade, *Images and Symbols*, pp. 45–46.
5. Purev, O. and G. Purvee. *Mongolian Shamanism* (Ulaanbaatar: Purvee, 2007), p. 100.
6. Purev and Purvee. *Mongolian Shamanism*, p. 100.
7. Eliade, M. *Shamanism: Archaic Techniques of Ecstasy*, Translated by Willard R. Trask, (Bollingen Series LXXVI, Princeton, NJ: Princeton University Press, 1974), p. 169.
8. Sarangerel, *Riding Windhorses* (Rochester VT: Destiny Books, 2000), p. 179.
9. Mithen, S., in: Maschner, H., ed. *Darwinian Archaeologies* (New York and London: Plenum Press, 1996), p. 204.
10. Turner, V. *Forest of Symbols* (Ithaca and London: Cornell University Press, 1967), p. 10.
11. Needham, R. *Symbolic Classification* (Santa Monica, CA: Goodyear Publishing Company, Inc., 1979), p. 5.
12. Cirlot, J. E, *A Dictionary of Symbols*, Translated by Jack Sage (New York: Philosophical Library, 1962), p. xiv.
13. Dissanayake, E. *What is Art For?* (Seattle and London: University of Washington Press, 1988), p. 126.
14. *Ibid.*, p. 118.
15. Eliade, *Images and Symbols*, p. 9.
16. Hyman, J. *The Imitation of Nature* (New York and Oxford: Basil Blackwell Ltd., 1989), pp. 66–67.
17. Lowie, R. H. *Primitive Religion* (New York: Liveright, 1970), p. 287.
18. *Ibid.*
19. Balzer M. M. ed. *Shamanic Worlds* (Armonk, NY and London: North Castle Books, 1997), p. 132.
20. Stein W. *Shamans* (San Diego, CA: Greenhaven Press, Inc., 1991), p. 56.
21. Young, D. *Origins of the Sacred* (New York: St. Martin's Press, 1991), p. 169.
22. Wilson, F. A. *Art as Revelation* (Fontwell (Sussex: Centaur Press Ltd., 1961), p. 4.
23. Wingert. P. S. *Primitive Art: Its Traditions and Styles* (New York: Oxford University Press 1962), p. 66.
24. Jung, C. G. ed. *Man and His Symbols*, J. Freemen coordinating editor (Garden City, NJ: Doubleday & Company, Inc., 1964), p. 23.
25. "Religious symbolism and iconography." *Encyclopaedia Britannica Library* from *Encyclopaedia Britannica 2005 Deluxe Edition CD-ROM*. Copyright © 1994–2003 Encyclopedia Britannica, Inc. (accessed March 26, 2007).
26. Fardon, R., ed. *Power and Knowledge* (Edinburgh: Scottish Academic Press, 1985) p. 157.
27. Forsyth, J. *A History of the Peoples of Siberia: Russia's North Asian Colony 1581–1990*. (Cambridge: Cambridge University Press, 1992), p. 85.
28. Michael, H. N. ed. *Studies in Siberian Shamanism* (Toronto: University of Toronto Press for the Arctic Institute of North America, 1963), p. 139.
29. Kharitonova, V. "'Black' Shamans, 'White' Shamans," in: Walter, M. N. and E. J. N. Fridman, eds. *Shamanism: An Encyclopedia of World Beliefs, Practices, and Culture*, Vol. II, pp. 536–539 (Santa Barbara, CA and Oxford: ABC CLIO, 2004), p. 537.
30. Kharitonova, "Black" Shamans, "White" Shamans, p. 537.
31. Grim, J. A. *The Shaman: Patterns of Siberian and Ojibway Healing* (Norman: University of Oklahoma Press, 1983), p. 39.
32. Grim, *The Shaman*, p. 39.
33. Eliade, *Shamanism*, p. 477.
34. Eliade, M. *Yoga: Immortality and Freedom*, Translated by Willard R. Trask, (Bollingen Series LVI, Princeton: Princeton University Press, 1990), p. 105.
35. Mackemzie, D. A. *China and Japan: Myths and Legends Series* (London: Bracken Books, 1985), pp. 72–73. See also: Fontana, D. *Secret Language of Symbols* (San Francisco: Chronicle Books, 1994) p. 95.
36. Cauquelin, J. "The Impact of Japanese Colonialism on Puyuma (Taiwan) Shamanism," in: Hoppál, M. and K. Howard, eds. *Shamans and Cultures*, pp. 97–104 (Budapest: Akadémiai Kiadó and Los Angeles: International Society for Trans-Oceanic Research, 1993), p. 99.
37. Jung, *Man and His Symbols*, p. 151.
38. Mumford, S. R. *Himalayan Dialogue: Tibetan Lamas and Gurung Shamans in Napal* (Madison: University of Wisconsin Press, 1989), p. 8.

39. "Religious symbolism and iconography." Encyclopaedia *Britannica Library* from *Encyclopaedia Britannica* 2005 Deluxe Edition CD-ROM. Copyright © 1994–2003 Encyclopedia Britannica, Inc. (accessed March 26, 2007).

40. Gimbutas, M. *The Language of the Goddess* (New York: Thames & Hudson, 1989), p. 3.

41. Emeagwale, G. and M. N. Walter. "Ancient Egyptian Shamanism," in: Walter, M. N. and E. J. N. Fridman, eds. *Shamanism: An Encyclopedia of World Beliefs, Practices, and Culture*, Vol. II, pp. 906–910 (Santa Barbara, CA and Oxford: ABC CLIO, 2004), p. 907.

42. Hart, G. *Dictionary of Egyptian Gods and Goddesses* (London and New York: Routledge, 1986), p. 154.

43. Emeagwale and Walter. "Ancient Egyptian Shamanism," p. 908.

44. Eliade, *Shamanism*, p. 159.

45. Budge, E. A. W. *Egyptian Magic* (New York: Dover Publications, Inc., 1971), pp. 230–231.

46. Levin, M. G. and L. P. Potapov. *The People of Siberia* (Chicago and London: University of Chicago Press, 1956.) p. 78

47. Eliade, *Shamanism*, p. 204.

48. Chesnov, Ya. B. "Dragon: Metaphor of the Eternal World," in: N. L. Zhulpvslaus ed. *Mify, Kul'ty, Oryady narodov zarubezhnoi azii*, pp. 59–72 (Moscow: Nauka, 1986), pp. 60–61. As quoted in C. Humphrey with Urgunge Onon. *Shamans and Elders: Experience, Knoweldge, and Power among the Daur Mongols* (Oxford: Clarendon Press, 1996), p. 280.

49. Mackenzie, *Myths and Legends Series*, p. 128.

50. Editors. *Encyclopedia of Magic and Superstition* (London: Octopus Books Limited, 1974), p. 158.

51. Stein, *Shamans*, p. 76.

52. Walker, B. G. *The Woman's Dictionary of Symbols and Sacred Objects*. (Edison NJ: Castle Books, 1988), p. 135.

53. Snow, D. 1976. *The Archaeology of North America* (New York: Viking Press, 1976), p. 65–68.

54. Torrance, R. M. *Spiritual Quest* (Berkeley and London: University of California Press, 1994), p. 224.

55. Nunley, J. W. *Moving with the Face of the Devil* (Urbana and Chicago: University of Illinois Press, 1987), p. 108.

56. Hoppál, M., ed. *Shamanism: Selected Writings of Vilmos Diószegi* (Budapest: Akadémiai Kiadó, 1998) p. xvii

57. Maringer, J. *The Gods of Prehistoric Man*. (New York: Alfred A. Knopf, 1960), p. 279.

58. Strathern, A., and M. Strathern. *Self-decoration in Mount Hagen* (Toronto and Buffalo: University of Toronto Press, 1971), p. 171.

59. Müller-Ebeling, C., C. Rätsch, and S. B. Shahi. *Shamanism and Tantra in the Himalayas* (London: Thames & Hudson, 2002), p. 41.

60. Burland, C. A. *Magic Arts: A Short History* (London: Arthur Barker Limited, 1966), p. 58.

61. AHED. *American Heritage Electronic Dictionary* (Houghton Mifflin Company. US Pat. No. 4,724,523, © 1991, Word Star International Inc., © 1992).

62. "Khnum," Encyclopaedia Britannica Library, from *Encyclopaedia Britannica* 2005 Deluxe Edition CD-ROM. Copyright © 1994–2003 Encyclopaedia Britannica, Inc. (accessed March 25, 2007).

63. Hoppál, Shamanism, p. xvii

64. Lindsay, *A Short History of Culture* (New York: Citadel Press, 1963), p. 111.

65. Hayden, B. *Shamans, Sorcerers and Saints*. (Washington: Smithsonian Books, 2003), p. 323.

66. Idowu, E. B. *African Traditional Religion* (Maryknoll, NY: Orbis Books, 1975), p. 174.

67. *Ibid.*

68. Ray, D. J. *Aleut and Eskimo Art: Tradition and Innovation in South Alaska* (Seattle: University of Washington Press, 1981), p. 21.

69. *Ibid.*

70. Blodgett, J. *The Coming and Going of the Shaman: Eskimo Shamanism and Art* (Winnipeg: Winnipeg Art Gallery Exhibition Catalog, 1978), p. 155.

71. Hunt. N. B. *Shamanism in North America* (Buffalo, NY: Firefly Book, 2002), p. 126.

72. Spence. L. *The Myths of the North American Indians* (New York: Barnes & Noble, 2005 [1914]), p. 76.

73. Webster. H. *Magic: A Sociological Study* (Stanford: Stanford University Press, 1948), p. 136.

74. *Ibid.*

75. Spence, L. *Myths of the North American Indians* (New York: Barnes and Noble, 2005 [1913]), p. 76.

76. *Ibid.*, p. 77.

77. *Ibid.*, p. 78.

78. *Ibid.*

79. *Ibid.*

80. Purev. O. and G. Purvee. *Mongolian Shamanism* (Ulaanbaatar: Purvee, 2007), p. 206.

81. Ibid., p. 207.

82. Ray, *Aleut and Eskimo Art*, p. 22.

83. Figes, O. *Natasha's Dance* (New York: Metropolitan Books, 2002), p. 365.

84. Eliade, *Shamanism*, p. 90.

85. *Ibid*

86. Dow, J. *Shaman's Touch* (Salt Lake City: University of Utah Press, 1989), p. 60.

87. *Ibid.*, p. 61.

88. Kister, D. "Korean Shamanism," in: Walter, M. N. and E. J. N. Fridman, eds. *Shamanism: An Encyclopedia of World Beliefs, Practices, and Culture*, Vol. II, 681–688 (Santa Barbara, CA and Oxford: ABC CLIO, 2004), p. 682.

89. Huhm, H. P. *Kut: Korean Shamanist Rituals* (Elizabeth, NJ and Seoul: Hollym, 1980), pp. 10–11.

90. Vitebsky, P. *The Shaman: Voyages of the Soul Trance, Ecstasy and Healing from Siberia to the Amazon* (Boston and London: Brown, Little and Company, 1995), p. 8.

91. Grim, J. *The Shaman: Patterns of Religious Healing Among the Ojibway Indians* (Norman: University of Oklahoma Press, 1983), p. 63.

92. *Ibid.*, p. 114.

93. Shepard, G. H. Jr. "Central and South American Shamanism," in: Walter, M. N. and E. J. N. Fridman, eds. *Shamanism: An Encyclopedia of World Beliefs, Practices, and Culture*, Vol. II, 382–392 (Santa Barbara, CA and Oxford: ABC CLIO, 2004), p. 389.

94. Meyer, L. *Black Africa: Masks, Sculpture, Jewelry* (Paris: Pierre Terrail, 1992), p. 74.

95. Hoppál, *Shamanism*, p. 119.

96. *Ibid.*

97. Blodgett, J. *Coming and Going of the Shaman: Eskimo Shamanism and Art* (Winnipeg: Winnipeg Art Gallery Exhibition Catalog, 1978), p. 76.

98. Riley, O. *Masks and Magic* (London: Thames & Hudson, 1955), p. 8.

99. Eliade, *Shamanism*, p. 165.

100. Müller-Ebeling, Rätsch, and Shahi. *Shamanism and Tantra*, pp. 227–228.

101. Lommel, A. *World of the Early Hunters*, translated by Michael Bullock (London: Evelyn, Adams & MacKay, 1967), p. 110.

102. Corbin, G. A. *Native Arts of North America, Africa, and the South Pacific: An Introduction* (New York: Harper and Row, Publishers, 1988), p. 59.

103. Edson, G. *Masks and Masking: Faces of Tradition*

and Belief Worldwide (Jefferson, NC and London: McFarland & Company, Inc. Publishers, 2005), pp. 171–172.
104. Hoppál, *Shamanism*, p. xix
105. Lommel, *World of the Early Hunters*, p. 110.
106. Eliade, *Symbolism*, p. 13.

Chapter 5

1. Lommel, A. *World of the Early Hunters* (London: Evelyn, Adams & Mackay, 1967), p. 128.
2. Levy-Bruhl, L. "What the natives think of pictures, names, and dreams," in: Mead, M. and N. Calas ed. *Primitive Heritage: An Anthropological Anthology* (New York: Random House, Inc., 1953), pp. 36–37.
3. Kehoe, A. *Shamans and Religion: An Anthropological Exploration in Critical Thinking* (Prospect Heights, IL: Waveland Press, Inc., 2000), p. 12.
4. Hoebel, E. A. Man in the Primitive World, 2d ed. (New York and London: McGraw-Hill Book Company, 1958), p. 252.
5. Wingert, P. *Primitive Art: Its Traditions and Styles* (New York: Oxford University Press, 1962), p. 57.
6. *Ibid.*
7. *Ibid.*
8. *Ibid.*
9. *Ibid.*, p. 17.
10. Cirlot, J. E. *Dictionary of Symbols*, translated by J. Sage (New York: Philosophical Library, 1962), p. xxi.
11. Hoppál, M. *Studies on Mythology and Uralic Shamanism*, Translation by Orsolya Frank, Bálint Sebestyén and Péter Simoncsics (Budapest: Akadémiai Kiadó, 2000), p. 5.
12. Walter, M. N. and E. J. N. Fridman, eds. *Shamanism: An Encyclopedia of World Beliefs, Practices, and Culture* (Santa Barbara, CA and Oxford: ABC CLIO, 2004), p. 22.
13. Gillette, D. *Shaman's Secret* (New York and London: Bantam Books, 1997), p. 117.
14. *Ibid.*, p. 27.
15. *Ibid.*
16. *Ibid.*
17. Gimbutas, M. *Languages of the Goddess* (London: Thames & Hudson, 1989), p. xv.
18. Lommel, *World of the Early Hunters*, p. 16.
19. *Ibid.*, p. 213.
20. Lewin, R. *Origins of Modern Humans* (New York: Scientific American Library, a division of HPHLP, 1993), p. 146.
21. *Ibid.*
22. *Ibid.*, p. 154; see also Eliade, M. *Symbolism, the Sacred, and the Arts*, (New York: Continuum, 1992), p. 63; Halifax, J. *Shaman: The Wounded Healer* (London: Thames and Hudson Ltd., 1982), p. 82; Marshack, A. *The Roots of Civilization* (New York and Dusseldorf: McGraw-Hill Book Company, 1972), pp. 272–273; Herskovits, M. J. *Man and His Works: the Science of Cultural Anthropology* (New York: Alfred A. Knopf, 1948), pp. 14–16.
23. Jung. C. G. *Man and His Symbols* (Garden City, NY: Doubleday & Company Inc., 1964), p. 151.
24. Markman, R. H. and Markman P. T. *The Flayed God: The Mesoamerican Mythological Tradition* (New York: HarperCollins Publishers, 1992), p. 5.
25. *Ibid.*
26. Levin, M. G. and Potapov, L. P. eds. *The Peoples of Siberia*, Translated by Scripta Technica, Inc., English translation edited by Stephen Dunn. Chicago and London: The University of Chicago Press, 1956), pp. 77–78.
27. Furst, P. T., in: Shafer, H. *Ancient Texans* (Austin, TX: Texas Monthly Press, 1986), p. 211.
28. Labbé, A. J. Colombia Before Columbus (New York: Rizzoli, 1986) p. 85.
29. Gillette, *Shaman's Secret*, p. 27.
30. Lommel, *World of the Early Hunters*, p. 27.
31. *Ibid.*
32. Gillette, *Shaman's Secret*, p. 39.
33. Hoppál, M. ed. 1998. *Shamanism: Selected Writings of Vilmos Diószegi* (Budapest: Akadémiai Kiadó, 1998), p. xix.
34. Eliade, M. *Shamanism*, Translated by Willard Trask (Princeton, NJ: Bollingen Series LXXVI Princeton University Press, 1974), p. 94.
35. Lewis, P. H. "The artist in New Ireland society," pp. 71–79, in: Smith, M. W. ed. The Artist in Tribal Society: Proceedings of a Symposium held at the Royal Anthropological Institute (London: Routledge & Kegan Paul, 1961), p. 71.
36. Gillette, *Shaman's Secret*, p. 121.
37. *Ibid.*, p. 117.
38. Eliade, *Shamanism*, p. 172.
39. Purev, O. and Purvee, G. *Mongolian Shamanism* (Ulaanbaatar: Purvee, 2007), p. 145.
40. Christensen, E. *Primitive Art* (New York: Thomas Y. Crowell Company, 1955), p. 327.
41. Lommel, *World of the Early Hunters*, p. 129.
42. Martynov, A. I. *The Ancient Art of Northern Asia*, Translated and edited by Demitri B. Shimkin and Edith M. Shimkin (Urbana and Chicago: University of Ilinois Press, 1991), p. 90.
43. Encyclopaedia Britannica, from Encyclopaedia Britannica Deluxe Edition 2005 CD. Copyright © 1994–2004 Encyclopaedia Britannica, Inc. (accessed May, 30, 2004).
44. Maxwell, R. J. ed. *American's Fascinating Indian Heritage* (Pleasantville, NY: The Reader's Digest Association, Inc., 1978), p. 285.
45. Gimbutas, M. *The Language of the Goddess* (New York: Thames & Hudson, 1989), p. 3–17.
46. *Ibid.*, p. 19–23.
47. Walter and Fridman, *Shamanism*, p. 336.
48. Eliade, M. *The Sacred and The Profane: The Natural of Religion*, Translated by Willard R. Trask (New York and London: A Harvest Book, Harcourt, Inc., 1987 [1957]), p. 12.
49. *Ibid.*
50. Monti, F. *African Masks*, Translated by A. Hale (London and New York: Hamlyn Publishing Group Limited, 1968), p. 25.
51. Edson, G. *Masks and Masking: Faces of Tradition and Belief Worldwide* (Jefferson, NC and London: McFarland & Company, Inc., Publishers, 2005), p. 21.
52. Walter and Fridman, *Shamanism*, p. 348.
53. Christensen, *Primitive Art*, p. 132.
54. Mack, J., ed. *Masks and the Art of Expression* (New York: Harry N. Abrams, Inc., Publishers, 1994), p. 126.
55. *Ibid.*, pp. 126–128.
56. *Ibid.*, p. 128.
57. Sarangerel. *Riding Windhorses: A Journey into the Heart of Mongolian Shamanism* (Rochester, VT: Destiny Books, 2000), p. 90.
58. Gillette, Shaman's Secret, p. 117.
59. *Ibid.*, p. 10.
60. Markman and Markman. *The Flayed God*, pp. 35–36.
61. Eliade, *Shamanism*, p. 165.
62. Serlin, I. A. "Dance and shamanism: ancient roots for a modern healing art," pp. 56–61, in: Heinze, R-I, Conference Coordinator and Editor. Proceedings of the Ninth International Conference on the Study of Shamanism and Alternative Modes of Healing (Berkeley: University of California 1992), p. 59.
63. Murphy, J. "Psychotherapeutic aspects of shamanism on the St. Lawrence Island, Alaska," pp. 53–83, in: Ari

Kiev, ed. *Magic, Faith and Healing: Studies in Primitive Psychiatry Today* (London: The Free Press of Glenscoe, 1964), p. 79.

64. Brandon, J. R. "The development of dance and theatre in the East Asian nations," in: *Encyclopaedia Britannica*, from Encyclopaedia Britannica Deluxe Edition 2005 CD. Copyright © 1994–2004 Encyclopaedia Britannica, Inc. (accessed May, 30, 2004).
65. *Ibid.*
66. David-Neel, A. *With Mystics and Magicians in Tibet.* (London, The Bodley Head, 1931) pp. 36–37.
67. Czaplicka, M. A. *Shamanism in Siberia* (Whitefish, MT: Kessinger Publishing, 1970 [reprint]), p. 45.
68. "Paleo-siberians," *Encyclopaedia Britannica*, from Encyclopaedia Britannica Deluxe Edition 2005 CD. Copyright © 1994–2004 Encyclopaedia Britannica, Inc. (accessed May, 30, 2004).
69. Czaplicka, *Aboriginal Siberia*, pp. 16–20.
70. *Ibid.*, p. 206.
71. *Ibid.*, p. 203.
72. *Ibid.*, p. 207.
73. *Ibid.*
74. *Ibid.*, p. 203.
75. Purev, O. and Purvee, G. *Mongolian Shamanism* (Ulaanbaatar: Purvee, 2007), p. 210.
76. *Ibid.*, p. 213.
77. *Ibid.*
78. Jochelson, W. *The Koryak* (Leiden: E. J. Brill and New York: G. E. Stechert and issued as v. 10 of Memoirs of the American Museum of Natural History, 1908), pp. 54–55.
79. Czaplicka, *Aboriginal Siberia*, p. 208.
80. Purev and Purvee. *Mongolian Shamanism*, p. 215–216.
81. Humphrey, C. with Urgunge, O. *Shamans and Elders: Experience, Knowledge, and Power among the Daur Mongols* (Oxford: Clarendon Press, 1996), p. 253.
83. Jochelson, *The Koryak*, p. 56.
84. Czaplicka, *Aboriginal Siberia*, p. 209.
85. *Ibid.*
86. Murdoch, J. "On the Siberian Origin of some customs of the Western Eskimo," in: *American Anthropologist*, (Washington, DC, 1888), p. 385
87. Jochelson, W. *The Koryak* (Leiden: E. J. Brill and New York: G. E. Stechert and issued as v. 10 of Memoirs of the American Museum of Natural History, 1908), p. 58.
88. Czaplicka, *Aboriginal Siberia*, p. 215.
89. Storm, R. *Mythology of Asia and the Far East* (London: Anness Publishing Ltd., 2006), p. 50.
90. Hoppál, *Shamanism*, p. xix
91. Eliade, *Shamanism*, p. 171.
92. Sieroszewski, W. L. *The Yakut: An Essay of an Ethnographical Investigation.* (St. Petersburg: I.R.G.S., 1896), p. 632.
93. *Ibid.*, p. 627.
94. Grim, J. A. *The Shaman: Patterns of Religious Healing Among the Ojibway Indians* (Norman: University of Oklahoma Press, 1983), p. 78.
95. Eliade, M. *Images and Symbols: Studies in Religious Symbolism*, Trans. by Philip Mairet (Princeton, NJ: Princeton University Press, 1991), p. 46.
96. Müller-Ebeling, C., Rätsch, C. and Shahi, S. B. *Shamanism and Tantra in the Himalayas* (London: Thames & Hudson, 2002), p. 212.
97. Eliade, *Shamanism: Archaic Techniques of Ecstasy*, p. 179.
98. *Ibid.*, p. 180.
99. "Sistrum," *Encyclopaedia Britannica Library*, from Encyclopaedia Britannica 2005 Deluxe Edition CD-ROM. Copyright © 1994–2003 Encyclopaedia Britannica, Inc. (accessed March, 25, 2007).
100. "Arts, Native American, Regional customs: Mexico and Middle America," *Encyclopaedia Britannica Library*, from Encyclopaedia Britannica 2005 Deluxe Edition CD-ROM. Copyright © 1994–2003 Encyclopaedia Britannica, Inc. (accessed March, 25, 2007).
101. "Arts, Native American, Regional customs: Mexico and Middle America," *Encyclopaedia Britannica Library*, from Encyclopaedia Britannica 2005 Deluxe Edition CD-ROM. Copyright © 1994–2003 Encyclopaedia Britannica, Inc. (accessed March, 25, 2007).
102. Diószegi, V. and Hoppál, M., eds. *Shamanism in Siberia* (Budapest: Akadémiai Kiadó, 1996), p. 66.
103. Müller-Ebeling, Rätsch, and Shahi. *Shamanism and Tantra*, p. 212.
104. Stein, W. *Shamans* (San Diego, CA: Greenhaven Press Inc., 1991), p. 72.
105. Hoppál, M. "Studies on Eurasian Shamanism," in: Hoppál, M. and Howard, K. eds. *Shamans and Cultures* (Budapest: Akadémial Kiadó and Los Angeles: International Society for Trans-Oceanic Research, 1993), p. 276.
106. Purev and Purvee. *Mongolian Shamanism*, p. 223.
107. *Ibid.*
108. *Ibid.*, p. 224.
109. Hoppál, *Shamanism*, p. 7.
110. Eliade, *Shamanism*, pp. 153–154.
111. <http://www.iras.ucalgary.ca/-volk/sylvia/Magic.htm>
112. Oakes, J. and R. Riewe. *Spirit of Siberia* (Washington, DC: Smithsonian Institution Press, 1998) p. 167.
113. *Ibid.*, p. 139.

Chapter 6

1. Edson, G. *Masks and Masking: Faces of Tradition and Belief Worldwide* (Jefferson, NC and London: McFarland & Company, Inc., Publishers, 2005) p. 164.
2. Aldhouse-Green, M. and S. Aldhouse-Green. *The Quest for the Shaman: Shape-Shifters, Sorcerers and Spirit-Healers of Ancient Europe* (London: Thames & Hudson, Ltd., 2005), p. 13.
3. Frazer, J. G. *The Golden Bough: A Study in Magic and Religion* (New York: The Macmillan Company, 1958), p. 477.
4. Alekseev. N. A. "The Role of the Shaman in the Life of the Turkic-speaking People of Siberia," in: M. M. Balzer, ed. *Shamanism: Soviet Studies of Traditional Religion in Siberia and Central Asia* (Armonk, NY and London: M. E. Sharpe, Inc., 1990), p. 96.
5. Hoppál, M. "Shamanism: Universal Structures and Regional Symbols," in: Hoppál, M and K. D. Howard eds. *Shamans and Cultures*, pp. 181–192 (Budapest: Akadémiai Kiadó and Los Angeles: International Society for Trans-Oceanic Research, 1993), p. 191.
6. "South American nomad social organization," Encyclopaedia Britannica Library, from *Encyclopaedia Britannica* 2005 Deluxe Edition CD-ROM. Copyright © 1994–2003 Encyclopaedia Britannica, Inc. (accessed June 9, 2007).
7. Hultkrantz, Å. *Shamanic Healing and Ritual Drama: Health and Medicine in Native North American Religious Traditions* (New York: The Crossroad Publishing Company, 1992), p. 131.
8. Langdon, E. J. and G. Baer. *Portals of Power: Shamanism in South America* (Albuquerque: University of New Mexico, 1992), p. 11.
9. Hultkrantz, *Shamanic Healing and Ritual Drama*, p. 30.

10. *Ibid.*, pp. 37–38.
11. *Ibid.*, p. 35.
12. Winkelman, M. and P. M. Peek eds. *Divination and Healing: Potent Vision* (Tucson: The University of Arizona Press, 2004), p. 128.
13. Anisimov, A. F. "The shaman's tent of the Evenks and the origin of the shamanistic rite," in: Michael, H. N. *Studies in Shamanism* (Toronto: Arctic Institute of North America, Anthropology of the North Translations from Russian Sources. No. 4. University of Toronto, 1963), p. 85.
14. Ibid.
15. *Ibid.*
16. *Ibid.*, p. 96.
17. Walter, M. N. and E. J. N. Fridman, eds. Shamanism: An Encyclopedia of World Beliefs, Practices, and Culture Vol I (Santa Barbara, CA and Oxford: ABC CLIO, 2004), p. 140.
18. Driscoll, J. T. "Shamanism," Transcribed by Douglas J. Potter, in: The Catholic Encyclopedia, Volume XIII. New York: Robert Appleton Company, 1912). <http://www.newadvent.org/cathen/index.html> Copyright © 2007 by Kevin Knight (accessed May 15, 2007).
19. Wu Bing-an. "Shamans in Manchuria," in: Hoppál, M. and O. von Sadovszky. *Shamanism Past and Present*, Part 2. pp. 263–269 (Budapest: Ethnographic Institute, Hungarian Academy of Science and Los Angeles/Fullerton: International Society for Trans-Oceanic Research, 1989), p. 263.
20. *Ibid.*
21. "Paleo-Siberians," Encyclopaedia Britannica Library, from *Encyclopaedia Britannica* 2005 Deluxe Edition CD-ROM. Copyright © 1994–2003 Encyclopedia Britannica, Inc. (accessed June 9, 2007).
22. Driscoll, "Shamanism," (accessed July 1, 2007).
23. Aldhouse-Green and Aldhouse-Green. *The Quest for the Shaman*, p. 12.
24. Walter and Fridman, *Shamanism*, p. 119.
25. Wallis, W. D. *Religion in Primitive Society* (New York: F. S. Crofts & Co., 1939), p. 147.
26. Kehoe, A. B. *Shamans and Religion* (Prospect Heights, IL: Waveland Press, Inc., 2000), p. 12.
27. Goodman, F. *Ecstasy, Ritual, and Alternate Reality: Religion in a Pluralistic World* (Bloomington and Indianapolis: Indiana University Press, 1988), p. 31.
28. Bäckman, L. and Å. Hultkrantz *Studies in Lapp Shamanism* (Stockholm: Almqvist & Wiksell, 1978), p. 17.
29. Lissner, I. *Man, God and Magic*, Translated by J. Maxwell Brownjohn (New York: G. P. Putnam's Sons, 1961), p. 89.
30. *Ibid.*
31. Eliade, M. T*he Sacred and The Profane: The Natural of Religion*, Translated by Willard R. Trask (New York and London: A Harvest Book, Harcourt, Inc., 1987 [1957]), p. 135.
32. Burland, C. A. *The Magical Arts: A Short History* (London: Arthur Barker Limited, 1966), p. 37.
33. Edson, G. *Masks and Masking*, p. 125.
34. Eliade, M. *Shamanism: Archaic Techniques of Ecstasy*, Translated by Willard R. Trask (Bollingen Series LXXVI, Princeton: Princeton University Press, 1974), p. 216.
35. *Ibid.*, p. 246.
36. Bäckman, L. and Å. Hultkrantz *Studies in Lapp Shamanism* (Stockholm: Almqvist & Wiksell, 1978), p. 46.
37. *Ibid.*
38. Eliade, *Shamanism*, p. 289.
39. Peters, L. *Ecstasy and Healing in Nepal* (Malibu. CA: Undena Publications, 1981), p. 13.
40. "Ritual." *Encyclopaedia Britannica Library* from Encyclopaedia Britannica 2005 Deluxe Edition CD-ROM. Copyright © 1994–2003 Encyclopedia Britannica, Inc. (accessed March 26, 2007).
41. *Ibid.*
42. Durkheim. E. *The Elementary Forms of Religious Life*. Translated by K. E. Field (New York: Free Press, 1995), p. 337.
43. Ibid., p. 226.
44. Eliade, *Shamanism*, p. 388.
45. "Apollo" *Encyclopaedia Britannica Library* from Encyclopaedia Britannica 2005 Deluxe Edition CD-ROM. Copyright © 1994–2003 Encyclopedia Britannica, Inc. (accessed March 30, 2007).
46. Eliade, *Shamanism*, p. 388.
47. Campbell, J. "The Historical Development of Mythology," in: Murray H., ed. *Myths and Mythmaking* (New York: George Braziller, 1960), p. 19.
48. Humphrey, C. "Chiefly and Shamanist Landscapes in Mongolia," pp. 135–162, in: Hirsch, E. and M. O'Hanlon, eds. *The Anthropology of Landscape: Perspectives on Place and Space* (Oxford: Clarendon Press, 1995), p. 136.
49. Balzer, M. M. ed. 1997. *Shamanic Worlds*. New York and London: North Castle Books, p. xvi.
50. Mason, D. A. *Spirit of the Mountains: Korea's San-Shin and Traditions of Mountain-Worship* (Elizabeth, NJ and Seoul: Hollym, 1999), p. 140.
51. Sargent, D. *Global Ritualism: Myth and Magic Around the World* (St. Paul, MN: Llewellyn Publications, 1994), p. 11.
52. Hoppál, M. and K. D. Howard. *Shamans and Cultures* (Budapest: Akadémiai Kiadó and Los Angeles: International Society for Trans-Oceanic Research, 1993), p. 243.
53. Ibid., p. 244.
54. Schafer, E. H. and Editors of Time-Life Books. *Ancient China* New York: Time Life Books, 1967), p. 60.
55. Purev, O. and G. Purvee. *Mongolian Shamanism* (Ulaanbaatar: Purvee, 2007), p. 26.
56. Purev and Purvee, *Mongolian Shamanism*, pp. 27–28.
57. Ibid., p. 28.
58. Bancroft-Hunt, N. *People of the Totem* (New York: G. Pl Putnam's Sons, 1979), p. 103.
59. Torrance, R. M. *The Spiritual Quest: Transcendence in Myth, Religion, and Science* (Berkeley, Los Angeles, and London: University of California Press, 1994), p. 72.
60. Dow, J. *The Shaman's Touch: Otomi Indian Symbolic Healing* (Salt Lake City: University of Utah Press, 1986), p. 7.
61. Edson, *Masks and Masking*, p. 112.
62. Shirokogoroff, S. M. *Psychomental Complex of the Tungus* (London: Kegan Paul, Trench, Trubner & Co., Ltd., 1935), p. 287.
63. "Shamanism," Heritage Series (Seoul: Korean Overseas Information Service, 1995), p. 3.
64. Humphrey, C. with U. Onon. *Shamans and Elders: Experience, Knowledge, and Power among the Daur Mongols* (Oxford: Clarendon Press, 1996), p. 202.
65. Purev and Purvee, *Mongolian Shamanism*, p. 193.
66. Ibid., p. 176.
67. Humphrey with Onon. *Shamans and Elders*, p. 206.
68. Ibid., p. 202.
69. Corbin, G. A. *Native Arts of North America, Africa, and the South Pacific: An Introduction* (New York: Harper and Row, 1988), p. 125.
70. Anisimov, A. F. "The Shaman's Tent of the Evenks and the Origin of the Shamanistic Rite," in: Michael, H. N. Studies in Shamanism (Toronto: Arctic Institute of

North America, Anthropology of the North Translations from Russian Sources. No. 4. University of Toronto, 1963), p. 97.
71. *Ibid.*
72. *Ibid.*
73. Vitebsky, P. *The Shaman: Voyages of the Soul Trance, Ecstasy, and Healing from Siberia to the Amazon.* (New York and London: Little, Brown and Company, 1995), p. 52.
74. Prokofyeva, Ye. D. "The Costume of the Enets Shaman," Translated by Barbara Krader, in: Michael, H. N. ed. *Studies in Siberian Shamanism* (Toronto: Published for the Arctic Institute of North America by University of Toronto Press, 1963), p. 129.
75. Jakobsen, M. D. *Shamanism: Traditional and Contemporary Approaches to the Mastery of Spirits and Healing* (New York and Oxford: Berghahn Books, 1999), p. 73.
76. *Ibid.*
77. *Ibid.*
78. Http://www.iras.ucalgary.ca/~volk/sylvia/Magic.htm
79. "Ritual" Encyclopaedia Britannica Library, from *Encyclopaedia Britannica* 2005 Deluxe Edition CD-ROM. Copyright © 1994–2003 Encyclopaedia Britannica, Inc. (accessed May 19, 2007).
80. Humphrey with Onon. *Shamans and Elders,* p. 204.
81. *Ibid.*
82. *Ibid.*, p. 224.
83. *Ibid.*
84. *Ibid.*, p. 225.
85. Corbin, *Native Arts of North America, Africa, and the South Pacific,* p. 59.
86. Walter and Fridman, *Shamanism,* p. 908.
87. *Ibid.*
88. Budge, E. A. W. *Osiris and the Egyptian Resurrection,* 2 Vols (London and New York: P. L. Warner and G. P. Putnam's Sons, 1911), p. 170. Also quoted in: Walter, M. N. and E. J. N. Fridman, eds. *Shamanism: An Encyclopedia of World Beliefs, Practices, and Culture,* Vol. II (Santa Barbara, CA and Oxford: ABC CLIO, 2004), p. 908.
89. Valadez, S. E. "Wolf Power and Interspecies Communication in Huichol Shamanism," in: Shaffer, S. B. and Furst, P. T. *People of the Peyote: Huichol Indian History, Religion & Survival* (Albuquerque: University of New Mexico Press, 1996), p. 271.
90. Vitebsky *The Shaman,* p. 64.
91. Hultkrantz, Å. "Ecological and Phenomenological Aspects of Shamanism," in: V. Diószegi and M. Hoppál. *Shamanism in Siberia* (Budapest: Akadémiai Kiadó, 1996), pp. 1–32.
92. *Ibid.*, p. 15.
93. Vitebsky *The Shaman,* p. 64.
94. Humphrey with Onon. *Shamans and Elders,* p. 30.
95. *Ibid.*
96. *Ibid.*
97. Bourguignon, E. "Trance Dance," in: Walter, M. N. and E. J. N. Fridman, eds. *Shamanism: An Encyclopedia of World Beliefs, Practices, and Culture,* Vol. II (Santa Barbara, CA and Oxford: ABC CLIO, 2004), p. 247.
98. Walter and Fridman, *Shamanism,* p. 140.
99. *Ibid.*
100. Bourguignon, "Trance Dance," p. 247.
101. *Ibid.*
102. Aldhouse-Green and Aldhouse-Green. *The Quest for the Shaman,* p. 12.
103. *Ibid.*
104. Driscoll, "Shamanism," (accessed June 20, 2007).
105. Kharitonova, V. "Black" Shamans, "White" Shamans, in: Walter, M. N. and E. J. N. Fridman, eds. *Shamanism: An Encyclopedia of World Beliefs, Practices, and Culture,* Vol. II (Santa Barbara, CA and Oxford: ABC CLIO, 2004), p. 537.
106. Shiokogoroff, S. M. *Psychmental Complex of the Tungus* (London: Kegan Paul, Trench, Trubner & Co., Ltd., 1935), p. 338.
107. Scarpari, M. *Ancient China: Chinese Civilization from its Origins to the Tang Dynasty* (New York: Barnes and Noble Publishing, 2006), p. 85.
108. Lemoine, J. "The Diagnosis of Disease as a 'Shamanic Equation' among the Hmong of Laos and Thailand," in: Hoppál, M. and Howard, K. D. *Shamans and Cultures* (Budapest: Akadémiai Kiadó and Los Angeles: International Society for Trans-Oceanic Research, 1993), p. 113.

Chapter 7

1. Walter, M. N. and Fridman, E. J. N. *Shamanism* (Santa Barbara, CA and Oxford: ABC CLIO, 2004), pp. 355–356.
2. Kiev, A. *Magic, Faith, and Healing: Studies in Primitive Psychiatry Today* (London: The Free Press of Glencoe, Collier-Macmillan Limited, 1964), p. 10.
3. Thompson, C. J. S. *Magic and Healing* (London and New York: Rider & Company, 1946), p. 9.
4. Winkelman, M. and Peek, P. M. *Divination and Healing: Potent Vision* (Tucson: The University of Arizona Press, 2004), p. 112.
5. Dow, J. *Shaman's Touch* (Salt Lake City: University of Utah Press, 1986), p. 139.
6. Hultkrantz, Å. *Shamanic Healing and Ritual Drama* (New York: Crossroad, 1992), p 106.
7. Kehoe, A. B. *Shamans and Religion* (Prospect Heights, IL, Waveland Press, Inc., 2000), 52.
8. Reichard, G. A. *Navaho Religion: A Study of Symbolism,* vol. 1 (Bollingen Series XVIII, New York: Pantheon Books, 1950), p. 80.
9. *Ibid.*, pp. 80–81.
10. Turner, V. *The Forest of Symbols* (Ithaca and London: Cornell University Press, 1967), p. 300.
11. *Ibid.*, p. 68.
12. de Waal Malefijt, A. *Religion and Culture* (New York: Macmillan Company, 1968), p. 251.
13. Kiev, *Magic, Faith, and Healing,* p. 406.
14. Park, W. Z. *Shamanism in Western North America* (Evanston and Chicago: Northwestern University, 1938), p. 26.
15. Reichard *Navaho Religion,* p. 80.
16. Eliade, M. *Shamanism: Archaic Techniques of Ecstasy,* Translated by Willard Trask (Bollingen Series LXXVI, Princeton, NJ: Princeton University Press, 1974), p. 216.
17. Lommel, A. *The World of the Early Hunters: Medicine-men, shamans, and artists,* Translated by Michael Bullock (London: Evelyn, Adams & MacKay,1967), p. 84.
18. Müller-Ebeling, C., C. Rätsch, and S. B. Shahi. *Shamanism and Tantra in the Himalayas,* translated by Annabel Lee (London: Thames & Hudson, 2002), p. 229.
19. Monter, E. W. *Witchcraft in France and Switzerland* (Ithaca and London: Cornell University Press, 1976) p. 167.
20. Thompson, C. J. S. *Magic and Healing* (London and New York: Rider & Company, 1946), p. 19.
21. Humphrey, C. with U. Onan. *Shamans and Elders: Experience, Knowledge, and Power among the Daur Mongols* (Oxford: Clarendon Press, 1996), p. 30.
22. Eliade, *Shamanism,* p. 164.
23. "Pre-Columbian Civilizations." *Encyclopaedia Britannica Library,* from Encyclopaedia Britannica 2005 Deluxe Edition CD-ROM. Copyright © 1994–2003 Encyclopaedia Britannica, Inc. (accessed March, 25, 2007).

24. Linton, R. *Tree of Culture* (New York: Alfred A. Knopf, 1957), p. 98.
25. *Ibid.*, p. 304.
26. *Ibid.*
27. de Wall Malefijt, A. *Religion and Culture* (New York: Macmillian Company, 1968), p. 216.
28. *Ibid.*
29. Hayden, B. *Shamans, Sorcerers, and Saints* (Washington, DC: Smithsonian Books, 2003), p. 363.
30. Bourke, J. G. *Apache Medicine-men* (New York: Dover Publications, Inc., 1993 [1892]), p. 4.
31. *Ibid.*
32. Wilbert, J. *Tobacco and Shamanism in South America* (New Haven and London: Yale University Press, 1987), p. 164.
33. Smith, R. J. *Fortune-tellers and Philosophers: Divination in Traditional Chinese Society* (Boulder and Oxford: Westview Press, 1991), p. 233.
34. *Ibid.*
35. Wales, H. G. Q. *Divination in Thailand: The Hopes and Fears of a Southeast Asian People* (London and Dublin: Curzon Press, 1983), p. 2.
36. *Ibid.*, p. 3.
37. Hill, D. *Magic and Superstition* (London and New York: The Hamlyn Publishing Group Ltd., 1968), p. 76.
38. *Ibid.*, pp. 76–77.
39. Middleton, J. ed. *Magic, Witchcraft, and Curing* (Garden City, NJ: The Natural History Press, 1967), p. 196–197.
40. Crawford, J. R. *Witchcraft and Sorcery in Rhodesia* (International African Institute, Oxford: Oxford University Press, 1967), p. 183.
41. Kiev, *Magic, Faith, and Healing*, p. 124.
42. Lindsay, J. *A Short History of Culture* (New York: Citadel Press, 1963), p. 111.
43. Eliade, *Shamanism*, p. 245
44. "Skull cult," *Encyclopaedia Britannica Library*, from Encyclopaedia Britannica 2005 Deluxe Edition CD-ROM. Copyright © 1994–2003 Encyclopaedia Britannica, Inc. (accessed March, 25, 2007).
45. Lissner, I. *Man, God and Magic*, Translated by J. Maxwell Brownjohn (New York: G. P. Putnam's Sons, 1961), p. 160.
46. Ryan, W. F. *The Bathhouse at Midnight: An Historical Survey of Magic and Divination in Russia* (University Park: Pennsylvania State University Press, 1999), p. 221
47. Eliade, *Shamanism*, p. 256.
48. "History of medicine," *Encyclopaedia Britannica Library*, from Encyclopaedia Britannica 2005 Deluxe Edition CD-ROM. Copyright © 1994–2003 Encyclopaedia Britannica, Inc. (accessed March, 25, 2007).
49. "Slavic religion," in: *Encyclopaedia Britannica Library*, from Encyclopaedia Britannica 2005 Deluxe Edition CD-ROM. Copyright © 1994–2003 Encyclopaedia Britannica, Inc. (accessed January, 2, 2008).
50. Fitzhugh, W. W. and Kaplan, S. A. *Inua: Spirit World of the Bering Sea Eskimo* (Washington, DC: Smithsonian Institution Press, 1982), p. 126.
51. Snow, D. *The Archaeology of North America* (New York: A Studio Book, Viking Press, 1976), pp. 54–55.
52. *Ibid.*
53. Hunt, N. B. *Shamanism in North America* (Buffalo, NY: Firefly Books Inc., 2003), p. 102
54. Pattee, R. "Ecstasy and Sacrifice," in: Doore, G. ed. *Shaman's Path: Healing, Personal Growth and Empowerment, pp. 17–31* (Boston and London: Shambhala, 1988), pp. 22–23.
55. Dow, *Shaman's Touch*, p. 139
56. *Ibid.*, p. 140
57. "Shamanic ritual" *Encyclopaedia Britannica Library*, from Encyclopaedia Britannica 2005 Deluxe Edition CD-ROM. Copyright © 1994–2003 Encyclopaedia Britannica, Inc. (accessed March, 25, 2007).
58. Walter and Fridman, *Shamanism*, p. 386.
59. "Shamanism" Korean Heritage Series, No. 15 (Seoul, ROK: Korean Overseas Information Service, 1995), p. 9.
60. *Ibid.*, p. 10.
61. Laderman, C. "Malay Shamans and Healers," in: Walter, M. N. and E. J. N. Fridman, eds. *Shamanism: An Encyclopedia of World Beliefs, Practices, and Culture* Vol II, pp. 818–824 (Santa Barbara, CA and Oxford: ABC CLIO, 2004), p. 818.
62. *Ibid.*, p. 819.
63. *Ibid.*, p. 821.
64. Maskarinec, G. "Healing and Shamanism," in: Walter, M. N. and E. J. N. Fridman, eds. *Shamanism: An Encyclopedia of World Beliefs, Practices, and Culture* Vol. I, pp. 137–142 (Santa Barbara, CA and Oxford: ABC CLIO, 2004), p. 140.
65. Benedict, R. *Patterns of Culture* 2d edition (Boston: Houghton Mifflin Company, 1959 [1934]), p. 268.
66. Lommel, *The World of the Early Hunter*. p. 7.
67. Grim, J. A. *The Shaman Patterns of Siberian and Ojibway Healing* (Norman: University of Oklahoma Press, 1983), p. 10.
68. Eliade, *Shamanism*, p. 182.
69. Alekeev, A. "Healing Techniques Among Evén Shamans," in: Balzer, M. M. ed. *Shamanic Worlds*, pp. 154–161 (Armonk, NY and London: North Castle Books, 1997), p. 156.
70. *Ibid.*
71. Hill, *Magic and Superstition*, p. 71.
72. Sandner, D. *Navaho Symbols of Healing* (Rochester, VT: Healing Arts Press, 1979), p. 62.
73. *Ibid.*, p. 61.
74. Torrance, R. M. *The Spiritual Quest: Transcendence in Myth, Religion, and Science* (Berkeley and London: University of California Press, 1994), p. 148.
75. *Ibid.*
76. *Ibid.*
77. Eliade, M. *Encyclopaedia Britannica Library*, from Encyclopaedia Britannica 2005 Deluxe Edition CD-ROM. Copyright © 1994–2003 Encyclopaedia Britannica, Inc. (accessed March, 25, 2007).
78. *Ibid.*
79. "South American forest peoples." *Encyclopaedia Britannica Library*, from Encyclopaedia Britannica 2005 Deluxe Edition CD-ROM. Copyright © 1994–2003 Encyclopaedia Britannica, Inc. (accessed March, 25, 2007).
80. Goodman, F. D. and S. Josephson. "Pueblo Religion and Spirit Worlds," in: Walter, M. N. and Fridman, E. J. N. *Shamanism*, pp. 346–350 (Santa Barbara, CA and Oxford: ABC CLIO, 2004), p. 349.
81. *Ibid.*
82. *Ibid.*
83. *Ibid.*
84. Underhill, R. *Red Man's Religion* (Chicago and London: University of Chicago Press, 1965), p. 83.
85. Melody, M. E. *The Apache* (New York and Philadelphia: Chelsea House Publishers, 1989), p. 34.
86. Bourke, *Apache Medicine-Men*, p. 49.
87. Melody, *The Apache*, pp. 35–37.
88. Lemoine, J. "The Diagnosis of Disease as a 'Shamanic Equation' among the Hmong of Laos and Thailand," in: Hoppál, M. and Howard, K. D. *Shamans and Cultures* (Budapest: Akadémiai Kiadó and Los Angeles: International Society for Trans-Oceanic Research, 1993), p. 111.
89. *Ibid.*
90. *Ibid.*, p. 112.
91. Kiev, *Magic, Faith, and Healing*, p. 13.

92. Service, E. R. *Profiles in Ethnology* (New York and London: Harper & Row, Publishers, 1963), pp. 23–24.
93. Sandner, *Navaho Symbols of Healing*, p. 106.
94. *Ibid.*
95. Langdon, E. J. M. and Baer, G. eds. *Portals of Power: Shamanism in South America* (Albuquerque: University of New Mexico Press, 1992), p. 129.
96. Middleton, *Magic, Witchcraft, and Curing*, p. 173.
97. Eliade, *Shamanism*, p. 256.
98. Müller-Edeling, Rätsch, and Sihahi. *Shamanism and Tantra in the Himalayas*, p. 124.
99. Lommel, *The World of the Early Hunters*, pp. 74–75.
100. *Ibid.*, p. 74.
101. *Ibid.*
102. *Ibid.*
103. Maskarinec, Gregory. "Healing and Shamanism," in: Walter, M. N. and E. J. N. Fridman, eds. *Shamanism: An Encyclopedia of World Beliefs, Practices, and Culture* Vol. I, pp. 137–142. Santa Barbara, CA and Oxford: ABC CLIO, 2004), p. 138.
104. "Healing cults" *Encyclopaedia Britannica Library*, from Encyclopaedia Britannica 2005 Deluxe Edition CD-ROM. Copyright © 1994–2003 Encyclopaedia Britannica, Inc. (accessed March, 25, 2007).
105. Lommel, *The World of the Early Hunters*, p. 73.
106. Hultkrantz, *Shamanic Healing and Ritual Drama*, p. 34.
107. *Ibid.*, p. 95.
108. Kiev, *Magic, Faith, and Healing*, p. 10.
109. "Southeast Indian Belief systems." *Encyclopaedia Britannica Library*, from Encyclopaedia Britannica 2005 Deluxe Edition CD-ROM. Copyright © 1994–2003 Encyclopaedia Britannica, Inc. (accessed March, 25, 2007).
110. Van Deusen, K. *Singing Story, Healing Drum: Shamans and Storytellers of Turkic Siberia* (Montreal & Kingston and London: McGill-Queen's University Press, 2004), p. 99.
111. Child, A. B. and I. L. Child. *Religion and Magic in the Life of Traditional Peoples* (Englewood Cliffs, NJ: Prentice Hall, 1993), 157.
112. *Ibid.*
113. *Ibid.*
114. Gillette, D. *Shaman's Secret* (New York and London: Bantam Books, 1997), p. 51.

Chapter 8

1. Walter, M. N. and E. J. N. Fridman, eds. *Shamanism: An Encyclopedia of World Beliefs, Practices, and Culture* (Santa Barbara, CA and Oxford: ABC CLIO, 2004), p. 921.
2. Antropova, V. V. and V. G. Kuznetsova "The Chukchi," in: Levin, M. G. and L. P. Potapov eds. *The Peoples of Siberia* pp. 799–835, Translated by Scripta Technica, Inc., English translation edited by Stephen Dunn. (Chicago and London: The University of Chicago Press, 1956), p. 821.
3. *Ibid.*
4. *Ibid.*
5. *Ibid.*, p. 822.
6. Purev, O. and G. Purvee *Mongolian Shamanism* (Ulaanbaatar: Purvee, 2007), p. 147.
7. Eliade, M. *Shamanism: Archaic Techniques of Ecstasy*, Translated by Willard Trask (Bollingen Series LXXVI, Princeton: Princeton University Press, 1974), p. 200.
8. Humphrey, C. and U. Onon. *Shamans and Elders: Experience, Knowledge, and Power among the Daur Mongols* (Oxford: Clarendon Press, 1996), p. 170.
9. *Ibid.*, p. 171.
10. Jones, G. H. "The Spirit Worship in Korea," in: *Transactions of the Korean Branch of the Royal Asiatic Society*, ii, i, p. 58. Quoted in: Lévy-Bruhl, L. *How Native Think*, translated by Lilian Clare (Princeton: Princeton University Press, 1985), p. 66
11. Kim, Tae-Kon. *Korean Shamanism-Muism* Translated and edited by Chang Soo-kyung Korean Studies Series No. 9 (Seoul: Jimoondang Publishing Company, 1998), pp. 20–21.
12. Winter, E. H. "Amba Religion," in: J. Middleton *Gods and Rituals* (Garden City, NY: The Natural History Press, 1967), p. 21.
13. *Ibid.*
14. *Ibid.*, p. 22.
15. Humphrey with Onon. *Shamans and Elders*, p. 30.
16. Winter, E. H. "Amba Religion," in: J. Middleton *Gods and Rituals*, pp. 21–40 (Garden City, NY: The Natural History Press, 1967), p. 22.
17. Hoppál, M. *Studies of Mythology and Uralic Shamanism*, Translation by O. Frank, B. Sebestyén and P. Simoncsics (Budapest: Akadémiai Kiadó, 2000), p. 133.
18. Gillette, D. *The Shaman's Secret: The Lost Resurrection Teachings of the Ancient Maya* (New York and London: Bantam Books, 1997), p. 108.
19. *Ibid.*
20. *Ibid.*
21. Beattie, J. H. M. "The Ghost Cult in Bunyoro," in: J. Middleton *Gods and Rituals* (Garden City, NY: The Natural History Press, 1967), pp. 255–256.
22. *Ibid.*, p. 257.
23. *Ibid.*, pp. 263–264.
24. Shirokogoroff, S. M. *Psychomental Complex of the Tungus* (London: Kegan Paul, Trench, Trubner & Co. Inc., 1935), p. 134.
25. *Ibid.*
26. *Ibid.*
27. *Ibid.*
28. Michael, H. N. ed. *Studies in Siberian Shamanism* (Toronto: University of Toronto Press, 1963), p. 5.
29. *Ibid.*, p. 6.
30. *Ibid.*, p. 7.
31. Shirokogoroff, *Psychomental Complex of the Tungus*, p. 139.
32. Covell, A. C. *Shamanist Folk Paintings: Korea's Eternal Spirits* (Elizabeth, NJ and Seoul: Hollym International Corporation, 1984), p. 112.
33. Alekseev, N. A. "Shamans and Their Religious Practices," in: Balzer, M. M. ed. *Shamanism: Soviet Studies of Traditional Religion in Siberia and Central Asia* (Armonk, NY and London: M. E. Sharpe, Inc., 1990), p. 49.
34. Eliade, *Shamanism*, pp. 5–6.
35. *Ibid.*
36. McGhee, R. *Ancient People of the Arctic* (Vancouver: U B C Press, Published in association with the Canadian Museum of Civilization, 1996), p. 157.
37. *Ibid.*
38. *Ibid.*
39. Eliade, *Shamanism*, p. 92.
40. *Ibid.*, p. 94.
41. "South American forest peoples." Encyclopaedia Britannica Library, from *Encyclopaedia Britannica* 2005 Deluxe Edition CD-ROM. Copyright © 1994–2003 Encyclopaedia Britannica, Inc. (accessed March 25, 2007).
42. Eliade, *Shamanism*, p. 85.
43. Jakobsen, M. D. *Shamanism: Traditional and Contemporary Approaches to the Mastery of Spirits and Healing* (New York and Oxford: Berghahn Books, 1999), p. 65.
44. Ibid., pp. 65–66.
45. Shirokogoroff, *Psychomental Complex of the Tungus*, p. 160.

46. Figes, O. *Natasha's Dance* (New York: Metropolitan Books, Henry Holt and Company, 2002), p. 360.
47. Eliade, *Shamanism*, p. 344.
48. *Ibid.*, p. 345.
49. Shah, S. I. *Oriental Magic* (New York: Philosophical Library Inc., 1957), p. 96.
50. Lissner, I. *Man, God and Magic*, translated by J. Maxwell Brownjohn (New York: G. P. Putnam's Sons, 1961), p. 268.
51. *Ibid.*
52. Ten Grotenhuis, E. *Japanese Mandalas: Representations of Sacred Geography* (Honolulu: University of Hawai'i Press, 1999), p. 70.
53. Bäckman, L. and Å. Hultkrantz *Studies in Lapp Shamanism* (Stockholm: Almqvist & Wiksell, 1978), p. 80.
54. Newton, D. *Crocodile and Cassowary* (New York: The Museum of Primitive Art, 1971), p. 10.
55. Ackerman, D. *A Natural History of the Senses* (New York: Random House, 1990), p. 6.
56. Frazer, J. G. *The Golden Bough: A Study in Magic and Religion* (New York: The Macmillan Company, 1958), p. 238.
57. Lommel, A. "Shamanism in Australia," in: Hoppál, M. and O. von Sadovszky eds. *Shamanism Past and Present*, Part 1 (Budapest Ethnographic Institute, Hungarian Academy of Science, Los Angeles and Fullerton: International Society for Trans-Oceanic Research, 1989), p. 25.
58. Shirokogoroff, *Psychomental Complex of the Tungus*, p. 161.
59. *Ibid.*, p. 161-162.
60. *Ibid.*, p. 162.
61. Antropova V. V. "The Koryaks," in: Levin, M. G. and L. P. Potapov eds. *The Peoples of Siberia*, Translated by Scripta Technica, Inc., English translation edited by Stephen Dunn, pp. 851–875 (Chicago and London: The University of Chicago Press, 1956), p. 866.
62. *Ibid.*, p. 867.
63. Vasilevich G. M. and A. V. Smolyak "The Evenks," in: Levin, M. G. and L. P. Potapov eds. *The Peoples of Siberia*, Translated by Scripta Technica, Inc., English translation edited by Stephen Dunn, pp. 620–654 (Chicago and London: The University of Chicago Press, 1956), p. 648.
64. *Ibid.*
65. Sharon, D. *The Wizard of the Four Winds* (New York: Free Press, 1978), p. 77.
66. Cququelin, J. "The Impact of Japanese Colonialism on Puyuma (Taiwan) Shamanism," in: Hoppál, M. and Howard, K. eds. *Shamans and Cultures* (Budapest: Akadémial Kiadó and Los Angeles: International Society for Trans-Oceanic Research, 1993), p. 98.
67. Jakobsen, *Shamanism: Traditional and Contemporary Approaches*, p. 43.
68. Bäckman, and Hultkrantz *Studies in Lapp Shamanism*, p. 43.
69. Boyll, L. "Bridging Worlds: Teaching Huichol Shamanism," in: R-I Heinze, ed. *Proceedings of the Ninth International Conference on the Study of Shamanism and Alternate Modes of Healing* (Berkeley: University of California, 1992), p. 143.
70. Torres, Y. G. "Altered States of Consciousness and Ancient Mexican Ritual Techniques," in: Hoppál, M. and O. von Sadovszky eds. *Shamanism Past and Present*, Part 2, pp. 349–353 (Budapest: Ethnographic Institute, Hungarian Academy of Sciences and Los Angeles and Fullerton: International Society for Trans-Oceanic Research, 1989), p. 349.
71. Hunt, N. B. *Shamanism in North America* (Buffalo, NY: Firefly Book, 2002), p. 10.
72. *Ibid.*
73. "Australian Aboriginal," Encyclopaedia Britannica Library, from *Encyclopaedia Britannica* 2005 Deluxe Edition CD-ROM. Copyright © 1994–2003 Encyclopaedia Britannica, Inc. (accessed June 20, 2007).
74. Sarangerel, *Riding Windhorses: A Journey into the Heart of Mongolian Shamanism* (Rochester, VT: Destiny Books, 2006), p. 8.
75. Eliade, *Shamanism*, p. 342.
76. *Ibid.*
77. Eliade, M. "Shamanism Southeast Asia and Oceania," in: Encyclopaedia Britannica Library, from *Encyclopaedia Britannica* 2005 Deluxe Edition CD-ROM. Copyright © 1994–2003 Encyclopaedia Britannica, Inc. (accessed May 19, 2007).
78. *Ibid.* (accessed January 12, 2008).
79. Bäckman, L. and Å. Hultkrantz *Studies in Lapp Shamanism* (Stockholm: Almqvist & Wiksell, 1978), p. 43.
80. Bäckman and Hultkrantz *Studies in Lapp Shamanism*, p. 43.
81. Lincoln, J. S. *The Dream in Primitive Cultures*. London: The Cresset Press, 1935), p. 22.
82. *Ibid.*
83. *Ibid.*, p. 23.
84. Souvay, C. L. "Interpretation of Dreams," Transcribed by Listya Sari Diyah, in: *The Catholic Encyclopedia*, Vol. V (New York: Robert Appleton Company, 1909). <http://www.newadvent.org/cathen/index.html> Copyright © 2007 by Kevin Knight.
85. Parman, S. *Dream and Culture: An Anthropological Study of the Western Intellectual Tradition* (New York and London: Praeger Publishers, 1991), p. 1.
86. Gillette, *Shaman's Secret*, p. 4.
87. *Ibid.*, p. 32.
88. "Dream," *Encyclopaedia Britannica Library*, from Encyclopaedia Britannica 2005 Deluxe Edition CD-ROM. Copyright © 1994–2003 Encyclopaedia Britannica, Inc. (accessed March 25, 2007).
89. Frazer, J. G. *The Golden Bough: A Study in Magic and Religion*. Vol. I (New York: The Macmillan Company, 1958), p. 211.
90. *Ibid.*, p. 212.
91. Castiglioni, A. *Adventures of the Mind* (New York: Alfred A. Knopf, 1946), p. 22.
92. Lincoln, J. S. *The Dream in Primitive Cultures* (London: The Cresset Press, 1935), p. 29.
93. "Dream," *Encyclopaedia Britannica.* (accessed March 26, 2007).
94. Lincoln, *The Dream in Primitive Cultures*, p. 29.
95. Frazer, *The Golden Bough*, pp. 640–641.
96. Ryan, W. F. *The Bathhouse at Midnight: An Historical Survey of Magic and Divination in Russia* (University Park: The Pennsylvania State University Press, 1999), p. 151.
97. Oberhelman, S. M. ed. *The Oneiroctriticon of Achmet: A Medieval Greek and Arabic Treatis on the Interpretation of Dreams*, Translated by Steven Oberlelman (Lubbock, TX: Texas Tech University Press, 1991), p. 36.
98. "Dream," Encyclopaedia *Britannica Library*, (accessed March 26, 2007).
99. Lincoln, *The Dream in Primitive Cultures*, p. 29.
100. Walter, and Fridman, *Shamanism*, p. 660.
101. *Ibid.*, p. 749.
102. Shirokogoroff, *Psychomental Complex of the Tungus*, p. 254.
103. *Ibid.*
104. Anisimov, A. F. "The Shaman's Tent of the Evenks and the Origin of the Shamanistic Rite," in: Michael, H. N. Studies in Shamanism (Toronto: Arctic Institute of North America, Anthropology of the North Translations from Russian Sources. No. 4. University of Toronto, 1963), p. 86.

105. Waters, F. *Masked Gods: Navajo and Pueblo Ceremonialism* (Chicago: The Swallow Press, Inc., 1950), p. 297.
106. Lincoln, *The Dream in Primitive Cultures*, p. 30.
107. Maskarinec, G. G. *The Rulings of the Night: An Ethnography of Nepalese Shaman Oral Texts* (Madison: The University of Wisconsin Press, 1995), p. 22.
108. Krippner, S. "The Use of Dreams in Shamanic Traditions," in: Hoppál, M. and O. von Sadovszky, eds. *Shamanism Past and Present*, Part 2, pp. 381–391 (Budapest: Ethnographic Institution, Hungarian Academy of Sciences/ Los Angeles/Fullerton: International Society for Trans-Oceanic Research, 1989), p. 382.
109. Bäckman, and Hultkrantz *Studies in Lapp Shamanism*, p. 14.
110. "Sakha." *Encyclopaedia Britannica Library*, from Encyclopaedia Britannica 2005 Deluxe Edition CD-ROM. Copyright © 1994–2003 Encyclopaedia Britannica, Inc. (accessed March 25, 2007).
111. Eliade, *Shamanism*, p. 292.
112. *Ibid.*
113. Bäckman and Hultkrantz. *Studies in Lapp Shamanism*, p. 11.
114. *Ibid.*, p. 93.
115. Siikala, A-L. *The Rite Technique of the Siberian Shaman*, FF Communications, Vol. 93. No. 220, Suomalainen Tiedeakatemia, (Helsinki: Academia Scientiarum Fennica, 1978), p 31.
116. "Dervish," *Encyclopaedia Britannica Library*, from Encyclopaedia Britannica 2005 Deluxe Edition CD-ROM. Copyright © 1994–2003 Encyclopaedia Britannica, Inc. (accessed March 25, 2007).
117. Bäckman and Hultkrantz *Studies in Lapp Shamanism*, p. 42.
118. *Ibid.*, p. 43.
119. *Ibid.*
120. Sander, D. *Navaho Symbols of Healing* (Rochester, VT: Healing Arts Press, 1991), p. 61.
121. Krippner, S. "Profiles of Three Contemporary Central American Shamans," in: R-I Heinze, ed. *Proceedings of the Ninth International Conference on the Study of Shamanism and Alternate Modes of Healing*, pp. 148–155 (Berkeley: University of California, 1992), p. 150.
122. *Ibid.*, p. 151.
123. "Shamanism," *Korean Heritage Series*, No. 15. (Seoul, ROK: Korean Overseas Information Service, 1995), p. 3.
124. Eliade, *Shamanism*, p. 88.
125. Sommarström, B. "The Sami Shaman's Drum and the Holographic Paradigm Discussion," in: Hoppál, M. and O. von Sadovszky, eds. *Shamanism Part and Present*, Part 1 (Budapest: Ethnographic Institute, Hungarian Academy of Science and Los Angeles/Fullerton: International Society for Trans-oceanic Research, 1989), 125.
126. Lewis, I. M. *Ecstatic Religion: A Study of Shamanism and Spirit Possession.* 2nd ed. (New York and London: Routledge, 1989), p. 8.

Chapter 9

1. Edson, G. Masks and Masking (Jefferson, NC and London: McFarland & Company, Inc., 2005), p. 177.
2. Collins, J. J. *Primitive Religion* (New York: Rowman and Littlefield, 1978), p. 7.
3. "Rites of passage: Primary rites of passage" Encyclopaedia Britannica Library, from *Encyclopaedia Britannica* 2005 Deluxe Edition CD-ROM. Copyright © 1994–2003 Encyclopaedia Britannica, Inc. (accessed April 29, 2007).
4. "Shinto Ritual practices and institutions" Encyclopaedia Britannica Library, from *Encyclopaedia Britannica* 2005 Deluxe Edition CD-ROM. Copyright © 1994–2003 Encyclopaedia Britannica, Inc. (accessed April 29, 2007).
5. Fried, M. N. and M. H. Fried *Transitions: Four Rituals in Eight Cultures* (New York and London: W.W. Norton & Company, 1980), p. 13.
6. *Ibid.*
7. "Rites of passage: Primary rites of passage" Encyclopaedia Britannica Library, (accessed April 29, 2007).
8. Turner, Victor. *The Forest of Symbols: Aspects of Ndembu Ritual* (Ithaca and London: Cornell University Press. 1967), p. 99.
9. "Rites of passage: Primary rites of passage" Encyclopaedia Britannica Library, (accessed April 29, 2007).
10. McGhee, R. *Ancient People of the Arctic* (Vancouver: UBC Press, Published in Association with the Canadian Museum of Civilization, 1996), p. 157.
11. *Ibid.*
12. Halifax, J. *Shamanic Voices* (New York: E. P. Dutton, 1979), p. 3.
13. Child, A.B. and Child I. L. *Religion and Magic in the Life of Traditional Peoples* (Eaglewood Cliffs, NJ: Prentice Hall, 1993), p. 160.
14. *Ibid.*, p. 160–161.
15. Cayne, B. S. ed dtr. *New Webster's Dictionary and Thesaurus of the English Language*, Revised (Danbury, CT: Lexicon Publications, Inc., 1992), p. 36.
16. Gimbutes, M. *The Language of the Goddess* (New York: Thames & Hudson, 1989), p. xxiii.
17. Steele, P. R. Handbook of Inca Mythology (Santa Barbara, CA and Oxford: ABC CLIO, 2004), p. 8.
18. Blodgett, J. *The Coming and Going of the Shaman: Eskimo Shamanism and Art* (Winnipeg: Winnipeg Art Gallery, 1978), p. 75.
19. Aldhouse-Green, M. and Aldhouse-Green S. *The Quest for the Shaman* (London: Thames & Hudson, 2005), p. 13.
20. Welter, M. N. and Friedman, E. J. N. *Shamanism: An Encyclopedia of World Beliefs, Practices, and Culture*, Vol. I (Santa Barbara, CA and Oxford: ABC CLIO, 2004), p. 255.
21. *Ibid.*, p. 256.
22. Valadez, S. E. "Wolf Power and Interspecies Communication in Huichol Shamanism," in: Shaffer, S. B. and Furst, P. T. *People of the Peyote: Huichol Indian History, Religion & Survival* (Albuquerque: University of New Mexico Press, 1996), p. 269.
23. *Ibid.*
24. *Ibid.*, p. 270.
25. Welter and Fridman, *Shamanism*, p. 257.
26. *Ibid.*
27. Mikhailov, T. M. *Buryat* Shamanism. 1990, p. 110.
28. Steele, *Handbook of Inca Mythology*, p. 8.
29. Lommel, A. *World of the Early Hunters*, Translated by Michael Bullock (London: Evelyn, Adams, and Mackay Ltd., 1967), p. 111.
30. Corbin, G. A. *Native Arts of North America, Africa, and the South Pacific: An Introduction* (New York: Harper and Row, 1988), p. 59.
31. Lommel, World of the *Early Hunters*, 1967, p. 10.
32. Pinch, G. *Magic in Ancient Egypt* (Austin: University of Texas Press, 1994), p. 51.
33. *Ibid.*
34. Eliade, M. *Shamanism: Archaic Techniques of Ecstasy*, Translated by Willard Trask (Bollingen Series LXXVI, Princeton: Princeton University Press, 1974), pp. 257–258.
35. Norbeck, E. 1961. Religion in Primitive Society. p. 110.
36. Turner, V. *The Forest of Symbols: Aspects of Ndembu Ritual* (Ithaca and London: Cornell University Press, 1967), p. 100.
37. Eliade, M. *Encyclopaedia Britannica Library*, from

Encyclopaedia Britannica 2005 Deluxe Edition CD-ROM. Copyright © 1994–2003 Encyclopaedia Britannica, Inc. (accessed March 25, 2007).
    38. Czaplicka, *Shamanism in Siberia*, p. 96.
    39. Eliade, *Shamanism*, p. 258.
    40. Schlesier, K. *The Wolves of Heaven: Cheyenne Shamanism, Ceremonies, and Prehistoric Origins* (Norman and London: University of Oklahoma Press, 1987), pp. 14–15
    41. Humphrey, C. with Urgunge Onon. *Shamans and Elders: Experience, Knowledge, and Power Among the Daur Mongols* (Oxford: Clarendon Press, 1996), p. 203.
    42. Driscoll, J. T. "Shamanism," Transcribed by Douglas J. Potter, in: The Catholic Encyclopedia, Volume XIII. New York: Robert Appleton Company, 1912), <http://www.newadvent.org/cathen/index.html> Copyright © 2007 by Kevin Knight (accessed April 27, 2007).
    43. *Ibid*.
    44. Rasmussen, K. *Netsilik Eskimos: Social life and Spiritual Culture*. Report of the fifth Thule Expedition 1921–24, Vol. VIII, 1923, p. 198, as quoted in: Blodgett, J. *The Coming and Going of the Shaman: Eskimo Shamanism and Art* (Winnipeg: Winnipeg Art Gallery, 1978), p. 63.
    45. Czaplicka, *Shamanism in Siberia*, p. 90.
    46. *Ibid*., p. 91.
    47. *Ibid*.
    48. Bessy, M. *A Pictorial History of Magic and the Supernatural* (London: Spring Books, 1986), p. 121.
    49. Czaja M. *Gods of Myth and Stone* (New York and Tokyo: Weatherhill, 1974), p. 163.
    50. Walker, B. *The Woman's Dictionary of Symbols and Sacred Objects* (Edison, NJ: Castle Books, 1988), p. 195.
    51. *Ibid*., pp. 195–196.
    52. *Ibid*., p. 196.
    53. *Ibid*.
    54. *Ibid*.
    55. Lang, A. *Myth, Ritual and Religion*, vol. II (London and Calcutta: Longmans, Green, 1913), p. 16.
    56. Walter and Feidman, *Shamanism*, p. 131.
    57. Roscoe, W. *Changing Ones: Third and Fourth Genders in Native North America*, Albuquerque: University of New Mexico Press as quoted in: Walter, N. W. and Feidman, E. J. N. *Shamanism: An Encyclopedia of World Beliefs, Practices, and Culture*, vol. 1 (Santa Barbara, CA and Oxford: ABC CLIO, 2004), p. 131.
    58. Benedict, R. *Patterns of Culture*, 2d (Boston: Houghton Mifflin Company, 1959), p. 263.
    59. Child, A. B. and I. L. Child. *Religion and Magic in the Life of Traditional Peoples* (Eaglewood Cliffs, NJ: Prentice Hall, Inc., 1993), p. 155.
    60. *Ibid*.
    61. *Ibid*., p. 156.
    62. Walker, *The Woman's Dictionary*, p. 241.
    63. Diószegu, V. and Hoppál, M. *Shamanism in Siberia*, Translated by S. Simon (Budapest: Akadémiai Kiadó, 1996), p. 125.
    64. Cququelin, J. "The Impact of Japanese Colonialism on Puyuma (Taiwan) Shamanism," in: Hoppál, M. and Howard, K. eds. *Shamans and Cultures* (Budapest: Akadémial Kiadó and Los Angeles: International Society for Trans-Oceanic Research, 1993), pp. 102–103.
    65. *Ibid*.
    66. Czaplicka, M. A. *Aboriginal Siberia: A Study in Social Anthropology* (Oxford: The Clarendon Press 1969 [1914]), p. 249
    67. Aldhouse-Green, M. and S. Aldhouse-Green. *The Quest for the Shaman: Shape-Shifters, Sorcerers and Spirit-Healers of Ancient Europe* (London: Thames & Hudson, Ltd., 2005), p. 13.
    68. Eliade, *Shamanism*, p. 125.
    69. *Ibid*., p. 351.
    70. Salamone, F. A. "Hausa Shamanistic Practices (Nigeria and Niger)," in: Walter, N. W. and Feidman, E. J. N. *Shamanism: An Encyclopedia of World Beliefs, Practices, and Culture*, vol. 1 (Santa Barbara, CA and Oxford: ABC CLIO, 2004), p. 923.
    71. Eliade, *Shamanism*, p. 351.
    72. Walter and Feidman, *Shamanism*, p. 132.
    73. Napier, A. D. *Masks, Transformation, and Paradox* (Berkeley and London: University of California Press, 1986), p. 177.
    74. Linton, R. *The Tree of Culture* (New York: Alfred A. Knopf, 1957), p. 155.
    75. Lang, *Myth, Ritual and Religion*, p. 90.
    76. Bowra, C. M. *Primitive Song* (Cleveland and New York: The World Publishing Company, 1962), p. 169–170.
    77. Lommel, *World of the Early Hunters*, p. 110.
    78. Lévi-Strauss, C. *Totemism* (Boston: Beacon Press, 1963b), p. 37.
    79. Humphrey with Onon. *Shamans and Elders*, p. 29.
    80. Walter and Feidman, *Shamanism*, p. 255.
    81. Valadez, "Wolf Power and Interspecies Communication in Huichol Shamanism," p. 267.
    82. Frazer, J. G. The Golden Bough: A Study of Magic and Religion, vol. I. (New York: Macmillan and Company, 1958), p. 628.
    83. Edson, Masks and Masking, p. 176.

Chapter 10

    1. Maxwell, J. A. ed. *America's Fascinating Indian Heritage* (Pleasantville, NY and Motreal: The Reader's Digest Association, Inc., 1978), p. 221
    2. Grim, J. A. *The Shaman Patterns of Siberian and Ojibway Healing* (Norman: University of Oklahoma Press, 1983), p. 120.
    3. Eliade, M. *Shamanism: Archaic Techniques of Ecstasy*, Translated by Willard R. Trask (Bollingen Series LXXVI, Princeton: Princeton University Press, 1974), p. 245.
    4. *Ibid*., p. 246.
    5. *Ibid*.
    6. Bogoras, W. *The Chukchee—Religion*. Memoirs of the American Museum of Natural History, No. 11, Part 2. (New York: American Museum of Natural History, 1907), p. 517.
    7. Czaplicka, M. A. *Aboriginal Siberia: A Study in Social Anthropology* (Oxford: The Clarendon Press, 1969 [1914]), p. 145.
    8. *Ibid*., p. 149.
    9. Jochelson, W. *The Koryak*. (Leiden: E. J. Brill and New York: G. E. Stechert and issued as v. 10 of Memoirs of the American Museum of Natural History, 1908 [1905]), p. 104.
    10. Chernetsov, V. N. "Concepts of the Soul Among the Ob Ugrians," in: Michael, H. N. ed. *Studies in Siberian Shamanism*, pp. 3–45 (Toronto: Arctic Institute of North America, Anthropology of the North Translations from Russian Sources. No. 4. University of Toronto, 1963b), p. 29.
    11. *Ibid*., p. 30.
    12. Gillette, D. *The Shaman's Secret: The Lost Resurrection Teachings of the Ancient Maya* (New York and London: Bantam Books, 1997), p. 150.
    13. *Ibid*.
    14. *Ibid*., p. 136.
    15. Hoppál, M. *Studies on Mythology and Uralic Shamanism*, Translated by O. Frank, B. Sebestyén, and P. Simoncsics (Budapest: Akadémiai Kiadó, 2000), p. 88.
    16. Barton, G. A. *The Religion of the World*, 4th ed. (Chicago: University of Chicago Press, 1937), p. 5.
    17. Macgowan K. and H. Rosse. *Masks and Demons*

(London: Martin Hopkinson and Company, Ltd., 1923), p. viii.
18. Alekseev. N. A. "The Role of the Shaman in the Life of the Turkic-speaking People of Siberia," in: M. M. Balzer, ed. *Shamanism: Soviet Studies of Traditional Religion in Siberia and Central Asia* (Armonk, NY and London: M. E. Sharpe, Inc., 1990), p. 96.
19. Sharon, D. *Wizard of the Four Winds* (New York: The Free Press, 1978), p. 50.
20. Child, A. B., and I. L. Child. *Religion and Magic in the Life of Traditional Peoples* (Englewood Cliffs, NJ: Prentice Hall, 1993), p. 17.
21. Wallis, W. D. *Religion in Primitive Society* (New York: F. S. Crofts & Co., 1939), p. 207.
22. Hultkrantz, Å. "Ecological and Phenomenological Aspects of Shamanism," in: Diószegi, V. and M. Hoppál, ed. *Shamanism in Siberia*, Selected Reprints, Translated by S. Simon (Budapest: Akadémiai Kiadó, 1996), p. 11.
23. Manuscript 4832, Smithsonian Institution National Anthropological Archive.
24. *Ibid.*
25. *Ibid.*
26. Shirokogoroff, S. M. *Psychomental Complex of the Tungus* (London: Kegan Paul, Trench, Trubner & Co. Ltd., 1935), p. 365.
27. *Ibid.*
28. Czaplicka, *Aboriginal Siberia*, p. 317.
29. Jochelson, *The Koryak*, p. 760.
30. Boas, F. "The Central Eskimo," Bureau of American Ethnology, pp. 409–669 (Washington, DC: *Sixth Annual Report*, 1884–85 [1888]), p. 615.
31. Czaplicka, *Aboriginal Siberia*, p. 318.
32. Pant, J. ed. *Himalayan Mysteries* (New Delhi: Roli & Janssen BV, 2001), p. 143.
33. Eliade, *Shamanism*, p. 291.
34. *Ibid.*
35. *Ibid.*
36. "Ancient Egypt" Encyclopaedia Britannica Library, from *Encyclopaedia Britannica* 2005 Deluxe Edition CD-ROM. Copyright © 1994–2003 Encyclopaedia Britannica, (accessed Inc. May 19, 2007).
37. Huxley, F. *The Way of the Sacred* (Garden City, NY: Doubleday and Company, Inc., 1974), p, 94.
38. *Ibid.*
39. Gillette, *The Shaman's Secret*, p. 117.
40. Oakes, J. and R. Riewe. *Spirit of Siberia* (Washington, DC: Smithsonian Institution Press, 1998), p. 64.
41. Gillette, *The Shaman's Secret*, p. 132.
42. *Ibid.*, p. 133.
43. *Ibid.*
44. Chagnon, N. A. *Yanomamö* (New York and London: Harcourt Brace Jovanovich College Publishers, 1992 [1968]), p. 2.
45. Reichard, G. A. *Navaho Religion: A Study of Symbolism* (Bollingen Series XVIII, New York: Pantheon Books, Inc., 1950), p. 41.
46. Hultkrantz, Å. *Shamanic Healing and Ritual Drama: Health and Medicine in Native North American Religious Traditions* (New York: The Crossroad Publishing Company, 1992), p. 15.
47. *Ibid.*
48. Parsons, E. C. *Pueblo Indian Religion*, vol. I (Lincoln and London: University of Nebraska Press, 1996 [1939]), p. 68.
49. *Ibid.*, p. 69.
50. Hultkrantz, *Shamanic Healing and Ritual Drama*, p. 167.
51. Kiev, A. *Magic, Faith, and Healing: Studies in Primitive Psychiatry Today* (London: The Free Press of Glencoe, Collier-Macmillan Limited, 1964), p. 159.
52. *Ibid.*, p. 161.
53. "Witchcraft, Witchcraft in Africa and the world," in: Encyclopaedia Britannica Library, from *Encyclopaedia Britannica* 2005 Deluxe Edition CD-ROM. Copyright © 1994–2003 Encyclopaedia Britannica, Inc. (accessed January 19, 2008).
54. Steele, P. R. *Handbook of Inca Mythology* (Santa Barbara, CA and Oxford: ABC CLIO, 2004), p. 201.
55. "ancient Egypt" Encyclopaedia Britannica Library, from *Encyclopaedia Britannica* 2005 Deluxe Edition CD-ROM. Copyright © 1994–2003 Encyclopaedia Britannica, Inc. (accessed May 19, 2007).
56. Walker, B. *The Woman's Dictionary of Symbols and Sacred Objects* (Edison, NJ: Castle Books, 1988), p. 396.
57. Kiev, *Magic, Faith, and Healing*, pp. 159–160.
58. Eliade, *Shamanism: Ancient Techniques of Ecstasy*, p. 206.
59. Walter, M. N. and E. J. N. Fridman, eds. *Shamanism: An Encyclopedia of World Beliefs, Practices, and Culture*, vol. I (Santa Barbara, CA and Oxford: ABC CLIO 2004), p. 375.
60. Eliade, *Shamanism: Ancient Techniques of Ecstasy*, Press, p. 441.
61. Harner, M. J. *The Jívaro: People of the Sacred Waterfalls* (Garden City, NY: Anchor Press/Doubleday, 1973), p. 134.
62. Maxwell, J. A. *America's Fascinating Indian Heritage* (Pleasantville, NY and Montreal: The Reader's Digest Association, Inc., 1978), p. 138.
63. *Ibid.*, p. 242.
64. *Ibid.*, p. 308.
65. Faron, L. C. "Death and Fertility Rites of the Mapuche Indians," in: J. Middleton ed. *Gods and Rituals* (Garden City, NY: The Natural History Press, 1967), pp. 229–230.
66. *Ibid.*, p. 230.
67. "Taoism," *Encyclopaedia Britannica Library*, from Encyclopaedia Britannica 2005 Deluxe Edition CD-ROM. Copyright © 1994–2003 Encyclopaedia Britannica, Inc. (accessed May 2, 2007).
68. Frazer, J. G. *The Golden Bough: A Study of Magic and Religion*, vol. 1, (New York: Macmillan and Company, 1958), p. 624.
69. Eliade, M. "Shamanism, Southeast Asia and Oceania," Encyclopaedia Britannica Library, from *Encyclopaedia Britannica* 2005 Deluxe Edition CD-ROM. Copyright© 1994–2003 Encyclopaedia Britannica, Inc. (accessed May 29, 2007).
70. "Pre-Columbian civilizations," Encyclopaedia Britannica Library, from *Encyclopaedia Britannica* 2005 Deluxe Edition CD-ROM. Copyright © 1994–2003 Encyclopaedia Britannica, Inc. (accessed September 5, 2007).
71. Radin, P. *Primitive Religion: Its Nature and Origin*, 2d ed. (New York: Dover Publications, 1957), p. 214.
72. Burkert, W. *Ancient Mystery Cults* (Cambridge and London: Harvard University Press, 1987), p. 101.
73. Hultkrantz, *Shamanic Healing and Ritual Drama*, p. 50–51.
74. *Ibid.*, p. 15–16.
75. Humphrey, C. with O. Urgunge. *Shamans and Elders: Experience, Knoweldge, and Power among the Daur Mongols* (Oxford: Clarendon Press, 1996), p. 241.
76. *Ibid.*
77. Campbell, J. *The Way of the Animal Powers, Historical Atlas of World Mythology*, Vol. 1 (Alfred Van Der Marck Editions, San Francisco: Harper & Row, 1983), p. 93.
78. Balzar, M. M. *Shamanic Worlds: Rituals and Lore of Siberia and Central Asia* (Armonk, NY and London: North Castle Books, 1997), p. 66.
79. *Ibid.*

80. "Sacred: Manifestation of the sacred." *Encyclopaedia Britannica Library*, from Encyclopaedia Britannica 2005 Deluxe Edition CD-ROM. Copyright © 1994–2003 Encyclopaedia Britannica, Inc. (accessed May 2, 2007).
81. "Sacrifice," http://www.themystica.com/mystica/articles/s/sacrifice.html, nd.
82. Humphrey with Onon. *Shamans and Elders*, p. 145.
83. *Ibid.*
84. *Ibid.*
85. *Ibid.*
86. Clottes, J. and Lewis-Williams, D. *Shamans of Prehistory: Trance and Magic in the Painted Caves*, translated by Sophie Hawkes (New York: Harry N. Abrams, Inc., Publishers, 1996), p. 101.
87. Gillette, *Shaman's Secret*, p. 38.
88. Markman, R. H. and P. T. Markman. *The Flayed God: The Mythology of Mesoamerica* (New York: HarperCollins Publishers, 1992), p. 180.
89. *Ibid.*, p. 181.
90. *Ibid.*
91. Frazer, J. G., in: Czaja, M. *Gods of Myth and Stone* (New York and Tokyo: Weatherhill, 1974), p. 216.
92. Beane, W. C. and W. G. Doty eds. *Myths, Rites, Symbols: A Mircea Eliade Reader*, vol. I (New York and London: Harper Colphon Books, Harper & Row, Publishers, 1976), p. 250.
93. Markman, and Markman. *The Flayed God*, p. 4.
94. Haberland, W. *The Art of North America*, Translated by Wayne Dynes (New York and London: Greystone Press, 1968), p. 48.
95. Werbner. R. P. *Ritual Passage, Sacred Journey: The Form, Process and Organization of Religions Movement* (Washington, DC: Smithsonian Institution Press, 1989), pp. 157–160.
96. Tanaka, S. "Ainu Shamanism," in: Walter, M.N. and E. J. N. Fridman, eds. *Shamanism: An Encyclopedia of World Beliefs, Practices, and Culture*, Vol. 1, pp. 657–665. (Santa Barbara, CA and Oxford: ABC CLIO, 2004), p. 661.
97. Huxley, *The Way of the Sacred*, p, 94.
98. Gillette, *Shaman's Secret*, p. 37.
99. *Ibid.*, p. 10.
100. *Ibid.*, p. 1.
101. *Ibid.*, pp. 132–133.
102. Sandner, D. *Navaho Symbols of Healing: A Jungian Exploration of Ritual, Image, and Medicine* (Rochester VT: Healing Arts Press, 1979), p. 34.
103. Maxwell, *America's Fascinating Indian Heritage*, p. 238.
104. *Ibid.*
105. *Ibid.*, p. 239.
106. Czaplicka, *Aboriginal Siberia*, p. 146.
107. *Ibid.*
108. Jochelson, *The Koryak*, p. 104.
109. Czaplicka, *Aboriginal Siberia*, p. 147.
110. *Ibid.*
111. Macgowan and Rosse, *Masks and Demons*, p. viii.
112. "Arts, Southeast Asia." Encyclopaedia *Britannica Library* from Encyclopaedia Britannica 2005 Deluxe Edition CD-ROM. Copyright © 1994–2003 Encyclopaedia Britannica, Inc. (accessed March 26, 2007).
113. Purev, O. and Purvee, G. *Mongolian Shamanism* (Ulaanbaatar: Purvee, 2007), p. 24.
114. Anisimov, A. F. "Cosmological Concepts of the Peoples of the North," in: Michael, H. N. ed. *Studies in Siberian Shamanism*, pp. 157–229 (Toronto: Arctic Institute of North America, Anthropology of the North Translations from Russian Sources. No. 4. University of Toronto, 1963b), p. 160.
115. Humphrey, C. "Chiefly and Shamanist Landscapes in Mongolia," pp. 135–162, in: Hirsch, E. and M. O'Hanlon, eds. *The Anthropology of Landscape: Perspectives on Place and Space* (Oxford: Clarendon Press, 1995), p. 143.
116. Czaplicka, *Aboriginal Siberia*, p. 168.
117. Winkelman, M. "Neuropsychology of Shamanism," in: Walter, M. N. and E. J. N Fridman, eds. *Shamanism: An Encyclopedia of World Beliefs, Practices, and Culture*, pp. 187–194, vol. 1 (Santa Barbara, CA and Oxford: ABC CLIO, 2004), p. 190.
118. Vyatkina, K. V. "The Buryats," in: Levin, M. G. and L. P. Potapov eds. pp. 203–242. Translated by Scripta Technica, Inc., English translation edited by Stephen Dunn. (Chicago and London: The University of Chicago Press, 1956), p. 226.
119. Winkelman, "Neuropsychology of Shamanism," p. 190.
120. Musi, C. C. "Finno-Ugric Shamanism," in: Walter, M. N. and E. J. N Fridman, eds. *Shamanism: An Encyclopedia of World Beliefs, Practices, and Culture*, pp. 486–494, vol. 1 (Santa Barbara, CA and Oxford: ABC CLIO, 2004), p. 487.
121. "Religious groups (from Mali)." Encyclopaedia *Britannica Library* from Encyclopaedia Britannica 2005 Deluxe Edition CD-ROM. Copyright © 1994–2003 Encyclopedia Britannica, Inc. (accessed December 23, 2007).
122. Rousselot, J-L. "Yupik Shamanism (Alaska)" Translated by Jane Ripken, in: Walter, M. N. and E. J. N Fridman, eds. *Shamanism: An Encyclopedia of World Beliefs, Practices, and Culture*, pp. 362–364, vol. 1 (Santa Barbara, CA and Oxford: ABC CLIO, 2004), p. 362
123. "Totemism," Encyclopaedia Britannica Library, from *Encyclopaedia Britannica* 2005 Deluxe Edition CD-ROM. Copyright © 1994–2003 Encyclopaedia Britannica, Inc. (accessed June 20, 2007).
124. *Ibid.*
125. Musi, C. C. "Finno-Ugric Shamanism," p. 487.
126. *Ibid.*
127. Balzer, *Shamanic Worlds*, p. 14.
128. Bancroft-Hunt, N. and W. Forman. *People of the Totem* (New York: G. Pl Putnam's Sons, 1979), p. 76.
129. de Waal Malefijt, A. 1968. Religion and Culture. p. 205.
130. Alekseev. N. A. "The Role of the Shaman in the Life of the Turkic-speaking People of Siberia," in: M. M. Balzer, ed. *Shamanism: Soviet Studies of Traditional Religion in Siberia and Central Asia* (Armonk, NY and London: M. E. Sharpe, Inc., 1990), p. 78.
131. *Ibid.*, p. 80.
132. *Ibid.*, p. 81.
133. *Ibid.*, p. 82.
134. Powers, W. K. *Yuwipi: Vision and Experience in Oglala Ritual* (Lincoln, NB: Bison Books, University of Nebraska Press, 1984), p. 19. Cited in Ryan, R. E. Shamanism and the Psychology of C. G. Jung (London: Vega, 2002), p. 41.
135. Alekseev, "The Role of the Shaman in the Life of the Turkic-speaking People of Siberia," p. 87.
136. Radin, P. *Primitive Religion: Its Nature and Origin* (New York: Dover Publications, Inc., 1957 [1937]), p. 145.

Chapter 11

1. Maikoff, V. "Similarities and Differences Between Shamanism and Totalitarianism: Two Psychotechnologies," in: Heinze, R-I. ed. *Proceedings of the Ninth International Conference on the Study of Shamanism and Alternate Modes of Healing*, pp. 291–294 (Berkeley: University of California, 1992) p. 291.
2. Bäckman, L. and Å Hultkrantz. *Studies in Lapp Shamanism* (Stockholm: Almqvist & Wiksell International, 1977), p. 27.

3. *Ibid.*, pp. 27–28.

4. Edson, G. *Masks and Masking: Faces of Tradition and Belief Worldwide* (Jefferson, NC and London: McFarland & Company, Inc. Publishers, 2005), p. 114.

5. Grim, J. *The Shaman: Patterns of Siberian and Ojibway Healing* (Norman: University of Oklahoma Press, 1983), p. 120

6. Lissner, I. 1961. *Man, God and Magic*, Translated by J. Maxwell Brownjohn. (New York: G. P. Putnam's Sons, 1961), p. 11.

7. Paolucci, H. *Hegel: On The Arts* (New York: Frederick Unger Publishing Co., 1979), p. 11.

8. Humphrey, C. with Urgunge Onon. *Shamans and Elders: Experience, Knowledge, and Power Among the Daur Mongols* (Oxford: Clarendon Press, 1996), p. 52.

9. Bäckman, L. and Å Hultkrantz. *Studies in Lapp Shamanism*, p. 11.

10. Aldhouse-Green, M. and Aldhouse-Green, S. *The Quest for the Shaman* (London: Thames & Hudson, 2005), p. 12.

11. Sullivan, L. E. "The attributes and power of the shaman: a general description of the ecstatic of the soul," in: Seaman, G. & J. S. Day, eds. *Ancient Traditions: Shamanism in Central Asia and the Americas* (Denver: University Press of Colorado and Denver Museum of Natural History, 1994).

12. Castiglioni, A. *Adventures of the Mind* (New York: Alfred A. Knopf, 1946), p. 22.

13. Gillette, D. *The Shaman's Secret: The Lost Resurrection Teachings of the Ancient Maya* (New York and London: Bantam Books, 1997), p. 108.

14. *Ibid.*

15. Csikszentmihalyi, M, "Why We Need Things," in: Lubar, S. and W. D. Kingery eds. *History from Things: Essays on Material Culture*, (Washington and London: Smithsonian Institution Press, 1993), p. 23.

16. Benedict, R. Patterns of Culture (Boston: Houghton-Mifflin 1954), p. vii.

17. "Kwakiutl," in: Encyclopaedia Britannica Library, from *Encyclopaedia Britannica* 2005 Deluxe Edition CD-ROM. Copyright © 1994–2003 Encyclopaedia Britannica, Inc (accessed February 21, 2008).

18. Czaplicka, M. A. *The Turks of Central Asia in History and at the Present Day* (London: Curzon Press and New York: Harper & Row Publishers, Inc., 1973 [1918]), p. 31.

19. Hoppál, M. and K. D. Howard. *Shamans and Cultures* (Budapest: Akadémiai Kiadó and Los Angeles: International Society for Trans-Oceanic Research, 1993), p. 189.

20. Karéryi, C. "Man and Mask," in: Campbell, J., ed. *Spiritual Disciplines* (Papers from the Eranos Yearbook, Bollingen Series XXX, Vol. 4, Princeton: Princeton University Press, 1960), p. 154.

21. Corbin, G. A. *Native Arts of North America, Africa, and the South Pacific: An Introduction* (New York: Harper and Row, 1988), p. 125.

22. Lang, A. *Myth, Ritual and Religion*, Vol. II (London and New York: Longmans, Green and Co., 1913), p. 38.

23. Eliade, M. *Shamanism: Archaic Techniques of Ecstasy*. Translated by Willard R. Trask. Bollingen Series LXXVI (Princeton NJ: Princeton University Press, 1964), p. 84.

24. "Sacred kingship: status and functions," in: Encyclopaedia Britannica Library, from *Encyclopaedia Britannica* 2005 Deluxe Edition CD-ROM. Copyright © 1994–2003 Encyclopaedia Britannica, Inc (accessed January 20, 2008).

25. Basilov, V. N. "Chosen by the Spirits," in: Balzer, M. M. ed. *Shamanic Worlds*, pp. 3–48 (Armonk, NY and London: North Castle Books, 1997), p. 14.

26. Humphrey with Onon. *Shamans and Elders*, p. 31.

27. Eliade, *Shamanism*, p. 84.

28. Ramírez de Jara, M. C. and C. E. Pinzón Castaño. "Sibundoy Shamanism and Popular Culture in Colombia," in: Langdon, E. J. M. and G. Baer eds. *Portals of Power: Shamanism in South America*, pp. 287–303 (Albuquerque: University of New Mexico Press, 1992), p. 289.

29. *Ibid.*, p. 289.

30. *Ibid.*

31. Wilbert, J. *Tobacco and Shamanism in South America* (New Haven and London: Yale University Press, 1987), 156.

32. Hoffman, M. and C. A. P. Ruck "Entheogens (Psychedelic Drugs) and Shamanism," in: Walter, M. N. and E. J. N. Fridman eds. *Shamanism: An Encyclopedia of World Beliefs, Practices, and Culture*, pp. 111–116 (Santa Barbara, CA and Oxford, ABC CLIO, 2004), p. 111.

33. *Ibid.*, p. 112.

34. Halifax, J. *Shaman: The Wounded Healer* (London: Thames and Hudson, 1988), p. 9.

35. Edson, G. *Masks and Masking*, p. 146.

36. Markman, R. H. and P. T. Markman. *The Flayed God: The Mesoamerican Mythological Tradition* (New York: HarperCollins, 1992), p. 42.

37. Jung, C. G. ed. *Man and His Symbols* (Garden City, NY: Doubleday & Company Inc., 1964), p. 149.

38. Purev, O. and G. Purvee. *Mongolian Shamanism* (Ulaanbaatar: Purvee, 2007), p. 25.

39. Humphrey with Onon, *Shamans and Elders, p.* 304.

40. Mikhailov, T. M. "Buryat Shamanism: History, Structure, and Social Function," in: Balzer, M. M. ed. *Shamanism: Soviet Studies of Traditional Religion in Siberia and Central Asia*, pp. 110–120 (Armonk, NY and London: M. E. Sharp, Inc., 1990), p. 117.

41. Bäckman and Hultkrantz, *Studies in Lapp Shamanism*, p. 30.

42. Lommel, A. *The World on the Early Hunters: Medicine-men, shamans and artists* (London: Evelyn, Adams & Mackay, 1967), p. 29.

BIBLIOGRAPHY

Abrahamsson, Hans. *The Origin of Death*. New York: Arno Press, 1977.

AHED, ©1991. American Heritage Electronic Dictionary. Houghton Mifflin, U.S. Pat. No. 44,7324,523, ©1992 Word Star International.

Ahmed, Rollo. *The Black Arts*. London: Studio Editions, 1994 [1936].

Ackerman, Diane. *A Natural History of the Senses*. New York: Random House, 1990.

Aldhouse-Green, Miranda, and Stephen Aldhouse-Green. *The Quest for the Shaman: Shape-Shifters, Sorcerers and Spirit-Healers of Ancient Europe*. London: Thames & Hudson. 2005.

Alekseev, Anatoly. "Healing Techniques Among Evén Shamans," in: Balzer, Marjorie M. ed. *Shamanic Worlds*, pp. 154–161. Armonk, NY and London: North Castle Books, 1997.

Alekseev, Nikolai Alekseevich. "The Role of the Shaman in the Life of the Turkic-speaking People of Siberia," in: Balzer, Marjorie M. ed. *Shamanism: Soviet Studies of Traditional Religion in Siberia and Central Asia*, pp. 78–109. Armonk, NY and London: M. E. Sharpe, 1990.

Alfrey, Judith, and Tim Putnam. *The Industrial Heritage: Managing Resources and Uses*. New York and London: Routledge, 1992.

Ambesi, Alberto Cesare. *Oceanic Art*. Translated by R. Montgomery. London and New York: Hamlyn, 1970.

"Ancestors' Spirits in the Sound of the Tambourine." Exhibition catalog, the collection of the Shaman Cult Accessories of Peoples of Siberia and North-east Asia Irkutsk: Regional Studies Museum, n.d.

Anisimov, Arkadiy Fedorovich. "The shaman's tent of the Evenks and the origin of the shamanistic rite," in: Michael, Henry N., ed. *Studies in Siberian Shamanism*, pp. 84–123. Toronto: Arctic Institute of North America, Anthropology of the North Translations from Russian Sources. No. 4. University of Toronto, 1963a.

———. "Cosmological concepts of the peoples of the north," in: Michael, Henry N. ed. *Studies in Siberian Shamanism*, pp. 157–229. Toronto: Arctic Institute of North America, Anthropology of the North Translations from Russian Sources. No. 4. University of Toronto, 1963b.

Ankarloo, Bengt, and Stuart Clark eds. *Witchcraft and Magic in Europe: The Eighteenth and Nineteenth Centuries*. Philadelphia: University of Pennsylvania Press, 1999a.

——— and ———, eds. *Witchcraft and Magic in Europe: The Twentieth Century*. Philadelphia: University of Pennsylvania Press, 1999b.

Antropova, V. V., and V. G. Kuznetsova "The Chukchi," in: Levin, Mikhail Grigor and Leonid Pavlovich Potapov, eds. *The Peoples of Siberia*, pp. 799–835. Translated by Scripta Technica, Inc., English translation edited by Stephen Dunn. Chicago and London: University of Chicago Press, 1956

Arendt, Hannah. *The Human Condition*. Chicago: University of Chicago Press, 1958.

Arieti, Silvano. *Creativity: The Magic Synthesis*. New York: Basic Books, 1976.

Asian Art in the Arthur M. Sackler Gallery. Washington, DC: Smithsonian Institution, 1987.

Atkinson, Jane M. "Shamanisms Today." *Annual Review of Anthropology*, 21, ed. Bernard J.S., Beals, A.R. and Tyler, S.A., pp. 307–330. Palo Alto: Annual Reviews.

———. *The Art and Politics of Wana Shamanship*. Berkeley and Oxford: University of California Press, 1989.

Awolalu, J. Omosade. *Yoruba Beliefs and Sacrificial Rites*. London: Longmans, 1979.

Bäckman, Louise, and Åke Hultkrantz. *Studies in Lapp Shamanism*. Stockholm: Almqvist & Wiksell International, 1978.

Bahn, Paul G. *The Cambridge Illustrated History of Prehistoric Art*. Cambridge: Cambridge University Press, 1998.

Baldwin, Gordon. C. *Schemers, Dreamers, and Medicine Men: Witchcraft and Magic among Primitive People*. New York: Four Winds Press, 1970.

Balikci, Asen. "Shamanistic Behavior Among the Netsilik Eskimos." *Southwest Journal of Anthropology*, 19: 380–395, 1963.

Baltimore Museum of Art. *The Alan Wurtzburger Col-*

lection of Oceanic Art, Baltimore: Baltimore Museum of Art 1956.

Balzar, Marjorie M., ed. *Shamanism: Soviet Studies of traditional Religion in Siberia and Central Asia*. Armonk, New York and London: M.E. Sharpe, 1990.

_____, ed. *Shamanic Worlds: Ritual and Lore of Siberia and Central Asia*. Armonk, NY and London: North Castle Books, 1997.

Bancroft-Hunt, Norman, and Werner Forman. *People of the Totem*. New York: G. P. Putnam's, 1979.

Barnett, Homer. *The Coast Salish of British Columbia*. Eugene: University of Oregon Monographs No. 4., 1955.

Barton, George A. *The Religions of the World*, 4th edition. Chicago: The University of Chicago Press, 1937.

Bascom, William. *African Art in Cultural Perspective*, New York: W.W. Norton, 1973.

Basilov, V. N. "Chosen by the Spirits," in: Marjorie M. Balzer ed. *Shamanic Worlds: Ritual and Lore of Siberia and Central Asia*, pp. 3–48. Armonk, New York and London: North Castle Books. 1997.

Baumer, Christoph. *Bön: Tibet's Ancient Religion*. Translated by Michael Kohn. Trumball, CT: Weatherhill, 2002.

Beane, Wendell C., and William G. Doty eds. *Myth, Rites, Symbols: A Mircea Eliade Reader*, Vol. I. New York and London: Harper Colophon Books, Harper and Row, 1976.

Bear Heart [with Molly Larkin]. *The Wind Is My Mother: The Life and Teachings of a Native American Shaman*. New York: Berkley Books, 1998 [1996].

Beattie, John H. M. "The Ghost Cult in Bunyoro," in: John Middleton, *Gods and Rituals*. Garden City, NY: Natural History Press, 1967.

Behringer, Wolfgang. *Shaman of Oberstdorf: Chonrad Stoeckhlin and the Phantoms of the Night*. Translated by H. C. Erik Midelfort. Charlottesville: University Press of Virginia, 1998.

Benedict, Ruth. *Patterns of Culture*, 2d edition. Boston: Houghton Mifflin, 1959 [1934].

Berger, Patricia, and Teresa T. Bartholomew, eds. *Mongolia: The Legacy of Chinggis Khan*. London: Thames and Hudson 1995.

Bessy, Maurice. *A Pictorial History of Magic and the Supernatural*. Translated by Margaret Crosland and Alan Daventry. London: Spring Books, 1968.

Bettelheim, Bruno. *Symbolic Wounds*. Glencoe: Free Press, 1954.

Birket-Smith, Kaj. *The Paths of Culture*. Madison and Milwaukee: University of Wisconsin Press, 1965.

Blacker, Carmine *The Catalpa Bow: A Study of Shamanistic Practices in Japan*. London: George Allen & Unwin, 1973.

Blanshard, Brand. *Reason and Belief*. New Haven: Yale University Press, 1975.

Bloch, Maurice, and Jonathan Parry, eds. *Death and the Regeneration of Life*. Cambridge: Cambridge University Press, 1982.

Blodgett, Jean. *The Coming and Going of the Saman: Eskimo Shamanism and Art*. Winnipeg: Winnipeg Art Gallery Exhibition Catalog, 1978.

Boas, Franz. "The Central Eskimo," Bureau of American Ethnology, pp. 409–669. Washington, DC: *Sixth Annual Report*, 1884–85 [1888].

Bogoras, Waldemar. "The Jesup North Pacific Expedition," Vol. 11, *The Chukchee*, New York and Leiden: American Museum of Natural History, 1907.

_____. *The Chukchee — Religion*. Memoirs of the American Museum of Natural History, No. 11, Part 2. New York: American Museum of Natural History, 1907.

_____. The *Chukchee*. New York: AMS Press, 1975 [1904–09].

Bouisson, Maurice. *Magic: Its History and Principal Rites*. Translated by G. Almayrac. New York: Dutton, 1961.

Bourguignon, Erika. "Trance Dance," in: Walter, M. N. and E. J. N. Fridman, eds. *Shamanism: An Encyclopedia of World Beliefs, Practices, and Culture*, Vol. I, pp. 247–250. Santa Barbara, CA, and Oxford: ABC CLIO, 2004.

Bourke, Joanna. *Fear: A Cultural History*. Emeryville, CA: Shoemaker Hoard, an imprint of Avalon, 2005.

Bourke, John G. *Apache Medicine-man*. New York: Dover, 1993 [1892].

Bowra, Cecil Maurice. *Primitive Song*. Cleveland and New York: The World, 1962.

Boyll, Larain. "Bridging Worlds: Teaching Huichol Shamanism," in: Ruth-Inge Heinze, ed. *Proceedings of the Ninth International Conference on the Study of Shamanism and Alternate Modes of Healing*, pp. 143–147. Berkeley: University of California, 1992.

Bradley, Richard. *Ritual and Domestic Life in Prehistoric Europe*. London and New York: Routledge, 2005.

Budge, E. A. Willis. *Egyptian Magic*. New York: Dover, 1971.

_____. *Osiris and the Egyptian Resurrection*, 2 Vols. London and New York: P. L. Warner and G. P. Putnam's, 1911.

Burkert, Walter. *Ancient Mystery Cults*. Cambridge and London: Harvard University Press, 1987.

Burland, Cottie A. *Beyond Science: A Journey into the Supernatural*. New York: Grossett & Dunlap, 1972.

_____. *The Magical Arts: A Short History*. London: Arthur Barker Limited, 1966.

_____. *Myths of Life and Death*. New York: Crown, 1974.

Bushnell, G.H.S. *Ancient Arts of the Americas*. New York and Washington: Frederick A. Praeger, 1965.

Campbell, Aidan. *Western Primitivism: African Ethnicity*. London: Cassell, 1997.

Campbell, Joseph. *Historical Atlas of World Mythology*, Vol. 1, The Way of the Animal Powers, Part 2: Mythologies of the Great Hunt, New York: Harper & Row, 1988b.

_____. *Historical Atlas of World Mythology*, Vol. II, The Way of the Seeded Earth, Part 2, Mythologies of the Primitive Planters: The North Americans, New York: Harper & Row, 1989.

_____. "The Historical Development of Mythology," in: Henry A. Murray ed. *Myth and Mythmaking*, pp. 19–45. New York: George Braziller, 1960.

_____. *The Masks of God: Occidental Mythology*. New York: Viking Press, 1964.

_____. *The Masks of God: Primitive Mythology*. New York: Penguin, 1976.

_____. *The Mystic Image*. Princeton, NJ: Bollingen Series C, Princeton University Press, 1974.

_____. *The Power of Myth*. New York, London, Toronto, Sydney, and Auckland: Doubleday, 1988a.

_____. *The Way of the Animal Powers: Historical Atlas of World Mythology*, Vol. 1. Alfred Van Der Marck Editions, San Francisco: Harper & Row, 1983.

_____, ed. "The Mystic Vision," Papers from the *Eranos Yearbook*, Bollingen Series XXX, Vol. 6, Translated by Ralph Manheim, Princeton: Princeton University Press, 1968.

_____, ed. "Spiritual Disciplines," Papers from the *Eranos Yearbook*, Bollingen Series XXX, Vol. 4, translated by Ralph Manheim, Princeton: Princeton University Press, 1960.

Capra, Fritjof. *The Tao of Physics*, 3d. ed. Boston: Shambhala, 1991.

Carr, Christopher, and D. Troy Case, eds. *Gathering Hopewell: Society, Ritual, and Ritual Interaction*. New York: Springer, 2004.

Castiglioni, Arturo. *Adventures of the Mind*. Translated by V. Gianturco. New York: Alfred A. Knopf, 1946.

Cauquelin, Josiane. "The Impact of Japanese Colonialism on Puyuma (Taiwan) Shamanism," in: Hoppál, M. and K. Howard, eds. *Shamans and Cultures*, pp. 97–104. Budapest: Akadémiai Kiadó and Los Angeles: International Society for Trans-Oceanic Research, 1993.

Chagnon, Napoleon A. *Yanomamö*, 4th edition. New York and London: Harcourt Brace Jovanovich College Publishers, 1992 [1968].

Chamalún, Luis Espinoza. *The Gate of Paradise: Secrets of Andean Shamanism*. Translated by Hilary Dyke. Bath, UK: Gateway Books, 1998.

Chernetsov, Valeriy Nikolayevich. "Concepts of the Soul Among the Ob Ugrians," in: Henry N. Michael ed. *Studies in Siberian Shamanism*, pp. 3–45. Toronto: Arctic Institute of North America by University of Toronto Press, 1963.

Chesnov, Ya. B. "Dragon: Metaphor of the Eternal World," in: N. L. Zhulpvslaus ed. *Mify, Kul'ty, Oryady narodov zarubezhnoi azii*, pp. 59–72. Moscow: Nauka, 1986.

Child, Alice B., and Child Irvin L. *Religion and Magic in the Life of Traditional Peoples*. Englewood Cliffs, NJ: Prentice-Hall, 1993.

Christensen, Erwin O. *Primitive Art*. New York: Thomas Y. Crowell, 1955.

Cirlot, Juan Edwardo. *A Dictionary of Symbols*. Translated by Jack Sage. New York: Philosophical Library, 1962.

Clifford, John. "Four Northwest Coast Museums," in: Karp, I. and S. D. Levine, eds. *Exhibiting Culture: the Poetics and Politics of Museum Display*. Washington and London: Smithsonian Institution Press, 1991,

Clottes, Jean, and David Lewis-Williams. *The Shamans of Prehistory: Trance and Magic in the Painted Caves*. Trans. by Sophie Hawkins. New York: Harry N. Abrams, 1998. [Originally, *Chamanes de la préhistoire*. Paris: Éditions du Senil, 1996].

Codd, Edward. *Magic in Names and Other Things*. Detroit, MI: Singing Tree Press, 1968.

Cole, Herbert M. *Mbari: Art and Life Among the Owerri Igbo*. Bloomington: Indiana University Press, 1982.

_____, and Chike Aniakor. *Igbo Arts: Community and Cosmos*, Los Angeles: Museum of Cultural History, University of California, 1984.

Collins, John J. *Primitive Religion*, New York: Rowman & Littlefield, 1978.

Conklin, Beth A. "Amazon Funeral Rites and Shamanism (Brazil)," in: M. N. Walter and E. J. N. Fridman, eds. *Shamanism: An Encyclopedia of World Beliefs, Practices, and Culture*, Vol. I, pp. 375–377. Santa Barbara, CA and Oxford: ABC CLIO, 2004.

Corbin, George A. *Native Arts of North America, Africa, and the South Pacific: An Introduction*. New York: Harper and Row, 1988.

Cordry, Donald. *Mexican Masks*. Austin and London: University of Texas Press, 1980.

Covell, Alan Carter. *Shamanist Folk Painting: Korea's Eternal Spirits*. Elizabeth, NJ and Seoul: Hollym International Corporation, 1984.

Crapanzano, Vincent, and Vivian Garrison. *Case Studies in Spirit Possession*. New York: Wiley, 1977.

Crawford, J. R. *Witchcraft and Sorcery in Rhodesia*. International African Institute: Oxford University Press, 1967.

Csikszentmihalyi, Mihaly. "Why We Need Things," in: Steve Lubar and W. David Kingery eds. *History from Things: Essays on Material Culture*. Washington and London: Smithsonian Institution Press, 1993.

Curtin, Jeremiah. *A Journey in Southern Siberia: The Mongols, Their Religion and Their Myths*. London: Sampson Low, Marston, 1909. An Eliboron Classics series, Adamant Media Corporation, 2005.

Czaja, Michael. *Gods of Myth and Stone*. New York and Tokyo: Weatherhill, 1974.

Czaplicka, Marie Antoninette. *Aboriginal Siberia: A Study in Social Anthropology*. Oxford: The Clarendon Press, 1969 [1914].

_____. *Shamanism in Siberia*. (reprint) Whitefish, MT: Kessinger, 2007 [1914].

_____. *The Turks of Central Asia in History and at the Present Day*. London: Curzon Press and New York: Harper & Row, 1973 [1918].

David-Neel, Alexandra. *Magic and Mystery in Tibet*. Baltimore: Penguin Books, 1971 [c1965].

_____. *With Mystics and Magicians in Tibet*, London: John Lane, 1931.

d'Aquili, Eugene G., C. D. Laughlin, and J. McManus. *The Spectrum of Ritual: A Biogenetic Structural Analysis*. New York: Columbia University Press, 1979.

Devereux, Paul. *Shamanism and the Mystery Lines*. St. Paul, MN: Llewellyn, 1993.

de Waal Malefijt, Annemarie. *Religion and Culture: An Introduction to Anthropology of Religion*. New York: Macmillan, 1968.

Diószegi, Vilmos, and Mihály Hoppál, eds. *Shamanism in Siberia*. Selected reprints, translated by S. Simon. Budapest Akadémiai Kiadó, 1996.

Dissanayake, Ellen. *What Is Art For?* Seattle and London: University of Washington Press, 1988.

Dobkin de Rios, Marlene. *Amazon Healer: The Life and times of an Urban Shaman*. Bridport, Dorset: Prism Press, 1992.

Dockstader, Frederick J. *Indian Art in Middle America*. Greenwich, CN: New York Graphic Society, 1964.

Doore, Gary. ed. *Shaman's Path: Healing, Personal Growth, and Empowerment*. Boston: Shambhala, 1988.

Douglas, Mary, ed. *Witchcraft: Confessions and Accusations*. London: Tavistock, 1970.

Douglas, Mary. *Natural Symbols: Explorations in Cosmology*. New York: Pantheon Books, 1982.

Dow, James. *The Shaman's Touch: Otomi Indian Symbolic Healing*. Salt Lake City: University of Utah Press, 1986.

Driscoll, John T. "Shamanism," Transcribed by Douglas J. Potter, in: *The Catholic Encyclopedia*, Volume XIII. New York: Robert Appleton, 1912. <http://www.newadvent.org/cathen/index.html> Copyright © 2007 by Kevin Knight.

Durkheim, Emile. *The Elementary Forms of the Religious Life*. Glencoe: Free Press, 1954.

Du Ry, Carel J. *Art of the Ancient Near and Middle East*. Translated by Alexis Brown. New York: Harry N. Abrams, 1969.

Edsman. Carl M. ed. *Studies in Shamanism*. Stockholm: Almqvist & Wiksell, 1967.

Edson, Gary. *Masks and Masking: Faces of Tradition and Belief Worldwide*. Jefferson, NC, and London: McFarland, 2005.

Eliade, Mircea. *A History of Religious Ideas*, Vol. 1. Chicago: University of Chicago Press, 1978.

_____. *Images and Symbols: Studies in Religious Symbolism*, Translated by Philip Mairet. Princeton, NJ: Princeton University Press, 1991.

_____. *Myths, Dreams, and Mysteries*, Translated by Philip Mairet. New York, London, and Toronto: Harpers & Brothers, 1960.

_____. "Recent Works on Shamanism," in: *History of Religion*, I, 1961. Chicago: University of Chicago Press, 1961.

_____. *The Sacred and the Profane: The Nature of Religion*, Translated by Willard R. Trask. New York and London: A Harvest Book, Harcourt, 1987 [1957].

_____. *Shamanism: Archaic Techniques of Ecstasy*. Translated by Willard R. Trask. Bollingen Series LXXVI, Princeton NJ: Princeton University Press, 1964.

_____. "Shamanism, Southeast Asia and Oceania," Encyclopaedia Britannica Library, from *Encyclopaedia Britannica* 2005 Deluxe Edition CD-ROM. Copyright © 1994–2003 Encyclopaedia Britannica, Inc. (accessed May 29, 2007).

_____. *Symbolism, the Sacred, and the Arts*, edited by Diane Apostolos-Cappadona. New York: Continuum, 1992.

_____. *Yoga: Immortality and Freedom*. Translated by Willard R. Trask. Bollingen Series LVI. Princeton NJ: Princeton University Press, 1990.

Eliot, Alexander. *Myths*. New York and Toronto: McGraw-Hill, 1976.

Emeagwale, Gloria, and Mariko Namba Walter. "Ancient Egyptian Shamanism," in: Walter, M. N. and E. J. N. Fridman, eds. *Shamanism: An Encyclopedia of World Beliefs, Practices, and Culture*, Vol. II, pp. 906–910. Santa Barbara, CA, and Oxford: ABC CLIO, 2004.

Encyclopaedia Britannica Library, from Encyclopaedia Britannica 2005 Deluxe Edition CD-ROM. Copyright © 1994–2003 Encyclopaedia Britannica.

Encyclopedia of Magic and Superstition: Alchemy, Charms, Dreams, Omans, Rituals, Talismans, Wishes. London: Octopus Books Limited, 1974.

Ennemoser, Joseph. *History of Magic*, Vol. II. Translated by William Howitt. New York: University Books, 1970.

Evans-Pritchard, Edward E. *Witchcraft, Oracles, and Magic Among the Azande*. Oxford: Clarendon Press, 1937.

Evans-Wentz, W. Y. *The Tibetan Book of the Dead*. New York: A Galaxy Book, Oxford University Press, 1960.

Fairchild, W. P. "Shamanism in Japan," *Folklore Studies* (Tokyo) 21, 1962.

Farb, Peter. *Man's Rise to Civilization as Shown by the Indians of North America from Primeval Times to the Coming of the Industrial State*. New York: E.P. Dutton, 1968.

Faron, Louis C. "Death and Fertility Rites of the Mapuche Indians," in: J. Middleton ed. *Gods and Rituals*. Garden City, NY: The Natural History Press, 1967.

Fienup-Riordan, Ann. *The Living Tradition of Yup'ik Masks*. Seattle and London: University of Washington Press in association with the Anchorage Museum of History and Art and the Anchorage Museum Association, 1996.

Figes, Orlando. *Natasha's Dance*. New York: Metropolitan Books, Henry Holt, 2002.

Fitzhugh, William W., and Aron Crowell. *Crossroads of Continents: Cultures of Siberia and Alaska*. Washington, DC, and London: Smithsonian Institution Press, 1988.

Fitzhugh, William W., and Susan A. Kaplan. *Inua: Spirit World of the Bering Sea Eskimo*. Washington, DC: Smithsonian Institution Press, 1982.

Flaherty, Gloria. *Shamanism and the Eighteenth Century*. Princeton: Princeton University Press, 1992.

Fontana, David. *The Secret Language of Symbols*. San Francisco: Chronicle Books, 1994.

Fontenrose, Joseph. "The Ritual Theory of Myth," in: *Folklore Studies*, Vol. 18, pp. 50–60. Berkeley and Los Angeles: University of California Press, 1966.

Forsyth, James. A *History of the Peoples of Siberia: Russia's North Asian Colony 1581–1990*. Cambridge: Cambridge University Press, 1992.

Forty, Jo. *Mythology: A Visual Encyclopedia*. London: PRC, 1999.

Fortune, Reo F. *Sorcerers of Dobu*. Prospect Heights, IL: Waveland Press, 1963.

Fraser, Douglas. *The Many Faces of Primitive Art*. Englewood Cliffs, NJ: Prentice-Hall, 1966.

Frazer, James George. *Fear of the Dead in Primitive Religion*, vol. III. London: Macmillan, 1936.

_____. *The Golden Bough: A Study of Magic and Religion*, vol. I. New York: Macmillan, 1958.

_____. *The Magic Art*, 3d ed. Vols. I and II, London: Macmillan, 1922.

Freidel, David L., Linda Schele, and Joy Parker. *Maya Cosmos: Three Thousand Years on the Shaman's Path*. New York: William Morrow, 1993.

Freud, Sigmund. *Totem and Taboo*. Translated and edited by J. Strachey. New York and London: W. W. Norton, 1989.

Fried, Martha N., and Morton H. Fried. *Transitions: Four Rituals in Eight Cultures.* New York and London: W. W. Norton, 1980.

Furst, Peter. T. "Introduction: An Overview of Shamanism," in: *Ancient Traditions: Shamanism in Central Asia and the Americas,* ed. by Gary Seaman and Jane S. Day, pp. 1–28. Niwot: University Press of Colorado, 1994.

Furst, Peter T., and Jill L. Furst. *North American Indian Art.* New York: Rizzoli International, 1982.

Furst, Peter T., and S. Nahmad, *Mitos y arte huicholes.* Mexico, DF: Secretaría de Educación Pública, 1972.

Gaisseau, Pierre-Dominique. *The Sacred Forest: Magic and Secret Rites in French Guinea.* Translated by Stephen Becker. New York: Alfred A. Knopf, 1954.

Gardner, Joseph L., ed. *Mysteries of the Ancient Americans: The New World before Columbus.* Pleasantville, NY, and Montreal: Reader's Digest Association, 1986.

Gayton, Anna H. *Yokuts-Mono Chiefs and Shamans.* University of California Publications in American Archaeology and Ethnology, 24 (1930), pp. 361–420.

Gerbrands, Adrianus A. *Art as an Element of Culture, Especially in Negro-Africa.* Leiden: E. J. Brill, 1957.

Gillette, Douglas. *The Shaman's Secret: The Lost Resurrection Teachings of the Ancient Maya.* New York and London: Bantam Books, 1997.

Gimbutas, Marija. *The Goddesses and Gods of Old Europe 6500–3500 BC: Myths and Cult of Images.* Berkeley and Los Angeles: University of California Press, 1982

———. *The Language of the Goddess.* London: Thames & Hudson, 1989.

Glaze, Anita J. 1981. *Art and Death in a Senufo Village.* Bloomington: Indiana University Press.

Gold, Peter. *Tibetan Reflections.* London: Wisdom Publication, 1984.

Goodman, Falicitas D., *Ecstasy, Ritual, and Alternate Reality: Religion in a Pluralistic World.* Bloomington and Indianapolis: Indiana University Press, 1988.

———, and Seth Josephson. "Pueblo Religion and Spirit Worlds," in: Walter, M. N. and E. J. N. Fridman. *Shamanism,* pp. 346–350. Santa Barbara, CA and Oxford: ABC CLIO, 2004.

Goudsblom, Johan, Eric Jones, and Stephen Mennell. *The Course of Human History.* New York and London: M.E. Sharpe, 1996.

Graceva, Galina. "Nganasan and Enets Shamans' Wooden Masks," in: Hoppál, Mihály and Otto von Sadovszky eds. *Shamanism Past and Present,* Part 1, pp.145–153. Budapest: Ethnographic Institute, Hungarian Academy of Sciences/Los Angeles and Fullerton: International Society for Trans-Oceanic Research, 1989

Graf, Fritz. *Magic in the Ancient World.* Translated by Franklin Philip. Cambridge and London: Harvard University Press, 1997.

Green, T. 2001. *Meeting the Invisible Man: Secrets and Magic in West Africa.* London: Weidenfeld & Nicolson.

Greub, Susanne, ed. *Art of the Sepik River: Papua New Guinea.* Basel: Tribal Art Centre, 1985.

Grim, John A. *The Shaman: Patterns of Siberian and Ojibway Healing.* Norman: University of Oklahoma Press, 1983.

———, ed. *Indigenous Traditions and Ecology.* Cambridge, MA: Harvard University Press, 2001.

Grimes, Ronald L. *Research in Ritual Studies: A Programmatic Essay and Bibliography.* Metuchen, NJ and London: American Theological Library Association and Scarecrow Press, 1985.

Guinca, Miguel Angel G. *Altamira.* Trans. Lynne Polak. Madrid: SILEX, 1979.

Gyaltsen, Shardza T. *Heart Drops of Dharmakaya.* Ithaca, NY: Snow Lion, 2002.

Haberland, Wolfgang. *The Art of North America.* Translated by Wayne Dynes. New York and London: Greystone Press, 1968.

Haeberlin, H. K. "SBeTeTDA'Q, A Shamanistic Performance of the Coast Salish." *American Anthropologist,* 20:249–257, 1918.

Hahn, T. 1971. *Tsuni-IIGoam The Supreme Being of the Khoi-Khoi.* Freeport, NY: Books for Libraries Press.

Halbwachs, Maurice. *The Collective Memory.* Translated by Francis J. Ditter, Jr. and Vida Yazdi Ditter. New York: Harper Colophon Books, 1980.

Halifax, Joan. *Shaman: The Wounded Healer.* London: Thames and Hudson, 1982.

———. *Shamanic Voices.* New York: E. P. Dutton, 1979.

Hansen, Henny Harald. *Mongol Costumes,* The Carlsberg Foundation's Nomad Research Project. London: Thames and Hudson, 1993

Harner, Michael J. *The Jivaro: People of the Sacred Waterfalls.* Garden City, NY: Anchor Press/Doubleday, 1973.

———. *The Way of the Shaman.* San Francisco: Harper San Francisco, A Division of HarperCollins Publishers, 1990.

Harrison, Jane Ellen. *Ancient Art and Ritual.* New York: Henry Holt, 1913.

Hart, George. *A Dictionary of Egyptian Gods and Goddesses.* London: Routledge, 1996.

Hartman, Günther. *Masken südamerikanischer Naturvölker,* Berlin: Veröffentlichungen des Museums für Völkerkunde, 1967.

Harvey, Graham, and Robert J. Wallis. *Historical Dictionary of Shamanism.* Lanham, MD and Plymouth, UK: Scarecrow, 2007.

Harwood, Alan. *Witchcraft, Sorcery, and Social Categories Among the Safwa.* Oxford: International African Institute by the Oxford University Press, 1970.

Hawthorn, Audrey. *Art of the Kwakiutl Indians and other Northwest Coast Tribes.* Vancouver: University of British Columbia; Seattle and London: University of Washington Press, 1967.

Hayden, Brian. *Shamans, Sorcerers and Saints: A Prehistory of Religion.* Washington, DC: Smithsonian Books, 2003.

Heidegger, Martin. *Being and Time [Sein und Zeit].* Translated by John Macquarrie and Edward Robinson. New York and London: Harper & Row, 1962.

Heinze, Ruth-Inge. ed. *Proceedings of the Ninth International Conference on the Study of Shamanism and Alternate Modes of Healing.* Berkeley: University of California, 1992.

———, ed. *The Nature and Function of Rituals: Fire from Heaven.* Westport, CN and London: Bergin & Garvey, 2000.

Heissig, Walter. *The Religions of Mongolia*. Translated by Geoffrey Samuel. Berkeley and Los Angeles: University of California Press, 1980.

———, and Dominique Dumas. *The Mongols Die Mongolen*, an exhibition catalogue published by the Staatliches Museum für Völkerkunde München [1989]. Innsbruck: Pinguin-Verlag and Frankfurt/Main: Umschau-Verlag, 1995.

Herskovits, Melville J. *Man and His Works: the Science of Cultural Anthropology*. New York: Alfred A. Knopf, 1948.

Hill, Douglas. *Magic and Superstition*. London and New York: Hamlyn, 1968.

Hirsch, Eric, and Michael O'Hanlon, eds. *The Anthropology of Landscape: Perspectives on Place and Space*. Oxford: Clarendon Press, 1995.

Hitchcock, John T., and Rex L. Jones, eds. *Spirit Possession in the Napal Himalaya*. London: Warminster, 1976.

Hobsbawm, Eric, and Terence Ranger. *The Invention of Tradition*. Cambridge: Cambridge University Press, 1983.

Hodgson, Janet. *The God of the Xhosa*. Cape Town: Oxford University Press, 1982.

Hoebel, Edward Adamson. *Man in the Primitive World*, 2d ed. New York and London: McGraw-Hill, 1958.

Hoffman, Mark, and Carl A. P. Ruck "Entheogens (Psychedelic Drugs) and Shamanism," in: Walter, M. N. and E. J. N. Fridman eds. *Shamanism: An Encyclopedia of World Beliefs, Practices, and Culture*, pp. 111–116. Santa Barbara, CA and Oxford: ABC CLIO, 2004.

Hogarth, Hyun–Key Kim. 1998. *Kut: Happiness Through Reciprocity*. Budapest: Akadémiai Kiadó.

Holtved, E. "Eskimo Shamanism," in: *Studies in Shamanism*. Edsman, C-M. (ed.) Stockholm: Almquist & Wiksell, 1967.

Hoppál, Mihály ed. *Shamanism: Selected Writings of Vilmos Diószegi*. Budapest: Akadémiai Kiadó, 1998.

———. *Studies of Mythology and Uralic Shamanism*, Translation by Orsolya Frank, Bálint Sebestyén and Péter Simoncsics. Budapest: Akadémiai Kiadó, 2000.

Hoppál, Mihály, and Gábor Kósa. 2003. *Rediscovery of Shamanic Heritage*. Budapest: Akadémiai Kiadó.

Hoppál, Mihály, and Kieth D. Howard, eds. *Shamans and Cultures*. Budapest: Akadémai Kiadó and Los Angeles: International Society for Trans-Oceanic Research. 1993.

Hoppál, Mihály, and Otto von Sadovszky eds. *Shamanism Past and Present*, Parts 1 and 2. Budapest: Ethnographic Institute, Hungarian Academy of Sciences/Los Angeles and Fullerton: International Society for Trans-Oceanic Research, 1989.

Houk, James Titus. *Spirits, Blood, and Drums: The Orisha Religion in Trinidad*. Philadelphia: Temple University Press, 1995.

Howells, William. *The Heathens: Primitive Man and His Religion*. Garden City, NY: Doubleday, 1948.

Huhm, Halla Pai. *Kut: Korean Shamanist Rituals*. Elizabeth, NJ and Seoul: Hollym, 1980.

Huizinga, Johan. *Homo Ludens*. New York: Roy, 1959.

Hultkrantz, Åke. "Ecological and Phenomenological Aspects of Shamanism," in: Diószegi, V. and M. Hoppál, ed. *Shamanism in Siberia*, Selected Reprints, Translated by S. Simon. Budapest: Akadémiai Kiadó, 1996.

———. "The Place of Shamanism in the History of Religions," in: Mohály Hoppál and Otto van Sadovszky. *Shamanism Past and Present*, Part 1. Budapest: Ethnographic Institute, Hungarian Academy of Sciences and Los Angeles/Fullerton: International Society for Trans-Oceanic Research, 1989.

———. *Shamanic Healing and Ritual Drama: Health and Medicine in Native North American Religious Traditions*. New York: Crossroad, 1992.

———. "Shamanism: A Religious Phenomenon?" in: G. Doore ed. *Shaman's Path: Healing, Personal Growth and Empowerment*, pp. 33–42. Boston and London: Shambhala, 1988

Humphrey, Caroline. "Chiefly and Shamanist Landscapes in Mongolia," pp. 135–162, in: Hirsch, E. and M. O'Hanlon, eds. *The Anthropology of Landscape: Perspectives on Place and Space*. Oxford: Clarendon Press, 1995.

———. *Karl Marx Collective: Economy, Society, and Religion in a Siberian Collective Farm*. Cambridge, Cambridge University Press, 1983.

———, with Urgunge Onon. *Shamans and Elders: Experience, Knoweldge and Power Among the Daur Mongols*. Oxford: Clarendon Press, 1996.

Hunt, Norman B. *Shamanism in North America*. Buffalo, NY: Firefly, 2003.

Hutton, Ronald. *Shamans: Siberian Spirituality and the Western Imagination*. London and New York: Hambledon and London, 2001.

Huxley, Francis. *The Way of the Sacred*. Garden City, NY: Doubleday, 1974.

Hyman, John. *The Imitation of Nature*. New York and Oxford: Basil Blackwell, 1989.

Idowu, E. B. *African Traditional Religion*. Maryknoll, NY: Orbis Books, 1975.

Ilyon. 13th Century. *Samguk yusa* (Legends and History of the Three Kingdoms of Ancient Korea). Trans. by Tae-Hung Ha and Granfton K. Mintz. Seoul: Yonsei University Press, 1972.

Jakobsen, Merete D. *Shamanism: Traditional and Contemporary Approaches to the Mastery of Spirits and Healing*. New York: Berghahn, 1999.

Jensen, Adolf E. *Myth and Cult Among Primitive Peoples*. Translated by M. T. Choldin and W. Weissleder. Chicago: University of Chicago Press. 1963, [1951].

Jochelson, Waldemar. *The Koryak*. Leiden: E. J. Brill and New York: G. E. Stechert and issued as v. 10 of Memoirs of the American Museum of Natural History, 1908 [1905].

Jordan, David K. *Gods, Ghosts and Ancestors: Folk Religion in a Taiwanese Village*. Berkeley: University of California Press, 1972.

Jung, Carl G., ed. *Man and His Symbols*. Garden City, NY: Doubleday, 1964.

Kakar, Sudhir. *Shamans, Mystics and Doctors*. Chicago: University of Chicago Press, 1982.

Kalweit, Holger. *Shamans, Healers, and Medicine Men*, Translated by Michael H. Kohn. Boston, MA: Shambhala, 1992.

Kan, Sergei. *Symbolic Immortality: The Tungit Potlatch of*

the *Nineteenth Century*. Washington and London: Smithsonian Institution Press, 1989.

Kapferer, Bruce. *The Feast of the Sorcerer: Practices of Consciousness and Power*. Chicago and London: University of Chicago Press, 1997.

Keesing, Roger M. *Kwaio Religion: The Living and the Dead in a Solomon Island Society*. New York: Columbia University Press, 1982.

Kehoe, Alice Beck. *The Ghost Dance: Ethnohistory and Revitalization*. Fort Worth: Holt, Rinehart and Winston, 1989.

———. *Shamans and Religion: An Anthropological Exploration in Critical Thinking*. Prospect Heights, IL: Waveland Press, 2000.

Kendall, Laurel. *The Life and Hard Times of a Korean Shaman*. Honolulu: University of Hawaii Press, 1988.

———. *Shamans, Housewives, and other Restless Spirits*. Honolulu: University of Hawaii Press, 1985.

Kenin-Lopsan, Mongush Borakhoevich. *Shamanic Songs and Myths of Tuva*, Mihály Hoppál ed. Budapest: Akadémiai Kiadó, International Society for Trans-Oceanic Research, Los Angeles, 1997.

Kerényi, C. 1960. "Man and Mask," in: Campbell, J., ed. *Spiritual Disciplines* (Papers from the Eranos Yearbook, Bollingen Series XXX, Vol. 4, Princeton: Princeton University Press.

Kharitidi, Olga. *Entering the Circle: Ancient Secrets of Siberian Wisdom Discovered by a Russian Psychiatrist*. London: Thorsons, 1996.

Kharitonova, Valentina. "Black and White Shamans," Shamans, in: Walter, M. N. and E. J. N. Fridman, eds. *Shamanism: An Encyclopedia of World Beliefs, Practices, and Culture*, Vol. II, pp. 536–539. Santa Barbara, CA and Oxford: ABC CLIO, 2004.

Kiev, Ari, ed. *Magic, Faith, and Healing: Studies in Primitive Psychiatry Today*. London: Free Press of Glencoe, Collier-Macmillan, 1964.

———. *Transcultural Psychiatry*. New York: The Free Press, 1972.

Kim, Tae-kon. *Korean Shamanism—Muism*, Translated and edited by Chang Soo-kyung. Seoul: Jimoondang, 1998.

Kirk, Geoffrey. S. *Myth: Its Meaning and Functions in Ancient and Other Cultures*. Berkeley and Los Angeles: University of California Press, 1970.

Kister, David A. "Korean Shamanism," in: Walter, M. N. and E. J. N. Fridman, eds. *Shamanism: An Encyclopedia of World Beliefs, Practices, and Culture*, Vol. II, 681–688. Santa Barbara, CA and Oxford: ABC CLIO, 2004.

———. *Korean Shamanist Ritual: Symbols and Dramas of Transformation*. Budapest: Akadémiai Kiadó, 1997.

Kitagawa, Joseph M. *Religion in Japanese History*. New York and London: Columbia University Press, 1966.

Klass, Morton. *Mind Over Mind: The Anthropology and Psychology of Spirit Possession*. New York and Oxford: Rowman & Littlefield, 2003.

Kluckhohn, Clyde. *Navajo Witchcraft*. Boston: Beacon Press, 1944.

———. "Recurrent Themes in Myths and Mythmaking," in: H. A. Murray, *Myth and Mythmaking*, pp. 46–60. New York: George Braziller, 1960.

Kottler, Jeffrey A, and Jon Carlson with Bradford Keeney. *American Shaman: An Odyssey of Global Healing Traditions*. New York and Hove: Brunner-Routledge, 2004.

Krader, Lawrence. "Buryat Religion and Society," in: J. Middleton ed. *Gods and Rituals*. Garden City, NY: The Natural History Press, 1967.

Kramer, Samuel Noah. *Mythologies of the Ancient World*. Chicago: Quadrangle, 1961.

Krippner, S. "Profiles of Three Contemporary Central American Shamans," in: R-I Heinze, ed. *Proceedings of the Ninth International Conference on the Study of Shamanism and Alternate Modes of Healing*. Berkeley: University of California, 1992, p.148.

———. "Shamans: The First Healers," in: Doore, G. ed. *Shaman's Path*, pp. 101–114. Boston and London: Shambhala, 1988.

Kuper, Adam. *The Invention of Primitive Society*. London: Routledge, 1988.

La Barre, Weston. *The Ghost Dance*, New York: Doubleday, 1970.

Labbé, Armand. 1986. *Columbia Before Columbus*. New York: Rizzoli.

———. *Shamans, Gods, and Mythic Beasts: Colombian Gold and Ceramics in Antiquity*. New York and Seattle: American Federation of Arts and University of Washington Press.

Laderman, Carol. "Malay Shamans and Healers," in: Walter, M. N. and E. J. N. Fridman, eds. *Shamanism: An Encyclopedia of World Beliefs, Practices, and Culture* Vol. II, pp. 818–824. Santa Barbara, CA and Oxford: ABC CLIO, 2004.

La Fontaine, J.S. *Initiation: Ritual Drama and Secret Knowledge Across the World*. Harmondsworth: Penguin Books, 1985.

Laing, John, and David Wire. *The Encyclopedia of Signs and Symbols*. London: Studio Editions, 1993.

Landes, Ruth. *Ojibwa Religion and the Midéwiwin*. Madison and London: University of Wisconsin Press, 1968.

Lanfer, B. 1917. "Origin of the Word Shaman," in: *American Anthropologist*, Vol. 19: pp. 361–371.

Lang, Andrew. *Myth, Ritual and Religion* (vols. I & II). New York and London: Longmans, Green, 1913.

Langdon, E. Jean. "Shamanism as the History of Anthropology," in: Mihály Hoppál and Otto van Sadovszky. *Shamanism Past and Present*, Part 1 (Budapest: ethnographic Institute, Hungarian Academy of Sciences and Los Angeles/Fullerton: International Society for Trans-Oceanic Research, 1989), p. 53.

———, and Gerhard Baer. *Portals of Power: Shamanism in South America*. Albuquerque: University of New Mexico Press, 1992.

Larson, Stephen. 1988. *The Shaman's Doorway*. Barrytown, NY: Station Hill Press.

Leenhardt, Maurice. *Folk Art of Oceania*, Translated by M. Heron. New York: Tudor, 1950.

Legg, S. *The Barbarians of Asia*. New York: Dorset Press, 1970.

Leiris, M., and J. Delange. *African Art: The Arts of Mankind*, eds. André Malraux and André Parrot, New York: Golden Press, 1968.

Lemoine, Jacques. "The Diagnosis of Disease as a 'Shamanic Equation' among the Hmong of Laos and Thailand," in: Hoppál, Mihály and Howard, Keith D.

Shamans and Cultures. Budapest: Akadémiai Kiadó and Los Angeles: International Society for Trans-Oceanic Research, 1993.

Levin, Mikhail Grigor, and Leonid Pavlovich Potapov, eds. *The Peoples of Siberia*, Translated by Scripta Technica, Inc., English translation edited by Stephen Dunn. Chicago and London: University of Chicago Press, 1956

Lévi-Strauss, Claude. *Structural Anthropology.* Translated by C. Johnson and B. G. Schoepf. New York: Basic Books, A Division of HarperCollins Publishers, 1963a.

———. *Totemism*, Translated by Rodney Needham. Boston: Beacon Press, 1963b.

Lévy-Bruhl, Lucien. *How Natives Think.* Translated by L. A. Clare. Princeton: Princeton University Press, 1985.

Lewin, Roger. *The Origin of Modern Humans.* New York: Scientific American Library, a division of HPHLP, 1993.

Lewis, I. M. *Ecstatic Religion: A Study of Shamanism and Spirit Possession.* 2nd. ed. New York and London: Routledge, 1989.

———. *Symbols and Sentiments.* New York and London: Academic Press, 1977.

Lewis, Philip H. "The Artist in New Ireland Society," in: M. W. Smith, ed. *The Artist in Tribal Society: Proceedings of a Symposium held at the Royal Anthropological Institute.* London: Routledge & Kegan Paul, 1961.

Lieban, Richard W. *Cebuano Sorcery: Malign Magic in the Philippines.* Berkeley and Los Angeles: University of California Press, 1967.

Lindsay, Jack. *A Short History of Culture.* New York: Citadel Press, 1963.

Linton, Ralph. *The Tree of Culture.* New York: Alfred A. Knopf, 1957.

Lissner, Iver. *Man, God and Magic.* Translated by J. Maxwell Brownjohn. New York: G.P. Putnam's, 1961.

Lommel, Andreas. *Masks: Their Meaning and Function.* New York and Toronto: McGraw-Hill, 1972.

———. "Shamanism in Australia," in: Hoppál, Mihály and Otto von Sadovszky eds. *Shamanism Past and Present*, Part 1 pp. 24–34 (Budapest Ethnographic Institute, Hungarian Academy of Science, Los Angeles and Fullerton: International Society for Trans-Oceanic Research, 1989.

———. *The World of the Early Hunters.* Translated by Michael Bullock. London: Evelyn, Adams & MacKay, 1967.

Lowie, Robert. H. *Primitive Religion.* New York: Liveright, 1970.

Lubar, Steve, and W. David Kingery, eds. *History from Things: Essays on Material Culture.* Washington and London: Smithsonian Institution Press, 1993.

Lubbock, John. *The Origin of Civilization and the Primitive Condition of Man.* London: Longman, 1870.

———. *Prehistoric Times.* London: Williams & Norgate, 1865.

Macgowan Kenneth, and Herman Rosse. *Masks and Demons.* London: Martin Hopkinson, 1924.

Mack, John, ed. *Masks and the Art of Expression.* New York: Harry N. Abrams, 1994.

Mackenzie, D. A. *Myths and Legends Series: China and Japan.* London: Bracken Books, 1985.

Maddox, John Lee. *Medicine Man: A Sociological Study of the Character and Evolution of Shamanism.* New York: Macmillan, 1923.

———. *Shamans and Shamanism.* Mineola, NY: Dover, 2003 [1923].

Magner, J. A. 1953. *Mental Health in a Mad World.* Milwaukee: Bruce.

Maikoff, Vladimir. "Similarities and Differences Between Shamanism and Totalitarianism: Two Psychotechnologies," in: Heinze, Ruth-Inge ed. *Proceedings of the Ninth International Conference on the Study of Shamanism and Alternate Modes of Healing*, pp. 291–294. Berkeley: University of California, 1992.

Mair, Lucy. *Witchcraft.* New York and Toronto: McGraw-Hill, 1971

Malinowski, Bronislaw. 1944. *A Scientific Theory of Culture.* Chapel Hill: The University of North Carolina Press.

Manuscript 4832. Washington: Smithsonian Institution National Anthropological Archive.

Maringer, Johannes. *The Gods of Prehistoric Man.* Translated and edited by Mary Ilford. New York: Alfred A. Knopf, 1960.

Markman, Roberta H., and Markman Peter T. *The Flayed God: The Mesoamerican Mythological Tradition.* New York: HarperCollins, 1992.

Marshack, A. *The Roots of Civilization.* New York and Dusseldorf: McGraw-Hill, 1972.

Marshall, Richard H., and associate editors, Thomas E. Bird and Andrew Q. Blane. *Aspects of Religion in the Soviet Union 1917–1967.* Chicago and London: The University of Chicago Press, 1971.

Martynov, Anatoly I. *The Ancient Art of Northern Asia*, Translated and edited by Demitri B. Shimkin and Edith M. Shimkin. Urbana and Chicago: University of Illinois Press, 1991.

Maskarinec, Gregory G. "Healing and Shamanism," in: Walter, M. N. and E. J. N. Fridman, eds. *Shamanism: An Encyclopedia of World Beliefs, Practices, and Culture* Vol. I, pp. 137–142. Santa Barbara, CA and Oxford: ABC CLIO, 2004.

———. *The Rulings of the Night: An Ethnography of Nepalese Shaman Oral Texts.* Madison: University of Wisconsin Press, 1995.

Mason, David A. *Spirit of the Mountains: Korea's San-Shin and Traditions of Mountain-Worship.* Elizabeth, NJ and Seoul: Hollym, 1999.

Mauldin, Barbara. *Masks of Mexico: Tigers, Devils, and the Dance of Life.* Santa Fe: Museum of New Mexico Press, 1999.

Maxwell, James A., ed. *America's Fascinating Indian Heritage.* Pleasantville, NY and Montreal: Reader's Digest Association, 1978.

Maxwell, Nicole. *Witch-Doctor's Apprentice.* 3d ed. New York: Library of the Mystic Arts Citadel Press, 1990.

McFarren, Peter, ed. *Mascaras de los Andes Bolivianos.* La Paz, Bolivia: Editorial Quipus/Banco Mercantil S.A., 1993.

McGhee, Robert. *Ancient People of the Arctic.* Vancouver: UBC Press, published in association with the Canadian Museum of Civilization, 1996.

McGill, Ormond. *The Mysticism and Magic of India.* South Brunswick and New York: A.S. Barnes, 1977.

McMillan, David W. *Emotion Rituals.* New York and London: Routledge, 2006.

Mead, Margaret, and Nicolas Calas, ed. *Primitive Heritage: An Anthropological Anthology.* New York: Random House, 1953.

Melody, Michael E. *The Apache.* New York and Philadelphia: Chelsea House, 1989.

Meyer, Laure. *Black Africa: Masks, Sculpture, Jewelry.* Paris: Pierre Terrail, 1992.

Meyer, Marvin, and Paul Mirecki. *Ancient Magic and Ritual Power.* Leiden and New York: E. J. Brill, 1995.

_____ and _____. *Magic and Ritual in the Ancient World.* Leiden and New York: E. J. Brill, 2002.

Michael, Henry N., ed. *Shamanism in Eurasia.* Göttingen, Edition Herodiot, 1984.

_____. *Studies in Siberian Shamanism.* Toronto: University of Toronto Press, 1963.

Middleton, John, ed. *Gods and Rituals.* American Museum Sourcebooks in Anthropology, published for the American Museum of Natural History, Garden City, NY: Natural History Press, 1967.

_____, ed. *Gods and Rituals.* Austin: University of Texas Press, 1981.

_____, ed. *Magic, Witchcraft and Curing.* Austin: University of Texas Press, 1982 [1967].

Middleton John, and E. H. Winter, eds. *Witchcraft and Sorcery in East Africa.* London: Routledge & Kegan Paul, 1978.

Mikhailov, Taras Maksimosvich. "Buryat Shamanism: History, Structure, and Social Functions," in: M.M. Balzer. *Shamanism: Soviet Studies of Traditional Religion in Siberia and Central Asia.* Armonk, NY and London: M. E. Sharpe, Inc., 1990.

Mithen, Steven. "The Origin of Art: Natural Signs, Mental Modularity, and Visual Symbolism," in: H.D.G. Maschner, ed. *Darwinian Archaeologies.* New York and London: Plenum Press, 1996.

Monter, E. William. *Witchcraft in France and Switzerland.* Ithaca and London: Cornell University Press, 1976.

Monti, Franco. *African Masks,* Translated by A. Hale. London and New York: Hamlyn, 1968.

Moodley, Roy, and William West, eds. *Integrating Traditional Healing Practices into Counseling and Psychotherapy.* Thousand Oaks and London: Sage, 2005.

Morgan, David. *The Mongols.* Oxford: Basil Blackwell, 1986.

Müller, Klaus. E., and Henning Christoph. *Soul of Africa: Magical Rites and Traditions.* Cologne: Könemann Verlagsgesellschaft mbH, 2000.

Müller-Edeling, Claudia, Christian Rätsch, and Surendra Bahadur Sihahi. *Shamanism and Tantra in the Himalayas.* Translated by Annabel Lee. London: Thames & Hudson, 2002,

Mumford, Stan R. *Himalayan Dialogue: Tibetan Lamas and Gurung Shamans in Nepal.* Madison: University of Wisconsin Press, 1989.

Murdoch, John. "Ethnological Results of the Point Barrow Expedition," in: General Report of the Bureau of Ethnology. Washington, DC, 1892.

_____. "On the Siberian Origin of some customs of the Western Eskimo," in: *American Anthropologist.* Washington, DC, 1888.

Murphy, Jane M. "Psychotherapeutic aspects of shamanism on the St. Lawrence Island, Alaska," pp. 53–83, in: Ari Kiev, ed. *Magic, Faith and Healing: Studies in Primitive Psychiatry Today.* London: Free Press of Glenscoe, 1964.

Murphy, Joseph M. *Santería: An African Religion in America.* Boston: Beacon Press, 1988.

Musée du quai Branly. Paris: Réunion des Musées Nationaux. 2000.

Musi, Carla Corradi. "Finno-Ugric Shamanism," in: Walter, M. N. and E. J. N. Fridman, eds. *Shamanism: An Encyclopedia of World Beliefs, Practices, and Culture,* pp. 486–494, vol. 1. Santa Barbara, CA and Oxford: ABC CLIO, 2004.

Mutwa, Vusamazulu C. *Zulu Shaman: Dreams, Prophecies, and Mysteries.* ed. Stephen Larsen. Rochester, VM: Destiny Books, 2003.

Nadel, S. "A Study of Shamanism in the Nuba Hills," *Journal of the Royal Anthropological Institute,* 76, 1946.

Napier, A. David. *Masks, Transformation and Paradox.* Berkeley and London: University of California Press, 1986.

Needham, Rodney. *Symbolic Classification.* Santa Monica, CA: Goodyear, 1979.

Newton, Douglas. *Crocodile and Cassowary.* New York: Museum of Primitive Art, 1971,

Nicholson, Shirley. *Shamanism: An Expanded View of Reality.* Wheaton, IL: Quest Books, 1987.

Noel, Daniel C., ed. *Paths of the Power of Myth.* New York: Crossroad, 1990.

Nooter, Mary H. *Secrecy: African Art That Conceals and Reveals.* Munich: Prestel, 1993.

Norbeck, Edward. *Religion in Primitive Society.* New York: Harper & Row, 1961.

Nunley, John W. *Moving with the Face of the Devil.* Urbana and Chicago: University of Illinois Press, 1987.

Oakes, Jill, and Rick Riewe. *Spirit of Siberia: Traditional Native Life, Clothing, and Footwear.* Washington, DC: Smithsonian Institution Press, 1998.

Oakes, Lorna, and Lucia Gahlin. *Ancient Egypt.* New York: Barnes and Noble, 2006.

Oberhelman, Steven M., ed. *The Oneiroctriticon of Achmet: A Medieval Greek and Arabic Treatise on the Interpretation of Dreams,* Translated by Steven Oberlelman. Lubbock: Texas Tech University Press, 1991.

Odgaard, U. "Palaeo-Eskimoic Shamanism," in: T. Vestergaard, ed. *North Atlantic Studies,* Vol. 4 No. 1+2. Højbjerg, Denmark: Aarhus University Press, 2001.

O'Keefe, Daniel L. *Stolen Lightning: The Social Theory of Magic.* New York: Continuum, 1982.

Oklandnikov, Alexei. *Art of the Amur: Ancient Art of the Russian Far East.* New York: Harry N. Abrams, and Aurora Art, Leningrad, 1981.

Olmos, Margarite F. and Lizabeth Paravisini-Gebert, eds. *Sacred Possessions: Vodou, Santería, Obeah, and the*

Caribbean. New Brunswick, NJ: Rutgers University Press, 1997.
Oman, John. *The Natural & the Supernatural.* New York: Macmillan, 1931.
Pant, Jitendra, ed. *Himalayan Mysteries.* New Delhi: Roli & Janssen BV, 2001.
Paolucci, Henry. *Hegel: On The Arts.* New York: Frederick Unger, 1979.
Park, Willard Z. *Shamanism in Western North America.* Evanston and Chicago: Northwestern University, 1938.
Parkin, David. *Sacred Void: Spatial Images of Work and Ritual Among the Giriama of Kenya.* Cambridge and New York: Cambridge University Press, 1991.
Parman, Susan. *Dream and Culture: An Anthropological Study of the Western Intellectual Tradition.* New York and London: Praeger, 1991.
Parrinder, Edward G. 1976. *West African Psychology: A Comparative Study of Psychological and Religious Thought.* London: Lutterworth Press.
Pattee, Rowena. "Ecstasy and Sacrifice," in: Doore, G. ed. *Shaman's Path: Healing, Personal Growth and Empowerment, pp. 17–31.* Boston and London: Shambhala, 1988.
Paul, Robert. A. 1982. *The Tibetan Symbolic World.* Chicago: University of Chicago Press.
Pearson, James L. *Shamanism and the Ancient Mind: A Cognitive Approach to Archaeology.* Walnut Creek, New York, and London: AltaMira Press, 2002.
Pemberton, John, ed. *Insight and Artistry in African Divination.* Washington and London: Smithsonian Institution Press, 2000.
Pentikäinen, Juha, ed. *Shamanism and Northern Ecology.* Berlin and New York: Mouton de Gruyter, 1996.
Perrin, Olivier. *Masques.* Paris: Musée Guimet in collaboration with l'École pratique de Hautes Études et son Centre documentaire d'Historie des religions, 1959.
Peters, Larry. *Ecstasy and Healing in Nepal: An Ethnopsychiatric Study of Tamang Shamanism.* Malibu, CA: Undena, 1981.
Pinch, Geraldine. *Magic in Ancient Egypt.* Austin: University of Texas Press, 1994.
Powers, William K. *Yuwipi: Vision and Experience in Oglala Ritual.* Lincoln: Bison Books, University of Nebraska Press, 1984.
Price, Neil, ed. *The Archaeology of Shamanism.* New York and London: Routledge, 2001.
Prokofyeva, Yekaterina Dmitriyevna. "The Costume of the Enets Shaman," Translated by Barbara Krader, in: Michael, Henry N., ed. *Studies in Siberian Shamanism.* Toronto: Published for the Arctic Institute of North America by University of Toronto Press, 1963.
Purev, Otgony, and Gurbadaryn Purvee. *Mongolian Shamanism,* Translated, edited and designed by Gurbadaryn Purvee, English edition by Richard Lawrence and Elaine Cheng. Ulaanbaatar: Purvee, Gurbadaryn, 2007.
Radin, Paul. *Primitive Religion: Its Nature and Origin,* 2d. ed. New York: Dover, 1957 [1937].
_____. *The World of Primitive Man.* New York: Grove Press, 1960.
Rajchman, John, ed. *The Identity in Question.* New York and London: Routledge, 1995.
Ramírez de Jara, Maria C., and Carlos E. Pinzón Castaño. "Sibundoy Shamanism and Popular Culture in Colombia," in: Langdon, E. J. M. and G. Baer, eds. *Portals of Power: Shamanism in South America,* pp. 287–303. Albuquerque: University of New Mexico Press, 1992.
Ratzel, Friedrich. *History of Mankind,* Translated by A. J. Butler. New York: Macmillan, 1896.
Ray, Dorothy Jean. *Aleut and Eskimo Art: Tradition and Innovation in South Alaska.* Seattle: University of Washington Press, 1981.
_____. *Artists of the Tundra and the Sea.* Seattle: University of Washington Press, 1961.
_____. *Eskimo Art: Tradition and Innovation in North Alaska.* Seattle and London: University of Washington Press, 1977.
_____. *Eskimo Masks: Art and Ceremony.* Seattle and London: University of Washington Press, 1967.
_____. *The Eskimos of Bering Strait, 1650–1898.* Seattle and London: University of Washington Press, 1975.
Read, Carveath. *Man and His Superstitions.* London: Senate, an imprint of Studio Editions, 1995 [1925].
Reichard, Gladys A. *Navaho Religion: A Study of Symbolism,* vol. 1. Bollingen Series XVIII, New York: Pantheon Books, 1950.
Reichel-Dolmatoff, Gerardo. *Amazonian Cosmos: The Sexual and Religious Symbolism of the Tukano Indians.* Chicago: University of Chicago Press, 1971.
_____. *Rainforest Shamans.* Totnes, England: Themis Books, 1997.
_____. *The Shaman and the Jaguar.* Philadelphia: Temple University Press, 1975.
Reid, Anna. *The Shaman's Coat: A Native History of Siberia.* New York: Walker, 2002.
Reik, Theodor. *Ritual: Psycho-Analytic Studies.* New York: International Universities Press, 1958.
Reynolds, Barrie. *Magic, Divination and Witchcraft Among the Barotse of Northern Rhodesia.* Berkeley and Los Angeles: University of California Press, 1963.
Riches, David. *Northern Nomadic Hunter-Gatherers.* London and New York: Academic Press, 1982.
Riley, Olive. *Masks and Magic.* London: Thames & Hudson, 1955.
Ripinsky-Nixon, Michael. *The Nature of Shamanism: Substance and Function of a Religious Metaphor.* Albany: State University of New York, 1993.
Rogers, Spencer L. *The Shaman.* Springfield: Charles C. Thomas, 1982.
Rosenthal, Judy. *Possession, Ecstasy, and Law in Ewe Voodoo.* Charlottesville and London: University Press of Virginia, 1998.
Rousselot, Jean-Loup. "Yupik Shamanism (Alaska)." Translated by Jane Ripken, in: Walter, M. N. and E. J. N Fridman, eds. *Shamanism: An Encyclopedia of World Beliefs, Practices, and Culture,* pp. 362–364, vol. 1. Santa Barbara, CA and Oxford: ABC CLIO, 2004.
Ryan, Robert E. *Shamanism and the Psychology of C. G. Jung.* London: Vega, 2002.
Ryan, William Francis. *The Bathhouse at Midnight: An Historical Survey of Magic and Divination in Russia.*

University Park: Pennsylvania State University Press, 1999.
"Sacrifice," http://www.themystica.com/mystica/articles/s/sacrifice.html.
Sagalayev, A. M., and I. V. Okryabr'skaya. *Traditional World View of the Turks of Southern Siberia: Sign and Ritual*. Nauka: Novosibirsk, 1990.
Sahlins, Marshall. *Culture and Practical Reason*. Chicago and London: The University of Chicago Press, 1976.
Sander, Donald, M.D. *Navaho Symbols of Healing: A Jungian Exploration of Ritual, Image, and Medicine*. Rochester, VT: Healing Arts Press, 1991.
Sandner, Donald F., and Stephen H. Wong, eds. *The Sacred Heritage: The Influences of Shamanism on Analytical Psychology*. New York and London: Routledge, 1997.
Sansonese, J. Nigro. *The Body of Myth: Mythology, Shamanic Trance, and the Sacred Geography of the Body*. Rochester, VA: Inner Traditions, 1994.
Sarangerel. *Riding Windhorses: A Journey into the Heart of Mongolian Shamanism*. Rochester, VT: Destiny Books, 2000.
Sargent, Denny. *Global Ritualism: Myth and Magic Around the World*. St. Paul, MN: Llewellyn, 1994.
Scarpari, Maurizio. *Ancient China: Chinese Civilization from its Origins to the Tang Dynasty*. New York: Barnes and Noble, 2006.
Schaefer, Stacy, and Peter Furst. *People of the Peyote*. Albuquerque: University of New Mexico Press, 1996.
Schafer, Edward H. and editors of Time-Life Books. *Ancient China*. New York: Time-Life Books, 1967.
Schlesier, Karl H. *The Wolves of Heaven: Cheyenne Shamanism, Ceremonies, and Prehistoric Origins*. Norman and London: University of Oklahoma Press, 1993.
Schmid, Robert, and Fritz Trupp. *Tribal Asia: Ceremonies, Rituals and Dress*, Translated by John Nicholson. London: Thames & Hudson, 2004.
Scholem, Gershom. *Major Trends in Jewish Mysticism*. New York: Schocken Books, 1946 [1941].
Schusky, Ernest, and Patrick Culbert. *Introducing Culture*, 3d ed. Englewood Cliffs, NJ: Prentice-Hall, 1978.
Seaman, Gary, and June S. Day, eds. *Ancient Traditions: Shamanism in Central Asia and the Americas*. Niwot: University Press of Colorado, 1994.
Seligmann, Kurt. *The History of Magic*. New York: Pantheon Books, 1948.
Serlin, Ilene. A. "Dance and Shamanism: Ancient Roots for a Modern Healing Art," pp. 56–61, in: Heinze, Ruth-Inge, ed. Conference Co-ordinator and Editor. *Proceedings of the Ninth International Conference on the Study of Shamanism and Alternative Modes of Healing*. Berkeley: University of California, 1992.
Service, Elman R. *Profiles in Ethnology*. New York and London: Harper & Row, 1963.
Shafer, Harry J. *Ancient Texans*. Austin: Texas Monthly Press, 1986.
Shaffer, Daniel, and Shila Scott, eds. *Asian Art: The Second HALI Annual*. London: Worldwide Hali, 1995.
Shah, Sayed Idries. *Oriental Magic*. New York: Philosophical Library, 1957.
"Shamanism," Korean Heritage Series, No. 15. Seoul, ROK: Korean Overseas Information Service, 1995.

Sharon, Douglas. *Wizard of the Four Winds: A Shaman's Story*. New York: Free Press, 1978.
Shaughnessy, James D., ed. *The Roots of Ritual*. Grand Rapids, MI: William B. Eerdmans, 1973.
Shepard, Glenn H., Jr. "Central and South American Shamanism," in: Walter, M. N. and E. J. N. Fridman, eds. *Shamanism: An Encyclopedia of World Beliefs, Practices, and Culture*, Vol. II, 382–392. Santa Barbara, CA and Oxford: ABC CLIO, 2004.
Shirokogoroff, Sergei M. *Psychomental Complex of the Tungus*. London: Kegan Paul, Trench, Trubner, 1935.
Shore, Bradd. 1996. *Culture in Mind: Cognition, Culture, and the Problem of Meaning*. New York and Oxford: Oxford University Press.
Sieroszewski, W. L. *The Yakut: An Essay of an Ethnographical Investigation*. St. Petersburg: I.R.G.S., 1896.
Siikala, Anna-Leena. *The Rite Technique of the Siberian Shaman*, FF Communications, Vol. 93. No. 220, Suomalainen Tiedeakatemia, Helsinki: Academia Scientiarum Fennica, 1978.
_____, and Mihály Hoppál. *Studies on Shamanism*. Budapest: Akaprint, 1992.
Silverman, J. "Shamanism and Acute Schizophrenia," *American Anthropologist*, 69, 1967.
Skultans, V. "Trance and the management of mental illness among Maharashtrian Families," *Anthropology Today*, Vol. 3, No. 1, 1987.
Slattum, Judy. *Masks of Bali: Spirits of an Ancient Drama*. San Francisco: Chronicle Books, 1992.
Smith, Marian W., ed. *The Artist in Tribal Society*: Proceedings of a Symposium held at the Royal Anthropological Institute. London: Routledge & Kegan Paul, 1961.
Smith, Richard J. *Fortune-tellers and Philosophers: Divination in Traditional Chinese Society*. Boulder and Oxford: Westview Press, 1991.
Smith, Susan V. H. *Masks in Modern Drama*. Berkeley and London: University of California Press, 1984.
Snow, Dean. *The Archaeology of North America*. New York: Viking Press, 1976.
Sommarström, Bo. "The Sami Shaman's Drum and the Holographic Paradigm Discussion," in: Hoppál, Mihály and Otto von Sadovszky, eds. *Shamanism Past and Present*, Part 1. Budapest: Ethnographic Institute, Hungarian Academy of Science and Los Angeles/Fullerton: International Society for Trans-oceanic Research, 1989.
Souvay, Charles L. "Interpretation of Dreams," Transcribed by Listya Sari Diyah, in: *The Catholic Encyclopedia*, Vol. V. New York: Robert Appleton, 1909. <http://www.newadvent.org/cathen/index.html> Copyright © 2007 by Kevin Knight.
Spence, Lewis. *The Myths of the North American Indians*. New York: Barnes & Noble, 2005 [1914].
The Spirit World, Alexandria, VA: Time-Life Books, 1992.
Spiro, Melford. E. *Burmese Supernaturalism*. New Jersey: Prentice-Hill, 1967.
Steele, Paul R. *Handbook of Inca Mythology*. Santa Barbara, CA and Oxford: ABC CLIO, 2004.
Stein, Wendy. *Shamans*. San Diego, CA: Greenhaven Press, 1991.

Stewart, K. "Spirit Possession in Native America," *Southwestern Journal of Anthropology*, 2, 1946.
Stewart, Omar. *Peyote Religion*. Norman: University of Oklahoma Press, 1987.
Stone, Peter G., and Brian Molyneaux, eds. *The Presented Past*. London and New York: Routledge, 1994.
Storm, Rachel. *Mythology of Asia and the Far East*. London: Anness, 2006.
Strathern, Andrew, and Marilyn Strathern. *Self-decoration in Mount Hagen*. Toronto and Buffalo: University of Toronto Press, 1971.
Sullivan, Lawrence E. "The Attributes and Power of the Shaman: A General Description of the Ecstatic of the Soul," in: Seaman, G. and J. S. Day, eds. *Ancient Traditions: Shamanism in Central Asia and the Americas*. Denver: University of Colorado and Denver Museum of Natural History, 1994.
_____. *Icanchu's Drum: An Orientation of Meaning in South American Religion*. New York: Macmillan, 1988.
Tambiah, S. J. 1970. *Buddhism and the Spirit Cults in Northeast Thailand*. Cambridge: Cambridge University Press.
Tanaka, Sakurako (Sherry). "Ainu Shamanism," in: Walter, M.N. and E. J. N. Fridman, eds. *Shamanism: An Encyclopedia of World Beliefs, Practices, and Culture*, Vol. 1, pp. 657–665. Santa Barbara, CA and Oxford: ABC CLIO, 2004.
Taussig, Michael. *Shamanism, Colonialism and the Wild Man: A Study in Terror and Healing*. Chicago and London: University of Chicago Press, 1987.
Taylor, Paul, and Lorraine Aragon. *Beyond the Java Sea: Art of Indonesia's Outer Islands*. Washington, DC: The National Museum of Natural History, Smithsonian Institution in association with Harry N. Abrams, New York, 1991.
Ten Grotenbuis, Elizabeth. *Japanese Mandalas: Representations of Sacred Geography* (Honolulu: University of Hawai'i Press, 1999), p. 70.
Teuten, Timothy. *The Letts Guide to Collecting Masks*. London: Studio Editions, 1991.
Thomas, Keith. *Religion and the Decline of Magic*. Oxford and New York: Oxford University Press, 1971.
Thompson, Charles J. S. *Magic and Healing*. London and New York: Rider, 1946.
Torbrügge, Walter. *Prehistoric European Art*, Translated by Norbert Guterman. New York: Harry N. Abrams, 1968.
Torgovnick, Marianna. *Primitive Passions: Men, Women, and the Quest for Ecstasy*. New York: Alfred A. Knopf, 1997.
Torrance, Robert M. *The Spiritual Quest: Transcendence in Myth, Religion, and Science*. Berkeley, Los Angeles, and London: University of California Press, 1994.
Torres, Eliseo with Timothy, L. Sawyer. *Curandero: A Life in Mexican Folk Healing*. Albuquerque: University of New Mexico Press, 2005.
Torres, Yolotl González. "Altered States of Consciousness and Ancient Mexican Ritual Techniques," in: Hoppál, M. and O. von Sadovszky, eds. *Shamanism Past and Present*, Part 2, pp. 349–353. Budapest: Ethnographic Institute, Hungarian Academy of Sciences and Los Angeles and Fullerton: International Society for Trans-Oceanic Research, 1989.

Tsultem, Niamosoryn. *Mongolian Sculpture*. Ulan-Bator: State Publishing House, 1989.
Turner, Victor. *The Forest of Symbols: Aspects of Ndembu Ritual*. Ithaca and London: Cornell University Press. 1967.
_____. *The Ritual Process: Structure and Anti-Structure*. Chicago: Aldine, 1969.
Underhill, Evelyn. *Mysticism: The Nature and Development of Spiritual Consciousness*. Oxford: Oneworld, 2002 [1961].
Underhill, Ruth. *Red Man's Religion: Beliefs and Practices of the Indians North of Mexico*. Chicago and London: University of Chicago Press, 1965.
Underwood, Horace G. *The Religions of Eastern Asia*. New York: Macmillan, 1910.
Urban, G., and Janet W. Hendricks. "Signal Functions of Masking in Amerindian Brazil" In: *Semiotica* 47–1/4: 181–218, 1983. Mouton: Amsterdam. Reprinted: Offprint Series No. 255, Institute of Latin American Studies, University of Texas at Austin.
Vadillo, A. E. 2002. *Santería y vodú; sexualidad y homoerotismo*. Madrid: Biblioteca Nueva.
Van Deusen, Kira. *Singing Story, Healing Drum: Shamans and Storytellers of Turkic Siberia*. Montreal: McGill-Queen's University Press, 2004.
Vasilevich, G. M., and A. V. Smolyak. "The Evenks," in: Levin, Mikhail Grigor and Leonid Pavlovich Potapov, eds. *The Peoples of Siberia*, pp. 620–654. Translated by Scripta Technica, Inc., English translation edited by Stephen Dunn. Chicago and London: University of Chicago Press, 1956.
Vetter, George B. *Magic and Religion: Their Psychological Nature, Origin, and Function*. New York: Philosophical Library, 1973.
Vestergaard, Torben A., ed. "Shamanism and Traditional Beliefs." *North Atlantic Studies*. vol. 4, no. 1+2. Højbjerg, Denmark: Aarhus University Press, 2001.
Vitebsky, Piers. *The Shaman: Voyages of the Soul Trance, Ecstasy, and Healing from Siberia to the Amazon*. New York and London: Brown, Little, 1995.
Vyatkina, K. V. "The Buryats," in: Levin, M. G. and L. P. Potapov, eds. *The Peoples of Siberia*, pp. 203–242. Translated by Scripta Technica, Inc., English translation edited by Stephen Dunn. Chicago and London: University of Chicago Press, 1956.
Wagley, C. "Tapirapé Shamanism," in: M. H. Fried, ed. *Readings in Anthropology*, vol. 2, 1959. New York: Thomas Y. Crowell, pp. 405–423.
Waite, Arthur E. *The Book of Ceremonial Magic*. New York: University Books, 1961.
Waite, Gary K. *Heresy, Magic, and Witchcraft in Early Modern Europe*. Houndmills, England: Palgrave Macmillan, 2003.
Wales, H. G. Quaritch. *Divination in Thailand: The Hopes and Fears of a Southeast Asian People*. London and Dublin: Curzon Press, 1983.
Walker, Barbara G. *The Woman's Dictionary of Symbols and Sacred Objects*. Edison, NJ: Castle Books, 1988.
Wallis, Robert J. *Shamans/Neo-Shamans: Ecstasy, Alternative Archaeologies and Contemporary Pagans*. London and New York: Routledge, 2003.

Wallis, Wilson D. *Religion in Primitive Society.* New York: F. S. Crofts, 1939.

Walter, Mariko Namba, and E. J. N. Friedman, eds. *Shamanism: An Encyclopedia of World Beliefs, Practices, and Culture.* 2 Vols. Santa Barbara, CA & Oxford: ABC CLIO, 2004.

Wassing, René S. *African Art: Its Background and Traditions.* London: Alpine Fine Arts Collection (UK), 1968.

Waters, Frank. *Masked Gods: Navajo and Pueblo Ceremonialism.* Chicago: The Swallow Press, 1950.

Wavell, Stewart, Audrey Butt and Nina Epton. *Trances.* London: Dutton, 1967.

Weber, Max. *The Sociology of Religion.* London: Methuen, 1922.

_____. *Magic: A Sociological Study.* Stanford, CA: Stanford University Press, 1948.

Webster, Hutton. *Primitive Secret Societies: A Study of Early Politics and Religion,* 2d ed. New York: Macmillan, 1932,

Werbner, Richard P. *Ritual Passage, Sacred Journey: The Form, Process and Organization of Religions Movement.* Washington, DC: Smithsonian Institution Press, 1989.

Wesselman, Hank. *Medicinemaker: Mystic Encounters on the Shaman's Path.* New York and London: Bantam Books, 1998.

Weyer, Edward M. *The Eskimos.* New Haven: Yale University Press, 1932.

Wherry, Joseph H. *Indian Masks and Myths of the West.* New York: Bonanza Books, 1969.

Whitehead, Neil L. *Dark Shamans.* Durham and London: Duke University Press, 2002.

_____, and Robin Wright, eds. *In Darkness and Secrecy: The Anthropology of Assault and Witchcraft in Amazonia.* Durham and London: Duke University Press, 2004.

Wilbert, Johannes. *Tobacco and Shamanism in South America.* New Haven and London: Yale University Press, 1987.

Williams, Joseph J. *Voodoos and Obeahs: Phases of West India Witchcraft.* New York: AMS Press, 1970.

Wilson, Frank Avray. *Art as Revelation.* Fontwell, Sussex: Centaur Press, 1981.

Wingert, Paul S. *Primitive Art: Its Traditions and Styles.* New York: Oxford University Press, 1962.

Winkelman, Michael. "Cross-cultural Perspectives on Shamans," in: Walter, M. N. and E. J. N Fridman eds. *Shamanism: An Encyclopedia of World Beliefs, Practices, and Culture*, Vol. 1, pp. 61–70. Santa Barbara, CA and Oxford: ABC CLIO, 2004.

_____. "Neuropsychology of Shamanism," in: Walter, M. N. and E. J. N Fridman, eds. *Shamanism: An Encyclopedia of World Beliefs, Practices, and Culture*, pp. 187–194, vol. 1. Santa Barbara, CA and Oxford: ABC CLIO, 2004.

_____. *Shamanism: The Neural Ecology of Consciousness and Healing.* Westport, CT and London: Bergin & Garvey, 2000.

_____, and Philip M. Peek, eds. *Divination and Healing: Potent Vision.* Tucson: University of Arizona Press, 2004.

Winter, Edward H. "Amba Religion," in: John Middleton. *Gods and Rituals.* pp. 21–40. Garden City, NY: Natural History Press, 1967.

Wissler, Clark. "Masks," in: Guide Leaflet Series of the American Museum of Natural History No. 96. New York. Reprinted from *Natural History*, Vol. XXVIII, No. 4, pp. 339–352, 1938.

Wolf, Arthur P., ed. *Religion and Ritual in Chinese Society.* Stanford: Stanford University Press, 1974.

Wu Bing-an. "Shamans in Manchuria," in: Hoppál, M. and O. von Sadovszky. *Shamanism Past and Present*, Part 2. pp. 263–269. Budapest: Ethnographic Institute, Hungarian Academy of Science and Los Angeles/Fullerton: International Society for Trans-Oceanic Research, 1989.

Young, Dudley. *Origins of the Sacred: The Ecstasies of Love and War.* New York: St. Martin's Press, 1991.

Young, Frank W. *Initiation Ceremonies: A Cross-cultural Study of Status Dramatization.* Indianapolis: Bobbs-Merrill, 1965.

Yuille, John, C., ed. *Imagery, Memory and Cognition.* Hillsdale, NJ and London: Lawrence Erlbaum Associates, 1983.

Zaehner, Robert C. *Mysticism, Sacred and Profane.* London: Oxford University Press, 1957.

Zimmer, Heinrich. *Myths and Symbols in Indian Art and Civilization.* Princeton, NJ: Bollingen Series VI, Princeton University Press, 1972.

Zuidema, R. T. (1983) "Masks in the Incan Solstice and Equinoctial Ritual," in: N. Ross Crumine and Marjorie Halpin, eds. *The Power of Symbols, Masks and Masquerade in the Americas*, pages 149–56, Vancouver: University of British Columbia Press, 1983.

About the Photographs

Plates

PLATE 1—Courtesy the Smithsonian Institution National Anthropological Archive NAA INV 06637100
PLATE 2—Courtesy the National Museum of Mongolian History, Ulaanbaatar. SCM D-1384
PLATE 3—Courtesy the National Museum of Finland. VKK 156:6
PLATE 4—Courtesy the National Museum of Mongolian History, Ulaanbaatar.
PLATE 5—Courtesy the National Museum of Finland SUK 205:1
PLATE 6—Courtesy the Smithsonian Institution National Anthropological Archive. NAA INV 01604504.
PLATE 7—Courtesy the National Museum of Finland. VKK 11:10
PLATE 8—Courtesy the National Museum of Finland. VKK 11:14
PLATE 9—Courtesy the Library of Congress. LC-USZ62-24875.
PLATE 10—Courtesy the Smithsonian Institution National Anthropological Archive. NAA INV 04113900
PLATE 11—Courtesy the Smithsonian Institution National Anthropological Archive. NAA INV 04114000
PLATE 12—Courtesy the Smithsonian Institution National Anthropological Archive. NAA INV 02265700
PLATE 13—Courtesy the Smithsonian Institution National Anthropological Archive. NAA INV 1508400
PLATE 14—Courtesy the Smithsonian Institution National Anthropological Archive. NAA INV 02265500.
PLATE 15—Courtesy the Institut für Ethnologie der Universität Göttingen. AS-957
PLATE 16—Courtesy the Institut für Ethnologie der Universität Göttingen. AS-957.
PLATE 17—Courtesy the National Museum of Mongolian History, Ulaanbaatar.
PLATE 18—Courtesy the National Museum of Mongolian History, Ulaanbaatar.
PLATE 19—(c) Staatliches Museum für Volkerkunde München, Photographic Archives. No. 27-46-1d.
PLATE 20—Courtesy the National Museum of Mongolian History, Ulaanbaatar. SCM D-1384
PLATE 21—(c) Staatliches Museum für Volkerkunde München, Photographic Archives. Mus. No. 5783. This drum is published in Lommel 1967, plate 41.
PLATE 22—(c) Staatliches Museum für Volkerkunde München, Photographic Archives. Mus. No. 26-3-34. This rattle is published in Lommel 1967, plate 22.
PLATE 23—Courtesy the National Museum of Mongolian History, Ulaanbaatar.
PLATE 24—Courtesy the National Museum of Mongolian History, Ulaanbaatar.
PLATE 25—Courtesy the Smithsonian Institution National Anthropological Archive. NAA INV 04227800.

Photographs

PHOTOGRAPH 1—Courtesy the Smithsonian Institution National Anthropological Archive. NAA INV 05010000.
PHOTOGRAPH 2—Museum of Texas Tech University. TTU1982-038-001-024
PHOTOGRAPH 3—Museum of Texas Tech University. TTU1982-083-004-025
PHOTOGRAPH 4—Museum of Texas Tech University TTU 1982-083-003-016.
PHOTOGRAPH 5—Courtesy the Library of Congress, LC-USZ62-124567
PHOTOGRAPH 6—Courtesy the Library of Congress LC-USZ62-52208
PHOTOGRAPH 7—Museum of Texas Tech University. TTU1982-083-002-036
PHOTOGRAPH 8—Museum of Texas Tech University. TTU1982-083-002-011
PHOTOGRAPH 9—Museum of Texas Tech University 1982-083-003-017
PHOTOGRAPH 10—Courtesy the National Museum of Mongolian History, Ulaanbaatar.
PHOTOGRAPH 11—Courtesy the National Museum of Mongolian History, Ulaanbaatar.
PHOTOGRAPH 12—Courtesy a private collector.
PHOTOGRAPH 13—Courtesy a private collector.
PHOTOGRAPH 14—Courtesy a private collector.
PHOTOGRAPH 15—Museum of Texas Tech University. TTU1981-083-004-075.
PHOTOGRAPH 16—Courtesy the Library of Congress, LC-USZ62-52215.
PHOTOGRAPH 17—Courtesy the Smithsonian Institution National Anthropological Archive. NAA INV 09907900.
PHOTOGRAPH 18—Courtesy the Smithsonian Institution National Anthropological Archive. NAA INV 06485400
PHOTOGRAPH 19—Courtesy the National Museum of Mongolian History, Ulaanbaatar.
PHOTOGRAPH 20—Courtesy the National Museum of Mongolian History.

About the Photographs

PHOTOGRAPH 21— Courtesy the Library of Congress. LC-USZ62-135992.

PHOTOGRAPH 22— Museum of Texas Tech University. TTU1982-083-002-034.

PHOTOGRAPH 23— Courtesy the Smithsonian Institution National Anthropological Archive NAA INV 07030100

PHOTOGRAPH 24— Courtesy the Library of Congress, LC-USZ62-52196.

About the Drawings

DRAWING 1.1— The drawing is after an illustration in Halifax 1982:50 and Edson 2005:114, drawing 6.3 of rock painting from Monsell site, Salish, Nanaimo River, British Colombia.

DRAWING 1.2— The drawing is after an illustration in Wingert 1962:213, plate 55. This artifact is said to be in the Routenstrauch-Joset-Museum für Volkenkunde, Cologne, but the location has not been verified.

DRAWING 1.3— The drawing is after the image in Leiris and Delange 1968:318. The artifact was in the Muse de l'Homme in Paris in 1968. The current location has not been verified.

DRAWING 1.4— The drawing is after an illustration in Martynov 1991:164.

DRAWING 1.5— The drawing is after an illustration in Okladnikov 1981, plate 14. A similar image is in Martynov 1991.

DRAWING 1.6— The drawing is after an illustration in Okladnikov 1981, plate 15.

DRAWING 1.7— The drawing is after photographs take at the site with permission of the Museum of Texas Tech University.

DRAWING 1.8— The drawing is after an illustration in Bahn 1998:180. The original tracing is attributed to B.N. Pyatkin and G.N. Kurochkin.

DRAWING 1.9— The drawing is after an illustration in Lommel 1967:11 and Lang and Wire 1993:25. A similar image is in Burland 1974:40–41.

DRAWING 2.1— The drawing is an artifact in the Museum of Texas Tech University.

DRAWING 2.2— The drawing is from the artifact in the Howard/Herr Collection at the Museum of Texas Tech University.

DRAWING 2.3— The drawing is after an illustration in Blodgett 1978, plate 136. The current location of the artifact is reported to be the National Museum of Man, Ottawa.

DRAWING 2.4— The drawing is after an illustration in Shaffer and Scott 1995:54. The location of this artifact is reported to be a private collection.

DRAWING 2.5— The drawing is after an illustration in Lommel 1967:115, plate 31, and Edson 2005:49, drawing 2.10. The current location of this artifact is reported to be the Museum of the American Indian, New York.

DRAWING 2.6— The drawing is after an illustration in Maringer 1960, figure 1; in Lissner 1961, plate 113; Lommel 1972:199; Marshack 1972:82; Campbell 1976:309; Halifax 1982:82; Larsen 1988:9; Walker 1988:390; Gimbutas 1991:176, figure 275; Edson 2005:31, drawing 1:12.

DRAWING 2.7— The drawing is after an illustration in Maxwell 1978:101. The location of the artifact is reported to be the Museum of the American Indian.

DRAWING 2.8— The drawing is after an illustration in Fienup-Riordan 1996:129. The current location of this artifact is reported to be the Smithsonian Institution.

DRAWING 2.9— The drawing is after an illustration in Hoppál 1998:47. The current location of this artifact is reported to be the Mörön Museum of Krassnoyarsk.

DRAWING 2.10— The drawing is after an illustration an image provided by the Staatl. Museum für Völkerkunde, Munich, Mus. No. 26-3-34, and Lommel 1967:90, plate 22.

DRAWING 3.1— The drawing is after an illustration in Melody 1989, cover image. The drawing is in Edson 2005:64, drawing 3.8. The current location of this artifact has not been verified.

DRAWING 3.2— Drawing is from the artifact. The current location of the artifact is the Museum of Texas Tech University, Lubbock, Texas.

DRAWING 3.3— The drawing is after an illustration in Graceva 1989:147.

DRAWING 3.4— The drawing is after an illustration in Clottes and Lewis-Williams 1996:36; Lommel 1967:129; Christensen 1955, figure 318, and Halifax 1982:11.

DRAWING 3.5— The drawing is after an illustration in Laing and Wire 1993:40; Bessy 1968:8; Lommel 1967:126.

DRAWING 3.6— The drawing is after an illustration in Hartmann 1967:250, plate 2. The same mask is in Urban and Hendricks 1983, plate 6 and Teuten 1991:71. The drawing is in Edson 2005:117, drawing 6.7. The current location of this artifact is reported to be the Museum für Volkerkunde, Berlin.

DRAWING 3.7— The drawing is after an illustration in Shaffer and Scott 1995:70. The artifact is reported to be in the Mort Golub Collection.

DRAWING 4.1— The drawing is after an illustration in Lommel 1967:33; Halifax 1982:84; and Lang and Wire 1993:40.

DRAWING 4.2— The drawing is after an illustration Dockstader 1964, figure 241. The location of the artifact is reported to be the Museum of the American Indian.

DRAWING 4.3— The drawing is after the image in Scarpari 2006:84–85.

DRAWING 4.4— The drawing is from the artifact. The current location of this artifact is the collection of the author.

DRAWING 4.5— The drawing is after an illustration in

Perrin 1959:85. A similar mask is shown in Wissler 1938:25. Figure 55. This drawing is in Edson 2005:151, drawing 8.3. The current location of this artifact has not been verified.

DRAWING 4.6—The drawing is after an illustration in Cole and Aniakor 1984:217, figure 332. The mask is thought made by Ekezi Ngwo of Awkuzu, circa 1940–1950. The current location of this artifact is reported to be the Museum of Cultural History, University of California, Los Angeles.

DRAWING 4.7—The drawing is from the artifact. The current location of this artifact is in the collection of the author.

DRAWING 4.8—The drawing is after an illustration in Dwyer and Dwyer 1973:32. The location of this artifact is reported to be the Fine Arts Museums of San Francisco.

DRAWING 4.9—The drawing is after an illustration in the exhibition catalog "Ancestors' Spirits in the Sound of the Tambourine," the Irkutsk Regional Studies Museum page 7. The current location of the artifact is unknown.

DRAWING 4.10—The drawing is after an illustration in Vitebsky 1995:14 and Bancroft-Hunt 2002:39. The current location of this artifact has not been verified.

DRAWING 4.11—The drawing is after an illustration in Vitebsky 1995:111; Bancroft-Hunt 2002:17; and Halifax 1982:74. The current location of this artifact has not been verified.

DRAWING 4.12—The drawing is after an illustration in Fitzhugh and Kaplan 1992:70, plate 71. The current location of this artifact is reported to be the Khabarovsk Regional Museum, but the location has not been verified.

DRAWING 4.13—The drawing is after an illustration in Mack 1994:108, figure 70. The location of this artifact has not been verified.

DRAWING 5.1—The drawing is after an illustration in Hartmann 1967, figure 42. The same mask is in Urban and Hendricks 1983:190, plate 7, and the drawing is in Edson 2005:168, drawing 9.5. The current location of this artifact is reported to be the Museum für Volkerkunde, Berlin.

DRAWING 5.2—The drawing is after an illustration in Lissner 1961:217, Lommel 1967:107; Bessy 1968:9; and Laing and Wire 1993:39.

DRAWING 5.3—The drawing is after an illustration in Marshack 1972:272.

DRAWING 5.4—The drawing is after an illustration in Gardner 1986:299.

DRAWING 5.5—The drawing is after illustration in Lommel 1967:133 and Campbell 1983:130, plate 225.

DRAWING 5.6—The drawing is after an illustration in Lommel 1967:131; Okladnikov 1981:44–45; Laing and Wire 1993:39.

DRAWING 5.7—The drawing is after a decoration on a Zuni pottery vessel in the Museum of Texas Tech University collection. Illustrations of similar images are found in Lommel 1967:132; Laing and Wire 1993:39, and Christensen 1955, figure 121.

DRAWING 5.8—The drawing is after an illustration in the exhibition catalog "Ancestors' Spirits in the Sound of the Tambourine," the Irkutsk Regional Studies Museum, page 5. The current location of the artifact is unknown.

DRAWING 5.9—The drawing is after an illustration in Bancroft-Hunt 1979: 35. The location of this artifact is reported to be the Museum of Anthropology, University of British Columbia, Canada.

DRAWING 5.10—This drawing is after an illustration in Holm 1987:178, plate 72. A similar piece appears on the cover of *Shamanism in North America* a Firefly Book published in 2002 by Norman Bancroft Hunt.

DRAWING 6.1—The drawing is after an illustration in Lissner 1961, plates 114 and 115; Lindsay 1963:21; Marshack 1972:273; Campbell 1976:276; Halifax 1982:54; Gimbutas 1991:176, figure 275; Christensen 1955, figure 322, and Edson 2005:50, drawing 2.11.

DRAWING 6.2—The drawing is after an illustration in Laing and Wire 1993:240.

DRAWING 6.3—The drawing is after an illustration in Bancroft-Hunt 1979:80. The current location of this artifact has not been verified.

DRAWING 6.4—The drawing is after an illustration in Scarpari 2006:83. The current location of this artifact has not been verified.

DRAWING 6.5—The drawing is after an illustration in a catalog for an exhibition titled "Ancestors' Spirits in the Sounds of the Tambourine" at the Irkutsk Regional Studies Museum. The mask is reported to be in the Irkutsk Regional Studies Museum.

DRAWING 6.6—The drawing is after an illustration in Schmid and Trupp 2004:244.

DRAWING 6.7—The drawing is after an illustration in Burland 1968:45. The current location of this artifact has not been verified.

DRAWING 6.8—The drawing is after an illustration in Lee 1973, plate 25; Huxley 1974:233; and Halifax 1982:43. The current location of this artifact has not been verified.

DRAWING 7.1—The drawing is after an illustration in Leenhardt 1950, plate 41. This drawing also appears in Edson 2004:39, drawing 2.3. The current location of this artifact has not been verified.

DRAWING 7.2—The drawing is after artifact and an illustration in Réunion des Musées Nationaux 2000:58. The current location of this artifact is reported to be the Musée du quai Branly, Paris.

DRAWING 7.3—The drawing is after an illustration in Leenhardt 1950, plate13. This drawing also appears in Edson 2004:130, drawing 7.2. The current location of this artifact has not been verified.

DRAWING 7.4—The drawing is after an illustration in Campbell 1983:202, plate 336. The same mask is illustrated in Halifax 1982:33; Campbell 1988:202, plate 336, and on the cover of Campbell 1988. A similar piece is included in Holm 1989:233, plate 98 and the same drawing is in Edson 2005:167, drawing 9.4. The current location of this artifact is reported to be the American Museum of Natural History.

DRAWING 7.5—This drawing is after a piece in the Howard-Herr Collection at the Museum of Texas Tech University.

DRAWING 7.6—This drawing is after the illustration in Wassing 1968:207, plate 113. The artifact is believed to be in the Museumvoor Land-en Volkenkunde, Rotterdam, The Netherlands.

DRAWING 7.7—The drawing is after an illustration in MacGowan and Rosse 1924:26. The drawing is in Edson 2005:40, drawing 2.4. The current location of this artifact is unknown.

DRAWING 8.1—The drawing is after an illustration in McFarren 1993:109. This drawing is in Edson 2005:169, drawing 9.6. The current location of this artifact has not been verified.

DRAWING 8.2—The drawing is after an illustration in Hawthorn 1967:131, figure 124. The current location of this artifact has not been verified.

DRAWING 8.3—The drawing is after an illustration in Waite 1961; Fraser 1966:280, figure 9a. A similar mask is in Perrin 1959:27, and the same drawing is in Edson 2005:171, drawing 9.8. The current location of this artifact is reported to be the Provincial Museum, Victoria, BC.

DRAWING 8.4—The drawing is after an illustration in Norman Bancroft Hunt 2002:122. The same image appears in Breton 2006:26–27. The current location of this artifact has not been verified.

DRAWING 9.1—The drawing is after an illustration in the Baltimore Museum of Art 1956:13. The drawing is in Edson 2005:24, drawing 1.10. The current location of the artifact has not been verified.

About the Drawings

DRAWING 9.2— The drawing is after an illustration in Wherry 1969:220 and Ray 1967:38. The current location of this artifact is reported to be the Robert H. Lowie Museum of Anthropology.

DRAWING 9.3— The drawing is after an illustration in Ray 1981:174, plate 145 and Fienup-Riordan 1996:301. The current location of this artifact is reported to be the University of Alaska Museum.

DRAWING 9.4— The drawing is after an illustration in Fienup-Riordan 1996:216. The current location of this artifact has not been verified.

DRAWING 9.5— The drawing is after an illustration in Berger and Bartholomew 1995:169, figure 40; see also Lommel 1970:114, figure 70. Similar pieces are illustrated in Tsultem 1989, figure 178 and 180, and the same drawing appears in Edson 2005:184, drawing 10.3. The current location of this artifact is the Chojin Lama Temple Museum, Ulaanbaatar, Mongolia.

DRAWING 9.6— The drawing is after an illustration in Quilter 2005:43.

DRAWING 9.7— The drawing is after an illustration in Riley 1955:56, plate 19; Bushnell 1965:131, figure126; and Edson 2005:55, drawing 3.2. The same mask is in Campbell 1983:218, plate 285. The current location of this artifact is reported to be the University Museum, Philadelphia.

DRAWING 9.8— The drawing is after an illustration in Taylor and Aragon 1991:161 and Edson 2005:57, drawing 3.3. The location of this artifact was reported to be the Barbier-Mueller Museum, Geneva.

DRAWING 9.9— The drawing is after the illustration in Gardner 1986:302. The current location of the ceramic figure is unknown.

DRAWING 9.10— The drawing is after an illustration in Teuten 1990:26. The drawing is in Edson 2005:89, drawing 4.12. The current location of this artifact has not been verified.

DRAWING 9.11— The drawing is after an illustration in Fitzhugh and Crowell 1988:272, figure 372 and Edson 2005:100, drawing 5.5. The current location if this artifact is reported to be the Museum of Anthropology and Ethnography in St. Petersburg, but the location has not been verified.

DRAWING 9.12— The drawing is after an illustration in Greub 1985:32. The drawing appears in Edson 2005:73, drawing 4.1. The current location of this artifact is reported to be the Museum für Volkskunde, Basel, Switzerland.

DRAWING 9.13— The drawing is after an illustration in Oakes and Gahlin 2006:397. The current location of this artifact has not been verified.

DRAWING 10.1— The drawing is after an illustration the catalog *Asian Art in the Arthur M. Sackler Gallery* 1987:121, figure 76. The current location of the artifact is reported to be the Arthur M. Sackler Gallery, Smithsonian Institution.

DRAWING 10.2— The drawing is after an illustration in Slattum 1992:80. This drawing is in Edson 2005:83, drawing 4.8. The current location of this artifact has not been verified.

DRAWING 10.3— The drawing is after an illustration in *Encyclopedia of Magic & Superstition* 1974:73.

DRAWING 10.4— After an illustration in Markman and Markman 1992:52, image 4: Bushnell 1967:34, figure 25, and Cordry 1980:77. The drawing is in Edson 2005:36, drawing 2.1. The current location of this artifact is reported to be the Museo Nacional de Antropologia, Mexico, DF.

DRAWING 10.5— The drawing is after an illustration in Fitzhugh and Kaplan 1982:195, plate 243. The drawing is in Edson 2005:81, drawing 4.6. The current location of this artifact has not been verified.

DRAWING 10.6— The drawing is after an illustration in Labbé 1986:41, figure 36.

DRAWING 10.7— The drawing is after an illustration in Boas 1955:225, figure 223.

DRAWING 11.1— The drawing is after an illustration in Hill 1968:73. The current location of this artifact has not been verified.

DRAWING 11.2— The drawing is after an illustration in Burland 1968:114; Haberland 1968:204, figure 85; Snow 1976:76; Halifax 1982:83; Corbin 1988:103; Campbell 1983:11 and 157; Walker 1988:370; Edson 2005:114, drawing 6.4, and others. The current location of this artifact has not been verified.

DRAWING 11.3— The drawing is after an illustration in Lommel 1967:8 and Lang and Wire 1993:25.

DRAWING 11.4— The drawing is after an illustration in Bancroft-Hunt 1979:72–73 and Vitebsky 1995:84. This artifact is reported to be in the Provincial Museum, Victoria, BC, Canada.

DRAWING 11.5— The drawing is after an illustration in Mauldin 1999:38. The location of this artifact is reported to be the Museum of New Mexico.

DRAWING 11.6— The drawing is after an illustration in a catalog for an exhibition titled "Ancestors' Spirits in the Sounds of the Tambourine" at the Irkutsk Regional Studies Museum. The artifact is reported to be in the Irkutsk Regional Studies Museum.

INDEX

Ainu people 179
Alekseev, Nikolai Alekseevich 228
ämägät 15, 88, 111, 175
amagyat see *ämägät*
amulets 85, 98
ancestor-worship 5, 228
ancestral spirits 16, 52, 82, 105, 130, 180
Andaman Islands 44, 48, 172, 175
androgyny 198–200, 202, 211, 221
animism 29, 53, 65, 174, 227
antlers 29, 30, 41, 53, 77, 81–83, 90, 92, 97, 203, 236, 238
Apache 47, 50, 86, 114, 141, 155, 215
Araucanian shaman 112
art and artists 11, 20, 32, 48, 51, 81, 92, 94, 95, 96, 98, 100–103, 123, 129, 160, 191; hunting cultures 102; object 93; spirituality 94, 99; symbolism 12

Bäckman, Louise 182, 231
Balzer, Marjorie Mandelstam 11, 12, 219
bears 41, 46, 66, 147
Benedict, Ruth 12, 38, 47, 200, 234
birds 17, 19, 65, 67, 80, 88, 98, 109, 113, 133, 135, 168, 174, 190, 193, 196, 204, 205, 222, 238; bones 79; carved 23; costume 191; feathers 41, 134; fetish 75; headdress 81; human-headed 214, 215; images 43, 77, 81; masks 57, 90, 97, 104, 187; sacred 75, 97; sculptures 77; skeleton 75; spirit 44, 79, 173, 218; supernatural 188; symbols 75, 78, 102; transformation 171; woman-bird 79
Black Darhad 43
black shaman 10, 27
Bogoraz, V.G. 12
Bön religion 5
bones 37, 41, 42, 48, 77–79, 85, 86, 101, 102, 122, 143, 148, 162, 164, 189, 208, 209, 216, 226, 238; divination 147; hollow 67, 159; human 82, 83; whistles 96
Borneo 154, 175, 178, 193, 197, 202
Bourguignon, Erika 137
breath 81, 102, 119, 166, 167, 171, 172, 200, 208
Buddhism 5, 29, 57, 74, 75, 83, 90, 109, 167, 226
Budge, Sir E.A. Wallis 136
Buryat 10, 40, 41, 74, 75, 79, 114, 162, 198, 202, 219, 227; *buge* and *bo* (shaman) 198; *ongon* 102; shaman 133, 134, 218

Campbell, Joseph 97
cannibals 213, 235
Cauquelin, Josiane 173
ceremonial boards 93, 94
ceremonies 7, 10, 11, 13, 16, 17, 19, 20, 26, 27, 37, 49, 54, 72, 73, 86, 93, 105, 114, 118, 120, 123, 125, 130, 136, 139, 145, 154, 162, 169, 173, 176, 206, 207, 209, 210, 214, 218, 224, 228, 230, 234, 237, 241; curing 61, 127, 155; healing 47, 155; initiating 106, 186; masking 96; *numblin* 133; potlatch 235; purification 126; religious 34; salmon 238; shamanistic 232; walking shaman 115
chants 17, 27, 35, 44, 56, 60, 63, 72, 126, 131, 154, 182, 237
Cherokee 34, 140, 159
Cheyenne 86, 157, 197, 198, 234
Chinese 5, 8, 26, 31, 79, 109, 115, 130, 144, 147, 191, 215; ancestor worship 4; characters 116; document (*Wei Chih*) 30; dragon 77; government 52; guardian figure 83; mirror 134; mythology 75, 199; ritual 139; shamanism 212; society 216; symbols 135
Christensen, Erwin 10
Chukchee 60, 90, 107, 111, 123, 124, 157, 162, 198, 202, 210, 228; drum 108, 109; funerary ritual 224, 226; *kelet* (spirit) 208; people 117, 161; sacrifice 65; self-determined death 210; shaman 149, 197
Confucianism 52
cosmic tree 30, 69, 81, 112, 161, 237
costume see paraphernalia
Covell, Alan Carter 166
Crow 43, 78
Curtis, Edward 34, 43, 64, 72, 78, 105, 121, 133, 176
Czaplicka, Marie Antoinette 198, 224

Daur Mongol 48, 135
death 15, 16, 19, 26, 46, 49–51, 67, 75, 81, 85, 104, 115, 123, 142, 143, 147, 148, 150, 151, 155, 161, 165–168, 170, 171, 173, 176, 183, 185, 187, 190, 191, 194, 196, 197, 202, 206, 210, 212, 214, 221, 222, 224, 228, 229, 232, 238, 240, 241; destruction 36; dismemberment 37, 189, 199; dream 45; human 35 ; illness 10, 54, 58, 65, 66, 141, 157, 160, 164, 175, 213; life after 36, 37, 137, 186, 216, 234; magic 101; prayed to death 60; resurrection 21, 163, 172, 208; ritual 78, 126, 218; shamans 77; sickness 38; trance 48; turning death into life 94, 106
deer 29, 83, 84, 86–88, 102, 114, 126, 132, 135, 136, 165, 195, 205, 222, 238; blood 194; costumes 41; dance 113, 236; head 42, 53; hoof rattles 113; mask 192; symbol 193
demons 10, 12, 50, 68, 73, 96, 114, 124, 126, 130, 140, 151, 161, 176; death 27; deities 26, 99, 117; disease 13; expelling 44; possession 13, 141, 151; spirit 9, 107, 139, 150
Diószegi, Vilmos 82, 91
diseases 13, 46, 50, 67, 85, 144, 149, 151, 152, 154, 155, 163, 166, 182, 208, 219, 226, 233, 243;

cure 86, 150, 139; dangerous 66; diagnose 116; "disease-object" 141, 159; healing 83; mental 202; misfortune 84; origin 140; shaman disease 20; spirit of the disease 153; theory of disease 21
divination 54, 62, 65, 145, 146, 154, 173; bones 83, 147; bowl 153; dreams 178, 179; healing 8, 122, 129, 143; magic 144; mirror 116; oracle bones 143; oracular consultation 66; power 21; shaman 139, 144, 161; shamanic activities 57; skull 147, 223; trance 139; Yoruba 140, 153
Dogon people 132, 238
dreaming places 178
dreams 31, 45, 87, 88, 91, 101, 142, 158, 168, 172, 179, 181, 182, 187, 197, 216, 239; "festival of dreams" 178; initiatory 8; prophetic 178; shaman's 177; visions 141, 157, 159, 165, 176, 190, 238
Driscoll, John T. 8
drums 21, 38, 39, 44, 47, 57, 58, 60, 69, 74, 88, 94, 99, 103, 107, 113, 114, 131, 144, 170, 182, 195, 202, 236, 239; beating 72, 122; drumstick 108–110, 115, 132; drum making 237; Koryak 110; Ojibway 112; round 109; shaman's 41, 72, 109, 111, 112, 162; single-faced 65; Yakut 111
Durkheim, Emile 15
Duwamish 93

eagles 32, 41, 43, 44, 75, 76, 79, 81, 87, 97, 113, 133, 174, 175, 205, 229
ecstasy 5, 9, 31, 38, 118, 127, 137, 150, 182, 187, 223, 228, 231, 233; belief 73; blood-ecstasy 221; emotional 117; rituals 32; shamanic 150, 181; states 8, 17, 21, 33, 136, 181; techniques 11, 107, 152, 167; trance 28, 54, 114, 136
Ecuador 84, 149, 195, 215, 223
Egypt 65, 66, 78, 79, 81, 99, 113, 130, 135, 136, 170, 178, 197, 203, 205, 208, 210, 214, 215
Eliade, Mircea 11, 54, 90, 101, 107, 112, 115, 128, 157, 167, 168, 170, 197, 208
Eskimos 75, 77, 84, 85, 108, 111, 114, 127, 178, 181, 192, 197, 203, 210, 222
Evenk 9, 39, 74, 89, 122, 123, 132, 147, 165, 172, 180, 239
evil spirits 8, 10, 20–22, 52, 55, 65, 75, 86, 91, 117, 137, 141, 142, 146, 151, 158, 161, 172, 175, 181, 208, 224, 228, 233; prisoner 235; shamanism 229

familiars 6, 41, 48, 67, 85, 87, 88, 115, 117, 172
fear 15, 16, 25, 27, 36, 51, 86, 126, 163, 165, 166, 178, 190, 209, 210, 234, 241; the dead 208, 212, 216; respect of death 211; uncertainty 14; unknown 26
feathers 44, 47, 61, 75, 79, 81, 86, 87, 95, 105, 106, 113, 126, 132, 134, 191, 195, 203; bird 41, 135; eagle 78; feathers and ribbons 80; owl 42, 80; wood grouse 43
fetishes 23, 41, 51, 55, 75, 86, 89, 125, 134; power 85
Figes, Orlando 168
Forsyth, James 74
Frazer, James George 34
Fridman, Eva Jane 227

Garuda 75, 79, 109
Gennep, Arnold van 125, 186
ghosts 140, 164, 167, 182, 190, 213, 218, 224; the dead 175; fear 209; local 11, 28; malevolent 14; spirits 50; witches 86
Gillette, Douglas 163, 212, 234
Gimbutas, Marija 95
Goldi 79, 91, 168, 169, 207, 209
Goodman, Falicitas 125
Grim, John A. 39, 75
guardian spirits 77, 78, 173, 175, 205, 228
Gurung 36

Halbwachs, Maurice 6
Halifax, Joan 32
hallucinogens 13, 18, 72, 89
Hamatsa secret society 164
Han Dynasty 52, 130
Hansen, Henry 41
healers and healing 7, 8, 10, 24, 28, 35, 44, 48, 49, 50, 58, 79, 83, 89, 116, 124, 128, 129, 139, 143, 150, 152, 155, 157, 159–179, 195, 205, 225, 229; acts of healing 48, 175; ceremony 47, 155; divining 23, 137; energy 49, 152; power 31, 96, 112; process 31, 36, 122, 125, 141, 152, 154, 155; rite 182; rituals 34, 173, 222; shamanic healing 158; the sick 11, 54 ; spirit song 159; symbolic healing 140, 150
helper spirits 20, 85, 87, 88, 132, 138, 146, 167, 168, 231
Hiller, John K. 59
Hinduism 57, 70
Hopewell site 149
Hopi 34, 86, 113, 114, 207, 234
Hopi Snake Dance 34
Hoppál, Mihály 82
horns 15, 42, 41, 47, 53, 75, 80–83, 87, 105, 110, 113, 134, 135, 159
Huichol 84, 114, 136, 194, 205
Hultkrantz, Åke 10, 136, 159, 182, 231, 241
Humphrey, Caroline 136, 219, 241
hunter culture 7, 193
huur 114, 115, 131; *see also* mouth organ
hysteria 5

Idowu, E. Bolaji 85
Igbo 16, 82, 84

image making 104
insanity 141, 221
Islam 29, 220
itzers 94

jackals 205
jaguars 75, 84, 88, 135, 194, 195, 205
Jakobsen, Merete D. 133
Japan 30, 31, 99, 107, 173, 179, 185, 199, 201
Jemez Pueblo 86
jinglers 114
Jivero 13, 84, 114, 215

kachina 104, 105
kami 30, 31, 185
Karagas , 99, 111
Kehoe, Alice Beck 25, 31, 33
Kingdom of Shadows 126, 208
Komi people 51
Korea 21, 77, 88, 107, 151, 163, 166, 185, 199
Koryak 90, 107–111, 124, 143, 172, 197, 208, 210
Krader, Lawrence 10
Krippner, Stanley 9, 11
Krivoshapkin, S.S. 153
Kuskokwim River 28
kut 89, 209, 215, 228
Kwaio 64, 67
Kwakiutl 90, 164, 174, 235

Lake Baikal 9, 40, 44, 74, 79, 114, 115, 207, 210, 218
Lascaux 57, 97
legends 75, 100, 128, 164, 208, 213, 229, 235, 238
Lewis, I.M. 29, 32, 183
Lewis, Philip H. 100
life and death 8, 9, 17, 31, 36, 55, 58, 59, 63, 64, 82, 91, 119, 130, 135, 149, 163, 204, 207, 209, 211, 215, 216, 217, 218, 223, 239
Lincoln, J.S. 176
Linton, Ralph 143
Lommel, Andreas 9, 30, 31, 37, 158
Lord of the Animals 99

Machu-Tungus 9
Maddox, John Lee 20, 47
Magdalenian Period 29, 102
magic 5, 6, 8, 10–12, 15, 28, 34, 35, 40–41, 47, 51, 53–54, 56, 59, 62, 64, 69, 70, 71, 77, 84, 85, 89, 93, 94, 97, 98, 100, 104, 106, 109, 111, 118, 119, 125, 127, 128, 136, 140, 142, 143, 144, 147, 159, 161, 170, 175, 184, 190, 193, 197, 199, 208, 212, 214, 216, 224, 227, 230, 234, 236, 240; arts 20, 34, 61; black 55, 154; curing 99; elements 57; elixir 153; energy 32, 58; fertility 101, 158; flight 75, 170, 191; healing 205; hunting 57, 83; incantation 225; intervention 59, 60, 61, 63; knowledge 4, 48, 55; medicinal 99; mortuary 65; music 113; mysteries 44; obser-

vance 59, 63, 64; plants 72; potions 65; power 36, 55, 81, 131, 132, 143, 239; practices 10, 52, 55, 63, 78, 98, 146, 192; procedure 56, 67; rite 60; rituals 157; religion 14, 16, 56; sacred worlds 93; shamanism 56, 58, 61, 62, 63, 66, 186; spell 78; sympathetic 54, 157; witchcraft 46, 56, 63, 67
Mahakala 90
Mair, Lucy 66
Malefijt, Annemarie de Waal 144
malevolent spirits 30, 63, 65, 66, 103, 134, 145, 211, 216
Manchu 8, 9, 39, 123, 129, 146, 162, 168
mansin 88, 133
Maori 58, 148, 171, 175, 176, 179
masks 62, 64, 72, 89, 95, 103, 105, 107, 119, 134–148, 150–167, 174, 190, 203, 207, 208, 221, 232, 237, 239; animal 17, 106; *Avaldai* 106; Baba 204; Ball-on-head 180; bark-cloth 16; bear 168; bird 57, 91, 97, 187; bronze 130; clown 104; dance 47; death 149; deer 53, 192; devil 238; Dharmapala 26; fish dance 96; forehead 138; funeral 176; ghost dance 164; Haida portrait 106; helping-spirit 28, 91, 196, 139; Hudo' dance 193; jackal 205; life and death 217; made in Mexico 117; Magemut 222; Meninaku 61; Mgbedike 82; Nightway 154; Northwest Coast 136; Puma 84; Rangda 214; raven 133, 189; shaman's 24, 55, 90, 132, 149, 196, 204; skull 164; spirit 61, 63, 188; Tlingit 127; transformation 236; White Maiden 201; wolf 57
"mastery of the spirits" 10
Maya 26, 94, 95, 149, 163, 173, 178, 211, 222, 234; Arapaho 159; art and spirituality 98; life 9, 106, 212, 229; medicine man 9, 12, 31, 43, 51, 54, 63, 77, 78, 86, 96, 140, 147, 150, 154, 168, 216; Navajo 225; Ojibway 159; shaman-kings 160; shamanism 14, 64, 175, 208, 212, 213, 223
McGhee, Robert 187
Mesolithic art 102
the metaphysical 7, 30, 63, 131, 214, 233; environment 33; events 49; influence 56; phenomenon 49; practice 12; question 123, 236; reference 92; sense 71; transformation 135; worlds 118
Mexico 42, 81, 170, 205, 238; Aztec 84; drums 144; Huichol 84, 114, 194; masks 117, 217; Otomi 88; peyote ritual 136; shaman 237; Tarahumara 53, 130; Vera Cruz 111; Yaqui 42, 113
Middleton, John 146
mirrors 23, 77, 115–117, 130, 134, 135, 165, 184, 185, 232, also See *toli*

Molhilov, T.M. 8
Mongolian shamans 43, 106, 109, 115, 130, 131, 132
Mongols 5, 8, 19, 40, 69, 130, 163, 174, 198, 218, 219, 226, 227
monks 26, 81
mouth organ 115; see also *huur*
mugyök 88
Murdoch, John 111
mysticism 7, 8, 11, 12, 19, 38, 40, 84, 89, 101, 106, 131, 157, 159, 177, 186, 198, 203, 205, 206, 219, 239, 241; beings 29; concept 6, 190; connection 15; duties 81; encounter 31; experience 25, 32, 171; flight 78; forces 59; influence 57; information 52; paraphernalia 144; power 160, 209; practices 216; reference 147; religious roles 48; shamanism 65; signs and symbols 57; state of being 241; tradition 199
mythmakers 100, 230
myths 6, 7, 25, 68, 74, 75, 105, 120, 121, 125, 126, 140, 150, 160, 166, 174, 188, 199, 211, 227; Abaris 128; ancient 107; androgynous 200; appeasement 136; cedar tree 112; creation 127; devouring spirits 238; experience 27; figures 119; Huichol 194; Kaggen 219; magical incantation 225; Osiris 78; procreation 189 ; reality 10, 49; rituals 118; sacred stories 73; shaman 200; spirits and the supernatural 96; superstition 217; Thai 146; tradition 6, 105, 188

Navaho 51, 59, 66, 105, 141, 142, 154, 157, 176, 177, 182, 212, 213, 224, 225
Neo Siberians 107
Nepal 5, 36, 66, 77, 132, 179, 181, 209, 222
New Guinea 16, 82, 102, 148, 160, 171, 189, 204
Nightway Chant 154
nkisi 23
Nootka 90

oaths 56
occult 6, 8, 14, 55, 100
octagonal drums 109, 110
Ojibwa 39, 75, 89, 103, 112, 113, 122, 159, 228
Oman, John 26
ongon 74, 75, 85, 86, 101–103, 109, 110, 115, 162
Onon, Urgunge 25, 63
oracles 84, 87, 136, 143, 146, 147, 160; bones 144
Osiris 78, 83, 136, 199, 221
Otomi 88
Overworld 81, 82, 222

Paleo-Asian peoples 9
Paleo-Siberians 107, 108, 124, 197
Panther Cave 98

paraphernalia 23, 52, 53, 60, 62, 87, 94, 107, 135, 188, 189, 232; mystical 144; ritual 41, 75, 104, 131, 137, 186; spirit attracting 103; shamanic 194, 196, 235, 239; shamanistic 108, 174; shaman's 105, 115, 132
pathogenic objects 67
Pinch, Geraldine 197
Popol Vuh 163, 234
power 9–12, 15, 22, 29, 30, 44, 46, 48, 49, 52, 54, 56, 58, 61, 62, 66, 67, 71, 72, 77, 82–83, 85, 90, 93, 103, 105, 106, 108, 109, 111, 113, 119, 122, 124, 132–134, 144, 147, 149, 150, 151, 161, 164, 172–177, 180, 184, 194, 199, 200, 204, 205, 211, 217, 224, 228, 229, 233, 237, 240; Apache 47; belief 59, 63; curing 21, 157, 179; divine 14, 130; divining 23, 155; evil 116, 192; healing 96, 112, 137; magical 131; magico-religious 51; Manitou 89; medicine man 159; mystic 78, 79; mystical 160, 209; natural 6, 63; occult 14, 55, 100; procreation 158; psychic 123; sacred 120; shaman 38, 121, 142, 149, 181, 218, 232; shamanic 24, 33, 114, 125, 152, 183; shamanistic 20, 24, 94, 121, 202; spiritual 16, 50, 148, 152, 159, 187, 209; sorcery 140; supernatural 8, 13, 23, 33, 45, 47, 50, 59, 84, 126, 143, 181, 239; transcendent 19, 21; transcendental 25, 51; transformation 91, 135, 171, 196; words 35, 60, 78
prayer 14, 19, 27, 86, 118, 153, 212
procreation 6, 101, 158, 160, 189, 197, 199, 211, 217
psychopomp 8, 10, 64, 128, 151, 152, 165, 209, 217, 226
psychotropic drugs 37, 137
Purev, Otgony 20, 43
Purvee, Gurbudaryn 43

Radin, Paul 229
rattles 32, 41, 42, 53, 95, 105, 109–114, 131, 162, 165, 237
Rattlesnake Canyon 98
Ray, Dorothy Jean 85
ritual paraphernalia see paraphernalia
rituals 7, 10, 13, 15–17, 19, 23–28, 32, 38, 49, 51, 52, 54, 56, 59, 63, 65, 68, 72, 74, 86, 96, 99, 105, 111, 118, 119, 136, 141, 143–145, 151, 155, 157, 160–163, 166, 173, 174, 176, 182, 188, 190, 193, 200, 204–206, 211, 213, 217, 219, 224, 227, 230, 232, 233, 235, 241; bathing 159; behavior 70; cannibalism 223; canoe 93; ceremonies 93, 234; dance 30, 107, 130; death 78, 125, 214, 216, 218; drama 121, 159; duties 122; fire 109; gratitude 42; headhunters 149; hut 170; initiation

286 INDEX

186; intervention 125; journey 93; *kut* 89; language 123; masks 237; murder 223; objects 71, 129, 148, 196; observances 37, 103, 123, 130; paraphernalia 75, 104, 130, 131, 137, 186; performance 11, 35, 62, 73, 122, 129, 132; peyote 194; practice 84, 124, 126, 127, 152, 187, 210; project 71; sacrifice 218, 221; shamanistic 29, 41, 57, 58, 61, 83, 120, 121, 126, 131, 137, 203, 207; substance 194; symbolism 237; trance 139; transformation 197; transition 185, 186; war spirit 164; world 128

Russia 5, 8, 9, 18, 39, 44, 51, 57, 74, 92, 97, 102, 108, 147, 165, 167, 170, 172, 176, 178, 207, 209, 211, 219, 220

sacrifices 14, 27, 54, 95, 118, 125, 126, 128, 129, 162, 178, 186, 211, 222, 238; blood 47, 99, 219; human 84, 123, 149
Scarpari, Maurizio 139
séances 41, 62, 113, 145, 168, 216, 239; divining 54; Kelantan 233; Malay 170; rituals 166
self-mutilation 27, 58, 184, 219
Selkups 41
sex change 133, 197, 198, 200, 201
"Shaking Tent" 121, 122
shaman-mirror 115
shamanism 88, 111, 112, 114, 151, 153, 175, 240; artists 100; beliefs 32, 38, 62, 102; intervention 24, 49, 59, 64, 93, 119, 120, 198; objects 78, 92; performances 62, 151, 234, 237; practices 10, 17, 26, 78, 81, 89, 100, 128, 150, 185, 232; *see also* rituals
shaman's coat 94
Shang dynasty 143
shape-shifting 202, 203
Shirokogoroff, Sergei 179
Shoshone 50, 157
Siberia 5, 14, 19, 21, 29, 38, 78, 92, 97, 99, 102, 112, 117, 120, 128, 170, 171, 173, 207, 224, 237; Aleutian Islands 87; burial mound 19; Buryat 227; Chukchee 65, 157, 161; drums 111; Goldi 168, 169; Lake Baikal 79; masks 91; paraphernalia 108; people 40, 41, 71, 86, 88, 90, 107, 147, 163, 208, 229; sacrificial activities 123; shamanism 4, 11, 30, 47, 74, 81, 95, 100, 113, 114, 132, 137, 144, 166, 172, 185, 197, 219, 226, 238; spiritual practitioners 31; Tatar 220; Tungus 39; Yakut 12, 172, 175, 215
Sieroszewski, W.L. 111
Silla Dynasty 88
Sioux 86, 157, 176, 221, 229, 234
skulls 44, 82–84, 122, 147–150, 164
sorcery 27, 28, 41, 47, 54, 55, 59, 63, 65, 66, 88, 140, 151, 157, 164, 175, 197, 213, 215, 223

Spence, Lewis 86
spirit helpers 6, 48, 64, 75, 86, 95, 96, 117, 122, 131, 139, 155, 168, 171, 195
spirit world 6, 9–11, 13, 17, 21, 44, 45, 52, 57–59, 63, 69, 74, 89, 101, 106, 117, 126, 131, 137, 141, 149, 152, 158, 180, 196, 232; communication 54; connection 83, 90, 151, 195, 203; journey 87, 114, 239; relationship 60, 237; shaman 31, 124, 125; transposition 24
spiritual forces 24, 47
spiritual leaders 10, 49, 211
supernatural 5, 6, 9, 10, 12, 29, 35, 36, 38, 47, 53, 62, 70, 79, 82, 87, 92, 93, 96, 118, 120, 121, 123–125, 127, 129, 134, 137, 140, 145, 150, 168, 177, 179, 180, 184, 186, 190, 196, 202, 206, 216, 224, 228, 230, 235, 238, 241; belief 22, 23, 27, 33, 52, 97, 185, 218, 240; communication 31; Crow belief 43; death 66; elements 60, 188; energy 14, 55, 59, 23; experiences 104; force 147, 151, 157, 178; guidance 72, 78; illness 152; intervention 37, 64, 103, 131, 231; legacy 222; magic 54, 58, 63; malevolent appeal 7, 48; power 8, 15, 24, 32, 44, 46, 52, 58, 61, 84, 90, 126, 144, 152, 159, 181, 183; practices 173; rituals 166; shamanism 4, 11, 17, 20, 21, 25, 45, 49, 50, 75, 85, 86, 94, 104, 105, 130, 143, 187, 232, 239; spiritism 8; spirits 13, 141, 163, 181, 187; strength and knowledge 21; transformation 106, 136, 203; world 119, 131, 158, 163, 171, 182, 185, 192, 197, 204, 215, 231, 233
symbols 5, 23, 30, 35, 38, 49, 53, 72, 79, 83, 84, 91, 94, 97, 99, 100, 104, 109, 110, 117, 120, 132, 135, 140, 151, 162, 166, 170, 172, 174, 177, 185, 189, 199, 205, 207, 214, 231, 232, 235; belief 200, 203, 217, 234; birds 43, 44, 75, 78, 79, 81, 102; communication 70; costume 131; cultural heritage 74; death 149; drum 114, 115; energy 82; flight 75; healing 150, 154; magic 125; mask 89; mythology 68, 69; power 85, 93; religion 28; ritual 28, 57, 73, 118, 128; shamanism 10, 60, 62, 71, 75, 77, 95, 147, 193, 206, 237; snakes 77; spirits 16; Tibetan Buddhism 75; transformation 75; values 70; word 71

taboos 13, 14, 20, 45, 55, 59, 74, 120, 121, 127, 140, 141, 146, 150, 179, 202, 205, 210, 211, 224, 235, 241
Tae-kon, Kim 22
Taiwan 77, 173, 201

talismans 43, 85, 98
tambourines 65, 73, 111, 162, 170, 172
Tarahumara 53, 130
Tibet 5, 62, 74, 80, 111, 170, 199, 213
Tlingit 66, 67, 74, 90, 105, 106, 113, 127, 138, 149, 204, 216, 218, 232, 237, 238
Tofa 91
toli 42, 77, 116, 117, 132, 135; *see also* mirrors
trances 7, 8, 11, 17, 40, 72, 89, 97, 114, 131, 136, 144, 151, 155, 158, 163, 173; death-like 48; divination 139; drums 237; non-ordinary psychic states 216; rituals 129, 137; shamanism 13, 21, 28, 29, 31, 33, 38, 52, 98, 124, 129, 132, 137, 145, 154, 175, 182, 183, 192, 239; spirit intrusion 141; spirit world 18, 137; Sufi 181; Tibetan lamas 5; tobacco 206; transmogrification 203; visionary journeys 9, 31, 127
Transbaykal caves 97
transcendentalism 21, 24, 25, 29, 37, 51, 75, 77, 143, 185, 219, 223, 231–233, 240
transformation 45, 66, 98, 104, 106, 107, 118, 125, 128, 136, 139, 191, 199, 206, 207, 209, 213, 222, 240; belief 173, 184, 200; cave paintings 189; Chinese 216; death 166, 223; drums 236; Korean *mansin* 133; masks 28, 81, 90, 91, 132, 135, 174, 187, 196, 236; mystical concepts 190; mythical times 100; myths 192; physiological and psychological 61, 217; power 91, 135, 171, 187, 196; quasi-totemic animals 205; rites of passage 186; rituals 197; self-mutilation 183; sexuality 198, 201; shamanism 8, 44, 91, 135, 137, 187, 188, 195, 196, 197, 204, 238, 241; shapeshifters 203; symbolism 60, 75, 221; werewolves 190; witches 65; wolves 205
transvestitism 198, 201
Les Trois Frères 29, 30
Tsimshian people 149
Tungus 8, 9, 39, 55, 74, 80, 99, 108, 122, 123, 131, 133, 134, 147, 165, 168, 172, 179, 198, 210, 226
tupilak 87, 88
Tuvan people 71

ukhan-budla 48
Underworld 15, 78, 151, 176, 191, 193, 204, 214, 215, 222, 228, 239

vampires 190
ventriloquism 58, 60, 89
Vetter, George 56
visionary journeys 9, 31, 127
Vitebsky, Piers 11, 33
voodoo 55
Vyatkina, K.V. 227

Walter, Mariko 227
Webster, Hutton 58, 86
werewolves 190, 206
witch doctors 12
witchcraft 24, 46, 55, 56, 59, 63, 65, 66, 67, 81, 85, 86, 140, 155, 213, 215, 223; *Dawi Durga* 214; England 54; evil spells 27, 151; illness 46; Navajo 213, 224; shamanism 66, 67; Tlingit 66; were-animals 65; Yoruba 81; Zande 67
wizards 178, 179
wolves 29, 30, 57, 62, 71, 75, 110, 135, 136, 194, 195, 205

xargi 84
Xipe Totec 221
x-ray style painting 101

Yakut 9, 12, 75, 79, 88, 90, 107, 108, 110, 111, 134, 137, 172, 175, 181, 198, 202, 215, 228
Yanomami 89
Yaqui 42, 113

Zelenin, D.K. 13